A GUIDE TO THE **HOY DÍA** ICONS

ACTIVITY TYPES

	Pair Activity	Indicates that the activity is designed to be done by students working in pairs.
	Group Activity	Indicates that the activity is designed to be done by students working in small groups.
	Audio	Indicates that related audio material is available in MySpanishLab as well as on CDs and on the Companion Website.
	World Wide Web	Includes helpful links and activities found on the *Hoy día* Companion Website and in MySpanishLab.
	Video	Indicates that the video resources are available on a DVD or in MySpanishLab.
	Student Activities Manual	Indicates that additional practice activities are available in the Student Activities Manual. The manual is available in MySpanishLab as well as in printed form.
¡Hola!	MySpanishLab	Indicates that additional resources are available in MySpanishLab. For example, in MySpanishLab you will find a pronunciation guide, a mnemonic dictionary with tips to help you learn each chapter's vocabulary, and specialized information related to professions and careers.

ANNOTATED INSTRUCTOR'S EDITION

Hoy día

Spanish for **Real Life**

John T. McMinn
Austin Community College

Nuria Alonso García
Providence College

Prentice Hall

Boston   Columbus   Indianapolis   New York   San Francisco
Upper Saddle River   Amsterdam   Cape Town   Dubai   London
Madrid   Milan   Munich   Paris   Montreal   Toronto   Delhi   Mexico City
Sao Paulo   Sydney   Hong Kong   Seoul   Singapore   Taipei   Tokyo

Executive Editor, Elementary Spanish: Julia Caballero
Editorial Assistant: Andrea Arias
Executive Marketing Manager: Kris Ellis-Levy
Senior Marketing Manager: Denise Miller
Marketing Coordinator: Bill Bliss
Development Editor: Celia Meana
Development Editor for Assessment: Melissa Marolla Brown
Senior Managing Editor for Product Development: Mary Rottino
Associate Managing Editor (Production): Janice Stangel
Senior Production Project Manager: Nancy Stevenson
Media/Supplements Editor: Meriel Martínez
Senior Media Editor: Samantha Alducin
Senior Art Director: Pat Smythe
Art Director: Miguel Ortiz
Art Manager: Gail Cocker
Line Art: Daisy DePuthod
Senior Manufacturing & Operations Manager, Arts & Sciences: Nick Sklitsis
Operations Specialist: Cathleen Petersen
Text & Cover Designer: Lisa Delgado, Delgado and Company, Inc.
Manager, Rights & Permissions: Zina Arabia
Manager, Visual Research: Beth Brenzel
Manager, Cover Visual Research & Permissions: Karen Sanatar
Image Permission Coordinator: Richard Rodrigues
Full-Service Project Management: Melissa Sacco, Pre-Press PMG
Composition: Pre-Press PMG
Printer/Binder: Courier Kendallville
Cover Printer: Lehigh-Phoenix Color
Publisher: Phil Miller

This book was set in Palatino 10/12.

Credits and acknowledgments borrowed from other sources and reproduced, with permission, in this textbook appear on appropriate page within text (or on page C-1).

10 9 8 7 6 5 4 3 2 1

Prentice Hall
is an imprint of

www.pearsonhighered.com

Student Edition, Volume 1 ISBN-10: 0-205-75602-6
Student Edition, Volume 1 ISBN-13: 978-0-205-75602-5
Student Edition, Volume 2 ISBN-10: 0-205-76152-6
Student Edition, Volume 2 ISBN-13: 978-0-205-76152-4
Annotated Instructor's Edition, Volume 1 ISBN-10: 0-205-76982-9
Annotated Instructor's Edition, Volume 1 ISBN-13: 978-0-205-76982-7
Annotated Instructor's Edition, Volume 2 ISBN-10: 0-205-76983-7
Annotated Instructor's Edition, Volume 2 ISBN-13: 978-0-205-76983-4

Brief Contents

Scope & Sequence

De viaje 188

La niñez 220

Today's text for today's instructors, students, and classrooms...

Hoy día: Spanish for Real Life

Instructors are busy, students are busy. Classes are bigger, courses meet less frequently, and students want to be able to apply what they learn in class immediately. Today's instructors and students need a solution that fits with real life. *Hoy día:* **Spanish for Real Life** focuses on the Spanish students' need for everyday communication. It teaches them to function in a variety of real-world settings—at work and in their neighborhoods, traveling abroad, or doing service in their local communities. *Hoy día* helps students focus on what they need to know now to use Spanish effectively in real life.

As Spanish becomes more and more indispensable in daily life, students will find *Hoy día:* **Spanish for Real Life** an excellent tool that facilitates both their immersion in the Spanish language and their connection to the people who speak it.

REAL LIFE CONNECTIONS...

help students use Spanish effectively in their daily lives.

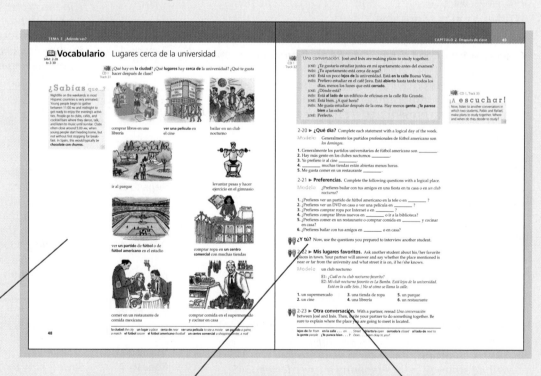

■ **Vocabulary** is presented via illustrations or photos and focuses on contexts in which a broad range of students—traditional college-aged students, working adults, or retirees returning to school—find themselves in real life.

■ *¿Y tú?* activities prompt students to personalize and share information with a partner. By making the activities personal, students see the connection between what they are practicing and its relationship to their own real lives.

■ *Otra conversación* activities have students adapt the communicative situation modeled in *Una conversación* to talk about their own real lives.

■ *En la vida real* sections integrate thematic review activities into real-life scenarios that help students understand the value of what they are learning and how it can be used in their daily lives.

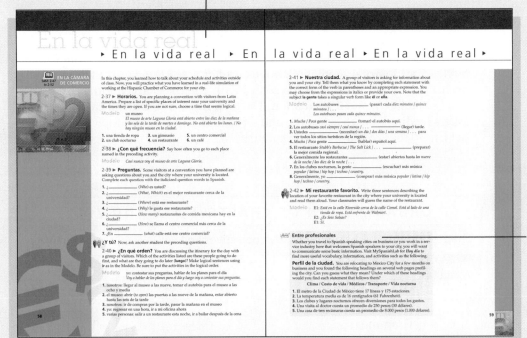

■ *Entre profesionales,* the last activity in the *En la vida real* section, focuses on expanding students' knowledge of Spanish for a particular career. Students are encouraged to go to MySpanishLab to learn more about this career path and practice with similar real scenarios and activities.

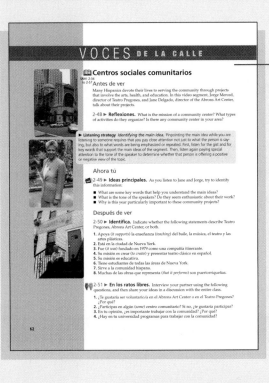

■ **Authentic video** segments in the *Voces de la calle* section feature real people using Spanish in their local communities in North America. By showing how important it is to be bilingual in our multicultural society, they help students tie what they are learning in class to their real lives.

ACCESSIBLE AND PRACTICAL ORGANIZATION...

makes it easy for students to organize their learning and for instructors to plan their classes.

▶ **Chapters 1–5 and 7–11** are divided into four interrelated sections or *Temas*. All material is presented in easy-to-follow two-page modules, with presentation of new material at the top of the left page of the spread, followed by practice on the facing page. The first three *Temas* of each chapter begin with a vocabulary presentation, followed by two grammar sections. The fourth *Tema* begins with a vocabulary presentation, but instead of new grammar presentations, it includes a review of material presented earlier in the chapter with activities integrated into a real-life situation. The final *Hoy día* section of each chapter offers readings, video activities, and structured composition topics through which students can apply their language skills to real life.

ORGANIZATION OF CHAPTERS 1–5 AND 7–11	
Chapter opener with communicative objectives and cultural advance organizer	
Tema 1	Title
	Vocabulary Grammar Grammar
Tema 2	Title
	Vocabulary Grammar Grammar
Tema 3	Title
	Vocabulary Grammar Grammar
Tema 4	Title
	Vocabulary *Resumen de gramática* *En la vida real*
Hoy día	
	Lectores de hoy *Voces de la calle* *Escritores en acción*
Vocabulary summary	

▶ **Review chapters 6 and 12** feature real-life scenarios spread over four *Temas*. Each review-chapter *Tema* recycles previously introduced vocabulary to encourage conversation while adding some new words to provide appropriate context and have students apply the comprehension strategies they have learned in previous chapters. Each of these chapters also reviews all of the grammar taught in the preceding five chapters.

ORGANIZATION OF REVIEW CHAPTERS 6 AND 12	
Chapter opener with communicative objectives and cultural advance organizer	
Tema 1	Title
	Thematic vocabulary *Repaso 1* *Repaso 2* *Repaso 3* *Repaso 4*
Tema 2	Title
	Thematic vocabulary *Repaso 1* *Repaso 2* *Repaso 3* *Repaso 4*
Tema 3	Title
	Thematic vocabulary *Repaso 1* *Repaso 2* *Repaso 3* *Repaso 4*
Tema 4	Title
	Thematic vocabulary *Repaso 1* *Repaso 2* *Repaso 3* *Repaso 4*

ADAPTABLE AND FLEXIBLE DESIGN...

supports instructors teaching face-to-face, hybrid, and fully online courses.

▶ **For classes with reduced contact hours,** the modular, two-page spreads in each *Tema* allow for maximum flexibility. The real-life communicative activities ensure that the content is immediately applicable. The wealth of additional content in MySpanishLab, including oral practice, tutorials, and more, allows you to assign meaningful practice outside of class, perfect for hybrid and fully online courses.

▶ **For classes with more contact hours,** the extensive instructor's annotations include numerous additional activities, allowing instructors to provide more practice in class with the meaningful linguistic input that students need. MySpanishLab also offers you premium content to enhance your class experience. Some of the content you can find includes the following:

  ▶ Mnemonic dictionary (memory aids designed to help students with chapter vocabulary)

  ▶ *Entre profesionales* (activities related to a variety of professions and careers)

  ▶ Podcasts

  ▶ *Escapadas* (a travelogue that takes students on a virtual voyage to different sites all over the Hispanic world)

  ▶ Games

  ▶ Pronunciation guide and practice

And much more...

MORE TOOLS FOR STUDENT SUCCESS...

support students as they learn Spanish through clearly organized review tools and meaningfully sequenced activities.

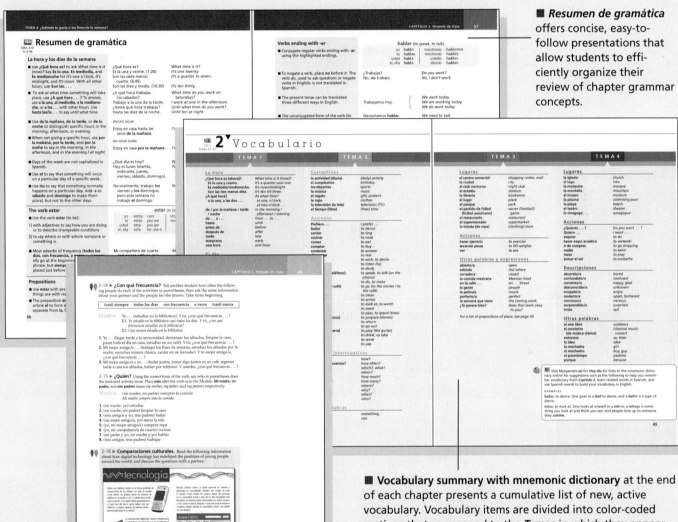

■ *Resumen de gramática* offers concise, easy-to-follow presentations that allow students to efficiently organize their review of chapter grammar concepts.

■ **Vocabulary summary with mnemonic dictionary** at the end of each chapter presents a cumulative list of new, active vocabulary. Vocabulary items are divided into color-coded sections that correspond to the *Temas* in which they appear, making it easy for students to study for quizzes and exams. Each vocabulary list also refers students to an online mnemonic dictionary that helps them remember new words more easily. For example, for the verb **mirar**, it points out that you *look at* yourself in a *mirror*. It also lists other Spanish words with the same root, helping students to make connections and expand their vocabulary. For **mirar**, it points out that **una mirada** is *a glance* or *a look*.

■ **Meaningful activities.** To support students as they use their new language skills, all vocabulary and grammar activities are designed to promote meaningful communication on topics about which students really have something to say. These activities are structured so that students must understand what they are saying in order to answer correctly. The numerous activities are carefully sequenced in order to build students' confidence as they use new structures, going from simple recognition, where students answer with a word or a brief phrase, to more global, personalized activities that allow students to speak about their own real experiences in Spanish.

Integrated program components give students and instructors what they need to make teaching and learning Spanish a meaningful, successful, and gratifying experience. *Hoy día* is available in two paperback volumes: Volume 1: Chapters 1–6, and Volume 2: Chapters 7–12.

Student Resources

▶ Student Activities Manual. The organization of the **Student Activities Manual** (SAM) parallels that of the student text. Activities corresponding to each *Tema* in the textbook recycle and reinforce the vocabulary and grammar presented in the textbook. The *Diario* at the end of the activities for *Temas* 2 and 4 guides students in writing paragraphs on the topics of the chapter. As in the textbook, the communicative nature of activities has been maintained so that students are required to think about the meaning of what they are writing, and grammatical forms are not practiced without relating them to meaning. The order of the activities follows directly the order of presentation of vocabulary and grammar in the corresponding *Tema* of the textbook, so that instructors who cover only part of a *Tema* during a class can easily assign the matching activities from that *Tema* of the SAM. As in the textbook, the final *Tema* of the SAM reviews material from throughout the chapter contextualized in a real-life setting.

▶ Answer Key for the Student Activities Manual. A separate, optional **Answer Key for the Student Activities Manual** allows students to check their own work if the instructor wishes.

▶ Audio CDs for the Student Activities Manual. CD recordings provide easy access to each listening comprehension activity in the Student Activities Manual. The recordings are also accessible in MySpanishLab and on the Companion Website.

▶ Audio CDs for the Student Textbook. CD recordings corresponding to each listening activity in the textbook, as well as the dialogues, vocabulary presentations, and the end-of-chapter vocabulary lists, allow students flexibility in practicing listening comprehension and pronunciation at home. The recordings are also accessible in MySpanishLab and on the Companion Website.

▶ Student Video DVD. Filmed especially for *Hoy día*, the *Voces de la calle* video features approximately 25 speakers from various Spanish-speaking countries and from diverse backgrounds and professions who use Spanish in their communities. Students can listen firsthand to the personal and professional experiences of journalists, students, artists, business owners, and others. Pre-, during-, and post-viewing activities are featured in the *Voces de la calle* section at the end of each chapter. The video script is also available for self-checking of the activities or to facilitate comprehension of the video content.

Instructor Resources

▶ Annotated Instructor's Edition

Available in two paperback volumes (Volume 1: Chapters 1–6, Volume 2: Chapters 7–12) the **Annotated Instructor's Edition** contains numerous marginal annotations with warm-up and expansion activities, as well as additional cultural information. Also included are an array of tips and ideas designed specifically for graduate teaching assistants or adjunct faculty who may have limited preparation time or who may be teaching Spanish for the first time.

▶ Instructor's Resource Manual

The Instructor's Resource Manual (IRM) includes sample syllabi and lesson plans, the scripts for the SAM audio program and the video, and a guide to rubrics.

▶ The Testing Program

The Testing Program is closely correlated with the content of the textbook and includes a bank of activities that assess the vocabulary, grammar, and listening, reading, and writing skills for each chapter of the text. This flexible, modular approach allows instructors to customize tests to fit their classes. Complete, ready-to-use tests are also provided, and can either be administered by the instructor or used as models.

▶ Audio CD for the Testing Program

This CD contains the audio that accompanies the listening comprehension section for each test.

▶ Instructor Resource Center

Several of the instructor supplements listed above—the Instructor's Resource Manual and the Testing Program, as well as the SAM audio script and the video script—are available for download at the access-protected *Hoy día* Instructor Resource Center (www.pearsonhighered.com). An access code will be provided at no charge to instructors once their faculty status has been verified.

Online Resources

▶ ¡Hola! MySpanishLab

MySpanishLab is Pearson's nationally hosted online learning system created specifically for students in college-level language courses. It brings together—in one convenient, easily navigable site—a wide array of language-learning tools and resources, an electronic version of the *Hoy día* student text, an interactive version of the *Hoy día* Student Activities Manual, and all materials from the *Hoy día* audio and video programs. Readiness checks, chapter tests, and tutorials for both Spanish and English grammar personalize instruction to meet the unique needs of individual students. Instructors can use the system to make assignments, set grading parameters, listen to student-created voice recordings, and provide feedback on student work. Instructor access is provided at no charge. Students can purchase access codes online or at their local bookstore.

▶ 🖥 Companion Website

The open-access Companion Website™ has been specifically created to accompany *Hoy día*. The Website features access to the *Hoy día* audio program (Textbook and SAM) as well as links for completing the *¡Navega!* activities within the textbook.

ACKNOWLEDGMENTS

Hoy día is the result of a collaborative effort among the authors, our publisher, and our colleagues and students. We are especially thankful to many members of the Spanish teaching community for their time and insightful suggestions as they reviewed the drafts of *Hoy día*. Their critiques and recommendations helped us to sharpen our pedagogical focus and improve the overall quality of the program. We gratefully acknowledge the contributions of our faculty reviewers.

Core panel of faculty reviewers

Darren Broome, *Gordon College, Georgia*
Lori Fry, *Indian River State College*
Khedija Gadhoum, *Clayton State University*
Frozina Goussak, *Collin County Community College*
David Migaj, *Wright City College of Chicago*
Dennis Miller, *Clayton State University*
Charles Molano, *Lehigh Carbon Community College*
Milagros Juan-Ojermark, *Diablo Valley College*
Sadie Nickelson-Requejo, *The University of Puget Sound*
Michele Shaul, *Queens University of Charlotte*
Sabrina Spannagel, *South Seattle Community College*

We also wish to acknowledge our student reviewers who gave us comprehensive feedback on the mnemonic dictionary. A total of 30 students from the following 15 colleges and universities participated.

Colleges and Universities
Arizona State University
Austin Community College
Miami Dade Community College
Oklahoma University
Providence College
The University of California, Los Angeles
University of Colorado, Boulder
University of Florida
University of Maryland, College Park
University of Nebraska, Lincoln
University of North Carolina, Greensboro
University of Pennsylvania
University of Pittsburgh
University of Texas, San Antonio
University of Washington

Students

Susan E Bendernagel, Rachel Brickner, Clint Cornett, Drue Dorsey, Alexis Fabrizio, Amanda Fakhir, Jessica Garza, Christopher Gast, Allissa Goldberg, Dianna He, Adam Hughes, Jason Hustedt, Amanda Kudron, Bridget D. Landry, Alex R. Langlois, Michael Long, Jr, Colleen R. McGreal, Samantha L. Mills, Laura Morel, Rachel Nekolaichuk, Timothy B. O'Mara, Meghana Reddy, Sasha Rodriquez, Drew Rudebusch, Evan Skinner, Nicolas Trilla, Caroleena Vargas, Cheryl Walker, Whitney E. Washousky, Alyssa Whitwell.

We are also grateful for the guidance of Celia Meana, development editor, for all of her work, suggestions, attention to detail, and dedication to the text. Her support and spirit helped us to achieve the final product. We would also like to thank the contributor who assisted us in the preparation the Student Activities Manual: Stéphanie Panichelli-Batalla. We are very grateful to other colleagues and friends at Prentice Hall: Meriel Martínez, Media Editor, for helping us produce such a great video, audio program, and Companion Website; and Melissa Marolla Brown, Development Editor for Assessment, for the diligent coordination among the text, Student Activities Manual, and Testing Program. We are very grateful to our MySpanishLab team, Bob Hemmer, Samantha Alducin, and Mary Reynolds, for the creation of *Hoy día* materials for MySpanishLab. Thanks to Andrea Arias, Editorial Assistant, for her hard work and efficiency in obtaining reviews and attending to many administrative details.

We are very appreciative of our marketing team, Kris Ellis-Levy, Denise Miller, and Bill Bliss, for their creativity and efforts in coordinating all marketing and promotion of the *Hoy día* program. Thanks, too, to our production team, Mary Rottino, Senior Managing Editor for Product Development, Janice Stangel, Associate Managing Editor, and Nancy Stevenson, Senior Production Project Manager, who guided *Hoy día* through the many stages of production; to our partners at Pre-Press PMG, especially Melissa Sacco, Senior Project Manager, for her careful and professional editing and production services. We also thank our art team, Pat Smythe, Miguel Ortiz, Gail Cocker, and Maria Piper. Special thanks to Lisa Delgado for the beautiful interior and cover designs. Finally, we would like to express our sincere thanks to Phil Miller, Publisher, and Julia Caballero, Executive Editor, for their guidance and support through every aspect of *Hoy día.*

John T. McMinn
Nuria Alonso García

1 En la universidad

In this chapter, you will learn about the growing importance of Hispanic cultures in the United States. It is important to understand some common cultural customs in order to avoid misunderstandings when meeting or working with Hispanics.

Hispanics generally expect people arriving at gatherings to shake hands or give kisses on the cheek to everyone in the group. When leaving, it is expected to say good-bye to everyone in the same manner.

► Do you feel comfortable giving or receiving kisses on the cheek?

► How often do you shake hands?

► How might a Hispanic feel if not acknowledged in this way?

Some Hispanics may move their hands more and stand closer when talking.

► What do you usually think when someone stands closer to you than most people?

► How might someone feel if you backed away?

In most Hispanic countries, people have a different sense of fashion and are less likely to wear shorts, T-shirts, and tennis shoes.

► Do people's clothes sometimes affect your impression of them? In what ways?

How to introduce new chapters.
Use the two pages that open each chapter as an advance organizer to connect what students already know with what they are going to learn. First, discuss the title and the various sections of the chapter. Ask students to brainstorm in English the most basic things related to the chapter theme that they should learn to communicate, and have them anticipate which of those they might learn in this chapter. Then, look at the photo and have students imagine who the people are and what they might be saying. Finally, have groups of students discuss the opening culture note and their own related observations. Ask each group to think of additional questions on the topic about which they would like to learn more.

Vocabulario Saludos y despedidas

SAM: 1-1
to 1-6

¿Sabías que...?

A greeting is a symbol of identity in different cultures. There are different types of greetings depending on the relationship between people. In Hispanic countries, the typical formal greeting among professionals is the handshake. Friends and family members usually give one or two kisses on the cheek, or male friends give one another a hug. How do you and your friends usually greet one another?

How to use ¿Sabías que...?
As you discuss each ¿Sabías que...?, ask students to make cross-cultural comparisons between Hispanic cultures and what is true for them.

¡Ojo!

■ You should learn all vocabulary appearing in the *Vocabulario* sections. Words needing additional explanations are boldfaced and glossed at the bottom of the page. You can also find a list with translations of all the new vocabulary from each *Tema* at the end of the chapter.
■ Note that the letter **h** is silent in Spanish and is not pronounced in **hola** or **hasta**, and the **ll** in words like **llamo** is pronounced similarly to an English **y** sound.

¿Cómo se pronuncia? ¡Hola!

The vowels a, e, i, o, u

The Pronunciation Guide for Spanish can be found in your MySpanishLab™ course. This guide will help you communicate more clearly in Spanish. Occasionally, marginal notes will suggest appropriate times to study pronunciation explanations. Now is a good time to learn how to pronounce the vowels **a, e, i, o, u** by accessing the Pronunciation Guide in *Capítulo 1*. The proper pronunciation of the vowels is the most basic key to good pronunciation in Spanish.

Una conversación informal

CD 1
Track 1

ANTONIO:	**Buenos días. Soy Antonio. ¿Y tú? ¿Cómo te llamas?**
DAVID:	**Hola.** Me llamo David.
ANTONIO:	**Mucho gusto,** David.
DAVID:	**Igualmente. ¿De dónde eres,** Antonio?
ANTONIO:	Soy **de aquí. ¿**Y tú?
DAVID:	Soy de Miami.
ANTONIO:	¿Eres estudiante?
DAVID:	Sí, soy estudiante de la universidad Panamericana.

Use the expressions in the preceding conversation to introduce yourself to a classmate or to other people with whom you have an informal relationship. Use **tú** to say *you* to a classmate or friend.

Una conversación formal

SR GONZÁLEZ:	**Buenas noches.** Soy Carlos González. ¿Y usted? ¿Cómo se llama?
SRA DELGADO:	Me llamo María Delgado.
SR GONZÁLEZ:	Mucho gusto.
SRA DELGADO:	Igualmente. ¿De dónde es usted, señor González?
SR GONZÁLEZ:	Soy de México. ¿Y usted, señora Delgado?
SRA DELGADO:	Soy de Puerto Rico.
SR GONZÁLEZ:	¿Es usted profesora o estudiante?
SRA DELGADO:	Soy profesora de español de la universidad Panamericana.

Use **usted** for *you* when talking to someone to whom you want to show respect, such as a professor or an adult you do not know well. A different form of the verb is also used with **usted.**

Más saludos y despedidas

JOSÉ:	¡Hola, Celia! **¡Cómo estás?**
CELIA:	**¡Buenas tardes,** José! **Estoy muy bien, gracias.** ¿Y tú?
JOSÉ:	**Regular. No estoy mal.**
CELIA:	**Pues, adiós. Hasta mañana.**
JOSÉ:	Sí, **hasta luego.**

Use **¿Cómo estás?** when asking how a friend, classmate, or someone with whom you have an informal relationship is doing, and **¿Cómo está (usted)?** when talking to a professor or an adult you do not know well.

Buenos días. *Good morning.*   **Soy** *I am*   **¿Y tú?** *And you?*   **¿Cómo te llamas?** *What's your name?*
Hola. *Hi.*   **Mucho gusto.** *Pleased to meet you.*   **Igualmente.** *Likewise.*   **¿De dónde eres?** *Where are you from?*   **de** *from, of*   **aquí** *here*   **Buenas noches.** *Good evening.*   **saludos** *greetings*   **despedidas** *saying good-bye*   **¿Cómo estás?** *How are you?*   **Buenas tardes.** *Good afternoon*   **Estoy muy bien, gracias** *I'm doing very well, thank you*   **Regular.** *As usual.*   **No estoy mal.** *I'm not bad.*   **Pues, adiós.** *Well, good-bye.*
Hasta mañana. *See you tomorrow.*   **hasta luego** *see you later, good-bye*

El alfabeto

Suggestions for presenting the alphabet.
Point out that *ch* and *ll* used to be considered separate letters and that some dictionaries will have them alphabetized as such.

Here is how you can ask people to spell their names or other words.

¿Cómo se escribe González? ¿Se escribe **con** o **sin** acento?

a	a	**k**	ka	**s**	ese
b	be (grande)	**l**	ele	**t**	te
c	ce	**m**	eme	**u**	u
d	de	**n**	ene	**v**	uve, ve (chica),
e	e	**ñ**	eñe		ve (corta)
f	efe	**o**	o	**w**	uve doble,
g	ge	**p**	pe		doble ve, doble u
h	hache	**q**	cu	**x**	equis
i	i	**r**	ere	**y**	i griega
j	jota	**rr**	erre	**z**	zeta

Suggestion for *Una conversación.*
Have students listen to the conversation first with books closed for the answers to the following questions: 1. ¿Cómo está Isabel? (bien) 2. ¿De dónde es? (Denver). Then, have students read along in their books as they listen a second time.

How to use *¡A escuchar!*
Each vocabulary presentation is always accompanied by an *¡A escuchar!* listening activity, which is a variation of the communicative task modeled by *Una conversación.* You may do *¡A escuchar!* immediately after reading the printed conversation, or you may wait until just before doing the *Otra conversación* activity to serve as another model. Answers are provided in Spanish. You may have students answer in Spanish or English.

Audioscript for *¡A escuchar!*
EDUARDO: *Hola.*
DANIEL: *Buenos días. Soy Daniel García. ¿Y tú? ¿Cómo te llamas?*
EDUARDO: *Me llamo Eduardo Martínez.*
DANIEL: *Mucho gusto, Eduardo. ¿De dónde eres?*
EDUARDO: *Soy de San Diego, California. ¿Y tú?*
DANIEL: *Soy de Monterrey, México.*

CD 1
Track 2

Una conversación. Two students are meeting for the first time.

JUAN: Buenos días. ¿Cómo estás?
ISABEL: Hola, estoy bien gracias. ¿Y tú?
JUAN: Bien, gracias. ¿Cómo te llamas?
ISABEL: Me llamo Isabel Ramos. ¿Y tú?
JUAN: Soy Juan Mosquera.
ISABEL: ¿Cómo se escribe Mosquera?
JUAN: Se escribe M-O-S-Q-U-E-R-A. ¿De dónde eres, Isabel?
ISABEL: Soy de Denver. ¿Y tú, Juan?
JUAN: Soy de aquí.
ISABEL: Mucho gusto.
JUAN: Igualmente.

CD 1, Track 3

¡A escuchar!

Listen to another conversation in which two students meet. What are their names and where are they from?

Possible answers for *¡A escuchar!*
Daniel García, Monterrey, México; Eduardo Martínez, San Diego, California

1-1 ▶ Respuestas. Which responses from the box are logical if someone says the following to you?

Adiós.	**Estoy regular.**	**Mucho gusto.**
Buenas tardes.	**Hola.**	**Soy Daniel Reyna.**
Buenos días.	**Igualmente.**	**Soy de aquí.**
Estoy muy bien, gracias.	**Me llamo Anita López.**	

Note for activities. Activities practicing new vocabulary and grammar are ordered from the more structured to the more open-ended. Instructors should feel free to do any activity in pairs, in groups, or as a whole class, according to the needs of the students.

Warm-ups for 1-2.
• Spell aloud the following course names that are cognates and have students write them down and give the English equivalents: *geología, antropología, astronomía, italiano, fotografía, justicia criminal, física.*
• Ask questions about words students have already seen or students' names:
¿Cómo se escribe llamo, con ll o con y?
¿Cómo se escribe aquí, con acento o sin acento?
• Spell the names of the five cities in the U.S. where the greatest percentage of the population speaks Spanish at home according to the U.S. Census Bureau. Have students write the name of the city as you spell it. Afterwards, give the percentage of people who speak Spanish in each city and the state where each is located. Discuss the growing importance of being bilingual. 1. *Hialeah, Florida (92%)* 2. *Laredo, Texas (91%)* 3. *Brownsville, Texas (87%)* 4. *East Los Angeles, California (86%)* 5. *McAllen, Texas (74%)*

1. ¡Hola!   **4.** ¿De dónde eres?   **7.** Mucho gusto.
2. ¿Cómo te llamas?   **5.** Soy Carlos González.   **8.** ¿Cómo estás?
3. ¿Cómo se llama usted?   **6.** Buenas tardes.   **9.** Hasta mañana.

1-2 ▶ ¿Cómo se escribe? Spell the names of your favorite people and things in Spanish. Your classmates will try to name them.

Modelo   tu restaurante favorito
          P-a-n-c-h-o-s (pe-a-ene-ce-hache-o-ese)

Answers for 1-2.
Answers will vary.

1. tu restaurante favorito   **2.** tu actor favorito   **3.** tu auto favorito

1-3 ▶ Otra conversación. With a partner, reread *Una conversación* between Juan and Isabel at the top of the page. Then change the conversation to talk about yourselves.

Answers for 1-1. 1. *Buenas tardes., Buenos días., Hola.;* 2. *Me llamo Anita López., Soy Daniel Reyna.;* 3. *Me llamo Anita López.; Soy Daniel Reyna.;* 4. *Soy de aquí.;* 5. *Mucho gusto., Soy Daniel Reyna., Me llamo Anita López., Buenos días., Buenas tardes., Hola.;* 6. *Buenas tardes., Hola.;* 7. *Igualmente., Mucho gusto.;* 8. *Estoy muy bien, gracias., Estoy regular.;* 9. *Adiós.*

¿Cómo se escribe . . . ? *How do you write . . . ? How is . . . spelled?*   **con** *with*   **sin** *without*

📖 Gramática 1

SAM: 1-7 to 1-8

Deciding how to address people: Using **tú** or **usted**

■ There are two ways to say *you* to someone in Spanish. Use the familiar form **tú** when talking to a friend, a classmate, a family member, or a child. Use the formal form **usted** to address an adult you do not know or someone to whom you wish to show respect. **Usted** is often abbreviated **Ud.**

■ Verb forms are different for each of the subject pronouns.

tú (*you, familiar*)	**usted** (*you, formal*)	
¿Cómo te llamas (tú)?	¿Cómo se llama (usted)?	*What is your name?*
¿Cómo estás (tú)?	¿Cómo está (usted)?	*How are you?*
¿De dónde eres (tú)?	¿De dónde es (usted)?	*Where are you from?*

■ In Spanish, subject pronouns like **yo** (*I*) and **tú** (*you,* familiar) are normally omitted because the verb ending indicates who the subject is. The pronoun **usted** (*you,* formal) is used more often than **yo** and **tú,** but it is often omitted as well. For example, both **soy** and **yo soy** are translated as *I am.* The word **yo** is included only when you want to put emphasis on the word *I.*

■ You should not expect to be able to translate word for word from English to Spanish. The lack of one-to-one correspondence can also be seen in the expressions used to give names.

SPANISH	LITERAL TRANSLATION	ENGLISH EQUIVALENT
(Yo) me llamo . . .	(*I*) *myself call. . . .*	*My name is. . . .*

1-4 ▶ ¿Tú o usted? In which situation would you more likely use the following phrases, A or B?

A

B

1. _A_ ¿Cómo te llamas?
2. _B_ ¿Cómo se llama usted?
3. _B_ ¿Cómo está usted?
4. _A_ ¿Cómo estás?
5. _B_ Me llamo Pablo Zamora, ¿y usted?
6. _A_ Me llamo Alicia, ¿y tú?
7. _B_ ¿De dónde es usted?
8. _A_ ¿Eres de México?
9. _A_ ¿De dónde eres?
10. _B_ ¿Es usted de Miami?

1-5 ▶ ¿Cómo se llama usted? ¿Cómo te llamas? How would you ask these people their names?

Modelo　　an elderly neighbor
　　　　　　¿Cómo se llama usted?

1. a professor
2. a classmate
3. your classmate's little brother
4. a salesclerk

5. your roommate's grandmother
6. your roommate's girlfriend/boyfriend
7. your father's boss
8. your mother's secretary

1-6 ▶ ¿Cómo está usted? ¿Cómo estás? How would you ask the people in the preceding activity how they are?

Modelo　　an elderly neighbor
　　　　　　¿Cómo está usted?

1-7 ▶ ¿Cómo estás? With a partner, prepare brief exchanges where these people greet each other and ask how they are doing. Do they use **¿Cómo estás?** or **¿Cómo está usted?**

Modelo　　E1: *Buenas tardes. ¿Cómo está*
　　　　　　　　usted?
　　　　　　E2: *Estoy muy bien, gracias.*
　　　　　　　　¿Y usted?
　　　　　　E1: *Estoy bien, gracias.*

1.

2.

3.

4.

📖 Gramática 2 Describing yourself and others: Introduction to **ser** and **estar**

SAM: 1-9
to 1-12

1. What are the two verbs meaning *to be* in Spanish? How do you say *I am, you are* (familiar), and *you are* (formal) with each?

2. Do you use the forms of **ser** or **estar** to say who people are? Where they are from? What they are like? How they are doing?

3. What are three adjectives you can use with **estar** to say how you are doing? Do you use the ending **-o** or **-a** for males? For females?

Note.
Students learn the full conjugation of *ser* later in this chapter and the full conjugation of *estar* in *Capítulo 2*. Their uses are compared in more detail in *Capítulo 4*.

■ There are two verbs meaning *to be* in Spanish.

ser *(to be)*			**estar** *(to be)*		
yo	soy	*I am*	yo	estoy	*I am*
tú	eres	*you are*	tú	estás	*you are*
usted	es	*you are*	usted	está	*you are*

■ The verbs **ser** and **estar** cannot be used interchangeably. Use the forms of **ser** to say who people are, where they are from originally, or what they are like. Use the forms of **estar** to say how people are feeling or doing. Remember that subject pronouns (**yo, tú, usted**) are often dropped in Spanish and you rely on the form of the verb to determine who the subject is.

Soy estudiante / profesor (profesora).	*I am a student / professor.*
Soy de Estados Unidos.	*I am from the United States.*
Estoy muy bien hoy.	*I am very well today.*

■ Whereas the verb *to be* is negated in English by placing *not* after it, verbs in Spanish are negated by placing **no** before them.

| Anita **no es** estudiante. Es profesora. | *Anita **is not** a student. She's a professor.* |
| **No soy** de aquí. | *I **am not** from here.* |

■ Some nouns and adjectives change forms depending on whether they describe males or females, such as **profesor** (*male*) and **profesora** (*female*). Here are some adjectives you might use with **estar** to say how you are doing. Use the ending **-o** for males and **-a** for females.

¿Cómo estás?

¿Cansado/a?

¿Enfermo/a?

¿Ocupado/a?

1-8 ▶ Presentaciones. Complete the following sentences by selecting the words in parentheses that describe you best, or by using others like them.

1. Soy ____. (estudiante, profesor, profesora)
2. Soy ____. (de aquí, de Chicago, de Dallas, de Atlanta, de Baltimore, . . .)
3. Hoy estoy ____. (bien, mal, regular, cansado/a, enfermo/a, ocupado/a)

 ¿Y tú? Now, ask another student the same information by completing the following questions with the appropriate verbs in the form of **tú**.

¿____ estudiante o profesor/a?
¿De dónde ____?
¿Cómo ____ hoy?

1-9 ► ¿Cómo estás?

Your friends are doing the following things when you call. How might they answer when you ask how they are? Using **cansado/a, enfermo/a, ocupado/a,** or **muy bien,** prepare short exchanges with a classmate, who will play the role of the person in the picture.

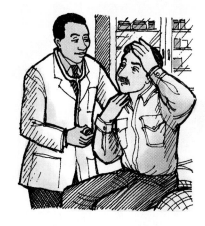

Modelo   Eduardo
E1: *Hola, Eduardo. ¿Cómo estás?*
E2: *Estoy enfermo.*

1. Ramón   **2.** Pedro   **3.** Alicia

1-10 ► Mucho gusto.

Get acquainted with a classmate using the following conversation as a model. Change the formal **usted** forms to familiar **tú** forms and make additional changes as needed.

— Buenas tardes. Soy Ximena Duarte. ¿Y usted? ¿Cómo se llama?
— Me llamo Enrique Contreras.
— Mucho gusto, señor Contreras.
— Igualmente. ¿Cómo está usted?
— Estoy muy bien. ¿Y usted?
— Bien, gracias. ¿De dónde es usted, señora Duarte?
— Soy de Miami. ¿Y usted?
— Soy de aquí.

1-11 ► Comparaciones culturales

Imagine that you are at an event at the Hispanic Chamber of Commerce in your area and you are meeting people from the following places. Ask each of them if they are from the capital city. Refer to the maps in the back of the book, if necessary.

Modelo   México
¿Es usted de la ciudad de México?

1. Puerto Rico
2. Cuba
3. El Salvador
4. la República Dominicana
5. Guatemala
6. Colombia
7. Honduras
8. Ecuador
9. Perú

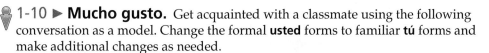

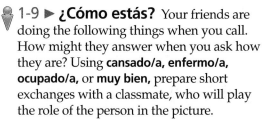

📖 Vocabulario En la clase

SAM: 1-13 to 1-16

 CD 1 Track 4 **¿Qué hay** en el salón de clase? ¿Hay muchos estudiantes en la clase de español?

¿Sabías que...?

In order to get maximum use out of classroom space, public school children in Mexico attend class in shifts. Morning school is approximately from 7:30 AM until 1:00–1:30 PM, and afternoon school from 1:00–1:30 PM until 7:30 PM. Do you think this system would work where you live? Why or why not?

¡Ojo!

Different words are sometimes used for certain things in different regions of the Spanish-speaking world. For example, in Mexico, people say **una pluma** instead of **un bolígrafo.** In Spain, people say **un ordenador** for **una computadora,** and **un computador** is used in parts of Latin America.

Suggestions for *Una conversación.*
• Have students listen to the conversation first with books closed and list as many things as they can that the roommates say they have *(un escritorio, una cama, una computadora* (for each), *un estante, varios libros, un estéreo, un televisor).* Then, have students read along in their books as they listen a second time.
• New words presented in the conversation include the boldfaced expressions and *un estéreo, un problema,* and *espacio.*

Audioscript for *¡A escuchar!*
ERNESTO: *Hola, Julio. ¡Qué mochila tan grande! ¿Qué hay en tu mochila?*
JULIO: *Tengo muchos libros para mis clases, una calculadora y varios cuadernos.*
ERNESTO: *¿Cuántas clases tienes?*
JULIO: *Tengo cuatro. ¿Y tú?*
ERNESTO: *Tengo cinco.*
JULIO: *¿Dónde están tus libros?*
ERNESTO: *Tengo libros electrónicos para mis clases. No necesito más libros, cuadernos ni calculadora. Sólo necesito mi computadora.*

 CD 1, Track 6

¡A escuchar!

Now, listen to two students talk about what they have and need for class. What does Julio have in his backpack? What does Ernesto have instead?

Possible answers for *¡A escuchar!*
Julio: (muchos) libros, una calculadora, (varios) cuadernos / Ernesto: una computadora.

10

En **mi cuarto,** en el escritorio, **tengo . . .**

 CD 1 Track 5

Una conversación. Two roommates are talking about what they have.

MARCO: Hola, Luis. **¿Tienes** muchas **cosas** para el cuarto?

LUIS: Tengo un escritorio, **una cama,** una computadora y un estante con **varios** libros. ¿Y tú?

MARCO: **Como** tú, tengo una computadora, **pero** no tengo muchos libros. **También** tengo un estéreo y un televisor. **Sólo necesito** una cama.

LUIS: No hay problema. Hay espacio **para tus** cosas y tengo **otra** cama.

---

qué *what* **hay** *there is, there are, is there, are there* **mi(s)** *my* **un cuarto** *a room* **tengo** *I have* **Tienes** *(do) you have* **una cosa** *a thing* **una cama** *a bed* **varios/as** *several* **Como** *like, as* **pero** *but* **También** *also, too* **Sólo** *only* **necesito** *I need* **para** *for* **tu(s)** *your* **otro/a** *another, other*

1-12 ▶ ¿Qué es? Which word from the list can be used to describe each item?

una computadora	una estudiante de mi clase
un cuarto	un estudiante de mi clase
un libro	una mesa con una silla para estudiantes
un señor	un profesor o una profesora con un grupo
una señora	de estudiantes

Modelo   Una profesora es *una señora*.

1. Un profesor es . . .
2. Un compañero de clase es . . .
3. Una compañera de clase es . . .
4. Un diccionario es . . .

5. Un salón de clase es . . .
6. Una calculadora es . . .
7. Una clase es . . .
8. Un pupitre es . . .

1-13 ▶ Productos. An international student is asking about product names. Which product from the list do you associate with each of these brand names?

un bolígrafo	un diccionario
una calculadora	un estéreo
una cama	un reloj
una computadora	

Modelo   Texas Instruments, Casio, Sharp
          una calculadora

1. Dell, Hewlett Packard, Gateway, Apple
2. Bic, Parker, Cross
3. Timex, Elgin, Rolex, Fossil, Pulsar
4. Merriam-Webster, American Heritage
5. Bose, Sony, Sharp, Panasonic
6. Serta, Sealy Posturepedic, Simmons

1-14 ▶ ¿Qué hay? A student is talking about what she has. Put each noun in parentheses in the logical blank. Then, indicate whether the sentence is true **(cierto)** or false **(falso)** for you. Note that **en** can mean both *in* or *on*.

Modelo   Tengo *un bolígrafo en mi mochila. (mochila, bolígrafo)*
          Cierto.

1. Tengo mucho ____papel____ en mi ____cuaderno____ . (papel, cuaderno)
2. Hay muchas ____cosas____ en mi ____mochila____ . (mochila, cosas)
3. Tengo una ____computadora____ en mi ____escritorio____ . (computadora, escritorio)
4. Hay muchos ____libros____ en mi ____estante____ . (estante, libros)
5. Tengo un ____televisor____ en mi ____cuarto____ . (cuarto, televisor)
6. No hay muchas ____ventanas____ en mi ____cuarto____ . (ventanas, cuarto)

1-15 ▶ Mis cosas. Say what items presented on the preceding page can be found in the following places.

Modelo   En mi pupitre, *hay un cuaderno y un bolígrafo.*

1. En mi pupitre . . .
2. En mi cuarto . . .
3. En mi mochila . . .

1-16 ▶ Otra conversación. With a partner, reread *Una conversación* between Marco and Luis. Then, imagine that one of you is moving in with the other and talk about what you have.

¡Ojo!

- Note that there are two different forms of the word for *a* (**un** and **una**). You will learn how to determine when to use **un** vs. **una** in the next grammar section. For now, use the form you see with each word in these vocabulary activities.
- The word **de** can mean either *from* or *of*, and it is also used before a noun that modifies another noun. In the second case, the modifying noun follows the noun it describes: **un salón de clase** *a classroom,* **un/a compañero/a de clase** *a classmate,* **una clase de español** *a Spanish class.*
- Use **mi** or **tu** before singular nouns to say *my* or *your* (familiar) and **mis** or **tus** before plural nouns.

Note for word lists.
Point out to students that words from lists of possible responses that have already been used in the *Modelo* are italicized, such as *una señora* in the list in activity 1-12 and *una calculadora* in activity 1-13.

Answers for 1-12.
1. *un señor;* 2. *un estudiante de mi clase;* 3. *una estudiante de mi clase;* 4. *un libro;* 5. *un cuarto;* 6. *una computadora;* 7. *un profesor o una profesora con un grupo de estudiantes;* 8. *una mesa con una silla para estudiantes*

Answers for 1-13.
1. *una computadora;* 2. *un bolígrafo;* 3. *un reloj;* 4. *un diccionario;* 5. *un estéreo;* 6. *una cama*

Answers for 1-15.
Answers will vary.

¿Cómo se pronuncia? ¡Hola!

Syllabification and Stress
It is easy to determine which syllable to stress in Spanish words with just a few simple rules. These rules are explained in the Pronunciation Guide found in MySpanishLab for your course.

 # Gramática 1

SAM: 1-17
to 1-20

Saying what there is: Gender and number of nouns, the indefinite article, and **hay**

Para averiguar

1. For nouns that do not refer to humans or animals, can you tell their gender from what they mean?
2. What endings generally indicate that a noun is masculine? That a noun is feminine? Are the following cognates masculine or feminine: **familia, actividad, video, definición**?
3. What is the plural ending for nouns ending with a vowel? For those ending with a consonant? What happens to a final **z** before the **-es** ending?
4. What are the two forms of the word for *a/an* in Spanish? For *some*? When do you use each?
5. How do you say *there is, there are, is there,* and *are there* in Spanish?
6. How do you say *not any* before a masculine noun? Before a feminine noun?

Suggestion for *Para averiguar.*
You may want to refer students to the *¡Ojo!* box on the next page for an explanation of cognates.

■ All nouns in Spanish have gender and are classified as masculine or feminine. Nouns naming humans or animals are generally masculine or feminine according to their sex, but you cannot guess the gender of nouns naming things from their meaning. For example, the word for *dress* (**vestido**) is masculine.

■ The words for *a/an* and *some,* known as indefinite articles, have different forms, depending on whether they are used with masculine or feminine nouns.

Indefinite Articles

	Masculine			Feminine		
SINGULAR	un	libro	*a book*	una	mesa	*a table*
PLURAL	unos	libros	*some books*	unas	mesas	*some tables*

■ Make nouns plural by adding **-s** if they end with a vowel and **-es** if they end with a consonant. A final **-z** changes to **-c-** before the **-es** plural ending.

una mesa	⟶	unas mesa**s**
un profesor	⟶	unos profeso**res**
un lápiz	⟶	unos lápi**ces**

■ Generally, nouns ending with **-o** or **-l** are masculine and those ending with **-a, -dad, -tad, -sión,** or **-ción** are feminine. There are exceptions, such as **un día** (*a day*) and many nouns ending with **-ma** like **un problema** (*a problem*), which are masculine. The gender of nouns ending with other vowels or consonants is usually not predictable, so you should learn them with the article.

■ Nouns referring to people generally have distinct forms for masculine or feminine. Masculine nouns ending in **-o** change the final **-o** to **-a** for the feminine form. An **-a** is added to a noun ending in a consonant for its feminine form.

un compañero de clase	*a classmate (male)*
una compañer**a** de clase	*a classmate (female)*
un profesor	*a professor (male)*
una profesor**a**	*a professor (female)*

■ Nouns ending with other vowels or the ending **-ista** generally have the same form for both males and females. Refer to **un** or **una** to determine gender.

un estudiante	*a student (male)*
una estudiante	*a student (female)*
un artista	*an artist (male)*
una artista	*an artist (female)*

■ Use **hay** to say what there is. **Hay** is used with both singular and plural nouns and can have four different translations: *there is, there are, is there,* or *are there.*

Hay un diccionario en mi mochila.	*There is a dictionary in my backpack.*
¿**Hay** muchos estudiantes?	*Are there a lot of students?*

Suggestion.
You may wish to point out that unlike in English, the singular forms *un / una* and the negative forms *ningún / ninguna* may also be dropped in Spanish. Ex. *Tengo (un) televisor en mi cuarto.* > I have a television set in my room. / *No tengo (ninguna) computadora.* > I don't have a computer.

■ To say that there is not something, place **no** before **hay.** To say *not any,* use **ningún** before a masculine noun or **ninguna** before a feminine noun instead of **un** or **una.**

No hay **ningún** libro aquí.	*There is not (isn't) any book here.*
No hay **ninguna** computadora.	*There is not (isn't) any computer.*

■ Like the word *some* in English, **unos** and **unas** are usually omitted in Spanish.

Hay (unos) libros en el estante.	*There are (some) books on the shelf.*

1-17 ► En la universidad. Here are some Spanish nouns that are cognates. You can determine whether the following nouns are masculine or feminine by their endings. Indicate whether you use **un** or **una** to translate *a* or *an* before each one.

Modelo   *una* residencia para estudiantes

1. _una_ cafetería
2. _un_ museo
3. _un_ teatro
4. _una_ administración
5. _una_ facultad de medicina
6. _un_ gimnasio
7. _un_ supermercado
8. _una_ discoteca
9. _un_ laboratorio de biología
10. _una_ orquesta sinfónica
11. _una_ competición de golf
12. _una_ estatua de un presidente

 ¿Y tú? Using **hay**, take turns with a partner to say whether the preceding items in this activity can be found at your university.

Modelo   *Hay una residencia para estudiantes. / Hay residencias para estudiantes. / No hay ninguna residencia para estudiantes.*

1-18 ► En la biblioteca. Say what there is in this library.

Modelo   *Hay una puerta.*

 1-19 ► En el salón de clase. A student will name one of the objects found in your classroom. The following students will repeat everything that has already been named and add one more item to the list until everything in your classroom has been named.

Modelo   E1: *En el salón de clase hay un escritorio.*
E2: *En el salón de clase hay un escritorio y pupitres.*
E3: *En el salón de clase hay un escritorio, pupitres y libros . . .*

Cognates are words that look similar and have the same meaning in two languages. You will learn more about cognates in the *Reading strategy* in this chapter.

Suggestion for 1-17.
Point out that when one noun modifies another, as in 9. *un laboratorio de biología*, the article agrees with the modified noun *laboratorio*, not its modifier *biología*.

How to use ¿Y tú?
¿Y tú? activities are often included as a second step within an activity and prompt students to apply newly practiced structures in a context that is real for them. Have students take turns sharing information with a partner.

Answers for 1-18.
1. *Hay un reloj.* 2. *Hay una computadora.* 3. *Hay un escritorio.* 4. *Hay una ventana.* 5. *Hay (unos/as) estudiantes.* 6. *Hay (unos) libros.* 7. *Hay una mesa.* 8. *Hay (unos) cuadernos.* 9. *Hay (unos) bolígrafos., Hay (unas) plumas.* 10. *Hay una calculadora.* 11. *Hay (unos) lápices.* 12. *Hay una mochila.*

📖 Gramática 2

SAM: 1-21
to 1-25

Saying how many: Numbers from 0 to 100

Para **averiguar**

1. Which numbers agree for masculine or feminine?
2. What are the forms of **uno** before masculine and feminine nouns?
3. Is there any difference in how you say *one class* and *a class*?
4. Which numbers between 16 and 99 are written as single words? Which must be written as three separate words?
5. When do you use **cien** to say *one hundred*? When do you use **ciento**?
6. Do you use **un/a** before **otro/a** to say *another*?

Suggestions for presenting and practicing numbers.
• Model pronunciation by saying pairs of numbers and having students repeat the one that is larger.
• Have students write five numbers between 1 and 30 on a sheet of paper. Randomly call out numbers, and the first student to have all five numbers called wins. Play again, having students write five multiples of 5 between 1 and 100.
• Have a student secretly write a number between 1 and 100 on a sheet of paper. As other students guess the number, the student who wrote it answers *más* or *menos* to indicate whether the number is greater or smaller. Use gestures to indicate *más* and *menos*. Students continue taking turns guessing until they narrow it down to the correct number.
• Say numbers and have students give the number that is greater by 10.
• Give math problems with two possible answers and have students repeat the answer that is correct. Modelo: 7 + 8 = 14/15 *(Siete más ocho ¿son catorce o quince?)*
• Send groups of students to the board. Give math problems aloud and have students write them and give the answer. Students at their desks should do the same problems on paper.

■ Here are the numbers 0–100 in Spanish. Use **cuántos** before a masculine noun and **cuántas** before a feminine noun to ask *how many*.

0 cero			
1 uno	11 once	21 veintiuno	31 treinta y uno
2 dos	12 doce	22 veintidós	32 treinta y dos . . .
3 tres	13 trece	23 veintitrés	
4 cuatro	14 catorce	24 veinticuatro	40 cuarenta (cuarenta y uno . . .)
5 cinco	15 quince	25 veinticinco	50 cincuenta (cincuenta y uno . . .)
6 seis	16 dieciséis	26 veintiséis	60 sesenta (sesenta y uno . . .)
7 siete	17 diecisiete	27 veintisiete	70 setenta (setenta y uno . . .)
8 ocho	18 dieciocho	28 veintiocho	80 ochenta (ochenta y uno . . .)
9 nueve	19 diecinueve	29 veintinueve	90 noventa (noventa y uno . . .)
10 diez	20 veinte	30 treinta	100 cien (ciento uno, ciento dos . . .)

■ The number **uno** changes to **un** before a masculine noun and **una** before a feminine noun. Note that **un** and **una** can be translated as *one* or *a/an* before a noun.

| Tengo **un** diccionario. | *I have one dictionary. / I have a dictionary.* |
| Hay **una** computadora. | *There is one computer. / There is a computer.* |

■ Similarly, **veintiuno** changes to **veintiún** and **veintiuna**, and numbers like **treinta y uno** change to **treinta y un** and **treinta y una** before masculine and feminine nouns. The numbers 16–29 are written as single words, but similar numbers above 30 are written as three separate words.

Hay **veintiún** estudiantes en mi clase.	*There are twenty-one students in my class.*
Hay **treinta y una** sillas.	*There are thirty-one chairs.*
Hay **cuarenta y cinco** días de clase.	*There are forty-five days of class.*

■ Use **cien** to say *one hundred* exactly, but **ciento** for the numbers 101–199. Do not use **y** directly after **ciento**

100 = cien
101 = ciento uno/a
145 = ciento cuarenta y cinco

■ If you do not know the exact number of something, you may also use the following words to express how many. These adjectives all agree with the nouns they describe for masculine or feminine.

mucho(s) / mucha(s)	*much, many*
poco(s) / poca(s)	*little, few*
varios / varias	*several*
otro(s) / otra(s)	*another, other*

| No tengo **mucho** papel. | *I don't have much paper.* |
| Hay **muchos** estudiantes internacionales. | *There are many international students.* |

■ Note that **otro** and **otra** mean *another* and you do not use **un** or **una** before them.

| ¿Hay **otro** examen? | *Is there another exam?* |

1-20 ► En la clase de matemáticas.

Use **más** (+) and **son** (=) to read the following math problems. Be sure to include the answers.

Modelo   10 + 12 = ___
          Diez más doce son veintidós.

1. 8 + 7 = ___   **5.** 15 + 12 = ___   **9.** 61 + 15 = ___
2. 6 + 10 = ___   **6.** 34 + 22 = ___   **10.** 84 + 15 = ___
3. 4 + 14 = ___   **7.** 49 + 13 = ___   **11.** 91 + 7 = ___
4. 13 + 11 = ___   **8.** 58 + 24 = ___   **12.** 63 + 37 = ___

1-21 ► ¿Cuál es tu número de teléfono?

Say the following telephone numbers aloud. Read the first digit alone, then read the last six as pairs.

Modelo   223-7607
          dos, veintitrés, setenta y seis, cero, siete

1. 907-1531   **4.** 305-6484   **7.** 257-1707
2. 759-4152   **5.** 414-9099   **8.** 654-1511
3. 878-9505   **6.** 302-1213   **9.** 512-6743

¿Y tú? Now, ask three classmates their telephone numbers in case you need to call them to ask something about class.

Modelo   — *¿Cuál es tu número de teléfono?*
          — *Es el 835-1324. (ocho, treinta y cinco, trece, veinticuatro)*

1-22 ► Comparaciones culturales.

Hispanics represent 15% of the population of the United States. Read the top ten states' rankings for the percentage of the population that is Hispanic. The first one has been done as an example. Note that commas are used instead of decimal points in Spanish.

Modelo   *Nuevo México es el número uno con el cuarenta y cuatro coma dos por ciento.*

1. Nuevo México: 44,2%   **6.** Florida: 20,1%
2. California: 35,9%   **7.** Colorado: 19,7%
3. Texas: 35,7%   **8.** Nueva York: 16,3%
4. Arizona: 29,7%   **9.** Nueva Jersey: 15,6%
5. Nevada: 24,4%   **10.** Illinois: 14,7%

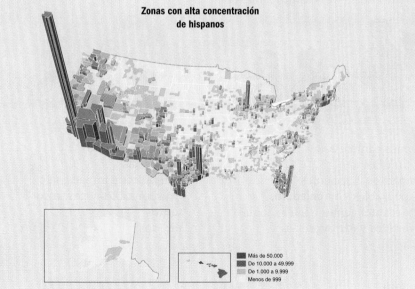

Zonas con alta concentración de hispanos

Más de 50.000
De 10.000 a 49.999
De 1.000 a 9.999
Menos de 999

(29,1%) 4. *Arizona (21,9%)* 5. *Nevada (19,3%)* 6. *Florida (18,7%)* 7. *Colorado (12,3%)* 8. *Nueva York (14,3%)* 9. *Nueva Jersey (13,0%)* 10. *Illinois (12,7%)* These statistics are from the U.S. Census Bureau (2006).

Vocabulario En el campus universitario

SAM: 1-26
to 1-28

 CD 1
Track 7

¿**Cómo es** la universidad? ¿el laboratorio de **lenguas**? ¿el gimnasio? ¿Cómo es **la comida** de la cafetería?

Los edificios son . . .

nuevos y modernos

viejos

La biblioteca es . . .

grande

pequeña

Las residencias son . . .

bonitas

feas

Los profesores y los estudiantes son . . .

buenos e interesantes
optimistas
simpáticos y pacientes
responsables y **trabajadores**
serios, inteligentes e intelectuales
divertidos y extrovertidos

malos y **aburridos**
pesimistas
antipáticos e impacientes
irresponsables y **perezosos**
tontos
tímidos

¿Sabías que...?

In Hispanic universities, there are generally no residence halls on campus for students. Local students usually live at home with their parents and non-local students live in **colegios mayores** located near campus. In addition to room and board, **colegios mayores** also provide cultural and sports activities for students. The **colegios mayores** are a very old Spanish tradition and can be found in many cities with important universities around Spain and Latin America.

¡Ojo!

In Spanish, the word *the* (**el, la, los, las**) and adjectives have various forms, depending on the nouns they modify. On what do you think their forms depend? You will learn more about how to use them in the next grammar section.

¡Ojo!

Normally **y** is used to translate *and*, but before words beginning with **i** or **hi** it changes to **e.** Similarly, **o** is used to say *or*, except before words beginning with **o** or **ho**, where it changes to **u.**

¿Cómo es/son . . . ? *How is/are . . . ? What is/are . . . like?* **una lengua** *a language* **la comida** *food* **pequeño/a** *little, small* **bonito/a** *pretty* **feo/a** *ugly* **aburrido/a** *boring* **simpático/a** *nice* **antipático/a** *unpleasant* **trabajador/a** *hardworking* **perezoso/a** *lazy* **tonto/a** *stupid, silly* **divertido/a** *fun*

CD 1
Track 8

Una conversación. Two friends are talking about their classes.

MARIELA: ¿Cómo son tus clases este semestre?
ADELMA: Tengo tres clases difíciles y dos **fáciles**.
MARIELA: ¿Y tus profesores? ¿Son interesantes?
ADELMA: **Todos** son interesantes menos uno **que** es aburrido.
MARIELA: ¿Y los estudiantes? ¿Son simpáticos?
ADELMA: Sí, tengo dos clases con mi **novio**, una con mi **mejor amiga**, otra con mi **compañera de cuarto** y hay otros amigos en todas mis clases.

 CD 1, Track 9

¡A escuchar!

Now, listen to a conversation in which two students are talking about their campus. What do they say about the buildings? What are three things they say about the library? What are Paloma's friend's dorm room and roommate like? What is the cafeteria like?

1-23 ▶ Mi universidad. Describe your university, your classes, and yourself by completing the following sentences with the appropriate words in italics.

1. La universidad es *grande / pequeña*. También es *moderna / vieja*.
2. Los edificios son *nuevos / viejos*. Muchos son *bonitos / feos*.
3. Hay *muchos / pocos* libros en la biblioteca. Es *grande / pequeña*.
4. Mis clases son *interesantes / aburridas*. Tengo clases *difíciles / fáciles*.
5. Mi clase de español es *grande / pequeña*. Hay *muchos / pocos* estudiantes.
6. Mis compañeros de clase son *inteligentes / tontos*. También son *divertidos / aburridos*.

1-24 ▶ ¿Cómo son? Claudia, a student, is describing her university. Complete each sentence with the most logical adjective in parentheses.

Modelo   La biblioteca es nueva y *moderna*. (vieja, moderna)

1. La biblioteca es grande y ___*buena*___. (pequeña, buena)
2. Los edificios son bonitos y ___*modernos*___. (modernos, feos)
3. Los estudiantes son extrovertidos y ___*divertidos*___. (tímidos, divertidos)
4. Los estudiantes son responsables y ___*trabajadores*___. (perezosos, trabajadores)
5. Los profesores son pacientes y ___*simpáticos*___. (simpáticos, antipáticos)
6. Las clases son difíciles, pero ___*buenas*___. (buenas, fáciles)
7. Las clases son interesantes y ___*divertidas*___. (aburridas, divertidas)
8. Mi compañera de cuarto es simpática y ___*buena*___. (mala, buena)

1-25 ▶ ¿Cómo eres? Complete the following sentences with the adjectives from the list that describe you best. Where two endings are given, use **-a** if you are female. Then, describe your best friend (*mejor amigo/a*). Answers for 1-25. Answers will vary.

aburrido/a	impaciente	paciente	simpático/a
antipático/a	inteligente	perezoso/a	tímido/a
divertido/a	interesante	responsable	tonto/a
extrovertido/a	irresponsable	serio/a	trabajador/a

Soy ———— y (e) ————. No soy ———— ni *(nor)* ————.

Mi mejor amigo/a es ———— y (e) ————. No es ———— ni ————.

 1-26 ▶ Otra conversación. With a classmate, reread *Una conversación* between Mariela and Adelma. Then, change the conversation so that it describes your classes.

---

fácil *easy*   **todo/a/os/as** *all*   **que** *that*   **un novio/una novia** *a boyfriend/a girlfriend*   **un/a mejor amigo/a** *a best friend*   **un/a compañero/a de cuarto** *a roommate*

Suggestions for *Una conversación*.
• Have students listen to the conversation first with books closed for the answers to the following questions. 1. ¿Cuántas clases tiene la estudiante? (5 clases) 2. ¿Cuántas clases son difíciles? (3 clases) 3. ¿Cuántos profesores son aburridos? (1 profesor) Then, have them read along in their books as they listen a second time.
• New words presented in the conversation include the boldfaced expressions, as well as *este semestre* and *menos* meaning *except, minus*.

Audioscript for *¡A escuchar!*
MARÍA: *Hola, Paloma. ¡Qué bien que ya estamos en la universidad! ¿Te gusta el campus? No es muy grande pero es muy bonito.*
PALOMA: *Para mí, los edificios viejos son bonitos, pero no me gustan los edificios nuevos. ¡Son feos!*
MARÍA: *Sí, y la biblioteca nueva no es muy bonita, pero es moderna y hay muchos libros. También hay muchas computadoras para los estudiantes.*
PALOMA: *¿Tienes un cuarto en la residencia nueva?*
MARÍA: *Sí, es bonito y grande y tengo una compañera de cuarto muy simpática.*
PALOMA: *¿Cómo es la cafetería? ¿Es buena la comida?*
MARÍA: *Sí, es buena.*

Possible answers for *¡A escuchar!*
(You may have students answer in Spanish or English. Answers are provided in Spanish.)
Los edificios viejos son bonitos, pero los edificios nuevos son feos. / La biblioteca nueva no es muy bonita, pero es moderna y hay muchos libros y computadoras para los estudiantes. / El cuarto es bonito y grande y la compañera de cuarto es muy simpática. / La comida es buena.

Follow-up for 1-23. Ask students: *¿Cómo es la universidad ideal?* 1. *¿La biblioteca es grande o pequeña?* 2. *¿La biblioteca es moderna o vieja?* 3. *¿Las clases son aburridas o interesantes?* 4. *¿Los profesores son buenos o malos?* 5. *¿Los profesores son simpáticos o antipáticos?* 6. *¿Los estudiantes son perezosos o trabajadores?* 7. *¿Los estudiantes son divertidos o aburridos?* 8. *¿Los edificios son nuevos o viejos?* 9. *¿Los edificios son bonitos o feos?* 10. *¿La comida de la cafetería es buena o mala?*

Suggestion for 1-25. Point out the *(e)* in parentheses and refer students to the *¡Ojo!* box on the preceding page.

📖 Gramática 1

SAM: 1-29
to 1-34

Specifying people and things and describing them: The definite article and adjectives

Para **averiguar**

1. What are the four forms of the word for *the* in Spanish? When do you use each?
2. When is the definite article used in Spanish, but not in English?
3. Which nouns and adjectives generally have different forms for masculine and feminine? Which do not?
4. When do you add **-s** to an adjective to make it plural? When do you add **-es**?
5. Where do you place adjectives with respect to the nouns they describe?
6. What are four adjectives that are placed before the noun? What happens to **bueno** and **malo** before masculine singular nouns? What does **grande** mean when it is after the noun? What does it mean before the noun? How does its form change before singular nouns?

Supplemental activities for adjectives.
• Tell students that a friend is talking about his/her parents. Have them write the following columns on a sheet of paper: *su padre* (his/her father), *su madre* (his/her mother), *sus padres* (his/her parents), *???*. Students write the number of each sentence they hear in the column of the person(s) it describes. If they cannot tell, they write it under *???*. 1. *Es muy serio.* 2. *Es trabajador.* 3. *Son intelectuales.* 4. *Es muy inteligente.* 5. *Es muy optimista.* 6. *Es tímido.* 7. *Es muy bonita.* 8. *Son buenos.* 9. *Es paciente.* 10. *Es extrovertida.*
• Have students say whether these words describe them more now than when they were 15 years old. *MODELO: responsable > Sí, soy más responsable ahora. / No, no soy más responsable.* (paciente, trabajador/a, optimista, intelectual, pesimista, perezoso/a, serio/a)
• Have students say whether these adjectives describe their best friend. *MODELO: viejo/a > No, mi mejor amigo/a no es viejo/a.* (grande, pequeño/a, feo/a, antipático/a, simpático/a, aburrido/a, interesante, perezoso/a, trabajador/a, bueno/a, malo/a)

■ There are four ways to say *the* (the definite article) in Spanish. The form you use depends on whether a noun is masculine or feminine and singular or plural.

Definite Articles

	Masculine	Feminine
SINGULAR	el edificio *the building*	la residencia *the residence hall*
PLURAL	los edificios *the buildings*	las residencias *the residence halls*

■ The definite article is not only used to translate the word *the,* it is also used when making a generalized description of a category of people or things. In such cases, there is no article in English.

Los cursos técnicos son difíciles.   *Technical courses are difficult.*
Los amigos son importantes.   *Friends are important.*

■ Adjectives also have different forms, depending on whether they describe a masculine or feminine noun, and whether the noun is singular or plural. Adjectives ending with **-o** or **-or** in the masculine form end with **-a** or **-ora** in the feminine form. Adjectives ending with other letters or **-ista** have just one form for both masculine and feminine.

	Masculine	Feminine	Masculine	Feminine
SINGULAR	tímido	tímida	inteligente	inteligente
PLURAL	tímidos	tímidas	inteligentes	inteligentes

Mi novio es tímido, inteligente, trabajador y optimista.   *My boyfriend is shy, intelligent, hardworking, and optimistic.*
Mi novia es tímida, inteligente, trabajadora y optimista.   *My girlfriend is shy, intelligent, hardworking, and optimistic.*

■ As with nouns, make adjectives plural by adding **-s** if they end with a vowel and **-es** if they end with a consonant. Use the masculine plural form of adjectives to describe a group with both males and females.

Juan es intelectual y serio.   ⟶   Juan y María son intelectual**es** y serio**s**.
Juan is intellectual and serious.   ⟶   *Juan and Maria are intellectual and serious.*

■ Unlike adjectives in English, most Spanish adjectives are placed after the nouns they modify.

una clase **difícil**   *a difficult class*
un edificio **feo**   *an ugly building*

■ The adjectives **bueno** (*good*), **malo** (*bad*), and **mejor** (*best*) may be placed before nouns. Like the number **uno**, the final **-o** of the masculine form of **bueno** and **malo** is dropped before singular nouns.

un **buen** amigo   una buena amiga   los buenos amigos   las buenas amigas
un **mal** día   una mala idea   los malos hábitos   las malas condiciones

■ The adjective **grande** means *big* or *large* when it is placed after the noun, but it means *great* when it is placed before it. Before masculine or feminine singular nouns it shortens to **gran**.

una universidad **grande**   *a big university*
una **gran** universidad   *a great university*

1-27 ▶ La universidad. Complete the following statements with the correct forms of the definite article.

Modelo   *Las* residencias son modernas.

1. __La__ universidad es grande.
2. __Los__ edificios son nuevos.
3. __La__ clase de español es divertida.
4. __Los__ estudiantes son trabajadores.
5. __La__ biblioteca es nueva y moderna.
6. __El__ laboratorio de lenguas es viejo.

¿Y tú? Take turns with a partner saying whether the preceding statements in this activity are true (**cierto**) or false (**falso**) for your university. Correct the false statements. Use **No hay . . .** to say there is not something at your university.

Modelo   *Cierto. Las residencias son modernas. | Falso. Las residencias son viejas. |*
          Falso. No hay residencias.

1-28 ▶ ¿Es igual? Compare studying at the university with studying at your high school using **más** *(more)* or **menos** *(less)* with the appropriate form of the adjective in parentheses. You may also respond with: **No hay mucha diferencia.**

Modelo   clases (fácil)
          Las clases son más fáciles en la universidad. | Las clases son menos fáciles
          en la universidad. | No hay mucha diferencia.

1. clases (difícil)
2. edificios (moderno)
3. biblioteca (pequeño)
4. estudiantes (trabajador)
5. clases (aburrido)
6. gimnasio (grande)

Answers for 1-28.
1. *más/menos difíciles;* 2. *más/menos modernos;*
3. *más/menos pequeña;* 4. *más/menos*
trabajadores; 5. *más/menos aburridas;*
6. *más/menos grande*

1-29 ▶ Dos universidades. In groups, prepare at least six sentences comparing these two universities. Which group can make the most comparisons?

Answers for 1-29.
Answers will vary.

Modelo   *Los edificios son más modernos en la Universidad Del Monte*
          y son más viejos en la Universidad Del Valle.

La Universidad del Monte   La Universidad del Valle

📖 Gramática 2

SAM: 1-35
to 1-40

Saying who it is: Subject pronouns and the verb **ser**

Para averiguar

1. What are three uses of the verb **ser** (to be)?
2. What are the forms of **ser** that go with each subject pronoun?
3. When do you use the **-as** ending instead of **-os** in **nosotros, vosotros,** or **ellos**? What form of these pronouns is used for mixed groups?
4. Where is **vosotros** used? What does it mean? What is used instead in Latin American Spanish?

■ You have already seen most of the forms of the verb **ser** (to be). Use **ser** to identify people, to say where they are from, or to describe what they are like. Here are all of its forms with the corresponding subject pronouns. The feminine pronouns **nosotras, vosotras,** and **ellas** are used for all-female groups. For groups containing males, use **nosotros, vosotros,** and **ellos.**

		ser (to be)			
yo	soy	*I am*	nosotros/as	somos	*we are*
tú	eres	*you are (familiar)*	vosotros/as	sois	*you are (plural, familiar)*
usted	es	*you are (formal)*	ustedes	son	*you are (plural)*
él	es	*he is*	ellos	son	*they are (males or mixed groups)*
ella	es	*she is*	ellas	son	*they are (females only)*

■ Subject pronouns are generally not used in Spanish, unless they are needed for clarity or to emphasize who you are talking about.

Somos amigos.   *We are friends.*
¿Eres de aquí?   *Are you from here?*

■ The form of the verb used with **usted, él,** and **ella** is the same for all verbs in all tenses. Similarly, the form for **ustedes, ellos,** and **ellas** is the same. Do not drop these pronouns if they are needed to clarify who the subject is.

Usted es muy bueno/a.   *You are very good.*
Él/Ella es muy bueno/a.   *He/She is very good.*

■ The pronoun **vosotros/as** is not generally used in Latin American Spanish. In Spain, it is used as the plural of familiar **tú** to talk to a group of friends or classmates, and **ustedes** is the plural of formal **usted.** In Latin American Spanish, use **ustedes** to say *you* (plural) to all groups, formal or familiar. Note that **ustedes** is often abbreviated **Uds**.

Vosotros/as sois mis amigos/as.   *You are my friends. (familiar, plural in Spain)*

Ustedes son mis amigos/as.   *You are my friends. (familiar, plural in America)*

Ustedes son mis mejores profesores.   *You are my best professors. (formal, plural, in all regions)*

■ When the names of people or things are the subjects of sentences, use the **él/ella** form of the verb if the subject is singular and the **ellos/ellas** form if it is plural. Use the **nosotros/as** form when including yourself in a group. Remember to place **no** before verbs to negate them.

Carlos es mi mejor amigo.   *Carlos is my best friend.*
Mis amigos son muy trabajadores.   *My friends are very hardworking.*
Mis amigos y yo no somos perezosos.   *My friends and I are not lazy.*

■ **Es** is also used to say *it is*. The subject pronoun *it* is not translated in Spanish.

Es una clase divertida.   *It's a fun class.*

Warm-up for *ser*.
• Ask students to give the pronoun they would use instead of the following names: *María, Juan, María y Anita, Juan y Carlos, Juan y María, Juan y tú, Juan y yo, tú y yo, María y tú, María y yo.*
• Reusing the subjects above, have students give the corresponding form of *ser* for each one.

1-30 ▶ ¿Cierto o falso?

Complete the following sentences with the correct forms of **ser**. Then, indicate whether each one is true (**cierto**) or false (**falso**) for you.

Modelo   Mi mejor amigo/a *es* paciente.
Cierto. Mi mejor amigo/a es paciente. /
Falso. Mi mejor amigo/a no es paciente.

1. Yo _____ soy _____ tímido/a.
2. Mi mejor amigo/a _____ es _____ de México.
3. Muchos de mis amigos _____ son _____ estudiantes.
4. Mis amigos y yo _____ somos _____ muy trabajadores.
5. Mi profesor/a de español _____ es _____ de Costa Rica.
6. Mis compañeros de clase _____ son _____ simpáticos.

1-31 ▶ Entrevista.

Complete the following questions with the correct forms of the verb **ser**.

1. ¿De dónde _____ eres _____ (tú)? ¿De dónde _____ es _____ tu mejor amigo/a? ¿_____ Es _____ (él/ella) estudiante también? ¿_____ Son _____ Uds. muy parecidos/as (*similar*)? ¿Quién (*Who*) _____ es _____ más paciente, él/ella o tú? ¿Quién _____ es _____ más extrovertido/a?

2. ¿Cómo _____ son _____ tus clases este semestre/trimestre? ¿_____ Eres _____ (tú) un/a buen/a estudiante? ¿_____ Eres _____ (tú) muy trabajador/a o un poco perezoso/a? ¿_____ Son _____ muy intelectuales tus amigos y tú? ¿_____ Son _____ (Uds.) muy serios? ¿_____ Son _____ tus clases más importantes o menos importantes que (*than*) tus amigos?

¿Y tú? Now, use the preceding questions to interview a classmate. Remember to use **mi** before a singular noun and **mis** before a plural noun to say *my*. Afterwards, report what you found out about your partner to the class. Use **su** before a singular noun and **sus** before a plural noun to say both *his* and *her.*

1-32 ▶ Comparaciones culturales.

A Latino is talking about Hispanics in the United States at a meeting of the Hispanic Chamber of Commerce. Complete each sentence with the appropriate form of the verb **ser**.

Modelo   Nosotros *somos* la minoría más grande de Estados Unidos. El 15% (por ciento) de la población *es* hispano y el 13% de la población es afro-americano.

1. El oeste (*west*) y el sur (*south*) _____ son _____ las dos regiones con más hispanos. La región con menos hispanos _____ es _____ el medio oeste (*midwest*).

2. Uno de cada (*each*) cuatro hispanos _____ es _____ monolingüe en español, uno _____ es _____ monolingüe en inglés y dos _____ son _____ bilingües.

3. Para la oficina del censo de Estados Unidos (*U.S. Census Bureau*), los términos **hispano** y **latino** _____ son _____ sinónimos, pero para muchas personas, los latinos _____ son _____ sólo de origen latinoamericano y los hispanos _____ son _____ de Latinoamérica, España y otras regiones también.

4. **Hispano** _____ es _____ el término preferido por el 22% de nosotros y **latino** _____ es _____ el término preferido por el 11%. Los dos términos _____ son _____ iguales (*equal*) para el 67% de nuestra (*our*) comunidad.

5. Cuatro de cada diez de nosotros _____ somos _____ inmigrantes y seis de nosotros _____ somos _____ originarios de Estados Unidos.

6. La edad promedio (*average age*) de la población de Estados Unidos _____ es _____ de 36 años (*years old*), pero la edad promedio de los hispanos _____ es _____ de sólo 27 años.

Follow-up for 1-30.
• Have students change the verb and adjective to the plural form in the following sentences. MODELO: *Soy trabajador. > Somos trabajadores.* 1. *Soy serio.* 2. *Eres bueno.* 3. *Ud. es pesimista.* 4. *Él es perezoso.* 5. *Ella es extrovertida.* 6. *No soy paciente.* 7. *No eres serio.* 8. *Él no es tonto.*

• Have students change the following sentences from plural to singular. 1. *Somos responsables.* 2. *Ellos son divertidos.* 3. *Ellas son inteligentes.* 4. *Somos intelectuales.* 5. *Ellos son optimistas.* 6. *Somos tímidas.*

• Tell students to contradict what you say. MODELO: *Ella es tímida. > No, ella no es tímida. Ella es extrovertida.* 1. *Ellos son pesimistas.* 2. *Él es serio.* 3. *Ellos son optimistas.* 4. *Ella es muy interesante.* 5. *Ellos son extrovertidos.* 6. *Ellos son perezosos.* 7. *Él es bueno.* 8. *Ellas son simpáticas.* 9. *Ella es tonta.* 10. *Él es divertido.*

Follow-up for 1-32.
• Have students say whether the following sentences are logical or accurate according to the information given in the activity. 1. *Hay muchos hispanos en Iowa, Minnesota y Wisconsin. Hay menos en California y Arizona.* 2. *El ochenta por ciento de los hispanos es bilingüe.* 3. *Una persona de México es hispana o latina. Una persona de España es hispana, pero no latina.* 4. *La mayoría (majority) de los hispanos es originaria de Estados Unidos.* 5. *Generalmente, más hispanos son viejos.*

• Discuss the following topics with students. 1. Why might some people prefer either the term *hispano* or *latino*? Which do you hear the most? 2. Why is the average age for Hispanics nearly ten years younger than the average age in the U.S.? What implications might this have for different sectors of society such as education? 3. Have you observed any cultural differences between the 60% of Hispanics from the United States and the 40% who immigrated?

 **Vocabulario** Los cursos universitarios y frases útiles

SAM: 1-41
to 1-49

 — **¿Qué estudias** en la universidad? ¿Qué clases tienes este semestre/trimestre?

CD 1
Track 10

— **Estudio** . . . Este semestre / trimestre tengo . . .

¿Sabías que...?

In many Hispanic countries, university studies are very specialized. Students complete three years of **Preparatoria** from the ages of 15 to 18, and then may enter directly into specialized degree programs like medicine or law, which have an average duration of five years. These degree plans are not postgraduate, as in the United States. Would you like your university studies to be more specialized?

¡Ojo!

- Do not use an article with course names after verbs like **estudio** (*I'm studying*) or **tengo** (*I have*). However, unlike in English, the definite article is used in Spanish when describing courses with an adjective as in the following sentences: **El español es interesante. / La física es difícil.**
- The word for *psychology* is spelled with a **p** in some regions and without a **p** in others.

How to use *Tema 4*.
In *Tema 4* of each chapter, the *Vocabulario* section presents new vocabulary related to the chapter theme, but no new grammar is introduced. Instead, the following *Resumen de gramática* summarizes all of the grammar presented in *Temas 1, 2,* and *3*. You may discuss the *Resumen de gramática* with students or ask them to review it outside of class. The last section of Tema 4, *En la vida real*, recycles chapter vocabulary and grammar in activities centered around a real life simulation.

Suggestions for *Una conversación* (on next page).
Have students listen to the conversation (on the next page) first with books closed for the answers to the following questions. 1. ¿Cómo es el profesor de historia? (No es muy interesante.) 2. ¿Cuánta tarea hay en la clase de historia? (Hay mucha tarea.) Then, have them read along in their books as they listen a second time.

Audioscript for *¡A escuchar!* (on next page)
NURIA: Hola, Maribel. ¿Cómo son tus clases este semestre? ¿Qué clases tienes?
MARIBEL: Son bastante buenas. Tengo matemáticas, historia, física y español.
NURIA: ¿Son interesantes?
MARIBEL: Mis clases de física e historia son interesantes, pero mi clase de matemáticas no es muy interesante y es muy grande. La clase de español es mi favorita. Es divertida y también es muy útil para mi profesión.

CIENCIAS SOCIALES:
historia
ciencias políticas
sociología
(p)sicología

LENGUAS:
español (*m*)
francés (*m*)
alemán (*m*)
japonés (*m*)
inglés (*m*)

CIENCIAS:
biología
química
física

BELLAS ARTES (*F PL*):
música
arte (*m*)
teatro

CURSOS TÉCNICOS:
matemáticas
informática

ADMINISTRACIÓN (*F*)
DE EMPRESAS:
contabilidad (*f*)
economía

HUMANIDADES (*F PL*):
literatura
filosofía

Suggestion.
Point out that *arte* is masculine in the singular, but feminine in the plural. Note also that gender is indicated with (*f*) and (*m*) for those courses whose forms may not clearly indicate gender.

Here are some instructions your Spanish instructor might give you in class:

¡Abran el libro en la página 37, por favor!	*Open the book to page 37, please!*
¡Lean cada pregunta	*Read each question!*
¡Repitan las siguientes palabras, por favor!	*Repeat the following words, please!*
¡Hagan el mismo ejercicio en parejas!	*Do the same exercise in pairs!*
¡Contesten en oraciones completas, por favor!	*Answer in complete sentences, please!*
¡Escriban las respuestas en la pizarra!	*Write the answers on the board!*
¡Aprendan estas palabras para mañana!	*Learn these words for tomorrow!*

Here are some things you might need to say to your instructor:

¿Hay tarea para la próxima clase?	*Is there homework for the next class?*
No comprendo. Repita, por favor.	*I don't understand. Please repeat.*
No sé la respuesta.	*I don't know the answer.*
¿Qué significa . . . en inglés?	*What does . . . mean in English?*
¿Cómo se dice . . . en español?	*How do you say . . . in Spanish?*

¿Qué estudias? *What do you study?, What are you studying?*   **Estudio** *I study, I am studying*
alemán *German*   **química** *chemistry*   **informática** *computer science*   **contabilidad** *accounting*

CD 1 Track 11

Una conversación. Two students are talking about their classes.

ENRIQUE: **¿Te gustan** tus clases?

VERÓNICA: **Me gustan** todas mis clases menos la clase de historia.

ENRIQUE: **¿Por qué no te gusta?**

VERÓNICA: El profesor no es muy interesante y hay mucha tarea que no es muy **útil.**

ENRIQUE: ¿Cuántos exámenes hay?

VERÓNICA: Sólo hay dos, **un examen parcial** y un examen final.

 CD 1, Track 12

¡A escuchar!

Listen to another conversation in which a student is talking to a friend about her classes. What classes does she have? Which ones does she like? Which one does she not like? Why? Which is her favorite (*favorita*)? Why?

1-33 ► Las clases. With which class(es) do you associate the following things?

Modelo   el cubismo → *arte*

1. un concierto de piano
2. una computadora
3. una calculadora
4. los débitos y los créditos
5. una novela realista
6. la lógica

7. la palabra *monsieur*
8. la inflación
9. las plantas y los animales
10. el oxígeno y el hidrógeno
11. la teoría de la relatividad
12. los procesos mentales

Possible answers for ¡A escuchar!
Tiene matemáticas, historia, física y español. Le gustan las clases de historia, física y español. / No le gusta la clase de matemáticas porque no es muy interesante y es muy grande. / Su clase favorita es la clase de español porque es muy útil y divertida.

¡Ojo!

Use **me gusta(n)** to say what you like and **te gusta(n)** to ask what a friend or classmate likes. Literally, **me gusta(n)** means that something *is* or some things *are pleasing to me.* Use **me/te gusta** (*is pleasing*) without **-n** if what you like is singular, and use **me/te gustan** (*are pleasing*) with **-n** if it is plural. In these structures, the definite article is used with the noun that follows (**Me gustan *los* exámenes fáciles.**), unless it is replaced by another word such as **tu(s)** or **mi(s)** (**Me gustan *mis* clases.**).

 1-34 ► ¿Te gusta(n)? Ask a classmate if he/she likes the following things. Use **te gusta** to ask about a singular noun and **te gustan** if it is plural.

Modelos   ¿la clase de español?
E1: *¿Te gusta la clase de español?*
E2: *Sí, me gusta.*

¿los cursos técnicos?
E1: *¿Te gustan los cursos técnicos?*
E2: *No, no me gustan.*

1. ¿la universidad?
2. ¿el campus?
3. ¿los edificios?
4. ¿las clases muy fáciles?

5. ¿las lenguas?
6. ¿más las ciencias o las artes?
7. ¿más la biología o la química?
8. ¿más la música o la literatura?

 ¿Y tú? Now in pairs, share with the class each other's preferences using **le gusta(n).** Note in the Modelo that if you include the name of the person you are talking about, **a** is inserted before it.

Modelo   *A Carlos le gusta mucho la clase de español.*

Possible answers for 1-33.
1. *música, bellas artes;* 2. *informática, cursos técnicos;* 3. *matemáticas, cursos técnicos;* 4. *contabilidad, administración de empresas, economía;* 5. *literatura, inglés, español;* 6. *filosofía;* 7. *francés, lenguas;* 8. *economía, administración de empresas;* 9. *biología, ciencias;* 10. *química, ciencias;* 11. *física, ciencias;* 12. *psicología/sicología, ciencias sociales*

 1-35 ► Instrucciones. Working with a partner, how many logical classroom commands can you form using words from each column? Include the article **el, la, los,** or **las** before each noun.

Modelo   *Hagan los ejercicios en el cuaderno.*

Abran	oraciones		página 54
Hagan	respuestas		pizarra
Escriban	tarea		cuaderno
Repitan	libro	en	escritorio
Lean	ejercicios		libro
Contesten	palabras		computadora
Aprendan	preguntas		

Supplemental activity for classroom instructions.
Write the following verbs in the imperative on the board: *Abran..., Escriban..., Lean..., Hagan..., Contesten..., Repitan....* Then, call out the following nouns and have students say which verbs might logically be used with them in classroom instructions. MODELO: *el libro > Abran el libro. / Lean el libro.* 1. *la puerta* 2. *la palabra* 3. *las ventanas* 4. *el cuaderno* 5. *las preguntas* 6. *la oración* 7. *el ejercicio* 8. *las respuestas* 9. *la tarea*

Suggestions for 1-35.
• Point out that the definite article is used when specifying a definite page, *en la página 54 (on page 54).*
• Make this activity a timed competition.

1-36 ► Otra conversación. With a partner, reread *Una conversación* between Enrique and Verónica. Then, change the conversation to talk about your own classes.

Te gusta(n) *do you like*   **Me gusta(n)** *I like*   **útil** *useful*   **un examen parcial** *a mid-term exam*

Resumen de gramática

How to use *Resumen de gramática*.
The *Resumen de gramática* summarizes all of the grammar presented in *Temas 1, 2,* and *3.* You may discuss the *Resumen de gramática* with students or ask them to review it outside of class.

Nouns and articles

- All nouns in Spanish have gender and are classified as masculine or feminine.

- The indefinite article (*a, some*), and the definite article (*the*) have different forms and must agree with the nouns that follow them.

Indefinite Articles

	Masculine		Feminine	
SINGULAR	un	ejercicio	una	pregunta
PLURAL	unos	ejercicios	unas	preguntas

Definite Articles

	Masculine		Feminine	
SINGULAR	el	ejercicio	la	pregunta
PLURAL	los	ejercicios	las	preguntas

¿Hay **un** diccionario?   *Is there a dictionary?*
¿Dónde está **el** diccionario?   *Where is the dictionary?*

Masculine	Feminine
-o: el libro	-a: la tarea
-l: el papel	-dad/-tad: la universidad
	-ción/-sión: la oración

- Generally, nouns ending with **-o** or **-l** are masculine and those ending with **-a, -dad, -tad, -sión,** or **-ción** are feminine. There are exceptions, such as **un día** (*a day*) and many nouns ending with **-ma** like **un problema** (*a problem*), which are masculine.

- Make nouns plural by adding **-s** if they end with a vowel and **-es** if they end with a consonant.

- A final **-z** changes to **-c-** before the **-es** plural ending.

Plurals of Nouns

ENDING WITH A VOWEL: la silla → las sillas
ENDING WITH A CONSONANT: el papel → los papeles
ENDING WITH -Z: el lápiz → los lápices

Numbers

- The number one (**uno**) changes to **un** before a masculine noun or **una** before a feminine noun, and looks like the indefinite article.

uno, dos, tres . . .
un libro, dos libros, tres libros . . .
una silla, dos sillas, tres sillas . . .

Adjective agreement

- Adjectives agree in number and gender with the nouns they modify.

- Adjectives ending with **-o** or **-or** change to **-a** or **-ora** for the feminine form.

- Adjectives ending with other letters or **-ista** generally have the same form for both genders.

	Masculine	Feminine
SINGULAR	nuevo	nueva
PLURAL	nuevos	nuevas

	Masculine	Feminine
SINGULAR	fácil	fácil
PLURAL	fáciles	fáciles

Mi profesor es simpático, intelectual y optimista.

My (male) professor is nice, intellectual, and optimistic.

Mi profesora es simpática, intelectual y optimista.

My (female) professor is nice, intellectual, and optimistic.

- Make adjectives plural by adding -s if they end with a vowel and -es if they end with a consonant.

Mis amigos son intelectuales y extrovertidos.

My friends are intellectual and extroverted.

Adjective placement

- Adjectives are placed after the nouns they modify.

un profesor simpático	*a nice profesor*
una clase aburrida	*a boring class*

- The adjectives **bueno** (*good*), **malo** (*bad*), and **mejor** (*best*) may be placed before nouns. The final **-o** of the masculine form of **bueno** and **malo** is dropped before singular nouns.

un buen examen	*a good exam*
un mal examen	*a bad exam*
una buena idea	*a good idea*
una mala idea	*a bad idea*

- After a noun, **grande** means *big* or *large*.

una universidad grande	*a big university*

- Before a noun, **grande** is shortened to **gran** and means *great*.

una gran universidad	*a great university*

Subject pronouns and the verb *ser*

- The verb **ser** means *to be* and is used to identify and describe people or things.

- Subject pronouns (**yo, tú** . . .) are generally omitted in Spanish. Insert them only to emphasize or clarify who the subject is.

- Use **nosotras, vosotras,** and **ellas** for all-female groups. For groups containing males, use **nosotros, vosotros,** and **ellos**.

- Use **tú** with a friend, a classmate, a family member, or a child. Use **usted** with an adult you do not know well or to show respect.

- **Vosotros/as** is used in Spain as the plural of **tú**. In Latin American Spanish, **ustedes** is used to say *you* (plural) to all groups.

- **Usted** and **ustedes** are abbreviated **Ud.** and **Uds.**

Subject Pronouns and *ser*

Singular			Plural		
yo	soy	*I am*	nosotros/as	somos	*we are*
tú	eres	*you are*	vosotros/as	sois	*you are*
usted	es	*you are*	ustedes	son	*you are*
él	es	*he is*	ellos	son	*they are*
ella	es	*she is*	ellas	son	*they are*

¿De dónde eres?	Where are you from?
Soy de Miami.	I'm from Miami.
¿Eres mi compañero de clase?	Are you my classmate?
¿Es Ud. mi profesor?	Are you my professor?

IN SPAIN:	Vosotros sois amigos.	You are friends.
IN LATIN AMERICA:	Ustedes son amigos.	You are friends.

Expressing *to be*

- Use **ser** (**yo soy, tú eres, Ud. es** . . .) to say who or what people or things are, where they are from, or what they are like.

Soy Mariela Martínez.	*I am Mariela Martínez.*
Soy de México.	*I'm from Mexico.*
Soy tímida.	*I'm shy.*

- Use **estar** (**yo estoy, tú estás, Ud. está** . . .) to say how people are feeling or doing, or where someone or something is.

Estoy un poco enferma hoy.	*I am a little sick today.*

- Use **hay** instead of **ser** or **estar** to say *there is, there are, is there,* or *are there.*

Hay veintiún estudiantes en mi clase.	*There are twenty-one students in my class.*

How to use *En la vida real*.
Since these are review activities, students may prepare many of them outside of class if you have limited class time.

SAM: 1-54
to 1-58

EN EL CENTRO DE ESTUDIANTES INTERNACIONALES

In this chapter, you learned how to greet people and get to know them, as well as describe yourself and your friends, your university, and your classes. Now, you will practice what you have learned in a real-life simulation of working at the international students' center at your university or college.

1-37 ▶ ¿Qué hay? Some new students are asking you about your school. Complete the following questions logically with either the correct form of the definite article (**el, la, los, las**) or the indefinite article (**un, una**).

Modelo   ¿Hay libros en español en *la* biblioteca?

1. ¿Hay _____ *una* _____ biblioteca grande en _____ *la* _____ universidad?
2. ¿Son todas _____ *las* _____ clases en inglés o hay clases en español?
3. ¿Hay computadoras para los estudiantes en _____ *la* _____ biblioteca?
4. ¿Hay residencias para _____ *los* _____ estudiantes?
5. ¿Hay _____ *una* _____ cafetería? ¿Es buena _____ *la* _____ comida?
6. ¿Son todas _____ *las* _____ clases por la mañana (*in the morning*) o por la tarde o hay clases por la noche también?
7. ¿Hay _____ *un* _____ laboratorio de lenguas para _____ *las* _____ clases de lengua?
8. ¿Hay clases de inglés como segunda lengua para _____ *los* _____ estudiantes internacionales?

¿Y tú? Now, ask a classmate the preceding questions about your school.

1-38 ▶ Descripciones. You are talking to a new student about your university. Use the correct form of one of the adjectives below to describe the italicized noun in each sentence. You may negate any sentence if you wish

aburrido	divertido	inteligente	pequeño
antipático	fácil	interesante	perezoso
bonito	feo	malo	simpático
bueno	grande	moderno	trabajador
difícil	intelectual	nuevo	viejo

Modelo   Hay muchos *estudiantes*.
Hay muchos estudiantes trabajadores. /
No hay muchos estudiantes antipáticos.

Answers for 1-38.
Answers will vary.

1. Hay muchos *profesores*.
2. Hay *una biblioteca*.
3. Me gustan *los edificios*.
4. Me gustan *las clases*.
5. Este semestre/trimestre tengo más *clases*.
6. Me gustan *los exámenes*.

1-39 ▶ Comparaciones culturales. You are meeting some international students from the following Hispanic countries. Guess which population in millions (**millones**) goes with each country. Your instructor will answer more (**más**) or less (**menos**) until you give the correct answer.

3 — 4 — 6 — 11 — 14 — 17 — 27 — 28 — 40 — 44 — 46 — más de 100

1. México _más de 100_
2. España _46_
3. Perú _28_
4. Ecuador _14_
5. Argentina _40_
6. Venezuela _27_
7. Costa Rica _4_
8. Cuba _11_
9. Colombia _44_
10. Uruguay _3_
11. Chile _17_
12. Paraguay _6_

1-40 ▸ Ciudades natales. You are filling out forms for some international students and they are spelling out the name of their hometowns. A classmate will spell the capital of a Hispanic country and the rest of the class will write it down and name the the country.

Modelo   E1:   L-I-M-A
            CLASS WRITES: *Lima, Perú*

1-41 ▸ Estudiantes internacionales. Some international students from Mexico are asking you the following things. Complete their questions using either **hay** or the correct form of the verb **ser** as appropriate.

Modelo   *¿Hay muchos estudiantes internacionales?*

1. ¿Hay muchos estudiantes de México? ¿___*Somos*___ (nosotros) el grupo de estudiantes internacionales más grande o ___*hay*___ más estudiantes internacionales de otro país (*country*)?
2. ¿___*Son*___ todas las clases de dos o tres días a la semana (*per week*) en la universidad o ___*hay*___ clases de un día a la semana o de cuatro o cinco?
3. ¿___*Son*___ muy importantes los deportes (*sports*) en la universidad?
4. ¿___*Hay*___ un estadio (*stadium*) grande?
5. ¿___*Son*___ caros (*expensive*) los libros para las clases?
6. ¿___*Hay*___ una librería (*bookstore*) en el campus?

 ¿Y tú? Now, play the role of an international student from Mexico and ask a classmate the preceding questions in this activity.

Modelo   *¿Hay muchos estudiantes internacionales?*
              Ustedes son el cinco o diez por ciento de los estudiantes.

¡Hola! Entre profesionales

With the fast-growing Hispanic populations in North America, sooner or later you will have a need for Spanish in your professional interactions. Visit MySpanishLab for *Hoy día* for links to *Entre profesionales* to learn useful Spanish for a particular field of work for each chapter. In this first chapter, instead of learning about a specific career, you will be introduced to the diverse groups of Hispanics you will encounter, and you will find more activities such as the following one.

 La diversidad hispana. You are at a gathering with students from different countries and you hear students use the following expressions to ask *What's up?* With a partner, prepare a conversation in which a student from one of these places greets you and asks "what's up" using one of the expressions below. You respond, and ask if he/she is from the appropriate place.

Una chilena:	*¿Qué hay (de nuevo)?*	Un cubano:	*¿Qué bolá?*
Un salvadoreño:	*¿Qué onda?*	Una puertorriqueña:	*¿Qué es la que hay?*
Una colombiana:	*¿Quiubo?*	Un dominicano:	*¿Qué lo que?*
Un mexicano:	*¿Qué pasó?*	Una española:	*¿Qué tal?*

Estudiar en el extranjero

SAM: 1-59
to 1-60

Antes de leer

Do you like to travel, see interesting places, and meet fascinating people? Studying abroad offers an unparalleled opportunity to do all of these things. Before reading the brochure for a study abroad program, read the following strategy to help you improve your comprehension.

> ▶ **Reading Strategy** *Recognizing cognates* There are many words in Spanish whose meaning can be guessed, because they are similar to an English word. Such words are called cognates. You have already seen some cognates in this chapter (**profesor, responsable, . . .**) Cognates can help you understand new texts in Spanish.

Ahora tú

1-42 ▶ **Cognados.** Note that the endings **-mente** and **-ado/a** correspond to *-ly* and *-ed* in English (**generalmente** = *generally,* **interesado/a** = *interested*). Skim the reading and identify as many cognates as possible as **verbos, sustantivos** (*nouns*), **adjetivos,** and **adverbios.**

How to use *Antes de leer.* Explain to students that they will learn a strategy in each chapter that will help them progress faster in learning to read Spanish.

Warm-up for 1-42. Point out the following patterns in cognates. Then give students the first two items from each group and have them guess the meaning of the last two. 1. *organizado/a* organized, *ocupado/a* occupied, *adaptado/a, interesado/a* 2. *generalmente* generally, *normalmente* normally, *aproximadamente, constantemente* 3. *universidad* university, *ciudad* city, *oportunidad, comunidad* 4. *tradición* tradition, *opción* option, *duración, civilización* 5. *estupendo* stupendous, *espíritu* spirit, *estudiado/a, especializado/a*

Suggestion. Point out to students that there are some false cognates, such as *realizar,* to do something or perform an activity, *embarazada,* pregnant, and *actualmente,* currently. Tell them that if a cognate does not seem right in a context, they should check it in a dictionary.

SIN FRONTERAS: ¿Necesitas perfeccionar tu español? ¿Estás interesado/a en aprender más de la cultura hispánica? SIN FRONTERAS tiene un programa para ti.

¿Quién habla español en el mundo? El español es la tercera[1] lengua del mundo[2] en número de hablantes[3] después del[4] chino mandarín y el inglés. Actualmente hay más de 400 millones de hablantes de español en el mundo. En Estados Unidos hablan español aproximadamente 34 millones de personas y el español es la lengua más estudiada en las universidades.

¿Por qué estudiar en el extranjero? Estudiar en el extranjero, conectar con la lengua en su elemento y aprender[5] la cultura de sus hablantes ofrecen la oportunidad de vivir[6] la lengua en todas sus dimensiones. SIN FRONTERAS prepara a los estudiantes para mirar[7] al mundo con una mente abierta[8].

¿Qué ofrece SIN FRONTERAS? SIN FRONTERAS ofrece programas en varios países[9] de Latinoamérica adaptados a los intereses del estudiante. ¿Interesado en estudiar la cultura maya? El programa de Mérida, en Yucatán, México es tu mejor opción. ¿Es tu interés aprender sobre las tradiciones incas? Lima, Perú, te espera[10].

La duración de los programas es flexible. Hay programas de semestre, año[11] académico o verano[12].

Todos los programas ofrecen:

- Clases diarias[13] con atención personalizada
- Profesorado especializado y dinámico
- Seminarios de cultura y civilización
- Excursiones a sitios de interés turístico

Las instalaciones incluyen:

- Residencias modernas y seguras[14]
- Cafetería
- Salas para actividades sociales
- Zonas Wi-Fi para acceso a Internet

Universidad de Guanajuato

Chichén Itzá, Yucatán, México

¡SIN FRONTERAS te conecta con el espíritu de la cultura hispana!

[1]*third* [2]*world* [3]*speakers* [4]*after* [5]*to learn* [6]*to live* [7]*to look at* [8]*an open mind* [9]*countries* [10]*awaits you* [11]*year* [12]*summer* [13]*daily* [14]*safe, secure*

Answers for 1-42. *Verbos: perfeccionar, conectar, prepara, estudiar, incluyen; Sustantivos: cultura, programa, millones, personas, universidades, elemento, oportunidad, dimensiones, Latinoamérica, intereses, opción, tradiciones, duración, semestre, clases, atención, seminarios, civilización, excursiones, sitios, instalaciones, residencias, cafetería, actividades, zonas Wi-Fi, acceso, Internet, espíritu; Adjetivos: interesado, hispánica, mandarín, estudiada, adaptados, maya, incas, flexible, académico, personalizada, especializado, dinámico, turístico, modernas, sociales; Adverbios: actualmente, aproximadamente.*

Después de leer

1-43 ► **¿Cierto o falso?** Complete the following sentences logically with either **hay** or a form of **ser.** Then, indicate whether the following statements are true (**cierto**) or false (**false**) and correct the false statements.

Answers for 1-43.
1. *Falso: El chino y el inglés son las dos lenguas con más hablantes.*; 2. *Cierto*;
3. *Falso: Hay un programa de Sin fronteras en Lima, Perú, para estudiar las tradiciones incas.*;
4. *Falso; Hay programas de semestre, año académico o verano.*; 5. *Cierto*; 6. *Cierto*;
7. *Falso; Hay residencias modernas y seguras.*;
8. *Cierto*

	Cierto (*True*)	Falso (*False*)
1. El español ___es___ la tercera lengua del mundo. El inglés y el francés ___son___ las dos lenguas con más hablantes.	☐	☐
2. Estudiar en el extranjero ___es___ una buena manera de conectar con una lengua y la cultura de sus (*its*) hablantes.	☐	☐
3. ___Hay___ un programa de *Sin fronteras* en Lima, Perú para estudiar las tradiciones mayas.	☐	☐
4. Todos los programas de *Sin fronteras* ___son___ de un año académico. No ___hay___ ningún programa durante el verano.	☐	☐
5. Las clases ___son___ todos los días.	☐	☐
6. ___Hay___ seminarios de cultura y civilización.	☐	☐
7. Los estudiantes viven (*live*) en casas particulares con familias. No ___hay___ ninguna residencia para los estudiantes.	☐	☐
8. Las instalaciones de *Sin fronteras* ___son___ modernas y seguras.	☐	☐

 1-44 ► **¿Qué hay?** Work in groups to see how many sentences you can create using **hay** to describe the **_Sin fronteras_** study abroad programs.

Modelo   *Hay programas en varios países.*
         Hay oportunidades de conectar con la lengua en su elemento . . .

 1-45 ► **¿No hay . . .?** In groups, write three additional questions you would like to ask a representative about **_Sin fronteras_**.

Modelo   *¿Cuántos estudiantes hay en las clases? ¿Son grandes?*
         ¿Hay un programa en Costa Rica?

 1-46 ► **Intereses.** Interview another student to find out his/her feelings about studying abroad.

1. ¿Estás interesado/a en estudiar en otro país?
2. ¿Tienes más interés en la cultura maya de México o en la cultura inca de Perú? ¿En qué otros países hispanos tienes interés?
3. En un programa de estudios en el extranjero, ¿es mejor vivir en una casa particular (*private*) con una familia local o en una residencia con otros estudiantes extranjeros? ¿Por qué?
4. ¿Hay oportunidades en Estados Unidos de estudiar español en un contexto de inmersión total?

 1-47 ► **Inmersión cultural.** Do you think that it is important to study abroad? Find words or phrases in the reading that suggest its value. Then, in groups, discuss these and other benefits of studying at a university in Latin America or Spain. Present your group's opinions to the class.

Suggestion for 1-47.
You may want to point out the following phrases from the reading as examples: *conectar con la lengua en su elemento, mirar al mundo con una mente abierta.*

VOCES DE LA CALLE

📖 Señas de identidad

SAM: 1-61
to 1-62

Antes de ver

The United States is home to many people of Hispanic origin who wish to preserve their language and traditions. In this first segment of *Voces de la calle*, various people will introduce themselves and talk about their Hispanic heritage and current lives.

1-48 ▶ Reflexiones. What are some indicators of the Hispanic presence in today's American society? Besides Hispanics, what other cultures are represented in the United States? What percentage of the population do Hispanics represent?

▶ **Listening strategy** *Anticipating content.* Working with a partner, list the five things people from around the world would most likely say when introducing themselves and what phrases they might use to express each in Spanish.

Ahora tú

🎬 **1-49 ▶ Verifica.** Listen to our video participants and check if the information that you have anticipated is given in the video.

Después de ver

1-50 ▶ ¿Qué dicen? Read the following statements from the video segment and identify the person who said each one: Jorge, Dennis, Edgar, or Analissa.

1. "Soy periodista (*journalist*), vivo (*I live*) en Nueva York, soy mitad (*half*) colombiano, mitad argentino, escribo para revistas como *Urban Latino* magazine."
2. "Como músico, me encanta (*I love*) estar con mi chelo, primeramente, tocar (*to play*) mi instrumento."
3. "¡Hola! [. . .]. Soy puertorriqueño. Vivo aquí en el Bronx, en Nueva York [. . .] desde 1982."
4. "Soy pintor y [. . .] estamos aquí en Queens, Nueva York, y estamos muy contentos de estar aquí."

Answers for 1-50.
1. *Dennis;* 2. *Analissa;* 3. *Jorge;*
4. *Edgar*

1-51 ▶ ¿De dónde son? Complete the following sentences indicating the origin of the people from the video. Use the appropriate form of **ser** and the place of origin or residence.

1. Analissa Martínez __es__ de __El Paso__, Texas.
2. Michelle y Alejandro __son__ de __la Ciudad de México__.
3. Edgar Alcaraz __es__ de __Paraguay__.
4. Gloria Celaya __es__ de __Nicaragua__ y su esposo Héctor __es__ de __Costa Rica__.

30

📖 Una consulta

SAM: 1-63

Antes de escribir

How to use *Antes de escribir*.
Explain to students that they will learn a strategy in each chapter that will help them to write more effectively in Spanish.

In this section of each chapter, you will use what you have learned to complete a writing task. For this first assignment, you are going to write an email to your professor introducing yourself and asking for a clarification about something in class. Use the writing strategy at the right to help you write more effectively.

Antes de escribir

1-52 ▶ ¡Prepárate! Before you write your email to your professor, review the topics and structures presented in this chapter and consider the following questions. Which did you find the most difficult to understand? What adjectives can you use in Spanish to describe how you feel about the class and the students in it? Which ones describe you as a foreign language learner?

Ahora tú

1-53 ▶ Una consulta. Write your email to your Spanish professor asking him/her a question about a grammar or vocabulary structure that you do not understand well. Remember to use expressions such as **No comprendo** or **¿Qué significa . . .?** Then, describe your personality as a foreign language student. Also include your views of the class in general.

Después de escribir

1-54 ▶ ¡Edita! Working with a partner, edit each other's emails and discuss possible errors or areas that are unclear.

1-55 ▶ ¡Repasa! Review your email using the checklist below to check your grammar:

❏ Did you use the verb **ser** to say who you are, and to identify yourself as a student from the class?
❏ Did you make the adjectives agree with the nouns in your descriptions?
❏ Did you include expressions such as **No comprendo** or **¿Qué significa . . . ?** to indicate the structure or vocabulary from the chapter that you do not understand well?
❏ Did you address your professor as **profesor** or **profesora**?

1-56 ▶ ¡Navega! Visit your online resource for *Hoy día* for the link to the *Centro Virtual Cervantes*. It offers a discussion forum, *Foro didáctico*, for students to search postings related to Spanish grammar and vocabulary, reading and writing. Click on *Foro didáctico*, and browse through the topics posted. Select one that might interest you, and see if you can grasp its content. Then, post the question that you have asked your professor by clicking on the **Nuevo mensaje** link at the top of the page. Fill out the **Nuevo mensaje** form. Send your question by clicking on **Enviar formulario**. See how other users around the world respond!

▶ Writing strategy
Identifying your audience.
When you write a letter or an email to a professor or a supervisor requesting information, it is essential to organize it logically and to use the correct tone. In this type of formal communication, you are expected to address the audience with the **usted** form rather than the **tú** form. Make your email polite and clear, and remember to address your professor as **profesor** or **profesora**. What phrases can you use to greet your professor and ask how he/she is?

Note for 1-56.
Another website you might wish to share with your students is *Wordreference.com* where they can find forums on how to translate from English to Spanish.

Saludos (Greetings)

Buenos días.	Good morning.
Buenas tardes.	Good afternoon.
Buenas noches.	Good evening. Good night.
Hola.	Hi.
¿Cómo estás?	How are you? (familiar)
¿Cómo está usted?	How are you? (formal)
hoy	today
Estoy . . .	I am . . . , I'm . . .
(muy) bien	(very) well
(un poco) cansado/a	(a little) tired
enfermo/a	sick, ill
mal	bad(ly)
ocupado/a	busy
regular	as usual
gracias	thank you
¿Y tú/usted?	And you? (familiar/formal)
Pues . . .	Well, . . . , So, ...

Presentaciones (Introductions)

¿Cómo te llamas?	What is your name? (familiar)
¿Cómo se llama usted?	What is your name? (formal)
señor (Sr.)	Mr., sir
señora (Sra.)	Mrs., Mme.
señorita (Srta.)	Miss
Me llamo . . .	My name is . . .
Soy . . .	I am, I'm . . .
¿Cómo se escribe?	How is that written?
con / sin acento	with / without an accent
Mucho gusto.	Pleased to meet you.
Igualmente.	Likewise.
¿De dónde eres?	Where are you from? (familiar)
¿De dónde es usted?	Where are you from? (formal)
Soy de . . .	I'm from . . .
aquí	here

Despedidas (Expressions for saying good-bye)

Adiós.	Good-bye.
Hasta luego.	See you later.
Hasta mañana.	See you tomorrow.

Otras palabras (Other words)

el estudiante	student (male)
la estudiante	student (female)
el profesor	professor (male)
la profesora	professor (female)
la universidad	university

En el salón de clase

un bolígrafo	pen
una calculadora	calculator
una cama	bed
una clase (de español)	(Spanish) class
un/una compañero/a de clase	classmate (male)
una computadora	computer
una cosa	thing
un cuaderno	notebook
un cuaderno de ejercicios	workbook
un cuarto	room
un diccionario	dictionary
un escritorio	desk
un estante	shelf
un estéreo	stereo
un lápiz	pencil
un libro	book
una mesa	table
una mochila	bookbag, backpack
un papel	(piece of) paper
una pizarra	blackboard
una planta	plant
una puerta	door
un pupitre	student desk
un reloj	clock, watch
un salón de clase	classroom
una silla	chair
un televisor	television set
una ventana	window

Otras palabras y expresiones

como	like, as
de	of, from
en	in, on, at
hay	there is, there are, is there, are there
más	more, plus
mi/s	my
mucho/a/os/as	much, many, a lot of
Necesito . . .	I need . . .
ningún/ninguna	no, not . . . any
otro/a	other, another
para	for
pero	but
poco/a/os/as	little, few
sólo	only
también	also, too
(no) tengo . . .	I (don't) have . . .
¿Tienes . . . ?	Do you have . . . ?
todo/a/os/as	all, every
tu/s	your (familiar)
un/a	a, an
unos/as	some
varios/as	several

For the numbers 0–100, see page 14.

En el campus universitario

la biblioteca	library
la cafetería	cafeteria
la comida	food
el/la compañero/a de cuarto	roommate
el edificio	building
el gimnasio	gym(nasium)
el laboratorio de lenguas	language lab
el/la mejor amigo/a	best friend
el/la novio/a	boyfriend/girlfriend
la residencia	residence hall, dormitory

Descripciones

¿Cómo es . . . ?	How is . . . ? What's . . . like?
aburrido/a	boring
antipático/a	unpleasant
bonito/a	pretty
bueno/a	good
difícil	difficult
divertido/a	fun
extrovertido/a	outgoing, extroverted
fácil	easy
feo/a	ugly
grande	big
(im)paciente	(im)patient
intelectual	intellectual
inteligente	intelligent
interesante	interesting
(ir)responsable	(ir)responsible
malo/a	bad
moderno/a	modern
nuevo/a	new
optimista	optimistic
pequeño/a	little, small
perezoso/a	lazy
pesimista	pessimistic
serio/a	serious
simpático/a	nice
tímido/a	shy, timid
tonto/a	stupid, silly
trabajador/a	hardworking
viejo/a	old

Otras palabras

menos	minus, less, except
que	that

*For the subject pronouns and the forms of **ser**, see page 20.*

Los estudios (*Studies*)

¿Qué estudias?	What are you studying?
Estudio . . .	I'm studying . . .
¿Qué clases tienes?	What classes do you have?
Este semestre/trimestre tengo . . .	This semester/trimester I have . . .

For a list of courses, see page 22.

En el libro de texto

el ejercicio	exercise
la oración	sentence
la página	page
la palabra	word
la respuesta	answer, response
la tarea	homework

Otras palabras y expresiones

cada	each
¿Cómo se dice . . . en español?	How do you say . . . in Spanish?
mismo/a	same
No comprendo.	I don't understand.
No sé.	I don't know.
por favor	please
próximo/a	next
¿Qué significa . . . en inglés?	What does . . . mean in English?
siguiente	following
¿Te gusta . . . ? / (+ singular noun)	
¿Te gustan . . . ? (+ plural noun)	Do you like . . . ?
(No) me gusta . . . / (+ singular noun)	
(No) me gustan . . . (+ plural noun)	I (don't) like . . .
útil	useful

For a list of classroom commands, see page 22

▶ Visit MySpanishLab for *Hoy día* for links to the mnemonic dictionary online and for suggestions to help you remember vocabulary from *Capítulo 1*, learn related words in Spanish, and use Spanish words to build your vocabulary in English.

EXAMPLES

día, day: This word is related to the English adjective *diurnal*. A *diurnal* animal is one that is active in the daytime. It is also related to *diary*, which is a daily journal. Related word in Spanish: **diario/a,** *daily*

noche, night: This word is related to the English adjective *nocturnal*. A *nocturnal* animal is one that is active at night. Related word in Spanish: **nocturno/a,** *nocturnal*

2 Después de clase

In this chapter, you will learn to talk about schedules and leisure activities. Although there are cultural differences among Hispanics, their concept of time regarding punctuality often varies significantly from that of other cultures.

Hispanics tend to be very flexible with time. It is not considered impolite to arrive ten or fifteen minutes late to informal gatherings.

▶ Do you consider yourself a punctual person?

▶ Is it important to be punctual? Why?

It is a common custom among Hispanic families to share mealtimes. In some Hispanic countries, work schedules allow time for people to have lunch at home with their families.

▶ How important do you think it is to share mealtimes with the family?

▶ What do you think of a work schedule that allows longer lunch hours?

In most Hispanic countries, people place a great emphasis on socializing with friends and family. Work schedules tend to be less demanding than in the United States.

▶ Do you think that work schedules in the United States are very demanding?

▶ Do you feel overwhelmed by the responsibilities of your schedule?

📖 **Vocabulario** Mi horario

SAM: 2-1
to 2-4

 ¿Qué hora es?
CD 1
Track 25

Son las ocho. Son las nueve y diez. Son las diez y cuarto. Son las once y veinte.

Es la una. Es la una y media. Son las dos menos veinte. Son las cinco menos cuarto.

¿Sabías que...?

In most Hispanic countries, Sunday is a day of rest. Traditionally, some people attend church in the morning, and then take a stroll around the town, visit the Sunday market, and go for a drink (**un aperitivo**). In the early afternoon, families gather around a special lunch that takes place between two and three, and usually lasts for hours. How do you usually spend your Sundays?

¡Ojo!

Use **es la una** to say *it is one o'clock*, but **son las . . .** to say *it is* with the other hours. Use **a la una** to say *at one o'clock* and **a las . . .** to say *at* with other hours. Use **hasta la una** or **hasta las . . .** to say *until* a certain hour. Also note that **mañana** might be translated as either *morning* or *tomorrow*, and **tarde** can mean either *afternoon* or *late.* The context will clarify the meaning. You will learn more about telling time in the next grammar explanation.

¿Qué día es? ¿Qué días tienes clases? ¿A qué hora? ¿Te gusta tu **horario**? ¿Tienes otra clase **antes** o **después de** la clase de español?

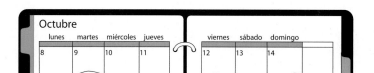

¿Dónde estás generalmente los lunes a las diez **de la mañana**? ¿a la una **de la tarde**? ¿a las diez **de la noche**?

¿en casa? ¿en la cama?   ¿en clase o en la biblioteca?

Suggestions for presenting time.
• Give each student a slip of paper with a different time on it to create a time line in front of the class. Students read their times aloud and place themselves in the appropriate places in line.
• Give two times and have students repeat the one that is later. The correct phrases are underlined. 1. *Es la una. / Son las dos.*
2. *Son las once. / Son las nueve.* 3. *Son las ocho y diez. / Son las ocho y cuarto.* 4. *Es la una y media. / Es la una y cuarto.* 5. *Son las siete menos diez. / Son las siete menos cinco.* 6. *Son las tres y cuarto. / Son las tres menos cuarto.*
7. *Son las nueve de la mañana. / Son las nueve de la noche.* 8. *Es la una y cinco. / Es la una menos cinco.*
• Give the following times and have students say what time it really is if your watch is thirty minutes behind. MODELO: *Son las dos y diez. > Son las tres menos veinte.* 1. *Es la una y media.*
2. *Son las dos y cuarto.* 3. *Son las tres menos diez.* 4. *Son las diez y diez.* 5. *Son las cuatro y cuarto.* 6. *Son las seis y veinte.* 7. *Son las siete menos cinco.* 8. *Son las ocho.* 9. *Es la una menos veinte.* 10. *Son las diez y veintiocho.*

¿en el trabajo? ¿en la oficina?   ¿con tus amigos?

el horario *the schedule*   **antes de** *before*   **después de** *after*   **de la mañana** *in the morning*   **de la tarde** *in the afternoon*   **de la noche** *at night*

CD 1
Track 26

Una conversación. Read the following conversation in which two students talk about their schedules.

JOSÉ: Hola, Inés. ¿Qué días tienes clases?

INÉS: Tengo clases de literatura, historia y biología los lunes, miércoles y viernes. Mi clase de ciencias políticas es los martes y jueves.

JOSÉ: ¿A qué hora son tus clases?

INÉS: Los martes y jueves, mi clase de ciencias políticas es a las nueve. Los lunes, miércoles y viernes estoy en clase **todo el día de** diez **a** tres.

JOSÉ: ¡Estás muy ocupada! ¿**Trabajas** también?

INÉS: Sí, **esta semana trabajo** cuatro **horas** el lunes, miércoles y viernes y todo el día el sábado. Con frecuencia trabajo los domingos también, pero **este fin de semana** no trabajo el domingo.

JOSÉ: ¿**Te gustaría estudiar conmigo** el domingo?

INÉS: Sí, me gustaría estudiar **juntos**. No me gusta estudiar **sola**. ¿A qué hora?

JOSÉ: No **demasiado temprano**. Estoy en la cama hasta **tarde** los domingos. ¿A las dos?

INÉS: Está bien.

2-1 ▶ Mis clases. Change the words in italics in the following sentences so that they describe you. If they are already true for you, read them as they are.

1. Mi clase de español es los *lunes y miércoles*.
2. Mi clase de español es a *las diez y cuarto de la mañana*.
3. Tengo *una clase* los martes y jueves.
4. No tengo ninguna clase los *viernes, sábados y domingos*.
5. Tengo *una clase* antes de la clase de español.
6. *No tengo ninguna clase* después de la clase de español.
7. Me gustan más las clases a *las nueve o diez de la mañana*.
8. No me gustan las clases a *las cuatro de la tarde*.

Answers for 2-1.
Answers will vary.

 2-2 ▶ ¿Dónde estás? Using the forms of **estar** as in the Modelo, ask where a classmate generally is at the indicated times. Some possible locations are provided in the box.

| con mi familia | en casa | en el trabajo | en la universidad, |
| con mis amigos | en clase | en la biblioteca | pero no en clase |

Modelo   los sábados a las 10:30 de la noche
            E1: *¿Dónde estás los sábados a las diez y media de la noche?*
            E2: *Los sábados a las diez y media de la noche, generalmente estoy con mis amigos.*

1. los lunes a las 9:00 de la mañana
2. los martes a la 1:15 de la tarde
3. los miércoles a las 7:30 de la mañana
4. los jueves a las 11:30 de la noche
5. los viernes a las 5:45 de la tarde
6. los domingos a las 3:20 de la tarde

Suggestion for 2-2.
You may have students work in pairs, or you may have the whole class work together, calling on individuals to ask the question and allowing them to pick any student to respond.

 2-3 ▶ Otra conversación. With a partner, reread *Una conversación* between José e Inés at the top of the page. Then, change it to talk about your schedule.

---

todo el día *all day*   **de . . . a . . .** *from . . . to . . .*   **trabajas** *(do) you work*   **esta semana** *this week*   **trabajo** *I work*   **horas** *hours*   **este fin de semana** *this weekend*   **¿Te gustaría . . . ?** *Would you like . . . ?*   **estudiar** *to study*   **conmigo** *with me*   **juntos/as** *together*   **solo/a** *alone*   **demasiado** *too, too much*   **temprano** *early*   **tarde** *late*

Suggestions for *Una conversación.*
• Have students listen to the conversation first with books closed for the answers to the following questions. 1. *¿Qué clases tiene Inés?* (literatura, historia, biología y ciencias políticas) 2. *¿Tiene más clases los lunes, miércoles y viernes o los martes y jueves?* (Tiene más clases los lunes, miércoles y viernes.) Then, have them read along in their books as they listen a second time.
• New words presented in the conversation include the boldfaced expressions, as well as *con frecuencia* and *está bien* meaning *it's okay/fine*.

CD 1, Track 27

¡A escuchar!

Listen to another conversation in which Sara asks Elena about her schedule this semester. What classes does Elena have, what days, and at what times? When does she work?

Audioscript for *¡A escuchar!*
SARA: *¿Cómo es tu horario este semestre, Elena? ¿Tienes muchas clases?*
ELENA: *Pues sí, pero este semestre no tengo clases los martes ni los jueves. Todas mis clases son los lunes, miércoles y viernes.*
SARA: *¿De qué hora a qué hora estás en clase?*
ELENA: *Tengo historia a las ocho de la mañana y ciencias políticas a las nueve y media. Por la tarde, mi clase de literatura es a la una y tengo matemáticas a las tres.*
SARA: *¿Trabajas los fines de semana también?*
ELENA: *Sí, trabajo quince horas los sábados y los domingos.*

Possible answers for *¡A escuchar!*
Tiene historia, ciencias políticas, literatura y matemáticas. Tiene clases los lunes, miércoles y viernes. Tiene clases a las ocho, a las nueve y media, a la una y a las tres. / Trabaja los sábados y los domingos.

Warm-up for 2-2.
First, have students draw four clocks in a row on a piece of paper and have them indicate the time they generally get up, arrive at the university, leave the university, and go to bed on the current day of the week. Give students the following phrases: *Estoy en la cama hasta . . . , Llego (I arrive) a la universidad a . . . , Estoy en la universidad hasta . . . , Estoy en la cama después de . . .* to accompany each clock. Next, have students draw another row of four clocks, leaving them blank. In pairs, have students take turns telling their partner the times they do each of the activities provided. Their partner will fill in the times they hear on their corresponding blank clocks. Afterwards, ask students to answer the following questions based on the information they recorded: *¿Quién (Who) está en la cama hasta más tarde? ¿Tú o tu compañero/a? ¿Quién está en la universidad más temprano? ¿más tarde? ¿más tiempo (time)? Por la noche, ¿quién está en la cama más temprano? ¿Quién está en la cama más tiempo?*

 Gramática 1   Describing your schedule:
SAM: 2-5
to 2-9
Time and the days of the week

Para averiguar

1. When do you use **es** instead of **son** to say what time it is?
2. When do you say **son las dos**? When do you say **a las dos**?
3. When do you say **de la mañana** for *in the morning*? When do you say **por la mañana**?
4. When do you use **el** with a day of the week? When do you use **los**?
5. What do **hasta, de . . . a, antes de,** and **después de** mean? After which of these do you drop **la, las, el, los** with hours and days?

Suggestion.
You may wish to point out that some speakers will say *¿Qué horas son?* instead of *¿Qué hora es?* and *en la mañana/tarde/noche* for *por la mañana/tarde/noche.*

Supplemental activities.
• Distribute photocopies of daily planners for a week. Working in pairs, have students take turns describing their class and work schedules while their partner fills in the schedule. Afterwards, the other student checks that it is correct.
• Ask students: *¿Qué día es hoy? ¿Qué día es mañana? ¿Qué día de la semana te gusta más? ¿Qué días trabajas? ¿Qué días estás en casa todo el día? ¿Dónde estás generalmente los lunes por la mañana? ¿por la tarde? ¿por la noche? ¿Dónde estás generalmente los sábados por la mañana? ¿Te gusta más estudiar por la mañana, por la tarde o por la noche? ¿Qué hora es ahora? ¿Estás en clase hoy todo el día? ¿De qué hora a qué hora estás en clase hoy? ¿Y mañana? ¿Tienes más clases por la mañana, por la tarde o por la noche?*

■ Use **¿Qué hora es?** to ask *What time is it (now)?* Say **Es la una** for *It's one o'clock,* **Es mediodía** for *It's noon,* and **Es medianoche** for *It's midnight.* With all other hours, use **Son las . . .** To express an amount of time until an hour, say that it's the hour minus (**menos**) the number of minutes.

— ¿Qué hora es?
— Es la una y cuarto. (1:15) / Son las tres menos diez. (2:50)

■ To ask at what time something takes place, use **¿A qué hora . . . ?** To answer, use **a la una, al mediodía, a la medianoche,** or **a las . . .** with other hours. Unlike *at* in English, **a** cannot be dropped in questions.

— ¿A qué hora es tu clase de historia?   — *(At) what time is your history class?*
— Es **a** las diez.   — *It's at ten.*

■ You may use the following expressions to distinguish times in the morning, afternoon, or evening.

de la mañana	A las ocho de la mañana.	*At eight in the morning.*
de la tarde	A la una de la tarde.	*At one in the afternoon.*
de la noche	A las once de la noche.	*At eleven in the evening.*

■ If you are not giving a specific hour, use **por la mañana, por la tarde,** and **por la noche** to say *in the morning, in the afternoon,* and *in the evening / at night.*

SPECIFIC HOUR: Trabajo a las ocho y media **de la mañana.**
    I work at eight thirty (half past eight) in the morning.
NO HOUR GIVEN: Trabajo **por la mañana.**
    I work in the morning.

■ Use the following expressions to ask and tell what day it is. Days of the week are not capitalized in Spanish and Monday (**lunes**) is the first day of the week on calendars, not Sunday (**domingo**).

— ¿Qué día es hoy?
— Hoy es lunes (martes, miércoles, jueves, viernes, sábado, domingo).

■ Use **el** to say that something will occur *on* a particular day. Although *on* may be dropped in English, **el** may not be dropped in this context in Spanish.

Esta semana, no tengo clase **el** miércoles.   *This week, I don't have class (on) Wednesday.*

■ To say that something normally happens every week *on* a day, use **los**. Add **-s** to **sábado** and **domingo** to make them plural, but not to days that already end with **-s**.

Trabajo **los** viernes y domingo**s**.   *I work (on) Fridays and Sundays.*

■ You may also use **hasta** (*until*), **antes de** (*before*), **después de** (*after*) or **de . . . a** (*from . . . to*) with days of the week or times. After **de . . . a**, the article is dropped before days or hours.

Estoy en clase **de** lunes **a** viernes **de** nueve **a** dos.   *I am in class Monday through Friday from nine to two.*

Estoy en casa **hasta** las ocho y **después de** las tres.   *I'm at home until eight and after three.*

2-4 ▶ ¿Qué hora es? Look at the clocks below and say what time it is.

Modelo   *Son las once y media de la mañana.*

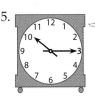

 1.   2.    3.   4.   5.

2-5 ▶ ¿Qué palabra es? Complete the following conversation by choosing the correct word in parentheses.

RAÚL: ¿Tienes más clases (1) ___por___ (de, por) la mañana o (2) ___por___ (de, por) la tarde este semestre/trimestre?

SERGIO: Tengo química (3) ___los___ (el, los) martes y jueves (4) ___a___ (son, a) las diez de la mañana. Mis clases de matemáticas e inglés son (5) ___por___ (de, por) la tarde (6) ___los___ (el, los) lunes, miércoles y viernes.

RAÚL: ¿Te gustaría estudiar química juntos en la biblioteca este fin de semana?

SERGIO: ¡Claro! ¿(7) ___El___ (El, Los) sábado o (8) ___el___ (el, los) domingo?

RAÚL: ¿(9) ___El___ (El, Los) domingo (10) ___a___ (a, son) las tres (11) ___de___ (de, por) la tarde está bien?

SERGIO: Me gusta más estudiar (12) ___a___ (son, a) las siete (13) ___los___ (el, los) domingos.

RAÚL: Está bien (14) ___a___ (son, a) las siete. ¿Qué hora es ahora?

SERGIO: (15) ___Son___ (Son, A) las dos y veinte.

RAÚL: Tengo clase (16) ___a___ (son, a) las dos y media. Hasta (17) ___el___ (el, los) domingo.

SERGIO: Hasta luego.

2-6 ▶ Entrevista. Ask another student the following questions. Afterwards, be prepared to tell the class about your partner. You will need these verb forms to talk about him/her: **le gusta(n), él/ella está, él/ella tiene, él/ella trabaja.**

1. ¿Te gusta tu horario este semestre? ¿Qué días estás en clase? ¿Qué días no tienes clase?
2. ¿Tienes más clases por la mañana, por la tarde o por la noche? ¿A qué hora te gustan más las clases? ¿A qué hora son tus clases este semestre?
3. ¿Qué días trabajas? ¿A qué hora?

2-7 ▶ Comparaciones culturales. In official schedules such as movie times or bus, train, and flight schedules, times in Hispanic countries are generally posted using the 24-hour clock. Do you think it would be good to use the 24-hour clock in official schedules here? Why or why not? Convert the following movie times from the 24-hour clock to conversational time.

Modelo   13:50
Las trece horas y cincuenta minutos son las dos menos diez de la tarde.

1. 19:00	**3.** 16:45	**5.** 21:35	**7.** 22:25
2. 20:30	**4.** 15:10	**6.** 14:40	**8.** 17:55

¡Ojo!

To convert from a 24-hour clock to a 12-hour clock, simply subtract 12 from the time given. For example, 15:00 is 3:00 PM (15 − 12 = 3). With the 24-hour clock, state the number of minutes (31–59 minutes) after the hour instead of using **menos** to say the number of minutes until the next hour.

Gramática 2 Saying where you are: The verb **estar**

SAM: 2-10
to 2-14

Para **averiguar**

1. What are two uses of the verb **estar**? What are its forms?
2. Which two adverbs indicating frequency are placed directly before the verb? Where may the other adverbs of frequency be placed?

¿Cómo se **pronuncia?** ¡Hola!

Written accent marks.

Written accents are used on some of the forms of **estar** to indicate which syllable is stressed. Refer to the Pronunciation Guide in your MySpanishLab course under Word Stress to learn the rules for using accent marks.

Suggestion for presenting *estar.*

Emphasize to students the two uses of *estar* listed here: 1) describing changeable conditions with adjectives, and 2) telling where or with whom. Tell them to remember these uses of *estar* and to use *ser* to translate *to be* in most other cases. The distinction between *ser* and *estar* is treated in more detail in *Capítulo 4.*

Warm-up for 2-8.

• Have students repeat the adverb that indicates the greater frequency. The correct answers are underlined. 1. *siempre/casi siempre;* 2. *nunca/casi nunca;* 3. *a veces/con frecuencia;* 4. *todos los días/de lunes a miércoles;* 5. *una vez a la semana/una vez al mes;* 6. *diez veces al año/una vez al mes*
• Have students repeat the following sentences inserting an appropriate adverb of frequency to describe themselves. 1. *Estoy cansado/a en clase.* 2. *Comprendo todas las preguntas.* 3. *Estoy en la biblioteca antes de clase.* 4. *Estoy en otra clase después de la clase de español.* 5. *Estudio toda la noche.* 6. *Tengo mucha tarea para mis clases.*

Follow-up for 2-8.

Ask students the following questions and have them answer in complete sentences. 1. *¿Estás . . . (en clase de lunes a viernes, en otra clase antes de la clase de español, en la biblioteca por la tarde, en casa todo el día los domingos)?* 2. *¿Y yo? Estoy . . . (en mi oficina antes de la clase de español, en mi oficina después de clase, en mi oficina mañana, en esta clase todos los días).* 3. *¿Y tus padres (parents)? ¿Están . . . (en [name your city], en el trabajo los lunes, en casa ahora, en casa los fines de semana, contigo los fines de semana generalmente)?* 4. *¿Tu mejor amigo/a y tú? ¿Están . . . (juntos/as con frecuencia, juntos/as más los lunes o los sábados, juntos/as en una clase, en todas las mismas clases)?*

■ You have already used the verb **estar** (*to be*) with adjectives to say how you are doing.

— ¿Cómo **estás**?
— **Estoy** un poco enferma y muy cansada.

■ Here is the full conjugation of **estar**.

estar *(to be)*

yo	estoy	*I am*	nosotros/as	estamos	*we are*
tú	estás	*you are (familiar)*	vosotros/as	estáis	*you are (familiar plural)*
usted	está	*you are (formal)*	ustedes	están	*you are (plural)*
él, ella	está	*he, she is*	ellos/as	están	*they are*

■ Also use **estar** to say where or with whom someone or something is.

— ¿**Estás** en clase los jueves?   — *Are you in class on Thursdays?*
— Sí, **estoy** en clase hasta las dos y   — *Yes, I'm in class until two and*
   después **estoy** con mis amigos.   *afterwards I'm with my friends.*

■ Use the following adverbs with verbs to say how often. **(Casi) siempre** and **(casi) nunca** are most commonly placed just before the verb. The other adverbs may go at the beginning or end of a clause.

(casi) siempre	*(almost) always*	**una vez a la semana**	*once a week*
(casi) nunca	*(almost) never*	**dos veces al mes**	*twice a month*
todo el día	*all day long*	**tres veces al año**	*three times a year*
todos los días	*every day*	**los lunes**	*on Mondays*
generalmente	*generally*	**los fines**	
con frecuencia	*frequently*	**de semana**	*on weekends*
a veces	*sometimes, at times*	**de lunes a viernes**	*Monday through Friday*

— ¿**Siempre** estás en casa por la   — *Are you always at home in the*
   mañana?   *morning?*
— No, **a veces** estoy en la biblioteca. — *No, sometimes I'm at the library.*

2-8 ▶ ¿Con qué frecuencia? Complete each sentence with the correct form of **estar** and an appropriate adverb of frequency to describe yourself and your acquaintances.

Modelo   (Yo) _____ muy cansado/a por la mañana.
         Casi siempre estoy muy cansado/a por la mañana.

1. (Yo) _____ muy ocupado/a los fines de semana.
2. Los domingos, mis padres _____ en casa todo el día.
3. Mi mejor amigo/a y yo _____ juntos/as los fines de semana.
4. Mi mejor amigo/a _____ en clase conmigo.
5. (Yo) _____ en la biblioteca antes de la clase de español.
6. El/La profesor/a de español _____ en el salón de clase cuando yo llego (*when I arrive*).
7. Mis compañeros de clase y yo _____ confundidos (*confused*) en clase.

Suggestions for 2-8.

You may prefer to have students first read the sentences with just the correct form of *estar*, then go back and insert the adverb of frequency. Adverbs of frequency will vary. The correct forms of estar are: 1. *Estoy* 2. *están* 3. *estamos* 4. *está* 5. *Estoy* 6. *está* 7. *estamos.*

2-9 ► ¿Dónde están? José is talking about himself and others. Refer to the illustrations and use the correct form of (**no**) **estar** with each item in parentheses to describe where or with whom these people are, or how they are doing.

Modelo   Mi compañero de cuarto . . . (conmigo, en la cama, cansado)
Mi compañero de cuarto no está conmigo. Está en la cama. Está cansado.

1. Mi padre . . . (en casa, en la oficina, ocupado, solo, con clientes)

2. Los clientes . . . (en un sofá, juntos en la misma mesa, interesados en la presentación)

3. Yo . . . (en un restaurante, en el trabajo, solo, con mi novia)

4. Mi novia y yo . . . (con otros amigos, solos en la mesa, solos en el restaurante)

2-10 ► Entrevista. Complete each question with the indicated form of the verb **estar**. After **me/te gusta**, leave **estar** unconjugated: **Me gusta estar . . .** (*I like to be . . .*).

1. ¿Dónde ___estás___ (tú) generalmente antes de la clase de español? ¿Dónde ___estás___ (tú) generalmente después de la clase? ¿Dónde ___están___ tus padres normalmente a la hora de la clase de español? ¿en casa? ¿en el trabajo? ¿en un café o un restaurante?

2. ¿___Está___ tu casa/apartamento/residencia cerca de (*near*) la universidad, lejos de (*far from*) la universidad o en el campus? ¿Hasta qué hora ___estás___ (tú) en tu casa/apartamento/residencia por la mañana? ¿Cuántas horas ___estás___ (tú) en la universidad generalmente los días que (nosotros) ___estamos___ en esta clase?

3. ¿Te gusta más ___estar___ con tus amigos o solo/a los fines de semana? Los fines de semana, ¿___estás___ (tú) más con tu familia o con tus amigos? ¿Qué días ___están___ ustedes juntos generalmente? A veces, ¿te gusta ___estar___ solo/a?

 ¿Y tú? Use the preceding questions to interview another student.

Hola, ¿cómo estás?

Vocabulario   Las actividades diarias

SAM: 2-15
to 2-18

 CD 1
Track 28

¿Qué te gusta **hacer** después de clase? ¿Con **quién** te gusta pasar **el tiempo libre**? ¿Cuáles son tus actividades **diarias**?

Generalmente después de clase, me gusta . . .

¿Sabías que...?

A very old tradition of universities in many Hispanic countries is **la tuna**. **Las tunas** are university bands, who in their free time, sing and play music in the streets to make some extra money to support their studies. Generally, only male students participate in **las tunas**, and they perform dressed in traditional costumes that resemble the French troubadours' attire from the Middle Ages. **Los tunos** (members of a **tuna**) have a repertoire of traditional songs developed by them and passed from one generation of members to the next. **La tuna** often brightens up town celebrations, weddings, and university parties.

tomar **algo** con otros estudiantes en un café

hablar por teléfono con mi mejor amigo/a

mirar la tele solo/a en casa

Hoy después de clase, necesito . . .

trabajar

regresar temprano a casa

estudiar

Este fin de semana, **deseo** . . .

Supplemental vocabulary activity.
Ask students: Do you generally like to do the following things or do you need to do them?
MODELO: mirar la televisión > Generalmente, me gusta mirar la televisión. (estudiar, limpiar la casa, trabajar, pasar mucho tiempo con los amigos, pasar mucho tiempo en la biblioteca, escuchar música, tomar algo con los amigos, descansar después de clase)

¿Cómo se pronuncia? ¡Hola!

The consonant r
To learn how to pronounce the letter **r** in words like **regresar, guitarra,** and the verb endings seen here, refer to the Pronunciation Guide in your MySpanishLab course under Consonants.

escuchar música y bailar con mi novio/a

tocar la guitarra y cantar con mis amigos

pasar tiempo solo/a en casa y **descansar**

hacer to do, to make   **quién** who, whom   **el tiempo** time   **libre** free   **diario/a** daily   **algo** something
desear to wish, to desire   **descansar** to rest

Este fin de semana, necesito . . .

limpiar la casa

cocinar / preparar **una cena** especial para **el cumpleaños** de un/a amigo/a

comprar **ropa** / **un regalo** para un/a amigo/a

CD 1
Track 29

Una conversación. In the following conversation, two friends are talking about weekend activities.

JOSÉ: ¿Qué te gusta hacer los fines de semana?

DIEGO: Los viernes casi siempre estoy cansado. Trabajo hasta las siete y después del trabajo, **prefiero** pasar la noche en casa.

JOSÉ: ¿No trabajas los sábados **ni** los domingos?

DIEGO: No, los sábados me gusta **salir**. Me gusta **ir al cine** o a un café con mis amigos. A veces me gusta **comer** en un restaurante.

JOSÉ ¿Te gusta descansar los domingos?

DIEGO: Sí, me gusta mirar **deportes** en la televisión, pero casi siempre necesito hacer mucha tarea.

JOSÉ: Yo también tengo mucha tarea los domingos.

2-11 ► ¿Qué haces? Change the italicized words so that the following sentences describe you. If the sentence is already true, answer **es cierto** and read the sentence as it is.

1. Hoy, después de clase, necesito *trabajar*.
2. Generalmente, después de clase, me gusta *descansar*.
3. No me gusta *bailar* con mis amigos.
4. Los fines de semana, me gusta *mirar la televisión*.
5. Tengo mucho tiempo para descansar *los jueves*.
6. Generalmente, necesito estudiar mucho *los lunes, miércoles y sábados*.
7. Me gusta pasar mucho tiempo con mis amigos *los viernes por la noche*.
8. Deseo pasar este fin de semana *solo/a en casa*.

 2-12 ► Entrevista. Interview another student with the following questions.

1. ¿Te gusta más tomar algo con tus amigos en un café o bailar con tus amigos en un club?
2. ¿Te gusta escuchar música clásica? ¿jazz? ¿rock? ¿música popular? ¿Te gusta más escuchar música de la radio o de tu iPod o MP3?
3. ¿Qué te gustaría hacer esta noche? ¿Y este fin de semana? ¿Qué necesitas hacer esta noche? ¿Y este fin de semana?

 2-13 ► Otra conversación. With a partner, reread *Una conversación* between José y Diego. Then, change it to talk about your weekend activities.

---

una cena *a dinner* **el cumpleaños** *the birthday* **la ropa** *clothes* **un regalo** *a gift, a present* **prefiero** *I prefer* **ni** *nor* **salir** *to go out* **ir al cine** *to go to the movies* **comer** *to eat* **los deportes** *sports*

 **Gramática 1**

SAM: 2-19
to 2-21

Talking about your activities:
Regular -**ar** verbs

Para **averiguar**

1. What is an infinitive?
2. What are the three infinitive endings in Spanish?
3. What are the endings of regular -**ar** verbs that go with each of the subject pronouns? How do you determine the stem to which you attach these endings?

 ¡Ojo!

You will learn later how to conjugate non -**ar** verbs like **ir** (to go), **comer** (to eat), and **hacer** (to do, to make). Until then, just use them in the infinitive after another verb to say what you need, would like, or like to do. (**Necesito comer. Me gustaría ir a la cafetería. Me gusta hacer mi tarea en un café.**)

■ **Infinitives:** The form of the verb that you find in Spanish dictionaries or vocabulary lists is called the infinitive. Some examples of infinitives in English are *to work, to do*, and *to write*. Spanish infinitives consist of single words that end in -**ar**, -**er**, or -**ir: trabajar, hacer, escribir.** Here you will learn the different forms of -**ar** verbs in the present tense.

■ To indicate the subject of -**ar** verbs you must conjugate them by dropping the -**ar** ending of the infinitive and adding the highlighted endings shown below. As with all verbs, the subject pronouns are not used, unless they are needed for clarity or emphasis.

trabajar *(to work)*

yo	trabaj**o**	*I work*	nosotros/as	trabaj**amos**	*we work*
tú	trabaj**as**	*you work*	vosotros/as	trabaj**áis**	*you work*
usted	trabaj**a**	*you work*	ustedes	trabaj**an**	*you work*
él, ella	trabaj**a**	*he, she works*	ellos/as	trabaj**an**	*they work*

■ These -**ar** verbs follow the same pattern as **trabajar.**

bailar	*to dance*	limpiar	*to clean*
cantar	*to sing*	llegar	*to arrive*
cocinar	*to cook*	mirar	*to look at, to watch*
comprar	*to buy*	necesitar	*to need*
contestar	*to answer*	pasar	*to pass, to spend (time)*
descansar	*to rest*	preparar	*to prepare*
desear	*to wish, to desire*	regresar	*to return*
escuchar	*to listen (to)*	tocar	*to play (music, an instrument)*
estudiar	*to study*	tomar	*to drink, to take*
hablar	*to speak*	usar	*to use*

■ Note that the simple present tense in English can be translated three different ways in Spanish.

Trabajamos hoy. { *We work today.*
                  We are working today.
                  We do work today.

■ To negate a verb, remember that you place **no** before it. Do not translate the verb *do* that is used to ask questions or negate verbs in English.

—¿**Pasas** mucho tiempo con tus padres?
—No, **no paso** mucho tiempo con ellos.

— *Do you spend much time with your parents?*
— *No, I don't spend much time with them.*

■ When there are two verbs together and the second one is the infinitive (*to . . .*) in English, it will be translated by an infinitive in Spanish.

Necesito **estudiar** muchos verbos.

I need to study a lot of verbs.

■ This does not mean, however, than you cannot have several conjugated verbs in a row.

Todos los días **estoy** en clase, **trabajo, regreso** a casa y **estudio.**

Every day, I'm in class, I work, (I) return home, and (I) study.

2-14 ► ¿Con qué frecuencia? Tell another student how often the following people do each of the activities in parentheses, then ask the same information about your partner and the people he/she knows. Take turns beginning.

(casi) siempre	todos los días	con frecuencia	a veces	(casi) nunca

Modelo   Yo . . . (estudiar en la biblioteca). Y tú, ¿con qué frecuencia . . . ?
E1: *Yo estudio en la biblioteca casi todos los días. Y tú, ¿con qué frecuencia estudias en la biblioteca?*
E2: *Casi nunca estudio en la biblioteca.*

1. Yo . . . (llegar tarde a la universidad, descansar los sábados, limpiar la casa, pasar todo el día en casa, estudiar en un café). Y tú, ¿con qué frecuencia . . . ?
2. Mi mejor amigo/a . . . (trabajar los fines de semana, estudiar los sábados por la noche, escuchar música clásica, cantar en un karaoke). Y tu mejor amigo/a, ¿con qué frecuencia . . . ?
3. Mi mejor amigo/a y yo . . . (bailar juntos, tomar algo juntos en un café, regresar tarde a casa los sábados, hablar por teléfono). Y ustedes, ¿con qué frecuencia . . . ?

2-15 ► ¿Quién? Using the correct form of the verb, say who in parentheses does the indicated activity more. Place **más** after the verb as in the Modelo. **Mi madre, mi padre,** and **mis padres** mean *my mother, my father,* and *my parents* respectively.

Modelo   (mi madre, mi padre) comprar la comida
Mi madre compra más la comida.

Answers for 2-15.
Answers will vary.

1. (mi madre, yo) estudiar
2. (mi madre, mi padre) limpiar la casa
3. (mis amigos y yo, mis padres) bailar
4. (mi mejor amigo/a, yo) mirar la tele
5. (yo, mi mejor amigo/a) comprar ropa
6. (yo, mi compañero/a de cuarto) cocinar
7. (mi padre y yo, mi madre y yo) hablar
8. (mis amigos, mis padres) trabajar

2-16 ► Comparaciones culturales. Read the following information about how digital technology has redefined the pastimes of young people around the world, and discuss the questions with a partner.

tecnología

Hablar por teléfono celular es la forma preferida de comunicación de los jóvenes en todo el mundo[1]. Como media[2], los jóvenes tienen 94 números de teléfono en su celular. ¿Y tú? ¿Cuántas veces al día usas tu celular? ¿Con quién hablas generalmente? ¿A qué hora del día te gusta hablar más por teléfono? ¿Cuántos números de teléfono tienes aproximadamente en tu celular?

La comunicación digital por Internet complementa, no reemplaza[3] a la televisión. Las personalidades de la televisión y los programas populares son temas[4] frecuentes en las salas de chat y las búsquedas[5] en línea. ¿Y tú? ¿Hablas con tus amigos de los programas de televisión? ¿Qué programas te gustan más? ¿Te gusta más mirar la televisión o pasar tiempo en la computadora? A veces, ¿miras episodios pasados de programas de televisión por Internet?

Muchos jóvenes tienen su perfil personal en Internet y participan en comunidades virtuales con amigos de todo el mundo. Como media, los jóvenes tienen 86 personas en su comunidad virtual y siete de las diez búsquedas más frecuentes en Internet están relacionadas con redes[6] sociales. ¿Y tú? ¿Usas *Facebook, MySpace* u otra red social en Internet? ¿Cuántos amigos forman tu comunidad virtual? ¿De dónde son tus amigos?

myspace.latino   Buscar
Inicio   Amigos   Foros   Música
¡Chisme!   ¡Buscar a tus amigos!   INICIAR SESIÓN REGÍSTRATE
Correo electrónico
¡Cargar fotos!   Especiales   Contraseña

[1]*worldwide* [2]*on average* [3]*replace* [4]*topics* [5]*searches* [6]*networks*

Gramática 2 Asking questions: Question formation

SAM: 2-22
to 2-27

Para averiguar

1. Where do you generally place the subject with respect to the verb in a question? In what sort of questions is the subject sometimes placed at the end?
2. What two expressions can you add to the end of a statement to check that you are right? How are they translated in English?
3. How do you say *who, what, which, where, when, why, how, how much, how many*, and *how often* in Spanish?
4. Do you use **qué** or **cuál** to translate *What is . . . ?* or *What are . . . ?* when asking for a definition? When asking for a selection out of a group of possibilities?

¡Ojo!

Note that all question words have written accent marks to distinguish them from other words in Spanish. For example, **cómo** means *how,* but **como** means *like,* and **qué** means *what* but **que** means *that* or *than.*

¿Cómo se pronuncia? ¡Hola!

The letters *cu* and *qu*

Most question words begin with **cu** and **qu**. Words spelled with **cu** have a [w] sound when they are pronounced but those with **qu** do not. There is more practice of **cu** and **qu** in the Pronunciation Guide in your MySpanishLab course under Consonants.

Supplemental activity.
Ask students the following questions about your class. Tell them that they may need to refer to their syllabi for some answers. 1. ¿Quién es? (Point at a student.) 2. ¿Cuántos estudiantes hay en clase hoy? 3. ¿Qué día es hoy? 4. ¿Qué hora es ahora? 5. ¿Dónde está mi oficina? 6. ¿Cuál es mi número de teléfono? 7. ¿Cuándo estoy en mi oficina? 8. ¿Cuántos exámenes hay este semestre? 9. ¿Cuántas semanas de clase hay? 10. ¿Cuándo estudias más, por la mañana, por la tarde o por la noche? 11. ¿De qué hora a qué hora estás en la universidad hoy? 12. ¿Cuántas clases tienes hoy? 13. ¿Cuál es tu día favorito? ¿Por qué es tu día favorito?

■ To ask a question that may be answered *yes* or *no,* use rising intonation just as in English. Rising intonation means that the pitch of your voice goes up at the end of the question. The word *do,* used to ask questions in English, is not translated in Spanish.

¿Trabajas todos los días? ——↗   *Do you work every day?* ——↗

■ Unlike in English, where questions and statements are worded differently, questions in Spanish are often worded the same as statements. For this reason, questions in Spanish begin with an inverted question mark to cue readers from the start to read them with the correct intonation.

STATEMENT: Trabajo mañana. ——↘   QUESTION: ¿Trabajo mañana? ——↗
            I work tomorrow.   *Do I work tomorrow?*

■ When the subject of a verb is stated, it is generally placed after the verb in a question. It may be placed at the end of a very short question.

STATEMENTS: Daniel estudia más   QUESTIONS: ¿Estudia Daniel
             que tú.   más que tú?
             Daniel estudia mucho.   ¿Estudia mucho Daniel?

■ If you think you already know the answer to a question and you are just asking to be sure, attach **¿verdad?** or **¿no?** to the end of a statement.

Daniel es tu novio, **¿verdad?**   *Daniel is your boyfriend, isn't he?*
Es de Guatemala, **¿no?**   *He's from Guatemala, right?*

■ Use the following interrogative words to ask questions that will be answered with new information, such as *where, when,* or *with whom.* **Cuál(es)** and **quién(es)** have plural forms when referring to plural nouns, and **cuánto/a** and **cuántos/as** agree for number and gender.

¿cuál(es)?	*which?, what?*	**¿dónde?**	*where?*
¿cuándo?	*when?*	**¿de dónde?**	*from where?*
¿con qué frecuencia?	*how often?*	**¿por qué?**	*why?*
¿cuánto/a?	*how much?*	**¿quién(es)?**	*who?*
¿cuántos/as?	*how many?*	**¿con quién(es)?**	*with whom?*
¿cómo?	*how?*	**¿qué?**	*what?*

■ Generally **qué** translates the English word *what;* however, **cuál(es)** translates as *what* when it is followed by the verb *to be* (**ser**) and one is making a selection from a group. Use **qué** to say *what* with other verbs and with **ser** when asking for a definition.

SELECTION: ¿Cuál es tu clase favorita?   *What is your favorite class?*
DEFINITION: ¿Qué es un infinitivo?   *What is an infinitive?*

■ Use **qué** rather than **cuál(es)** directly before a noun.

¿Qué días trabajas?   *What days do you work?*

2-17 ► La tarde de Ramón. Use the following illustrations to complete each question with the correct question word. Then, answer each question with a complete sentence in Spanish.

Answers for questions in 2-17.
1. *Regresa a las cinco y media.* 2. *Regresa en el autobús.* 3. *Compra comida.* 4. *Paga menos de veinticinco dólares.* 5. *Ramón prepara la comida.* 6. *Prepara la comida en el patio.*

1. ¿A ___qué___ hora regresa Ramón del trabajo?
2. ¿ ___Cómo___ regresa? ¿en su coche (*his car*) o en el autobús?
3. ¿ ___Qué___ compra antes de regresar a su casa? ¿un libro o comida?
4. ¿ ___Cuánto___ paga (*does he pay*)? ¿más de veinticinco dólares o menos?
5. ¿ ___Quién___ prepara la comida, Ramón o su esposa (*his wife*)?
6. ¿ ___Dónde___ prepara la comida? ¿en la casa o en el patio?

2-18 ► ¿Qué o cuál(es)? Complete the following questions students might have for the professor with **qué** or **cuál(es)** to say *what*. Use **qué** to say *what* with verbs other than **ser.** Before a form of **ser,** use **cuál(es)** to ask for a selection and **qué** for a definition.

Follow-up for 2-17.
Have students see how many logical questions they can think of for another student with the following verbs in a set time: *estudiar, trabajar, hablar por teléfono, bailar, comprar ropa, descansar, tocar. MODELO: preparar la comida: ¿Quién prepara la comida en tu casa? ¿Cuándo preparas la comida? ¿Dónde preparas la comida? ¿Qué comida preparas?. . .*

1. ¿ ___Cuál___ es la tarea para la próxima clase?
2. ¿ ___Qué___ necesitamos estudiar para mañana?
3. ¿ ___Qué___ es un infinitivo?
4. ¿ ___Cuáles___ son los verbos que necesitamos estudiar para el examen?
5. ¿ ___Qué___ más necesitamos estudiar para el examen?
6. ¿ ___Qué___ significa el verbo *llegar*?
7. ¿ ___Cuáles___ son sus (*your*) horas de oficina?
8. ¿ ___Qué___ le gusta hacer después del trabajo?

2-19 ► Preguntas. Write the questions you would ask another student to obtain the underlined information.

Modelo   Soy <u>de Baltimore.</u>
         ¿De dónde eres?

Answers for 2-19.
1. *¿Cómo eres?* 2. *¿Cuántas clases tomas este semestre?* 3. *¿Qué clases tienes?* 4. *¿Cuándo estás en clase? / ¿Qué días estás en clase?* 5. *¿A qué hora llegas a la universidad? / ¿Cuándo llegas a la universidad?* 6. *¿Dónde trabajas?* 7. *¿Con quién estudias?* 8. *¿A qué hora regresas a casa hoy? / ¿Cuándo regresas a casa hoy?*

1. Soy <u>tímido/a, paciente y optimista.</u>
2. Este semestre, tomo <u>tres</u> clases.
3. Tengo clases <u>de francés, matemáticas e historia.</u>
4. Estoy en clase <u>los lunes, miércoles y viernes por la mañana.</u>
5. Llego a la universidad <u>a las ocho y media.</u>
6. Trabajo <u>en un restaurante.</u>
7. Estudio con <u>mi mejor amigo.</u>
8. Hoy regreso a casa <u>después de clase.</u>

 ¿Y tú? Now, use the questions you prepared to interview a classmate.

Follow-ups for 2-19.
• Have students report back what they found out about their partners. Give them the possessive adjective *su(s).*
• Have other students ask individuals about their partners.
• What question was asked to elicit these responses? 1. *Me llamo* [your name]. 2. *Estoy bien hoy.* 3. *Soy de* [your city]. 4. *Hoy estoy en la universidad* [number] *horas.* 5. *Hoy estoy en mi oficina a* [time]. 6. *Hay* [number] *estudiantes en esta clase.* 7. *Mi clase favorita es esta clase.* 8. *Es mi clase favorita porque los estudiantes son simpáticos.*
• Have students make three statements of what they know about you or their classmates and check that they are right using *¿verdad?* or *¿no?*

📖 Vocabulario Lugares cerca de la universidad

SAM: 2-28
to 2-30

🔊 ¿Qué hay en **la ciudad**? ¿Qué **lugares** hay **cerca de** la universidad? ¿Qué te gusta hacer después de clase?

CD 1
Track 31

Supplemental activities.
• Name places in your city and have students say what they are. *MODELOS: Tinseltown > Es un cine. Old Navy > Es una tienda de ropa.*
• Have students complete the following statements with logical places from those presented here. 1. *Hay muchas tiendas en . . .* 2. *Hay libros en . . .* 3. *Hay música para bailar en . . .* 4. *Hay películas en . . .* 5. *Hay partidos de fútbol profesional en . . .* 6. *Hay pesas para hacer ejercicio en . . .* 7. *Hay comida y otros productos en . . .* 8. *Hay mesas para comer en . . .* 9. *Hay mesas para picnic en . . .* 10. *Hay menús en . . .*
• Have students name a place presented here that they associate with the following things: *una cena elegante, dinero, los tacos y las enchiladas, los fanáticos de fútbol, estantes con libros, plantas y animales.*

comprar libros en una librería

ver una película en el cine

bailar en un club nocturno

ir al parque

levantar pesas y hacer ejercicio en el gimnasio

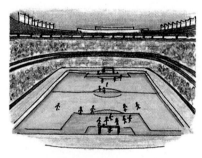

ver **un partido** de **fútbol** o de **fútbol americano** en el estadio

comprar ropa en **un centro comercial** con muchas tiendas

comer en un restaurante de comida mexicana

comprar comida en el supermercado y cocinar en casa

48

la ciudad *the city* **un lugar** *a place* **cerca de** *near* **ver una película** *to see a movie* **un partido** *a game, a match* **el fútbol** *soccer* **el fútbol americano** *football* **un centro comercial** *a shopping center, a mall*

CD 1
Track 32

Una conversación. José and Inés are making plans to study together.

JOSÉ: ¿Te gustaría estudiar juntos en mi apartamento antes del examen?

INÉS: ¿Tu apartamento está cerca de aquí?

JOSÉ: Está un poco **lejos de** la universidad. Está **en la calle** Buena Vista.

INÉS: Prefiero estudiar en el café Java. Está **abierto** hasta tarde todos los días, menos los lunes que está **cerrado**.

JOSÉ: ¿Dónde está?

INÉS: Está **al lado de** un edificio de oficinas en la calle Río Grande.

JOSÉ: Está bien. ¿A qué hora?

INÉS: Me gusta estudiar después de la cena. Hay menos **gente**. ¿**Te parece bien** a las ocho?

JOSÉ: Perfecto.

2-20 ▶ ¿Qué día? Complete each statement with a logical day of the week.

Modelo   Generalmente los partidos profesionales de fútbol americano son *los domingos.*

1. Generalmente los partidos universitarios de fútbol americano son _____.
2. Hay más gente en los clubes nocturnos _____.
3. Yo prefiero ir al cine _____.
4. _____ muchas tiendas están abiertas menos horas.
5. Me gusta comer en un restaurante _____.

2-21 ▶ Preferencias. Complete the following questions with a logical place.

Modelo   ¿Prefieres bailar con tus amigos en una fiesta en tu casa o en *un club nocturno?*

1. ¿Prefieres ver un partido de fútbol americano en la tele o en _____ ?
2. ¿Prefieres ver un DVD en casa o ver una película en _____ ?
3. ¿Prefieres comprar ropa por Internet o en _____ ?
4. ¿Prefieres comprar libros nuevos en _____ o ir a la biblioteca?
5. ¿Prefieres comer en un restaurante o comprar comida en _____ y cocinar en casa?
6. ¿Prefieres bailar con tus amigos en _____ o en casa?

 ¿Y tú? Now, use the questions you prepared to interview another student.

 ### 2-22 ▶ Mis lugares favoritos. Ask another student about his/her favorite places in town. Your partner will answer and say whether the place mentioned is near or far from the university and what street it is on, if he/she knows.

Modelo   un club nocturno

E1: *¿Cuál es tu club nocturno favorito?*
E2: *Mi club nocturno favorito es La Bamba. Está lejos de la universidad. Está en la calle Seis. / No sé cómo se llama la calle.*

1. un supermercado   3. una tienda de ropa   5. un parque
2. un cine   4. una librería   6. un restaurante

2-23 ▶ Otra conversación. With a partner, reread *Una conversación* between José and Inés. Then, invite your partner to do something together. Be sure to explain where the place you are going to meet is located.

---

lejos de *far from*   **en la calle . . .** *on . . . Street*   **abierto/a** *open*   **cerrado/a** *closed*   **al lado de** *next to*
la gente *people*   **¿Te parece bien . . . ?** *Does . . . seem okay to you?*

Suggestions for *Una conversación.*
Have students listen to the conversation first with books closed for the answers to the following questions. 1. ¿Dónde prefiere estudiar Inés? (Prefiere estudiar en el café Java.) 2. ¿Le gusta estudiar por la tarde o por la noche? (Por la noche.) Then, have them read along in their books as they listen a second time.

CD 1, Track 33

¡A escuchar!

Now, listen to another conversation in which two students, Pablo and Rafael, make plans to study together. Where and when do they decide to study?

Audioscript for *¡A escuchar!*
PABLO: Hola Rafael, ¿quieres estudiar conmigo hoy después de clase? Hay un examen el lunes y no comprendo nada. Estoy muy confundido.
RAFAEL: Sí, cómo no, pero trabajo después de clase hoy. Prefiero estudiar este fin de semana.
PABLO: ¿Quieres estudiar en mi apartamento el domingo por la tarde?
RAFAEL: ¿Está lejos de aquí?
PABLO: No, está en los apartamentos Del Prado, aquí al lado de la universidad en la calle Seis.
RAFAEL: Sí, está bien, ¿a qué hora?
PABLO: ¿A las dos?
RAFAEL: De acuerdo. ¿Cuál es el número de tu apartamento?
PABLO: Es el apartamento 59.
RAFAEL: ¿Y cuál es tu teléfono?
PABLO: 454-6026.
RAFAEL: Bien. ¡Hasta el domingo!

Possible answers for *¡A escuchar!*
Estudian en el apartamento de Pablo el domingo a las dos de la tarde.

Answers for 2-20.
Answers will vary.

Answers for 2-21.
1. un/el estadio; 2. un/el cine; 3. un/el centro comercial / una tienda; 4. una/la librería; 5. un/el supermercado; 6. un club (nocturno)

Follow-up for 2-22.
Ask students: ¿Hay cafetería en la universidad? ¿Te gusta la comida de la cafetería? ¿Cuál es tu restaurante favorito cerca de la universidad? ¿Cuál es tu tienda de ropa favorita? ¿Hay muchos clubes nocturnos cerca de aquí? ¿Cuál es el club más popular? ¿Hay un parque cerca de la universidad? ¿Te gusta estudiar en el parque? ¿Hay gimnasio en la universidad? ¿Hasta qué hora está abierto el gimnasio? ¿Te gustan las películas románticas? ¿Cuál es tu película favorita?

📖 Gramática 1   Indicating location: Prepositions of place and the contraction with **de**

SAM: 2-31
to 2-33

Para averiguar

1. Do you use **ser** or **estar** with prepositions to say where something is?
2. What happens to the word **de** when it is followed by **el** (*the*)? Does **de** contract with **la, los,** or **las?**

¿Cómo se pronuncia? ¡Hola!

The consonant d

Many prepositions contain the letter **d.** You can find an explanation of how to pronounce it in the Pronunciation Guide in your MySpanishLab course under Consonants.

Note. Prepositions are recycled in *Capítulo 3* where they are practiced with prepositional pronouns.

■ Use **estar** with these prepositions to say where something is.

a la derecha de	*to the right of*	a la izquierda de	*to the left of*
al lado de	*next to*	enfrente de	*across from, facing*
al este de	*east of*	al oeste de	*west of*
al norte de	*north of*	al sur de	*south of*
cerca de	*near*	lejos de	*far from*
con	*with*	sin	*without*
delante de	*ahead of, in front of*	detrás de	*behind*
encima de	*on top of*	debajo de	*below, under*
en	*at, in, on*	entre	*between*

■ **De** contracts with the singular article **el** (*the*) to form **del**. **De** does not contract with **la, los,** or **las.**

Tu lápiz está debajo **del** libro.   *Your pencil is under the book.*
Mi mochila está encima **de la** mesa.   *My backpack is on top of the table.*

2-24 ▶ Lugares. Name the building that is located in the following places in the illustration.

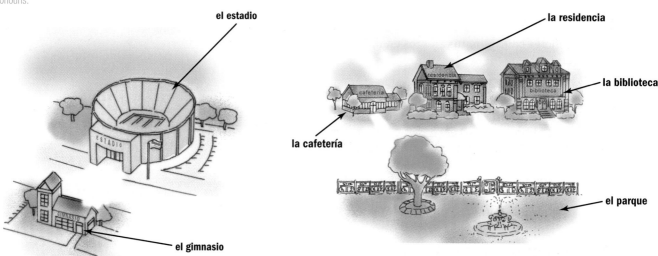

el estadio

la residencia

la biblioteca

la cafetería

el parque

el gimnasio

Supplemental activity. Ask several questions such as the following, completing them with students' names. *¿Quién está delante de . . . ? ¿Quién está detrás de . . . ? ¿Quién está a la derecha de . . . ? ¿Quién está a la izquierda de . . . ? ¿Quién está entre . . . y . . . ? ¿Quién está más lejos de la puerta? ¿Quién está al lado de la ventana?*

Answers for 2-24.
1. *El gimnasio está delante del estadio.* 2. *La biblioteca y la cafetería están al lado de la residencia.* 3. *El parque está enfrente de la residencia.* 4. *La cafetería está a la izquierda de la residencia.* 5. *La residencia está entre la cafetería y la biblioteca.* 6. *La biblioteca está a la derecha de la residencia.* 7. *La biblioteca está más lejos del gimnasio.* 8. *El estadio está más cerca del gimnasio.*

Modelo   Está detrás del gimnasio.
El estadio está detrás del gimnasio.

1. Está delante del estadio.
2. Están al lado de la residencia.
3. Está enfrente de la residencia.
4. Está a la izquierda de la residencia.
5. Está entre la cafetería y la biblioteca.
6. Está a la derecha de la residencia.
7. Está más lejos del gimnasio.
8. Está más cerca del gimnasio.

2-25 ▶ ¿Quién es? Write the name of a classmate on a sheet of paper. The rest of the class will ask questions about the location of the person whose name is on your paper until they can identify who it is. Use **ti** and **mí** as in the Modelo to say *you* and *me* after prepositions.

Modelo   E1: *¿Está detrás o delante de ti?*
          E2: *Está detrás de mí.*
          E3: *¿Está a la derecha de Raquel? . . .*

2-26 ▶ En la calle Molino. Sketch the street below on a sheet of paper. In random order, label each of the buildings using the names from the list. Make another sketch of the street, this time leaving out the names of the buildings. Then, working in pairs, ask each other questions using prepositions to discover where your partner's buildings are located. Continue until you have filled in the names of all the buildings on your blank sketch. When you have finished, compare papers.

| la biblioteca | el cine | el gimnasio | el restaurante | la tienda |
| el café | el club nocturno | la librería | el supermercado | de ropa |

Modelo   E1: *¿Qué está enfrente del hotel?*
          E2: *El restaurante está enfrente del hotel.*

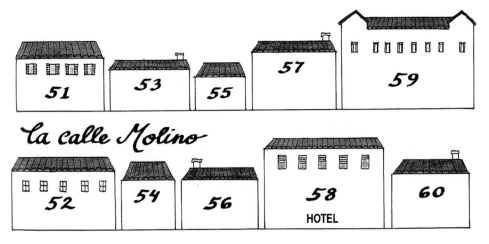

2-27 ▶ Comparaciones culturales. Read the description of the geographic locations of different Hispanic countries or territories, and identify which one is being described. Refer to the maps in the back of the book, if necessary.

Modelo   Está al norte de Costa Rica.
          Es Nicaragua.

1. Está entre Costa Rica y Colombia.
2. Está al lado de Haití.
3. Está al norte de Ecuador y Perú.
4. Está al oeste de Argentina.
5. Está entre Honduras y Costa Rica.
6. Está al sur de Nicaragua.
7. Está al este de la República Dominicana.
8. Está al norte de Guatemala y al sur de Estados Unidos.

Supplemental activities for prepositions.
• Have students refer to the drawing of the classroom in *Capítulo 1* on p. 10 and read the following true/false statements. 1. *El estante está delante de las ventanas.* (falso, Está al lado de las ventanas.) 2. *La profesora está delante de la pizarra.* (cierto) 3. *Hay un papel encima del escritorio de la profesora.* (cierto) 4. *Hay cuatro libros encima de la mesa.* (falso, Hay tres.) 5. *Hay una mochila debajo de la silla de una estudiante.* (falso, No hay ninguna mochila.)
• Continue by asking the following either/or questions such as: *¿La pizarra está enfrente de los estudiantes o a la derecha de los estudiantes?* (enfrente); *¿Las ventanas están a la derecha del estante o a la izquierda del estante?* (a la izquierda); *¿Hay unos libros o una computadora encima del estante?* (unos libros); etc.
• Tell students that *pongan* is the command *put*. Then give them commands such as the following: *Pongan su bolígrafo encima de (a la derecha de, a la izquierda de, debajo de, detrás de) su libro.*
• Give students pairs of objects or people and have them say where they are in relation to each other. MODELO: *tu mochila / tu silla > Mi mochila está debajo de mi silla.* 1. *tu libro / tu cuaderno;* 2. *la puerta / la pizarra;* 3. *tú / la(s) ventana(s);* 4. *yo (el profesor / la profesora) / mi escritorio;* 5. *yo (el profesor / la profesora) / la puerta*

Warm-up for 2-26.
Have students sketch *la calle Molino* with five boxes on each side of the street. Read the following sentences and have students fill in the name of each place. 1. *Enfrente del hotel, hay una biblioteca.* 2. *A la derecha de la biblioteca, hay un supermercado.* 3. *Al otro lado de la biblioteca, hay un café.* 4. *A la izquierda del café, hay un restaurante.* 5. *El restaurante está entre el café y un club nocturno.* 6. *Enfrente del club nocturno, hay un cine.* 7. *Al lado del cine, hay una tienda de ropa.* 8. *Entre la tienda de ropa y el hotel, hay una librería.* 9. *A la derecha del hotel hay un gimnasio.* (Quick reference answers: 51–club nocturno, 52–cine, 53–restaurante, 54–tienda de ropa, 55–café, 56–librería, 57–biblioteca, 58–hotel, 59–supermercado, 60–gimnasio)

Answers for 2-27.
1. *Panamá;* 2. *la República Dominicana;* 3. *Colombia;* 4. *Chile;* 5. *Nicaragua;* 6. *Costa Rica;* 7. *Puerto Rico;* 8. *México*

Follow-up for 2-27.
Give blank copies of a map of Latin America that includes Mexico and the Caribbean to students and have them, working in groups, write the names of the countries mentioned in the previous exercise on the map. Then, ask them to describe the locations of the Hispanic countries that have not been mentioned (Cuba, Venezuela, Bolivia, Paraguay, Uruguay). Encourage them to ask other students about the locations of the countries that they cannot figure out by themselves.

 Gramática 2

SAM: 2-34
to 2-36

Saying what you are going to do:
Ir, the contraction with a, ir a + infinitive

Para **averiguar**

1. What are the forms of the verb **ir?**
2. How do you say *I go*? How do you say *I am going*?
3. What word is placed between the conjugated form of **ir** and the infinitive that follows it when saying what someone is going to do?
4. How do you say *where* when asking where someone is going?
5. With which form of the word for *the* does **a** (*to*) contract?

Suggestion.
Point out that the forms of *ir* rhyme with the forms of *estar* learned earlier in this chapter. You may also wish to point out that the old slang expression in English *vamoose*, meaning *let's get out of here*, comes from *vamos*. Tell students that a good way to remember the form *van* is to think about how large families get around. They go in a van. Also, point out that the name of the old *Chevrolet* model *Nova* was not good for marketing to Hispanics, because *no va* means *it doesn't go*.

Supplemental activities.
• Repeat the expression of time that will arrive first in the future. 1. *esta tarde / esta noche;* 2. *este sábado / este domingo;* 3. *este fin de semana / el lunes que viene;* 4. *en dos semanas / la semana que viene;* 5. *en dos semanas / el mes que viene;* 6. *el año que viene / en tres meses;* 7. *esta noche / mañana;* 8. *a la medianoche / al mediodía*
• According to a survey in Chile, the following percentages of respondents commonly do the following activities on weekends. Give students the activities and the percentages in random order and have them guess which percentage goes with which activity: *ir a parques, plazas o áreas verdes* (green) *(53.4%), ir a restaurantes (39.4%), ir a clubes nocturnos (26.2%), ir a la iglesia (24.2%), ir al cine (19.8%), ir al estadio a ver fútbol (10.0%).* (See IRM for sources relating to the statistical data provided.)

Answers for 2-28.
Answers will vary.

■ Use the verb **ir** to say where people go.

ir *(to go)*

yo	voy	nosotros/as	vamos
tú	vas	vosotros/as	vais
usted	va	ustedes	van
él, ella	va	ellos, ellas	van

■ Use **adónde** with **ir** to ask where someone is going. To answer, use the preposition **a** (*to*). Like **de** which contracts with **el** to form **del**, **a** contracts with **el** to form **al**. It does not contract with **la, los,** or **las**.

— ¿**Adónde** van ustedes?   — *Where are you going?*
— Vamos **al** parque y luego vamos   — *We're going to the park and then we're*
   a la biblioteca.   *going to the library.*

■ Note that the forms of **ir** are used to say where someone *is going* at the moment, as well as where someone *goes* in general. To say what someone *is going to do*, conjugate **ir** followed by the preposition **a** and an infinitive.

— ¿**Vas a comer** en casa?   — *Are you going to eat at home?*
— No, **voy a comer** con mi novia.   — *No, I'm going to eat with my girlfriend.*
— ¿Qué **van a hacer** después?   — *What are you going to do afterwards?*
— **Vamos a** ir al centro comercial.   — *We're going to go to the mall.*

■ Use the infinitive of **hay, haber,** to say *there is/are going to be*.

Va a haber una fiesta el sábado.   *There's going to be a party on Saturday.*

■ The following adverbs express when something is going to happen.

esta mañana	*this morning*
esta tarde	*this afternoon*
esta noche	*tonight, this evening*
este fin de semana	*this weekend*
mañana (por la mañana, por la tarde, por la noche)	*tomorrow (morning, afternoon, night)*
la semana (el mes, el año) que viene	*next week (month, year)*

2-28 ▶ Lugares favoritos. Complete the following statements with the correct form of the verb **ir** and the name of a specific place to say where these people go in order (**para**) to do each activity.

Modelos   Para bailar, muchos estudiantes *van al club Carnaval.*
                Para comer comida italiana, yo *voy al restaurante Casa Toscana.*

1. Para ver una película, mis amigos y yo . . .
2. Para pasar una tarde tranquila, yo . . .
3. Para comprar ropa, mi mejor amigo/a . . .
4. Para tomar algo, mis amigos y yo . . .
5. Para comprar libros, muchos estudiantes . . .
6. Para comer comida mexicana, yo . . .

2-29 ► ¿Con qué frecuencia? Say how often these people go to the indicated places. Use an expression from the list and the correct form of **ir**.

(casi) siempre	con frecuencia	(casi) nunca
todos los días	a veces	

Modelo   después de clase, mis amigos y yo / la biblioteca
Después de clase, mis amigos y yo vamos a la biblioteca a veces.

1. mi padre / el trabajo
2. mi mejor amigo y yo / el gimnasio
3. yo / un restaurante de comida mexicana
4. mis padres / el parque
5. los sábados por la tarde, yo / el estadio
6. los sábados, mis amigos y yo / un club
7. mis amigos y yo / el cine
8. mi mejor amigo/a / el centro comercial

Answers for 2-29.
Answers will vary.

2-30 ► **Predicciones.** Say whether the following people are going to do each activity in parentheses tomorrow.

Answers for 2-30.
Answers will vary.

Modelo   Yo . . . (ir al trabajo, estar en clase)
No voy a ir al trabajo mañana. Voy a estar en clase mañana.

1. Yo . . . (estar ocupado/a, estar en casa por la mañana, ir al parque, salir con mis amigos, comer en un restaurante)
2. Mi mejor amigo/a . . . (trabajar, ir a la universidad, estar en la cama hasta el mediodía, pasar el día conmigo, comer conmigo, salir a bailar, estudiar mucho)
3. Mi mejor amigo/a y yo . . . (hablar por teléfono, tomar algo en un café, ir al centro comercial, estar juntos/as todo el día)
4. Mis padres (*my parents*) . . . (trabajar, estar en casa por la mañana, comer conmigo, descansar, estar en casa por la noche)

2-31 ► ¿Qué vas a hacer? In pairs, ask what your partner is going to do at the following times.

Modelo   esta noche
E1: *¿Qué vas a hacer esta noche?*
E2: *Voy a pasar esta noche en casa. No voy a hacer nada en especial.*

1. hoy después de clase
2. esta noche
3. mañana por la mañana
4. este sábado por la tarde
5. este sábado por la noche
6. la semana que viene

2-32 ► **Entrevista.** Complete the following questions with the correct forms of **ir**.

1. ¿Adónde ___vas___ (tú) generalmente después de la clase de español? ¿a casa? ¿a otra clase? ¿al trabajo? ¿a la biblioteca? ¿Prefieres estudiar con tus amigos en la biblioteca o prefieres ___ir___ a un café?
2. ¿ ___Vas___ (tú) a salir con tus amigos este fin de semana? ¿Adónde ___van___ ustedes generalmente los fines de semana? ¿ ___Van___ (ustedes) en tu coche (*car*), en el coche de un amigo o en el autobús?
3. ¿ ___Vas___ (tú) al cine con frecuencia? ¿ ___Vas___ (tú) más al cine por la tarde o por la noche? ¿Quién ___va___ más contigo (*with you*) al cine? ¿ ___Vas___ (tú) solo/a al cine a veces? ¿ ___Vas___ (tú) a ver una película hoy?

 ¿Y tú? Now, ask a classmate the preceding questions in this activity.

Follow-up for 2-30.
• Would a student who is making resolutions to be more responsible and live better say that he/she is going to do the following things or that he/she is not going to do them? MODELO: *pasar el día en la cama > No voy a pasar el día en la cama* (llegar a clase a tiempo, escuchar bien en clase, mirar mi teléfono todo el tiempo en clase, estudiar más para la clases, salir hasta tarde con los amigos todas las noches, tomar menos, comer mejor, comer mucho en restaurantes de comida rápida, preparar buena comida en casa, limpiar la casa con frecuencia, mirar la tele todo el día, ser más paciente, ser irresponsable)
• Point out that the singular form of verbs is used with the subject *la gente*. Then, have students do the following activity: Predict whether people are going to do the following things more (*más*) o less (*menos*) 25 years from now. (*trabajar más/menos, estar más/menos ocupada, necesitar más/menos la computadora, hacer más/menos cosas por Internet, pasar más/menos tiempo sola con la computadora, comer más/menos comida orgánica, comer más/menos comida artificial, estar más/menos enferma, ser más/menos independiente, ser más/menos optimista*)

Follow-up for 2-31.
Say or predict the next time you are going to do the following things. MODELO: *comer en un restaurante > Voy a comer en un restaurante hoy después de clase. / Voy a comer en un restaurante mañana por la noche. / No sé cuándo voy a comer en un restaurante la próxima vez.* (*estar muy ocupado/a, pasar el día en casa, ir al trabajo, hablar con tus padres, hacer la tarea de español, ir al cine, ir al supermercado, preparar la cena en casa, ir al centro comercial, comprar ropa nueva, comprar un coche nuevo, ir al gimnasio, ver un partido de fútbol americano/básquetbol, salir con los amigos, regresar tarde a casa*)

Follow-up for 2-32.
• Have students refer to their syllabus and ask them either/or questions such as the following. Remind them that the immediate future of *hay* is *va a haber*. 1. ¿*Va a haber cinco o seis exámenes este semestre?* 2. ¿*El próximo examen va a ser la semana que viene o en dos semanas?* 3. ¿*Vamos a estudiar cinco o seis capítulos del libro este semestre / trimestre?* 4. ¿*Vamos a regresar a clase mañana o el lunes?* 5. ¿*Cuándo vas a hacer la tarea para la próxima clase, hoy después de clase o más tarde?* 6. ¿*Vas a hacer la tarea solo/a o vas a estudiar con compañeros de clase?* 7. ¿*Vas a estudiar español el semestre / trimestre que viene o no vas a estudiar español?* 8. ¿*Vas a estudiar en esta universidad el semestre / trimestre que viene o vas a estudiar en otra universidad?*
• Put students in groups of 3–5 and have them work together to make predictions for one student from each of the other groups.

📖 Vocabulario   Los pasatiempos

SAM: 2-37
to 2-40

Note for *¿Sabías que . . . ?*
Sources: Statistics for Mexico: *Censo Nacional de Población y Vivienda* (2000) and *Study for Worldwide Rates of Religiosity*, University of Michigan, 1997. Statistics for Argentina: *Cultural Values at the Turn of the Millennium*, Marita Carballo, Gallup International, 1999. Statistics for Spain*: Study of Religion*, Centro de Investigaciones Sociológicas, Madrid, 2005.

Supplemental activities.
• Ask students: *¿Cuál es mejor ejercicio físico? ¿nadar o tomar el sol? ¿ver una película o esquiar? ¿ir al teatro o trabajar en el teatro? ¿bailar o tomar algo con los amigos? ¿levantar pesas o escuchar música? ¿hacer esquí acuático o tomar el sol? ¿hacer esquí acuático o tomar el sol? ¿comer o cocinar? ¿limpiar la casa o descansar?*
• Ask students:*¿Prefieres hacer estas cosas en grupo, en pareja o solo/a? (ir a un café, hacer ejercicio, tomar algo en un café, ir a la playa, bailar, cantar, tomar el sol, levantar pesas, ir al cine, ir al centro comercial, estudiar)*
• Have students give names of famous people they associate with these activities: *cantar ópera, bailar bien, cantar bien, cantar mal, cantar en español, tocar la guitarra, rezar, hacer ejercicio, nadar, cocinar.*
• Ask students: *Generalmente, ¿estás contento/a o aburrido/a si vas a los siguientes lugares con tus amigos los fines de semana? (al museo, a un concierto de música clásica, a un club nocturno, a un partido de fútbol americano, a un partido de básquetbol, a la playa, al lago, al cine, a la iglesia / la sinagoga / la mezquita, al centro comercial, al parque, a la biblioteca, a un café)*
• Review the adverbs of frequency and their placement and have students say how often they, their parents, or their friends go to each of the places listed above.

🔊 CD 1 Track 44

¿Te gustan las actividades **al aire libre**? ¿Te gusta . . . ?

ir a **la piscina** (al **lago**, a **la playa**) y **nadar, tomar el sol** o hacer esquí acuático

ir a la montaña y esquiar

¿Te gustan más las actividades culturales o espirituales? ¿Te gusta . . . ?

ir al museo, al teatro o a un concierto de música clásica

ir a la iglesia (a la sinagoga, a la mezquita), cantar y **rezar**

Si estás solo/a en casa los sábados por la noche . . .

Si **un/a muchacho/a desconocido/a** habla contigo . . .

¿estás **aburrido/a** y **triste porque** estás solo/a en casa?
¿estás **enojado/a** o **molesto/a** porque prefieres salir?

¿estás nervioso/a porque eres tímido/a?
¿estás **contento/a** porque eres muy sociable?
¿estás **sorprendido/a** o **confundido/a**?

---

los pasatiempos *pastimes* **al aire libre** *outdoors* **la piscina** *the swimming pool* **el lago** *the lake* **la playa** *the beach* **nadar** *to swim* **tomar el sol** *to sunbathe* **rezar** *to pray* **aburrido/a** *bored* **triste** *sad* **porque** *because* **enojado/a** *angry, mad* **molesto/a** *bothered, upset* **un muchacho** *a boy, a guy* **una muchacha** *a girl* **desconocido/a** *unknown* **contento/a** *happy, glad* **sorprendido/a** *surprised* **confundido/a** *confused*

CD 1
Track 35

Una conversación. José and Inés are making plans for this evening.

JOSÉ: Bueno Inés, ¿qué **quieres** hacer esta noche?

INÉS: No sé. ¿Por qué no vamos al centro comercial?

JOSÉ: No, no **quiero ir de compras**. ¡Vamos al cine! Quiero ver la nueva película de Benicio del Toro.

INÉS: Está bien. ¿Quieres ir a comer algo antes?

JOSÉ: ¡Buena idea! ¿A qué hora paso por tu casa?

INÉS: ¿A las seis y media?

JOSÉ: Muy bien. **Entonces**, hasta las seis y media.

INÉS: Sí. Hasta luego.

2-33 ▶ ¿Dónde? Ask a classmate where he/she prefers to do these things.

Modelo   nadar (en la piscina, en el lago o en la playa)
E1: *¿Prefieres nadar en la piscina, en el lago o en la playa?*
E2: *Generalmente, prefiero nadar en la piscina. / No me gusta nadar.*

1. tomar el sol (en la piscina, en el lago, en la playa o en el patio)
2. hacer ejercicio (en casa, en un gimnasio, en una piscina o en un parque)
3. tomar algo con los amigos (en casa, en un club o en un café)
4. cantar (en la iglesia / la sinagoga / la mezquita, en un bar o en casa)
5. ver una exposición (en un museo de arte o en un museo de ciencias naturales)
6. hablar con los amigos (por teléfono, en casa, en un café o en un bar)
7. ver una película (en el cine o en la televisión)
8. comer con los amigos (en casa, en un restaurante o en un parque)
9. bailar (en casa o en un club nocturno)

2-34 ▶ Reacciones. Describe how you feel in the following situations. Use **estoy** with an adjective from this list: **aburrido/a, nervioso/a, contento/a, triste, enojado/a, molesto/a, sorprendido/a,** or **confundido/a.**

Modelo   Un/a estudiante desconocido/a quiere tu número de teléfono.
Estoy nervioso/a.

1. Una persona desconocida llama por teléfono a las dos de la mañana.
2. Estás solo/a en casa el sábado por la noche, pero te gustaría salir con tus amigos.
3. Vas a una fiesta y todos miran un partido de fútbol americano en la tele.
4. Vas a la casa de un amigo para estudiar y hay una fiesta para tu cumpleaños.
5. Tu novio/a está con otro/a muchacho/a.

2-35 ▶ Otra conversación. With a partner, reread *Una conversación* between José and Inés. Then, change the conversation to make plans to do something together.

2-36 ▶ Comparaciones culturales. You are planning a trip to Mexico City. Compare the schedules of the following places of interest and services there with those of similar ones in your own city.

1. El Museo Nacional de Antropología es el museo más importante de la ciudad. Está abierto todos los días de nueve de la mañana a siete de la tarde, menos los lunes que está cerrado.
2. Muchos centros comerciales en la ciudad de México están abiertos de once de la mañana a nueve de la noche. Los domingos están cerrrados.
3. El metrobús (*city bus*) funciona desde (*starting from*) las cuatro y media de la mañana hasta la medianoche.

quieres *(do) you want*   quiero *I want*   ir de compras *to go shopping*   Entonces *so, then*

Resumen de gramática

SAM: 2-41
to 2-46

La hora y los días de la semana

- Use **¿Qué hora es?** to ask *What time is it (now)?* Say **Es la una, Es mediodía,** and **Es medianoche** for *It's one o'clock, It's midnight,* and *It's noon.* With all other hours, use **Son las. . . .**

- To ask *at* what time something will take place, use **¿A qué hora . . . ?** To answer, use **a la una, al mediodía, a la medianoche,** or **a las . . .** with other hours. Use **hasta las/la . . .** to say *until* what time.

- Use **de la mañana, de la tarde,** or **de la noche** to distinguish specific hours in the morning, afternoon, or evening.

- When not giving a specific hour, use **por la mañana, por la tarde,** and **por la noche** to say *in the morning, in the afternoon,* and *in the evening / at night.*

- Days of the week are not capitalized in Spanish.

- Use **el** to say that something will occur *on* a particular day of a specific week.

- Use **los** to say that something normally happens *on* a particular day. Add -s to **sábado** and **domingo** to make them plural, but not to the other days.

¿Qué hora es?	*What time is it?*
Es la una y veinte. (1:20)	*It's one twenty.*
Son las siete menos cuarto. (6:45)	*It's a quarter to seven.*
Son las diez y media. (10:30)	*It's ten thirty.*
¿A qué hora trabajas los sábados?	*What time do you work on Saturdays?*
Trabajo a la una de la tarde.	*I work at one in the afternoon.*
¿Hasta qué hora trabajas?	*Until what time do you work?*
Hasta las diez de la noche.	*Until ten at night.*

SPECIFIC HOUR:

Estoy en casa hasta las once **de la mañana**.   *I'm at home until eleven in the morning.*

NO HOUR GIVEN:

Estoy en casa **por la mañana**.   *I'm at home in the morning.*

¿Qué día es hoy?	*What day is today?*
Hoy es lunes (martes, miércoles, jueves, viernes, sábado, domingo).	*Today is Monday (Tuesday, Wednesday, Thursday, Friday, Saturday, Sunday).*
Normalmente, trabajo **los** viernes y **los** domingos, pero esta semana no trabajo **el** domingo.	*Normally, I work (on) Fridays and Sundays, but this week I don't work (on) Sunday.*

The verb *estar*

- Use the verb **estar** (*to be*):

1) with adjectives to say how you are doing or to describe changeable conditions

2) to say where or with whom someone or something is.

- Most adverbs of frequency (**todos los días, con frecuencia, a veces . . .**) generally go at the beginning or end of a phrase, but **siempre** and **nunca** are placed just before the verb.

estar *(to be)*

yo	estoy	*I am*	nosotros/as	estamos	*we are*
tú	estás	*you are*	vosotros/as	estáis	*you are*
usted	está	*you are*	ustedes	están	*you are*
él, ella	está	*he, she is*	ellos/as	están	*they are*

Mi compañero de cuarto **casi nunca** está en casa los sábados.   *My roommate is almost never at home on Saturdays.*

Con frecuencia trabaja todo el día.   *He frequently works all day.*

Prepositions

- Use **estar** with prepositions to say where things are with respect to one another.

- The preposition **de** contracts with the article **el** to form **del**, but it remains separate from **la, los,** or **las.**

¿Tu residencia está al lado del gimnasio o de la biblioteca?   *Is your dorm next to the gym or the library?*

Está a la derecha **del** gimnasio.   *It's to the right of the gym.*

Verbs ending with -ar

■ Conjugate regular verbs ending with -ar using the highlighted endings.

hablar *(to speak, to talk)*

yo	hablo	nosotros/as	hablamos
tú	hablas	vosotros/as	habláis
usted	habla	ustedes	hablan
él, ella	habla	ellos/as	hablan

■ To negate a verb, place **no** before it. The verb *do*, used to ask questions or negate verbs in English, is not translated in Spanish.

¿Trabajas?
No, **no** trabajo.

Do you work?
No, I don't work.

■ The present tense can be translated three different ways in English.

Trabajamos hoy.

We work today.
We are working today.
We do work today.

■ The unconjugated form of the verb (*to work, to do . . .*) is the infinitive. When there are two verbs together and the second one is in the form *to . . .* in English, it will generally be translated by an infinitive in Spanish. However, you can have several conjugated verbs in a row.

Necesitamos **hablar**.
Quiero **bailar**.

We need to talk.
I want to dance.

Hablamos, bailamos y cantamos.

We talk, (we) dance, and (we) sing.

The verb *ir*

■ Use **adónde** with **ir** (*to go*) to ask where someone goes.

ir *(to go)*

yo	voy	nosotros/as	vamos
tú	vas	vosotros/as	vais
usted	va	ustedes	van
él, ella	va	ellos, ellas	van

■ The preposition **a** (*to*) contracts with **el** to form **al**, but it does not contract with **la, los,** or **las**.

¿**Adónde** vas?
Voy **al** gimnasio.

Where are you going?
I'm going to the gym.

■ To say what someone is going to do, conjugate **ir** followed by the preposition **a** and an infinitive. The infinitive of **hay** is **haber**.

Va a haber un concierto en el parque. ¿**Vas a ir?**

There's going to be a concert at the park. Are you going to go?

Asking questions

■ Questions are preceded by an inverted question mark (¿) in Spanish. The words *do* and *does*, used to ask questions in English, are not translated in Spanish. The subject is generally placed after the verb in a question. It may be placed at the end of very short questions.

¿Trabaja Joel en una tienda o en un café?

Does Joel work at a store or at a café?

¿Por qué nunca baila contigo tu novio?

Why doesn't your boyfriend ever dance with you?

■ Attach **¿verdad?** or **¿no?** to the end of a statement to confirm information.

Vas a trabajar mañana, **¿verdad?**

You're going to work tomorrow, aren't you?

■ **Cuál(es)** translates *what* when it is followed by the verb *to be* (**ser**) and one is asking for a selection from a group.

SELECTION:

¿**Cuál** es tu restaurante favorito?

What is your favorite restaurant?

■ Use **qué** to say *what* with other verbs and with **ser** to ask for a definition.

DEFINITION:

¿**Qué** es la paella?

What is paella?

SAM: 2-47 to 2-52

EN LA CÁMARA DE COMERCIO

In this chapter, you learned how to talk about your schedule and activities outside of class. Now, you will practice what you have learned in a real-life simulation of working at the Hispanic Chamber of Commerce for your city.

2-37 ▸ Horarios. You are planning a convention with visitors from Latin America. Prepare a list of specific places of interest near your university and the times they are open. If you are not sure, choose a time that seems logical.

Modelo   un museo

Answers for 2-37.   *El museo de arte Laguna Gloria está abierto entre las diez de la mañana*
Answers will vary.   *y las seis de la tarde de martes a domingo. No está abierto los lunes. / No*
                       hay ningún museo en la ciudad.

1. una tienda de ropa   3. un gimnasio   5. un centro comercial
2. un club nocturno   4. un restaurante   6. un café

2-38 ▸ ¿Con qué frecuencia? Say how often you go to each place named in the preceding activity.

Modelo   *Casi nunca voy al museo de arte Laguna Gloria.*

Answers for 2-38.
Answers will vary.

2-39 ▸ Preguntas. Some visitors at a convention you have planned are asking questions about you and the city where your university is located. Complete each question with the italicized question words in Spanish.

1. ¿_____*Quién*_____ (*Who*) es usted?
2. ¿_____*Cuál*_____ (*What, Which*) es el mejor restaurante cerca de la universidad?
3. ¿_____*Dónde*_____ (*Where*) está ese restaurante?
4. ¿_____*Por qué*_____ (*Why*) le gusta ese restaurante?
5. ¿_____*Cuántos*_____ (*How many*) restaurantes de comida mexicana hay en la ciudad?
6. ¿_____*¿Cómo*_____ (*How*) se llama el centro comercial más cerca de la universidad?
7. ¿En _____*qué*_____ (*what*) calle está ese centro comercial?

 ¿Y tú? Now, ask another student the preceding questions.

2-40 ▸ ¿En qué orden? You are discussing the itinerary for the day with a group of visitors. Which of the activities listed are these people going to do first, and what are they going to do later (**luego**)? Make logical sentences using **ir** as in the Modelo. Be sure to put the activities in the logical order.

Modelo   yo: contestar sus preguntas, hablar de los planes para el día
         Voy a hablar de los planes para el día y luego voy a contestar sus preguntas.

1. nosotros: llegar al museo a las nueve, tomar el autobús para el museo a las ocho y media
2. el museo: abrir (*to open*) las puertas a las nueve de la mañana, estar abierto hasta las seis de la tarde
3. nosotros: ir de compras por la tarde, pasar la mañana en el museo
4. yo: regresar en una hora, ir a mi oficina ahora
5. varias personas: salir a un restaurante esta noche, ir a bailar después de la cena

2-41 ▸ Nuestra ciudad. A group of visitors is asking for information about you and your city. Tell them what you know by completing each statement with the correct form of the verb in parentheses and an appropriate expression. You may choose from the expressions in italics or provide your own. Note that the subject **la gente** takes a singular verb form like **él** or **ella**.

Modelo   Los autobuses _____ (pasar) cada *diez minutos / quince minutos / . . .*
          Los autobuses pasan cada quince minutos.

1. *Mucha / Poca* gente _____*toma*_____ (tomar) el autobús aquí.
2. Los autobuses *casi siempre / casi nunca / . . .* ____*llegan*____ (llegar) tarde.
3. Ustedes ____*necesitan*____ (necesitar) *un día / dos días / una semana / . . .* para ver todos los sitios turísticos de la región.
4. *Mucha / Poca* gente ____*habla*____ (hablar) español aquí.
5. El restaurante *Stubb's Barbecue / The Salt Lick / . . .* ____*prepara*____ (preparar) la mejor comida regional.
6. Generalmente los restaurantes ____*están*____ (estar) abiertos hasta *las nueve de la noche / las diez de la noche / . . .*
7. En los clubes nocturnos, la gente ____*escucha*____ (escuchar) más música *popular / latina / hip hop / techno / country.*
8. Generalmente, yo ____*compro*____ (comprar) más música *popular / latina / hip hop / techno / country.*

2-42 ▸ Mi restaurante favorito. Write three sentences describing the location of your favorite restaurant in the city where your university is located and read them aloud. Your classmates will guess the name of the restaurant.

Modelo   E1: *Está en la calle Riverside cerca de la calle Comal. Está al lado de una tienda de ropa. Está enfrente de Walmart.*
        E2: *¿Es Seis Salsas?*
        E1: *Sí.*

¡Hola! Entre profesionales

Whether you travel to Spanish speaking cities on business or you work in a service industry here that welcomes Spanish speakers to your city, you will want to communicate some basic information. Visit MySpanishLab for *Hoy día* to find more useful vocabulary, information, and activities such as the following.

Perfil de la ciudad. You are relocating to Mexico City for a few months on business and you found the following headings on several web pages profiling the city. Can you guess what they mean? Under which of these headings would you find each statement that follows them?

Clima / Costo de vida / Médicos / Transporte / Vida nocturna

1. El metro de la Ciudad de México tiene 17 líneas y 175 estaciones.
2. La temperatura media es de 16 centígrados (61 Fahrenheit).
3. Los clubes y lugares nocturnos ofrecen diversiones para todos los gustos.
4. Una visita al doctor cuesta un promedio de 250 pesos (30 dólares).
5. Una casa de tres recámaras cuesta un promedio de 8.000 pesos (1.000 dólares).

Moda global

SAM: 2-53
to 2-55

Antes de leer

Do you think that our society is driven by consumerism? Do you think that the same trend can be observed in other countries?

> ▶ **Reading Strategy** *Guessing meaning from context.* When you approach a text in Spanish, it is important to learn to use the context to guess possible meanings of unfamiliar words. By focusing on what you understand and the accompanying visual clues, you will often be able to figure out the meanings of new words.

2-43 ▶ **¡Practica!** Determine the meanings of the boldfaced words by looking at the context in each sentence.

1. Las familias españolas **gastan** casi 2.000 euros al año en ropa.
2. El dominicano Óscar de la Renta es uno de los iconos de **la moda** global.
3. En **una sociedad de consumo** muchas personas compran cosas que no necesitan.
4. Si vamos a ir de compras, **¿a qué esperamos?** ¿Por qué no vamos ahora?

Answers for 2-43.
1. spend; 2. fashion; 3. a consumer society;
4. what are we waiting for?

Ahora tú

2-44 ▶ **Una viñeta.** Now, read the following comic strip.

Después de leer

2-45 ▶ ¿De qué hablan? Answer the following questions based on Leticia and Aida's conversation.

1. ¿De qué hablan Leticia y su amiga por teléfono?
2. ¿Qué es Zara? ¿Qué cosas compra la gente en Zara?
3. ¿Qué van a hacer las muchachas?
4. ¿Qué le pregunta Aida a Leticia en el autobús?
5. ¿Compran las muchachas algo en Zara?
6. ¿Cuál es el comentario de Leticia al final de la viñeta?

2-46 ▶ ¡Cuánta tarea! Two friends, Marisol and Julia, are studying together and one of them wants to take a break. Complete their conversation with the correct question words from the box below. Some words may be used more than once.

cuál	cuántas	dónde	qué
cuándo	cuánto	por qué	verdad

MARISOL: (1) ¿ _____Qué_____ hora es?

JULIA: Son las seis y media. Estás cansada de estudiar, (2) ¿ _____verdad_____ ?

MARISOL: Sí, un poco. (3) ¿ _____Cuántas_____ actividades más necesitamos completar para la clase de mañana?

JULIA: Sólo dos más. Y después, (4) ¿ _____qué_____ quieres hacer?

MARISOL: ¡Ir de compras! Necesito un teléfono nuevo. (5) ¿ _____Qué_____ opinas (do you think)? ¿Vamos?

JULIA: No sé. (6) ¿ _____Cuándo_____ vamos a terminar (to finish) la tarea?

MARISOL: Más tarde. (7) ¿ _____Por qué_____ no vamos a buscar (to look for) mi teléfono ahora? ¡Por favor!

JULIA: Está bién. Y (8) ¿ _____cuál_____ vas a comprar?

MARISOL: No sé. Me gustaría tener un modelo compacto con todas las funciones modernas.

JULIA: (9)¿ _____Cuánto_____ quieres gastar (to spend)?

MARISOL: Pues, no mucho. (10) ¿ _____Dónde_____ hay una tienda de teléfonos por aquí cerca?

JULIA: En el centro Las Arenas. ¿A qué esperamos? ¡Vamos! (Let's go!)

2-47 ▶ La moda pasa . . . Interview your partner using the following questions, and then share the information with the rest of the class.

1. ¿Qué tipo de cosas te gusta comprar? ¿Ropa, música, libros, productos electrónicos?
2. ¿Con que frecuencia vas de compras?
3. De las marcas (brands) de ropa, ¿cuál prefieres? ¿Por qué?
4. ¿Cuáles son tus tiendas favoritas?
5. ¿Prefieres comprar en centros comerciales o en Internet? ¿Por qué?
6. ¿Con quién te gusta más ir de compras: con tus amigos, con tu familia, solo/a? ¿Por qué?
7. ¿Qué opinas de la siguiente frase de Yves Saint Laurent: "La moda pasa, el estilo es eterno"?

📖 Centros sociales comunitarios

SAM: 2-56 to 2-57

Antes de ver

Many Hispanics devote their lives to serving the community through projects that involve the arts, health, and education. In this video segment, Jorge Merced, director of Teatro Pregones, and Jane Delgado, director of the Abrons Art Center, talk about their projects.

2-48 ► Reflexiones. What is the mission of a community center? What types of activities do they organize? Is there any community center in your area?

> ► **Listening strategy** *Identifying the main idea.* Pinpointing the main idea while you are listening to someone requires that you pay close attention not just to what the person is saying, but also to what words are being emphasized or repeated. First, listen for the gist and for key words that support the main ideas of the segment. Then, listen again paying special attention to the tone of the speaker to determine whether that person is offering a positive or negative view of the topic.

Ahora tú

2-49 ► Ideas principales. As you listen to Jane and Jorge, try to identify this information:

■ What are some key words that help you understand the main ideas?
■ What is the tone of the speakers? Do they seem enthusiastic about their work?
■ Why is this year particularly important to these community projects?

Después de ver

2-50 ► Identifica. Indicate whether the following statements describe Teatro Pregones, Abrons Art Center, or both.

1. Apoya (*it supports*) la enseñanza (*teaching*) del baile, la música, el teatro y las artes plásticas.
2. Está en la ciudad de Nueva York.
3. Fue (*it was*) fundado en 1979 como una compañía itinerante.
4. Su misión es crear (*to create*) y presentar teatro clásico en español.
5. Su misión es educativa.
6. Tiene estudiantes de todas las áreas de Nueva York.
7. Sirve a la comunidad hispana.
8. Muchas de las obras que representa (*that it performs*) son puertorriqueñas.

Answers for 2-50.
1. Abrons Art Center; 2. Teatro Pregones and Abrons Art Center; 3. Teatro Pregones; 4. Teatro Pregones; 5. Teatro Pregones and Abrons Art Center; 6. Abrons Art Center; 7. Teatro Pregones and Abrons Art Center; 8. Teatro Pregones

2-51 ► En los ratos libres. Interview your partner using the following questions, and then share your ideas in a discussion with the entire class.

1. ¿Te gustaría ser voluntario/a en el Abrons Art Center o en el Teatro Pregones? ¿Por qué?
2. ¿Participas en algún (*some*) centro comunitario? Si no, ¿te gustaría participar?
3. En tu opinión, ¿es importante trabajar con la comunidad? ¿Por qué?
4. ¿Hay en tu universidad programas para trabajar con la comunidad?

Tu perfil en Internet

SAM: 2-58

Antes de escribir

Are you on *Facebook, MySpace,* or any other social network? How often do you use it if so? What features do social networks offer, and what makes them attractive? In this chapter, you are going to create your profile for a social network in Spanish.

2-52 ► ¡Prepárate! When you think about what information you would like to share about yourself in such a profile, what words or ideas come to your mind? Think about the following topics and jot down all of the words and ideas that occur to you in Spanish.

- tu personalidad y el tipo de estudiante que eres
- tus estudios, las clases que tomas este trimestre/semestre/año
- tu universidad y el área donde está situada
- tus actividades de tiempo libre

Ahora tú

2-53 ► Tu perfil en Internet. Now, complete the spaces with your personal information and write four paragraphs corresponding to the last four questions on the following screen.

myspace.latino — Buscar

| Inicio | Amigos | Foros | Música |

Cargar foto

Nombre
Fecha de nacimiento
Correo electrónico
¿Cómo soy?
¿Qué estudio?
¿Cómo es mi universidad?
¿Qué me gusta hacer en mi tiempo libre?

Después de escribir

2-54 ► ¡Edita! Exchange your Internet profile with a partner, and peer-edit what he/she wrote. Is there any relevant information missing? Offer suggestions to improve the grammar and organization of your partner's writing.

2-55 ► ¡Revisa! Review your profile, including the suggestions that your partner has given you, and make sure that it contains the following elements:

- ❏ vocabulary to describe yourself
- ❏ vocabulary to describe your classes and talk about your schedule
- ❏ vocabulary to describe the university
- ❏ verbs to talk about your after-class activities

2-56 ► ¡Navega! Visit your online resource for *Hoy día* for links to social networks in Spanish. Compare each site with the social network site that you currently use. Does it contain similar information? How is it different? Do you like it better?

63

2 Vocabulario

La hora

¿Qué hora es (ahora)?	What time is it (now)?
Es la una y cuarto.	It's a quarter past one.
Es mediodía/medianoche.	It's noon/midnight.
Son las tres menos diez.	It's ten till three.
¿A qué hora?	At what time?
a la una, a las dos . . .	at one, o'clock, at two o'clock . . .
de / por la mañana / tarde / noche	in the morning / afternoon / evening
de . . . a . . .	from . . . to . . .
hasta	until
antes de	before
después de	after
tarde	late
temprano	early
una hora	one hour

El día

¿Qué día es hoy?	What day is today?
lunes	Monday
martes	Tuesday
miércoles	Wednesday
jueves	Thursday
viernes	Friday
sábado	Saturday
domingo	Sunday
¿Qué días trabajas?	What days do you work?
Trabajo el lunes.	I work on Monday. (a particular week)
Trabajo los lunes.	I work on Mondays.

Adverbios de frecuencia

(casi) siempre	(almost) always
(casi) nunca	(almost) never
todo el día	all day
todos los días	every day
generalmente	generally
con frecuencia	frequently
a veces	sometimes, at times
los fines de semana	on weekends
una vez a la semana / al mes / al año	once a week / a month / a year

Otras palabras y expresiones

conmigo	with me
demasiado	too, too much
en el trabajo / la oficina	at work / the office
esta semana	this week
el horario	schedule
juntos/as	together
Me / Te gustaría . . .	I / You would like . . .
solo/a	alone

Sustantivos

la actividad (diaria)	(daily) activity
el cumpleaños	birthday
los deportes	sports
la música	music
el regalo	gift, present
la ropa	clothes
la televisión (la tele)	television (TV)
el tiempo (libre)	(free) time

Acciones

Prefiero . . .	I prefer . . .
bailar	to dance
cantar	to sing
cocinar	to cook
comer	to eat
comprar	to buy
contestar	to answer
descansar	to rest
desear	to wish, to desire
escuchar	to listen (to)
estudiar	to study
hablar (por teléfono)	to speak, to talk (on the phone)
hacer	to do, to make
ir (al cine / al café)	to go (to the movies / to the café)
limpiar	to clean
llegar	to arrive
mirar	to look at, to watch
necesitar	to need
pasar	to pass, to spend (time)
preparar (la cena)	to prepare (dinner)
regresar	to return
salir	to go out
tocar (la guitarra)	to play (the guitar)
tomar	to drink, to take
trabajar	to work
usar	to use

Palabras interrogativas

¿cómo?	how?
¿con qué frecuencia?	how often?
¿cuál(es)?	which?, what?
¿cuándo?	when?
¿cuánto/a?	how much?
¿cuántos/as?	how many?
¿dónde?	where?
¿por qué?	why?
¿qué?	what?
¿quién(es)?	who?

Otras palabras

algo	something
ni	nor

Lugares

el centro comercial	*shopping center, mall*
la ciudad	*city*
el club nocturno	*night club*
el estadio	*stadium*
la librería	*bookstore*
el lugar	*place*
el parque	*park*
el partido de fútbol (fútbol americano)	*soccer (football) game*
el restaurante	*restaurant*
el supermercado	*supermarket*
la tienda (de ropa)	*(clothing) store*

Acciones

hacer ejercicio	*to exercise*
levantar pesas	*to lift weights*
ver	*to see*

Otras palabras y expresiones

abierto/a	*open*
adónde	*(to) where*
cerrado/a	*closed*
la comida mexicana	*Mexican food*
en la calle . . .	*on . . . Street*
la gente	*people*
la película	*movie*
perfecto/a	*perfect*
la semana que viene	*the coming week*
¿Te parece bien?	*Does that seem okay to you?*

For a list of prepositions of place, see page 50.

Lugares

la iglesia	*church*
el lago	*lake*
la mezquita	*mosque*
la montaña	*mountain*
el museo	*museum*
la piscina	*swimming pool*
la playa	*beach*
el teatro	*theater*
la sinagoga	*synagogue*

Acciones

¿Quieres . . . ?	*Do you want . . . ?*
Quiero . . .	*I want . . . .*
esquiar	*to ski*
hacer esquí acuático	*to waterski*
ir de compras	*to go shopping*
nadar	*to swim*
rezar	*to pray*
tomar el sol	*to sunbathe*

Descripciones

aburrido/a	*bored*
confundido/a	*confused*
contento/a	*happy, glad*
desconocido/a	*unknown*
enojado/a	*angry*
molesto/a	*upset, bothered*
nervioso/a	*nervous*
sorprendido/a	*surprised*
triste	*sad*

Otras palabras

al aire libre	*outdoors*
el concierto (de música clásica)	*(classical music) concert*
entonces	*so, then*
la idea	*idea*
la muchacha	*girl*
el muchacho	*boy, guy*
el pasatiempo	*pastime*
porque	*because*

 ▶ Visit MySpanishLab for *Hoy día* for links to the mnemonic dictionary online for suggestions such as the following to help you remember vocabulary from *Capítulo 2*, learn related words in Spanish, and use Spanish words to build your vocabulary in English.

EXAMPLES

bailar, *to dance:* One goes to a **ball** to dance, and a **bal**let is a type of dance.

mirar, *to look at:* One looks at oneself in a **mir**ror, a **mir**age is something you look at and think you see, and people look up to someone they ad**mire**.

3 En familia

In this chapter, you will learn about Hispanic families.

Con frecuencia, afirmaciones como las siguientes (*the following*) se usan para describir las relaciones entre las familias hispanas. ¿Crees que (*Do you think that*) son ciertas? ¿Son ciertas estas afirmaciones sobre (*about*) tu familia?

▸ En las familias hispanas, las necesidades de la familia tienen prioridad sobre las necesidades de los individuos.

▸ Los abrazos (*hugs*) y las interacciones son más importantes que el espacio personal.

▸ Para los hispanos la palabra *familia* incluye a todos los miembros de la familia y no solamente a la familia nuclear.

▸ Para los jóvenes hispanos es menos importante independizarse (*to become independent*) de sus padres que para los jóvenes norteamericanos.

Suggestion for chapter opener.
Starting in this chapter, the cultural information presented in the chapter opener will be introduced in Spanish. Discuss the chapter opener photo with students asking them questions such as: *¿Cómo es la familia? ¿Qué relación hay entre las personas de la foto? ¿Dónde están? ¿Están contentas o tristes? ¿Por qué?* Then, have students work in groups to discuss what their family does when they get together, and whether each statement in the culture note is also true about them and their family. Finally, have students express their own observations about Hispanic families, and ask each group to think of additional questions on the topic about which they would like to learn more.

📖 Vocabulario Los familiares

SAM: 3-1 to 3-4

Note.
You may also want to give students the word *parientes* as a synonym for *familiares*.

🔊 ¿Cuántos son ustedes en tu familia? ¿Cuántos hermanos tienes? ¿Tienes muchos **familiares?** ¿Tienes más primos **por parte de tu madre** o por parte de tu padre?

CD 1
Track 52

¿Sabías que...?

En muchos hogares (*homes*) hispanos de Estados Unidos, el español es la lengua de comunicación entre padres e hijos porque los padres comprenden que preservar el español es preservar sus raíces (*roots*). Santa Ana, California, El Paso, Texas y Miami, Florida son las tres ciudades de más de 300.000 habitantes donde el español se habla con más frecuencia en los hogares hispanos. Más de 34 millones de personas hablan español en casa en Estados Unidos.

Note for *¿Sabías que . . . ?*
Starting in this chapter, *¿Sabías que . . . ?* notes are in Spanish. Remind students to use what they already know, the context, and cognates to guess the meanings of unfamiliar words. For example, use *No comprendo* to help students guess the meaning of *comprenden.* You may always ask for a volunteer to translate the note into English or you may do so yourself if it is not clear for the class. Additional statistics indicate that Spanish is spoken in 67% to 70% of the homes in the cities cited. (Source: U.S. Census Bureau, the 2007 American Community Survey)

Supplemental activities.
• Ask students the following questions about Alicia in the family tree. 1. *¿Quiénes son los abuelos de Alicia?* 2. *¿Manuel y Rosa son los padres de su padre o de su madre?* 3. *¿Cómo se llama el tío de Alicia?* 4. *¿Quién es la esposa de su tío?* 5. *¿Su tía Carmen es la hermana de la madre o del padre de Alicia?* 6. *¿Cuántos hijos tienen los tíos de Alicia?* 7. *¿Cómo se llama su primo?* 8. *¿Cómo se llama su prima?* 9. *¿Cuántos hermanos tiene Alicia?* 10. *¿Cuántos nietos tienen sus padres?* 11. *¿Quién es Lorena?*
• Have students complete the following sentences with an opposite adjective. *MODELO: Mi mejor amigo no es alto, es bajo.* 1. *No es joven ni de mediana edad . . .* 2. *No es menor que yo . . .* 3. *No es optimista . . .* 4. *No es delgado . . .* 5. *No es impaciente . . .* 6. *No es serio . . .* 7. *No es tímido . . .* 8. *No es perezoso . . .*

¡Ojo!

Use the expression **tener . . . años** (*to have . . . years*) to express age in Spanish, rather than translating the verb *to be* from English. For example: **Tengo veinte años.** *I'm twenty years old.*

CUATRO GENERACIONES

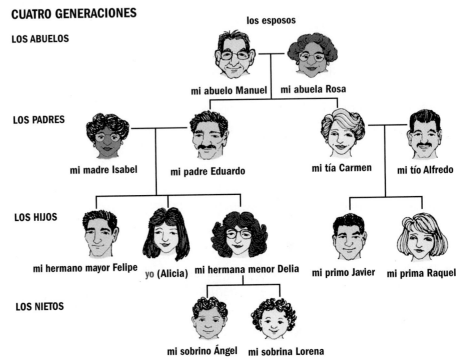

los esposos

LOS ABUELOS

mi abuelo Manuel   mi abuela Rosa

LOS PADRES

mi madre Isabel   mi padre Eduardo   mi tía Carmen   mi tío Alfredo

LOS HIJOS

mi hermano mayor Felipe   yo (Alicia)   mi hermana menor Delia   mi primo Javier   mi prima Raquel

LOS NIETOS

mi sobrino Ángel   mi sobrina Lorena

¿Eres más como tu padre o como tu madre? ¿Cómo son tus hermanos? **¿Cuántos años tienen?**

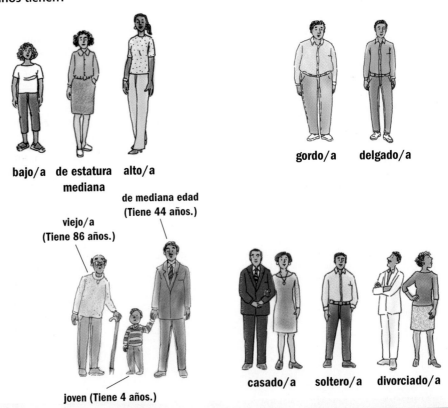

bajo/a   de estatura mediana   alto/a

gordo/a   delgado/a

de mediana edad (Tiene 44 años.)

viejo/a (Tiene 86 años.)

joven (Tiene 4 años.)

casado/a   soltero/a   divorciado/a

los familiares *family members*   **por parte de tu madre** *on your mother's side*   **¿Cuántos años tienen?** *How old are they?*

CD 1
Track 53

Una conversación. Dos amigos, Daniel y Carmen, hablan de la familia de Carmen.

DANIEL: ¿Cuántos son ustedes en tu familia?
CARMEN: Somos cinco. **Vivo** con mis padres y tengo una hermana **mayor** y un hermano **menor**.
DANIEL: ¿Cómo se llaman tus hermanos?
CARMEN: Mi hermana mayor se llama Anita y mi hermano menor se llama Alberto.
DANIEL: ¿Cuántos años tienen?
CARMEN: Anita tiene veintitrés años y Alberto **sólo** tiene diez.
DANIEL: ¿Tienen **mascotas**?
CARMEN: Sí, tenemos dos **perros** y un **gato**.

3-1 ▶ Aclaración. Complete the following questions with the correct words to clarify the relationships between these people.

Modelo   ¿Tu sobrina es *la hija* de tu hermano o de tu hermana?

1. ¿Tu abuela es __*la madre*__ de tu padre o de tu madre?
2. ¿Tu tío es __*el hermano*__ de tu padre o de tu madre?
3. ¿Tu primo es __*el sobrino*__ de tu padre o de tu madre?
4. ¿Tu nieta es __*la hija*__ de tu hijo o de tu hija?
5. ¿Tu sobrino es __*el hijo*__ de tu hermano o de tu hermana?
6. ¿Tu medio (*half*) hermano es __*el hijo*__ de tu madre o de tu padre?

3-2 ▶ Otra conversación. In pairs, reread *Una conversación* between Daniel and Carmen. Then, change the conversation to describe your own families.

3-3 ▶ Comparaciones culturales. What is the average household (**hogar medio**) like in Mexico, Spain, and the United States? In groups, read the following statistics for Spain and Mexico, then guess the same statistics for the United States. Afterwards, your instructor will give the correct response. Explain which of them you find the most surprising and why.

1. En España una persona vive sola en el 12 por ciento de los hogares y en México en el 6 por ciento. ¿Y en Estados Unidos?
2. En España, el 19 por ciento de los hogares son de parejas (*couples*) sin hijos y en México, el 13 por ciento. ¿Y en Estados Unidos?
3. El promedio de edad (*average age*) del primer matrimonio en España es 32 años para los hombres y 29 años para las mujeres. En México, el promedio de edad es 23 años para los hombres y 20 para las mujeres. ¿Y en Estados Unidos?
4. En España hay 24 divorcios por 100 matrimonios y en México hay 12. ¿Y en Estados Unidos?
5. Como promedio, en España, las mujeres tienen su primer hijo a los 31 años y en México a los 24 años. ¿Y en Estados Unidos?

Suggestions for 3-3.
• Give students a few minutes to read the sentences and decide on their answers. You may also give students cues using *más* or *menos* until they guess correctly. If needed, have a student translate each sentence to verify comprehension.
• After students know the correct statistics for the United States, have each student select the statistic they find most surprising and write it on a sheet of paper. Then, have students share what they wrote with the class.

Vivo *I live*   **mayor** *older*   **menor** *younger*   **sólo** *only*   **una mascota** *a pet*   **un perro** *a dog*   **un gato** *a cat*

Suggestion for *Una conversación*.
Have students listen to the conversation first with books closed for the answers to the following questions. 1. ¿Cuántos son en la familia de Carmen? (cinco) 2. ¿Cómo se llaman sus hermanos? (Anita y Alberto) Then, have them read along in their books as they listen a second time.

 CD 1, Track 54

¡A escuchar!

Ahora escuchen otra conversación en la cual (*in which*) dos amigos hablan de la familia. ¿Cómo es la familia de Roberto? ¿Y la de Andrea? ¿Cuál de los dos quiere tener más hijos?

Note for *¡A escuchar!*
Starting in this chapter, directions for *¡A escuchar!* sections are in Spanish.

Audioscript for *¡A escuchar!*
ANDREA: *Hola, Roberto. ¿No vas a pasar el fin de semana con tu familia?*
ROBERTO: *No, no paso mucho tiempo con ellos. Mis padres siempre están ocupados con el trabajo y no tengo hermanos.*
ANDREA: *¿No tienes primos tampoco?*
ROBERTO: *Mi madre no tiene hermanos y los dos hermanos de mi padre y sus hijos viven muy lejos. Tú pasas mucho tiempo con tu familia, ¿verdad?*
ANDREA: *Sí, para nosotros es muy importante estar juntos. Mis hermanos Andrés y Mónica viven con mis padres y yo siempre regreso a su casa los fines de semana. Siempre hay una fiesta en casa de uno de mis tíos.*
ROBERTO: *¿Cuántos tíos tienes?*
ANDREA: *Mi madre tiene cinco hermanos y mi padre tres. Tengo dieciocho primos. Siempre hay algo que celebrar.*
ROBERTO: *¿Quieres tener muchos hijos algún día?*
ANDREA: *Quiero uno o dos. ¿Y tú?*
ROBERTO: *No sé, dos o tres.*

Possible answers for *¡A escuchar!* La familia de Roberto es pequeña. No tiene hermanos. / La familia de Andrea es grande y divertida. Tiene muchos tíos y primos. / Roberto quiere tener más hijos.

Follow-up for 3-1
Point out that Spanish has distinct words to talk about *in-laws* (*cuñado/a, suegro/a, nuera,* and *yerno*) and that the suffix *-astro/a* is used like the English prefix *step-*. You may want to write these words on the board and then give sentences to explain the relationships. MODELO: *Mi cuñado es el hermano de mi esposo y mi cuñada es su hermana. ¿Cómo se dice cuñado y cuñada en inglés?*

Answers for 3-3.
Correct percentages for the United States:
1. 27%; 2. 29%; 3. 27 *para los hombres* / 25 *para las mujeres*; 4. 48; 5. 25. (See IRM for sources relating to the statistical data provided.)

Gramática 1

SAM: 3-5
to 3-6

Saying whose it is: The possessive adjectives

Para **averiguar**

1. How do you say *my, your, his, her, its, our,* and *their* in Spanish?
2. Does the ending of a possessive adjective agree for number and gender with the owner or the object possessed? Would you use **su** or **sus** to translate *their house*?
3. What do you use in Spanish instead of *'s* to show possession?
4. What can **su(s)** mean? How can you clarify its meaning?

■ The following possessive adjectives are useful when talking about belongings or relationships. You have already seen **mi(s)**, **tu(s)**, and **su(s)**. Only **nuestro/a(s)** (*our*) and **vuestro/a** (*your* pl. fam.) have different forms for masculine and feminine nouns.

Possessive Adjectives

Before singular nouns	Before plural nouns	
mi	mis	*my*
tu	tus	*your (sing., fam.)*
su	sus	*your (sing., form.),his, her, its*
nuestro/a	nuestros/as	*our*
vuestro/a	vuestros/as	*your (pl., fam.)*
su	sus	*your (pl.), their*

■ The endings of possessive adjectives agree for number and gender with the object possessed, not the owner. Note that you use **su casa** to say *their house* as well as *his house* or *her house.*

Sus padres tienen cinco gatos.	*His / Her / Their / Your parents have five cats.*
Nuestra casa no está lejos de aquí.	*Our house isn't far from here.*

■ In Spanish, use **el / la / los / las** + *noun* + **de** instead of *'s* to show possession. Remember that **de** contracts with **el** (*the*) to form **del**.

Es **la** casa **de** Ramón.	*It's Ramón's house.*
Son **los** padres **del** esposo **de** mi hermana.	*They are my sister's husband's parents.*

■ Since **su(s)** can mean *your, his, her, its,* or *their,* it is often rephrased as shown below. **De** contracts with **el** (*the*) but not with **él** (*he, him*).

	las cosas de usted(es)	*your things*
sus cosas	las cosas de él	*his things*
	las cosas de ella	*her things*
	las cosas de ellos/ellas	*their things*
¿Es **la** casa **de él** o es **la** casa **de ella**?		*Is it his house or is it her house?*

Recycle: Adjectives
Activity 3-4 recycles descriptive adjectives from *Capítulo 1, Tema 3.*

Answers for 3-4.
1. *Tu familia es simpática.* 2. *Tus hermanas son divertidas.* 3. *Tu madre es trabajadora.* 4. *Tus hijos son buenos.* 5. *Tu perro es inteligente.* 6. *Tu computadora es excelente.* 7. *Tu casa es bonita.* 8. *Tu cuarto es grande.*

3-4 ▶ Cumplidos. Give a compliment to a friend with **tu(s)** and the correct form of the logical adjective.

Modelo   padres (interesante, aburrido)
          Tus padres son interesantes.

1. familia (antipático, simpático)
2. hermanas (aburrido, divertido)
3. madre (trabajador, perezoso)
4. hijos (bueno, malo)

5. perro (tonto, inteligente)
6. computadora (viejo, excelente)
7. casa (feo, bonito)
8. cuarto (grande, pequeño)

¿Y tú? Now, describe to a partner what you know about your best friend's family and belongings using the adjectives in the preceding activity.

Modelo   *Sus padres son aburridos. | No sé si sus padres son interesantes o aburridos. | Mi mejor amigo/a no tiene padres.*

3-5 ► ¿La familia de quién?
Do these sentences describe Felicia's family or Marco's family? Rephrase each sentence to clarify whose family is being described.

Modelo   Su padre es alto.
          El padre de Felicia es alto.

1. Su familia es más grande.
2. Son cinco en su familia.
3. Sus hermanos son mayores.
4. Sus hermanos son menores.
5. Su madre es más alta que su padre.
6. Su hermana está con su esposo y el bebé de ellos.
7. Sus abuelos están con su familia.
8. Su familia está en el patio.
9. Su familia está en el sofá.
10. Hay muchas plantas en su casa.

La familia de Marco

La familia de Felicia

3-6 ► Nuestra clase.
Complete the following sentences with **nuestro**, **nuestra**, **nuestros**, or **nuestras** and the appropriate ending from the choices in parentheses, or use one of your own.

Modelo   _____ clase es (por la mañana / por la tarde / por la noche).
          Nuestra clase es por la mañana.

1. ___Nuestra___ tarea (es muy larga todos los días / no es muy larga generalmente / es muy larga a veces / . . .).
2. Las horas de oficina de ___nuestro/a___ profesor/a son (antes de clase / después de clase / antes y después de clase / . . .).
3. ___Nuestro/a___ profesor/a contesta ___nuestras___ preguntas (en inglés generalmente / en español generalmente / en inglés a veces y en español a veces).
4. ___Nuestros___ exámenes (son fáciles / son difíciles / no son fáciles ni difíciles).
5. ___Nuestro___ próximo examen es (esta semana / la próxima semana / en dos o tres semanas / . . .).

3-7 ► ¿Cierto o falso?
Complete the following sentences with the logical possessive adjective.

Modelo   Tengo cinco tíos por parte de mi padre. Todos *sus* hermanos son mayores que él.

1. Tengo una tía por parte de mi madre. ___Mi___ tía es menor que ella.
2. Somos cinco en mi familia, mis dos hermanos y yo y ___mis / nuestros___ padres.
3. Mis hermanos invitan a ___sus___ amigos a la casa con frecuencia.
4. Mis hermanos y yo pasamos mucho tiempo con ___nuestros / mis___ primos.
5. Mis abuelos vienen a mi casa con frecuencia porque ___su___ casa está cerca de donde vivo.
6. Tengo tres sobrinos. Son los hijos de ___mi___ hermana mayor.

¿Y tú?
With a partner, take turns telling each other whether the sentences in the preceding activity are true (**cierto**) or false (**falso**) for you. If a sentence is false, change it so that it describes your family.

Modelo   Tengo cinco tíos por parte de mi padre. Todos *sus* hermanos son mayores que él.
          Falso. Tengo dos tíos por parte de mi padre. Uno de sus hermanos es mayor que él. / No tengo tíos por parte de mi padre. / No tengo padre.

📖 Gramática 2 Describing relationships: The verbs tener and venir

SAM: 3-7 to 3-11

Para averiguar

1. How do you say *to have* and *to come* in Spanish? What are their forms? In which two forms do they have different endings?
2. What word precedes an infinitive after **tener** when saying what someone *has to do*?

■ The verb **tener** (*to have*) is useful when describing family or possessions. You have already seen some of its forms. Below is its full conjugation. The verb **venir** (*to come*) is similar to **tener**.

tener (to have)

yo	tengo		nosotros/as	tenemos
tú	tienes		vosotros/as	tenéis
Ud., él, ella	tiene		Uds., ellos/as	tienen

venir (to come)

yo	vengo		nosotros/as	venimos
tú	vienes		vosotros/as	venís
Ud., él, ella	viene		Uds., ellos/as	vienen

Tengo muchos primos que **vienen** a nuestra casa con frecuencia.   *I have a lot of cousins that come to our house frequently.*

■ It is common to leave out the indefinite article (**un/una**) when saying what someone does or does not have with an unmodified noun. In the singular, the indefinite article (**un, una**) is generally used if the noun is modified.

WITHOUT THE ARTICLE: No tengo gato. Tengo perro.
I don't have a cat. I have a dog.

WITH THE ARTICLE: Tengo un perro viejo y gordo.
I have an old, fat dog.

■ Use **tener que** followed by an infinitive to say that someone *has to do* something.

Tenemos que limpiar la casa.   *We have to clean the house.*

3-8 ▶ ¿Qué tienen? Say whether the following people have each relative or item indicated in parentheses.

Modelo   mis abuelos (muchos nietos, una casa grande)
Mis abuelos tienen muchos nietos. No tienen una casa grande.

1. yo (muchos primos, hijos, sobrinos, padres estrictos, perro, gato)
2. mis padres (nietos, mucho trabajo, una casa grande, muchas plantas)
3. mi madre y yo (mucho en común, una buena relación, muchas diferencias de opinión)
4. mi mejor amigo/a (hijos, mucho dinero, muchos problemas, mucha paciencia)

3-9 ▶ La clase de español. Complete each sentence with the correct form of venir.

1. (Nosotros/as) ___*Venimos*___ a la clase de español todos los días.
2. A veces (yo) ___*vengo*___ a clase enfermo/a porque no me gusta faltar a (*to miss*) clase.
3. Nadie ___*viene*___ a clase conmigo. (Yo) ___*Vengo*___ solo/a.
4. A veces mis compañeros de clase ___*vienen*___ a mi casa / apartamento / residencia para estudiar conmigo los fines de semana.
5. Muchos estudiantes están contentos si sus profesores no ___*vienen*___ a clase porque no tienen que trabajar. El/La profesor/a de español siempre ___*viene*___ a clase.

👥 ¿Y tú? With a partner, take turns changing the preceding sentences so that they describe your class. If a sentence is already true, read it as it is and say **Es cierto**.

Follow-ups for 3-8.
• Ask students: ¿Quién de tu familia tiene . . . ? (*más ropa, más dinero, más paciencia, menos paciencia, más trabajo, más videojuegos, nietos, un bebé, un iPod, más tiempo para descansar, más tarea de español*)
• Remind students of the words *nadie* and *todos (nosotros)* and the form of the verb used with each. Then, have them say who has the following things in your class. 1. *una mochila debajo de su silla*; 2. *una mochila al lado de su silla*; 3. *un lápiz (un cuaderno, un libro, un café, una Coca-Cola) encima de su mesa*; 4. *muchas preguntas*; 5. *una copia del próximo examen*; 6. *mucha tarea esta noche*; 7. *estudiantes excelentes*; 8. *un/a profesor/a loco/a*

3-10 ▶ ¿Qué tienes? ¿Cómo es? Ask another student whether the following people have the things or pets shown. Your partner should describe what they have using an adjective.

Modelo E1: *¿Tienen computadora tus abuelos?*
E2: *Sí, tienen una computadora vieja. | No, mis abuelos no tienen computadora.*

MODELO:
tus abuelos

1. tus padres

2. tú

3. tu mejor amigo

4. tú

3-11 ▶ Una fiesta de cumpleaños. What do these people have to do? Complete each sentence with **tener que** and the logical activity from the list.

comprar un regalo para ella	limpiar	preparar las enchiladas
decorar la casa para la fiesta	llegar temprano	trabajar
hablar español		

Modelo El cumpleaños de mi madre es mañana. Mis hermanos y yo *tenemos que comprar un regalo para ella.*

1. La fiesta para mi mamá es una sorpresa (*surprise*). Si vienes, (tú) . . .
2. Mis abuelos no hablan inglés. Con ellos, (yo) . . .
3. Mi hermano mayor no viene a la fiesta porque (él) . . .
4. Vamos a servir comida mexicana en la fiesta. Mis hermanos . . .
5. La fiesta va a ser en mi casa y ahora es un desastre. Esta noche, (yo) . . .
6. Casi todos mis hermanos van a venir temprano mañana. (Nosotros) . . .

3-12 ▶ Entrevista. Complete each pair of questions logically using the correct form of **tener** in one blank and the correct form of **venir** in the other. Be sure to use the appropriate verb in each blank.

1. ¿Cuántos tíos y primos ___tienes___ (tú)? ¿___Vienen___ (ellos) a visitar a tu familia con frecuencia?
2. ¿___Tienes___ (tú) casa, apartamento o cuarto en una residencia? ¿Quiénes ___vienen___ a pasar más tiempo contigo, tus primos o tus amigos?
3. ¿Qué días ___vienes___ (tú) a la universidad? ¿Qué día(s) ___tienes___ (tú) más clases?
4. ¿___Tienes___ (tú) compañero/a de cuarto? ¿___Vienen___ (Uds.) juntos/as a la universidad?
5. ¿Qué días ___viene___ el/la profesor/a a su oficina? ¿A qué hora ___tiene___ (él/ella) horas de oficina?
6. ¿___Tienes___ (tú) que trabajar los días que hay clase de español? ¿___Vienes___ (tú) a la clase de español antes de ir al trabajo o después?

¿Y tú? Now, use the questions to interview another student.

Note for 3-11.
Remind students that words from lists of possible responses that have already been used in the *Modelo* are italicized, such as *comprar un regalo para ella* in this list.

Possible answers for 3-11.
1. *tienes que llegar temprano;* 2. *tengo que hablar español;* 3. *tiene que trabajar;* 4. *tienen que preparar las enchiladas;* 5. *tengo que limpiar;* 6. *tenemos que decorar la casa para la fiesta.*

Follow-ups for 3-11.
• Ask students: *¿Quién de tu familia tiene que hacer estas cosas generalmente? (trabajar mucho, trabajar los sábados, limpiar la casa generalmente, preparar la comida generalmente, comprar la comida, tomar mucho café por la mañana, estudiar mucho, venir a la universidad mañana, tomar el autobús con frecuencia, descansar con frecuencia)*
• Preguntas personales: *¿Qué tienes que hacer esta noche? ¿Tienes que trabajar / estudiar para un examen / hacer mucha tarea / ir a otra clase / limpiar la casa / preparar la comida para tu familia / ir a la casa de un amigo?*

📖 Vocabulario Un día típico

SAM: 3-12
to 3-13

¿Sabías que...?

Una situación bastante (*fairly*) común para los hijos en España y en muchos países (*countries*) de Latinoamérica es vivir con sus padres hasta los 25 o los 30 años. Independizarse no es la tendencia general entre los jóvenes hispanos, como ocurre en Estados Unidos, y los hijos viven en la casa de sus padres sin presión (*pressure*) hasta encontrar (*until finding*) un buen trabajo.

¡Ojo!

Both **tomar** and **beber** mean *to drink*, but **tomar** is commonly used in expressions such as **tomar un café, un té** or in the expression **tomar algo** *to have a drink*. In Latin America, **tomar** is used in most contexts to refer to drinking.

Suggestion for Una conversación.
● Have students listen to the conversation first with books closed for the answers to the following questions. 1. *¿Qué días tiene Ernesto más clases? (los lunes, miércoles y viernes)* 2. *¿Para qué clase necesita comprar más libros? (la clase de literatura)* Then, have them read along in their books as they listen a second time.

Audioscript for ¡A escuchar!
CD 1, Track 57
CARLOS: *Beatriz, ¿qué planes tienes para hoy? ¿Tienes clase?*
BEATRIZ: *Bueno, esta mañana tengo dos clases.*
CARLOS: *¿Quieres comer conmigo después?*
BEATRIZ: *Sí, pero no tengo mucho tiempo. Tengo que escribir un ensayo para mi clase de sociología y tengo que leer más de cien páginas para mi clase de filosofía.*
CARLOS: *Sí, comprendo. Vamos a comer algo rápido. Yo tampoco tengo mucho tiempo porque necesito aprender el nuevo vocabulario para mi clase de francés.*

🔊 CD 1, Track 56

¡A escuchar!

Ahora escuchen otra conversación en la cual (*in which*) Beatriz habla con su novio de su día. ¿Cuántas clases tiene Beatriz hoy? ¿Qué desea hacer su novio? ¿Por qué no tienen mucho tiempo?

Possible answers for ¡A escuchar!
Beatriz tiene dos clases. / Su novio desea comer con ella. / Porque tienen que estudiar.

🔊 Por la mañana . . .
CD 1
Track 55

Leo el periódico o **una revista** y tomo café. Tomo mucho café porque **tengo sueño**.

Por la tarde . . .

Como con mis amigos. Nunca **bebo vino** al mediodía.

Por la noche . . .

Escribo y leo correos electrónicos. Recibo muchos correos electrónicos.

Corro temprano por el parque.

Asisto a mis clases. Vivo cerca de la universidad.

Leo mis libros de texto, escribo **ensayos** para mis clases y aprendo vocabulario para mi clase de español.

Una conversación. Ernesto habla con su padre de sus clases durante la primera semana del semestre.

PADRE: Ernesto, ¿tienes clases todos los días?

ERNESTO: Sí, asisto a dos clases los lunes, miércoles y viernes por la mañana y a una por la tarde. Los martes y jueves tengo una clase a las nueve de la mañana.

PADRE: Ah, y ¿tienes que comprar muchos libros para las clases?

ERNESTO: Necesito leer cinco libros para mi clase de literatura pero sólo uno en cada otra clase.

PADRE: ¿Tienes que escribir muchos ensayos para las clases?

ERNESTO: Sí, tres para mi clase de literatura, uno para mi clase de historia y otro para mi clase de ciencias políticas.

PADRE: ¿Vas a hablar con tus profesores durante sus horas de oficina si no comprendes algo?

ERNESTO: Sí, pero hasta ahora todo va bien.

PADRE: ¿Te gustan todas tus clases?

ERNESTO: Me gustan todas menos la clase de ciencias políticas. No aprendo mucho en **esa** clase.

---

una revista *a magazine*   **tener sueño** *to be sleepy*   **beber vino** *to drink wine*   **asistir a** *to attend*
un ensayo *an essay, a paper*   **ese/esa** *that*

3-13 ▶ ¿Por qué? Select the most logical ending for each sentence from the choices on the right.

1. Como en un restaurante . . .
2. Corro por el parque . . .
3. Tomo café por la mañana . . .
4. Leo las explicaciones del libro . . .
5. Aprendo bien el vocabulario . . .
6. Escribo muchos correos electrónicos . . .

a. porque tengo sueño.
b. porque necesito ejercicio.
c. porque no me gusta preparar la comida.
d. porque no me gusta hablar por teléfono.
e. porque estudio todos los días.
f. si no comprendo algo.

Answers for 3-13.
1. c; 2. b; 3. a; 4. f; 5. e; 6. d

Follow-up for 3-13.
Ask students: ¿Es lógico? Contesten sí o no para indicar si las siguientes oraciones son lógicas.
1. Leo muchos libros para la clase de literatura.
2. Corro a mi próxima clase porque tengo dos horas entre las clases. 3. A veces no asisto a clase si estoy enfermo. 4. Escribo muchos poemas para la clase de matemáticas. 5. Escribo un ensayo sobre el socialismo para la clase de ciencias políticas. 6. Comprendo bien el material de la clase de sociología porque es fácil.
7. Aprendo mucho en la clase de historia porque el profesor no es muy bueno.

3-14 ▶ ¿Con qué frecuencia? Insert one of the following adverbs or adverbial phrases in each of the following sentences to say how often you do each activity.

(casi) siempre	todos los días	con frecuencia	a veces	(casi) nunca

Modelo   Como mucho por la mañana.
Nunca como mucho por la mañana.

1. Como solo/a al mediodía.
2. Corro por el parque o la calle.
3. Asisto a mi clase de español.
4. Aprendo mucho en mis clases.
5. Escribo ensayos para mis clases.
6. Asisto a un partido de básquetbol.
7. Como pizza.
8. Recibo correos electrónicos.
9. Leo novelas románticas.
10. Escribo poemas.
11. Asisto a un concierto.
12. Leo el periódico.

Recycle: Adverbs of frequency
Activity 3-14 recycles adverbs of frequency from *Capítulo 2, Tema 1.*

Follow-ups for 3-15.
• Read the following sentences and have students repeat the one that describes them best.
1. *Leo más el periódico. / Leo más revistas. / Casi nunca leo.* 2. *Leo más para la clase de español. / Leo más para otra clase.* 3. *Leo más en casa. / Leo más en la biblioteca.* 4. *Aprendo vocabulario para la clase de español fácilmente. / Aprendo vocabulario para la clase de español con dificultad.* 5. *Aprendo mejor cuando estudio solo/a. / Aprendo mejor cuando estudio con otros estudiantes.* 6. *Escribo más para la clase de español. / Escribo más para otra clase.* 7. *Escribo más ensayos para mis clases. / Escribo más correos electrónicos.* 8. *Recibo más correos electrónicos de mis amigos. / Recibo más correos electrónicos de mi familia. / Recibo más correos electrónicos de mis profesores.* 9. *Como más comida mexicana. / Como más comida italiana. / Como más comida china.* 10. *Al mediodía, como con mi familia. / Al mediodía, como solo/a. / Al mediodía, como con mis amigos.* 11. *Asisto a más clases por la mañana. / Asisto a más clases por la tarde. / Asisto a más clases por la noche.* 12. *Asisto a más partidos de fútbol americano. / Asisto a más partidos de básquetbol. / Asisto a más conciertos.*
• Tell students: *Completa las siguientes oraciones con por la mañana, por la tarde o por la noche. 1. Como en un restaurante más . . . ; 2. Asisto a más clases . . . ; 3. Tomo más café . . . ; 4. Escribo y leo correos electrónicos más . . . ; 5. Aprendo mejor si estudio . . . ; 6. Leo el periódico más . . . ; 7. Leo mis libros de texto más . . . ; 8. Corro más . . .*

Generalmente, ¿dónde comes al mediodía?

3-15 ▶ ¿En qué clases? In which classes do you do these things?

Modelo   Escribo más ensayos.
Escribo más ensayos en mi clase de inglés. / Escribo muchos ensayos en todas mis clases. / No escribo ningún ensayo para ninguna clase.

1. Aprendo mucho.
2. Leo más.
3. A veces no asisto a clase.
4. Casi siempre comprendo bien.
5. A veces no comprendo.
6. A veces tengo sueño.

Suggestion. Point out the difference between *¿cómo?* (how?), *como* (as, like, since), and *como* (I eat). Tell students that *coco* means *coconut* and have them try to translate these tongue twisters. *Como poco coco como, poco coco compro. / ¿Cómo como? ¡Como como como!*

3-16 ▶ Otra conversación. In pairs, reread *Una conversación* between Ernesto and his father. Then, imagine one of you is talking to a family member about your classes and prepare a similar conversation.

📖 Gramática 1 Describing your daily activities: Regular -er and -ir verbs

SAM: 3-14 to 3-18

Para averiguar

1. How do -er verb endings differ from those for the -ar verbs you learned in *Capítulo 2*?
2. Verbs ending with -ir are conjugated like -er verbs except in two forms. Which ones?

■ The endings for regular -er verbs are similar to those for -ar verbs. Just replace the letter a in the -ar verb endings with an e. Regular -ir verbs are conjugated like -er verbs, except in the **nosotros/as** and **vosotros/as** forms.

comer (to eat)

yo	como	nosotros/as	comemos
tú	comes	vosotros/as	coméis
Ud., él, ella	come	Uds., ellos/as	comen

vivir (to live)

yo	vivo	nosotros/as	vivimos
tú	vives	vosotros/as	vivís
Ud., él, ella	vive	Uds., ellos/as	viven

■ The following -er and -ir verbs are conjugated like **comer** and **vivir**.

-ER VERBS

aprender (a . . .)	to learn (to . . .)
beber	to drink
comprender	to understand
correr	to run
creer	to believe
deber	must, should
leer	to read
vender	to sell

-IR VERBS

abrir	to open
asistir (a)	to attend
compartir	to share
escribir	to write
recibir	to receive

¿Cómo se pronuncia? ¡Hola!

The letters b and v

In Spanish, the letters **b** and **v** are pronounced alike. Refer to the Pronunciation Guide in your MySpanishLab course under Consonants to learn more about their pronunciation in words like **beber, vivir,** and **escribir**.

■ Use the preposition **a** before nouns following **asistir** and before infinitives following **aprender**.

Mis padres asisten **a** clases de baile. *My parents are attending dance classes.*
Aprenden **a** bailar salsa. *They are learning to dance salsa.*

■ Like the verb *must* in English, **deber** can be followed by an infinitive to indicate obligation or supposition (a guess). When it indicates obligation, it is similar in meaning to **tener que**. When it indicates supposition, it is generally followed by **de** before the infinitive.

OBLIGATION:
Uds. **deben** pasar más tiempo juntos. *You must spend more time together.*
(Tienen que pasar más tiempo juntos.) (*You have to spend more time together.*)

SUPPOSITION:
Ellos **deben de** ser hermanos. *They must be brothers.*

3-17 ▶ ¿Sí o no? Say whether the following people do each of the activities listed in parentheses in your Spanish class.

Modelo Yo . . . (comer antes de venir a clase)
Sí, como antes de venir a clase. | No, no como antes de venir a clase.

1. Yo . . . (comprender todas las preguntas en clase, vender mis libros al final del semestre, deber escuchar bien en clase para aprender, deber mirar mi celular constantemente en clase)
2. Nosotros . . . (aprender francés en esta clase, leer muchos libros, asistir a clase todos los días, escribir muchos ensayos en español)
3. El/La profesor/a . . . (escribir mucho en la pizarra, recibir a muchos estudiantes en su oficina, deber repetir si los estudiantes no comprenden)

3-18 ▶ ¿Quién? Ask your partner who in his/her family does the following things. To say nobody, use **nadie** with the same verb form as for **él/ella**.

Modelo   leer mucho
E1: ¿Quién de tu familia lee mucho?
E2: Yo leo mucho. | Todos leemos mucho. |
Nadie lee mucho.

1. comer mucha comida mexicana
2. correr con frecuencia
3. asistir a muchos conciertos
4. creer en Santa Claus
5. aprender español
6. vivir solo/a
7. leer el periódico todos los días
8. comprender otra lengua

3-19 ▶ Entrevista. Complete these questions logically with the correct forms of the verbs in parentheses. Note that the verbs are not in the correct order.

1. ¿_____Vives_____ (tú) con tus padres? ¿_____Tienes_____ (tú) tu propio (*own*) cuarto o _____compartes_____ (tú) el cuarto con otra persona? (compartir, vivir, tener)
2. ¿_____Viven_____ muchos de tus tíos y primos cerca de aquí? ¿_____Escriben_____ Uds. más correos electrónicos o _____hablan_____ (Uds.) más por teléfono? (escribir, vivir, hablar)
3. ¿_____Lees_____ (tú) todos los correos electrónicos que _____recibes_____ (tú) de tus amigos y familiares? ¿_____Abres_____(tú) los correos no deseados (o el spam) generalmente? (recibir, abrir, leer)
4. ¿Siempre _____compartes_____ (tú) todos tus problemas con tus padres o no _____debes_____ (tú) hablar de algunas (*some*) cosas con ellos? ¿Quién de tu familia _____comprende_____ mejor tus problemas? (compartir, comprender, deber)

 ¿Y tú? Now, use the preceding questions to interview a classmate.

3-20 ▶ Comparaciones culturales. Read the following statistics about schedules and life in Spain and translate the verbs in parentheses in the appropriate forms.

Modelo   En España el 62,5% de las estudiantes y el 55,7% de los estudiantes varones (*male*) _asisten_ (*attend*) regularmente a clase. ¿Y los estudiantes de tu universidad? ¿_Asisten_ (*Do they attend*) más regularmente a clase?

1. El 49% de las mujeres y el 34% de los hombres en España _____comparten_____ (*share*) mucho tiempo con sus familias. ¿Y tú? ¿Cuánto tiempo _____compartes_____ (*do you share*) con tu familia? ¿Quién _____comparte_____ (*shares*) más tiempo contigo, tu padre o tu madre?
2. Los días laborales, el 24% de las mujeres y el 26% de los hombres _____comen_____ (*eat*) durante una hora o más al mediodía, pero el 42% de cada grupo se toma sólo un cuarto de hora o menos para _____comer_____ (*to eat*). Y tú, ¿durante cuánto tiempo _____comes_____ (*do you eat*) al mediodía?
3. El 9% de las mujeres y el 14% de los hombres _____creen_____ (*believe*) que los españoles _____viven_____ (*live*) mejor que el resto de Europa y el 23% de las mujeres y el 24% de los hombres _____creen_____ (*believe*) que el resto de Europa _____vive_____ (*lives*) mejor. ¿_____Vivimos_____ (*do we live*) mejor aquí que en otras regiones? ¿Qué _____crees_____ (*do you believe*)?

 ¿Y tú? With a partner, take turns answering the preceding questions to express your opinion or situation.

Modelo   Creo que los estudiantes asisten más regularmente a clase aquí. | Creo que los estudiantes asisten menos regularmente a clase aquí.

Follow-ups for 3-18.
• Ask students: ¿Quién hace estas cosas con más frecuencia, tu mejor amigo/a o tú? MODELO: correr más > Yo corro más. (Él/Ella corre más. / Nosotros/as no corremos. / Los/Las dos corremos mucho.) 1. leer más el periódico; 2. leer más libros; 3. asistir a más clases todos los días; 4. comer más pizza; 5. escribir más correos electrónicos; 6. asistir a más conciertos; 7. asistir a más partidos de fútbol americano; 8. comer más en restaurantes
• Preguntas personales. ¿Lees más el periódico o revistas? ¿Qué revistas lees con frecuencia? ¿Escribes muchos correos electrónicos? ¿Escribes más correos electrónicos o recibes más correos electrónicos? ¿Comprendes otras lenguas? ¿Aprendes otra lengua? Generalmente, ¿aprendes mejor si estudias por la mañana, por la tarde o por la noche? ¿Qué deseas aprender a hacer? ¿tocar un instrumento musical? ¿bailar? ¿cocinar? ¿En qué restaurante comes con frecuencia? ¿Comes más comida mexicana o más comida italiana? ¿Comes antes o después de clase? ¿Comes mucho por la mañana?
• Write the following sentences on the board and challenge students in pairs to see how many logical ways they can complete them using different -ar, -er, or -ir verbs. 1. (Yo) (no) _____ muchos correos electrónicos. 2. En esta clase, nosotros (no) _____ muchas preguntas. 3. A veces, algunos (some) estudiantes (no) _____ mucho. 4. En esta clase, el/la profesor/a (no) _____ español.

Note for 3-20.
The statistics for the MODELO are from a study by the Universidad Complutense de Madrid and the rest are taken from a study by the Comisión Nacional para la Racionalización de los horarios españoles y la Normalización con los demás países de la UE. Ask students if any of the statistics surprise them.

📖 Gramática 2 Describing people: Idiomatic expressions with **tener**

SAM: 3-19 to 3-23

■ There are a few idiomatic expressions in Spanish with **tener** (*to have*) followed by a noun that say how old people are or describe conditions they have. In English, these conditions are expressed using the verb *to be*.

tener . . . años	*to be . . . years old*	tener prisa	*to be in a hurry*
tener calor	*to be hot*	tener razón	*to be right*
tener frío	*to be cold*	tener sed	*to be thirsty*
tener hambre	*to be hungry*	tener sueño	*to be sleepy*
tener miedo (de)	*to be afraid (of)*	tener suerte	*to be lucky*

¿Tienes prisa?   *Are you in a hurry?*
Sí, tengo miedo de llegar tarde.   *Yes, I'm afraid of arriving late.*

■ Since the words following **tener** in the preceding expressions are nouns, rather than adjectives, use **mucho/a** rather than **muy** to modify them.

                     LITERALLY:
Tengo **mucha** hambre.   *I have a lot of hunger. = I'm very hungry.*

■ Use the expression **tener ganas de** (+ infinitive) to say what someone *feels like doing* or is *in the mood to do*.

Tengo ganas de comer.   *I feel like eating.*

■ Remember that you use **tener que** before an infinitive to say what someone has to do.

Tengo que aprender estas   *I have to learn these expressions.*
expresiones.

3-21 ▶ ¿Deseo o necesidad? Indicate whether you generally feel like doing the following activities or you have to do them.

Modelo   trabajar   *Tengo que trabajar.*
                  descansar   *Tengo ganas de descansar.*

1. estudiar para un examen
2. ir al cine
3. limpiar la casa
4. preparar la comida
5. comer en un restaurante
6. asistir a clase
7. asistir a un concierto
8. leer mis libros de texto
9. leer una revista
10. escribir un ensayo para una clase

3-22 ▶ En otras palabras. Give another way to express the same idea using an expression from the list.

tener ganas de	tener miedo de	tener razón	tener sueño
tener hambre	tener prisa	tener sed	

Modelo   ¿Estás nervioso cuando hablas en clase?
                  ¿Tienes miedo de hablar en clase?

1. ¿Tienes ganas de comer algo?
2. ¿Necesitas una siesta?
3. ¿Tienes ganas de tomar algo?
4. Tu respuesta es correcta.
5. ¿Deseas ir al cine esta noche?
6. ¿Por qué corres?

3-23 ▶ El día de Ramón. Describe Ramón's day by completing each sentence logically with the expressions in parentheses.

Modelo   Ramón siempre *tiene mucho sueño* por la mañana y *tiene miedo* de quedarse dormido (*oversleep*). (tener miedo, tener mucho sueño)

1. Ramón casi siempre _____ por la mañana porque si no llega a tiempo para el autobús _____ esperar (*to wait*) veinte minutos por el siguiente. (tener prisa, tener que)

2. Al mediodía, (él) _____ comer en la oficina porque siempre está muy ocupado y _____ por terminar su presentación para la tarde. (tener mucha prisa, tener que)

3. Come una ensalada con frecuencia porque no _____. Generalmente no bebe mucho tampoco (*either*) porque no _____. (tener mucha hambre, tener mucha sed)

4. Por la tarde, Ramón _____ hacer una presentación para sus colegas. Todos respetan las ideas y la opinión de Ramón porque casi siempre _____. (tener que, tener razón)

5. A veces sus colegas _____ tomar café durante la presentación porque Ramón tiene una voz (*voice*) monótona y porque (ellos) _____ después de comer. (tener que, tener sueño)

6. Ramón casi siempre _____ pasar por el supermercado después del trabajo porque sus hijos siempre _____ y comen mucho. (tener mucha hambre, tener que)

7. Generalmente, Ramón _____ preparar la comida porque su esposa regresa tarde del trabajo. A veces comen en un restaurante cuando (ellos) no _____ de cocinar. (tener ganas, tener que)

8. Su esposa casi siempre _____ después de comer y no _____ de hablar mucho por la noche. (tener ganas, tener sueño)

3-24 ▶ Una pareja (*couple*) incompatible. Complete each sentence logically with an idiomatic expression with **tener** to describe this incompatible couple. Some expressions are used more than once.

Modelo   Él siempre pone (*puts*) el aire acondicionado al máximo porque *tiene calor*.

1. Ella pone el aire acondicionado al mínimo porque _____.
2. Él siempre come solo porque ella nunca _____.
3. Ella está enojada si él no está de acuerdo (*doesn't agree*) con ella porque ella cree que siempre _____.
4. Ella siempre _____ durante las películas de terror.
5. Él siempre _____ durante las películas de amor porque está aburrido.
6. Él siempre se toma su tiempo cuando ella _____.
7. Ella siempre está en la cama antes de las diez de la noche, pero él nunca _____ hasta la una o las dos de la mañana.
8. Ella _____ de divorciarse y él también.

📖 Vocabulario   Más pasatiempos

SAM: 3-24
to 3-27

🔊 ¿Qué haces los sábados?

CD 1
Track 58

¿Sabías que...?

En los países (*countries*) hispanos la gente vive los deportes de forma muy intensa. Mirar el fútbol o el béisbol es una actividad muy común del fin de semana. Como resultado del contacto con la cultura norteamericana, el béisbol es hoy el deporte más popular entre los hispanos de Estados Unidos. ESPN es el primer canal estadounidense con información deportiva en español para el público hispano.

¿Cómo se pronuncia? ¡Hola!

The letter g

Many of the verb forms shown here contain the letter **g**. Refer to the Pronunciation Guide in your MySpanishLab course under Consonants for an explanation of how to pronounce it.

A veces, **traigo** mucho trabajo a casa los fines de semana.

Hago ejercicio.

Veo la tele o una película.

Pongo mi iPod (la radio, un CD).

Salgo con mis amigos a un restaurante (al cine, a un bar, a bailar, a un evento deportivo).

A veces, hago un viaje en coche a las montañas o a la playa.

Si estoy cansado/a, no hago nada en especial. Paso mucho tiempo en casa.

80

traigo *I bring*

CD 1
Track 59

Una conversación. Dos primos, Laura y Rafael, hablan de los fines de semana.

LAURA: Rafael, ¿qué haces generalmente los fines de semana?
RAFAEL: Pues, con frecuencia los sábados y a veces los viernes por la noche salgo con mis amigos a comer o a bailar. Si estoy cansado, a veces no hago nada en especial los viernes. Veo la tele o un DVD en casa.
LAURA: A veces, ¿regresas muy tarde a casa?
RAFAEL: Sí, a veces regreso a las dos o las tres de la mañana.
LAURA: ¿Qué haces los domingos por la tarde?
RAFAEL: Los domingos hago mi tarea y leo mucho para mis clases. Si no tengo mucha tarea, a veces veo un partido de fútbol en la tele.

3-25 ▶ Qué haces? Select the words in italics that describe you best or provide your own if you prefer.

1. Para escuchar música en el coche, generalmente pongo *la radio / un CD / mi iPod / . . .*
2. Veo más *películas de terror / dramas / comedias / películas de aventuras / películas de acción.*
3. Veo más partidos de *fútbol americano / fútbol / básquetbol / béisbol / tenis* en la televisión.
4. Hago más viajes *a la playa / a las montañas / a Nueva York / a Los Ángeles / . . .*
5. Generalmente *los fines de semana / los sábados por la noche / los domingos por la tarde / . . .*, no hago nada en especial.
6. Salgo más con mis amigos *los sábados por la noche / los domingos por la tarde / . . .*
7. Salgo más con mis amigos *al cine / a bailar / a un café / a un restaurante / . . .*

3-26 ▶ En otras palabras. Rephrase the following sentences by replacing the words in italics with the verb phrases from the list that express the same ideas.

hago algo	hago un viaje	no pongo	veo
hago ejercicio	*no hago nada*	no salgo	

Modelo Generalmente, *descanso* los fines de semana.
Generalmente, no hago nada los fines de semana.

1. Generalmente, *no me gusta mirar* la tele durante la cena (*dinner*).
2. A veces *voy* en coche a otra ciudad si no hay nada interesante que hacer aquí.
3. Casi siempre *paso tiempo* con mi mejor amigo los fines de semana.
4. Con frecuencia *asisto a* un partido de fútbol americano en el estadio.
5. *Corro o voy al gimnasio* todos los días.
6. Generalmente, *estoy en casa* los domingos.

¿Y tú? Tell your partner whether the sentences in the preceding activity are true (**cierto**) for you. Change the false statements to describe yourself correctly, and then ask about your partner.

Modelo E1: *No es cierto. Casi siempre salgo con mis amigos los sábados. ¿Y tú?*
E2: *Yo casi siempre trabajo los fines de semana, pero no hago nada si no trabajo.*

3-27 ▶ Otra conversación. With a partner, reread *Una conversación* between Laura and Rafael. Then, change it to talk about your own weekends.

Suggestion for *Una conversación.*
Have students listen to the conversation first with books closed for the answers to the following questions. 1. ¿Por qué a veces pasa Rafael los viernes en casa? (Porque está cansado.) 2. ¿Qué día del fin de semana lee más para sus clases? (los domingos) Then, have them read along in their books as they listen a second time.

CD 1, Track 60

¡A escuchar!

Ahora escuchen otra conversación en la cual dos amigos, Ernesto y Javier, hacen planes. ¿Adónde van esta tarde? ¿Con quién? ¿Adónde van esta noche? ¿Con quién?

Audioscript for ¡A escuchar!
JAVIER: Ernesto, ¿estás muy ocupado esta tarde? ¿Quieres ir al parque a correr conmigo?
ERNESTO: Sí, no hago nada en especial esta tarde y necesito hacer más ejercicio.
JAVIER: ¿Está bien si traigo a mi perro? Le gusta correr conmigo.
ERNESTO: No hay problema. Me gustan los perros . . . Oye, esta noche salgo con mi hermana y su amiga a un concierto de un grupo que toca salsa. ¿Tienes ganas de ir con nosotros? Tú sabes que a mi hermana le gusta mucho bailar.
JAVIER: Sí, a mí también me gusta. ¿A qué hora?
ERNESTO: ¿A las ocho?
JAVIER: ¡Perfecto!

Possible answers for ¡A escuchar!
Esta tarde van al parque con el perro de Javier. / Esta noche van a un concierto con la hermana de Ernesto y su amiga.

Answers for 3-26.
1. no pongo; 2. hago un viaje; 3. hago algo; 4. veo. 5. Hago ejercicio; 6. no salgo

¿Sales más al cine o ves más películas en casa?

 **Gramática 1**

SAM: 3-28
to 3-31

Talking about your activities: The verbs **hacer, salir, poner, traer, ver,** and **oír;** and the personal **a**

Para averiguar

1. What is irregular about the verbs **hacer, poner, traer, salir,** and **ver** in the present tense?
2. What are the forms of the verb **oír**? What does **oír** mean?
3. What are three idiomatic expressions with **hacer**?
4. Which verb can be used to say that you *turn on* something?
5. What word precedes direct objects referring to people? What happens to **a** when it is followed by **el** (*the*)?

Suggestion.
Point out that the verb *ver* is commonly used instead of *mirar* to talk about watching television.

■ The following verbs are conjugated like regular **-er** and **-ir** verbs in the present indicative, except for the **yo** forms.

	hacer (*to do / to make*)	**poner** (*to put / to set*)	**traer** (*to bring*)	**salir** (*to go out / to leave*)	**ver** (*to see*)
yo	hago	pongo	traigo	salgo	veo
tú	haces	pones	traes	sales	ves
Ud., él, ella	hace	pone	trae	sale	ve
nosotros/as	hacemos	ponemos	traemos	salimos	vemos
vosotros/as	hacéis	ponéis	traéis	salís	veis
Uds., ellos/as	hacen	ponen	traen	salen	ven

— ¿Qué **haces** los fines de semana? — *What do you do on weekends?*
— No **hago** nada en especial. ¿Y tú? — *I don't do anything special. And you?*
— Casi siempre **salgo** con mis amigos. — *I almost always go out with my friends.*

■ The verb **oír** has a slightly different pattern.

oír (*to hear*)			
yo	oigo	nosotros/as	oímos
tú	oyes	vosotros/as	oís
Ud., él, ella	oye	Uds., ellos/as	oyen

— ¿**Oyes** algo? — *Do you hear something?*
— No, no **oigo** nada. — *No, I don't hear anything.*

■ **Hacer** is used in the following idiomatic expressions:

hacer una pregunta	*to ask a question*
hacer un viaje	*to take a trip*
hacer una fiesta	*to have a party*

■ After **salir,** you must use the preposition **de** before the name of the place you are leaving.

Salimos **de** la casa a las siete.   *We leave the house at seven.*

■ The verb **poner** can be used to say that you put on music or you turn on the radio or television.

¿Por qué **pones** la tele si vamos a salir?   *Why are you turning on the TV if we're going to leave?*

■ In Spanish, when the object of a verb is a person, the preposition **a** precedes the noun. In this context, it is called the personal **a**, and has no English equivalent. Do not use the personal **a** after the verb **tener** to talk about friends or family members you have. Also, remember that when **a** is followed by **el** (*the*), the two words contract to form **al**.

¿**Oyen** ustedes bien **al** profesor?   *Do you hear the professor well?*
Siempre traigo **a** mis hijos.   *I always bring my children.*

Supplemental activities.
You may wish to have students open their books to the maps at the end of the book before asking: *¿A qué país* (country) *hacen un viaje estas personas si visitan estas capitales?* MODELO: *Nosotros visitamos Asunción. > Hacemos un viaje a Paraguay.* 1. *Mi hermano visita San José.* 2. *Mis amigos visitan Managua.* 3. *Yo visito La Paz.* 4. *Mis padres visitan Montevideo.* 5. *Mi prima visita Quito.* 6. *Todos visitamos Buenos Aires.*

3-28 ▶ ¿Qué hacen ustedes? Ask a classmate whether he/she and the following people do the first activity in parentheses. After responding, your partner will ask whether you and others do the second activity.

Modelo tú (hacer la comida en casa, salir mucho a comer)
    E1: *¿Haces la comida en casa?*
    E2: *A veces yo hago la comida y a veces mi esposo hace la comida. (No, generalmente no hago la comida en casa.) ¿Y tú? ¿Sales mucho a comer?*
    E1: *Con frecuencia salgo a comer los fines de semana.*

1. tú (poner tu iPod a veces durante las clases, traer un iPod en tu mochila)
2. tus amigos y tú (salir más los viernes o los sábados, salir a bailar con frecuencia)
3. tus padres y tú (salir mucho a comer juntos, comer en un restaurante con frecuencia)
4. tus amigos (hacer algo en especial para tu cumpleaños generalmente, hacer una fiesta para tu cumpleaños)

3-29 ▶ ¿A quién? Complete the following sentences with the personal **a** and the names of people.

Modelo A veces oigo . . . tarde por la noche.
    A veces oigo a la gente que vive al lado tarde por la noche. / Generalmente no oigo a nadie tarde por la noche.

1. Veo . . . todos los días.
2. Me gustaría ver más . . .
3. A veces, no comprendo . . .
4. Con frecuencia invito . . . a salir conmigo.
5. Traigo . . . a la universidad en mi coche.
6. Visito . . . con frecuencia.

3-30 ▶ Comparaciones culturales. Complete the following sentences about families in Spain by translating the verbs in parentheses in the correct form. Then, answer the questions to compare the situations in Spain with those of your own family and friends.

Modelo Según un estudio publicado por la Fundación la Caixa, en España, los padres *salen* (leave) del trabajo, por término medio (*on average*), a las 6:20 de la tarde y las madres a las 5:30. ¿Y tus padres? ¿A qué hora *salen* (do they leave) del trabajo?
    Mi madre sale del trabajo más o menos a la misma hora que en España, pero mi padre sale más temprano.

1. Los hijos ___ven___ (see) la televisión un promedio (*an average*) de 1 hora y 54 minutos al día. ¿Y tú? ¿Cuánto tiempo ___ves___ (do you see) la televisión todos los días?
2. El 35% de las hijas y el 44% de los hijos varones mayores de 15 años ___salen___ (go out) con sus amigos casi todos los fines de semana por la noche. ¿Y tú? ¿___Sales___ (do you go out) con tus amigos casi todos los fines de semana?
3. Los padres españoles ___ponen___ (put) una hora límite de llegar a casa por la noche al 80% de las hijas y al 71% de los hijos varones. ¿Y tus padres? ¿___Ponen___ (do they put) una hora límite de llegar a casa?
4. Sólo el 8% de las hijas y el 5% de los hijos varones ___creen___ (believe) que su padre es muy estricto. El 57% de las hijas y el 61% de los hijos varones ___creen___ (believe) que su padre es poco estricto o que no es nada estricto. ¿Y tú? ¿___Crees___ (do you believe) que tu padre es muy estricto?
5. El 36% de los abuelos maternos y el 16% de los abuelos paternos ___ven___ (see) a sus nietos casi todos los días. ¿Y tú? ¿Con qué frecuencia ___ves___ (do you see) a tus abuelos?

Follow-ups for 3-28.
• Have students repeat the sentence that describes them best. 1. *Sólo traigo mi libro de español a la clase de español. / También traigo otros libros a la clase de español.* 2. *Traigo mis libros en una mochila. / No traigo mochila.* 3. *Traigo mi coche a la universidad. / No traigo mi coche a la universidad.* 4. *Hago más tarea para la clase de español. / Hago más tarea para otra clase.* 5. *Hago mi tarea solo/a. / Hago mi tarea con mis amigos.* 6. *Pongo música a veces cuando estudio. / Nunca pongo música cuando estudio.* 7. *En clase, pongo mi mochila debajo de la silla. / Pongo mi mochila al lado de la silla.* 8. *Salgo para la universidad todos los días a la misma hora. / No salgo para la universidad todos los días a la misma hora.*
• Have students say how often they do the following things in Spanish class. Modelo: *salir de clase temprano > Nunca salgo de clase temprano. / A veces salgo de clase temprano.*
1. *traer mi libro a clase;* 2. *oír bien al profesor / a la profesora;* 3. *poner algo debajo de mi silla;* 4. *salir de clase durante los exámenes;* 5. *hacer preguntas;* 6. *traer un diccionario a clase;* 7. *hacer la tarea durante la clase*
• Ask students: 1. ¿*Traes las siguientes cosas en tu mochila a la clase de español?* (el cuaderno de ejercicios, el libro de español, mucho dinero, comida, una calculadora, una computadora, un teléfono celular) 2. ¿*Oyes a veces estas cosas en la clase de español?* (teléfonos celulares, música, muchas preguntas en español, mucho inglés, el / la profesor/a del salón de clase de al lado) 3. ¿*Hacemos nosotros las siguientes cosas en esta clase?* (muchos ejercicios en grupos, muchos ejercicios en la pizarra, mucha tarea, muchos exámenes, muchas preguntas, muchas fiestas)
• Preguntas personales. 1. ¿*A qué hora sales de tu última clase hoy? ¿Qué haces generalmente después de las clases?* 2. ¿*Haces muchos viajes? ¿Haces más viajes a la playa, a las montañas o a otra ciudad? ¿Te gustaría más hacer un viaje a México o a España? ¿a Puerto Rico o a Bolivia?* 3. ¿*Haces muchas fiestas en tu casa? ¿Qué hacen tus amigos y tú en las fiestas generalmente? ¿Traen tus amigos algo a las fiestas?*

Follow-up for 3-29.
Preguntas personales. 1. ¿*Visitas a tu mejor amigo/a con frecuencia?* 2. ¿*Traes a otro estudiante a la universidad en tu coche?* 3. ¿*Ves más a tus padres o a tu mejor amigo/a los fines de semana?* 4. ¿*Ves a tus vecinos* (neighbors) *con frecuencia?* 5. ¿*Oyes a tus vecinos a veces cuando escuchan música?* 6. ¿*Cuándo no tienes ganas de ver a nadie?*

Note for 3-30. This information was taken from the report *Padres e hijos en la España actual* by Gerardo Meil Landwerlin published by the *Fundación la Caixa* (2006).

Follow-up for 3-30.
The following is a list of the main reasons parents and children argue in Spain according the report *Comunicación y conflictos entre hijos y padres* (2003) by the *Fundación de Ayuda contra la Drogadicción*. They are listed in order of frequency, with 1 as the most common. Give students the list in random order and have them guess the correct order. Then, compare the results. 1. *la colaboración doméstica;* 2. *los estudios;* 3. *la hora de llegar por la noche;* 4. *el dinero;* 5. *la hora de levantarse* (to get up); 6. *la relación con sus hermanos;* 7. *el consumo de alcohol;* 8. *los amigos*

Gramática 2

SAM: 3-32
to 3-34

Talking about what you do with friends and family: Pronouns used after prepositions

Para **averiguar**

1. Which two pronouns used after prepositions are different from the subject pronouns?
2. How do you say *with me* and *with you* (singular, familiar)? How do you say *with him (her, us, them)*?
3. After which three prepositions do you use the pronouns **yo** and **tú**, rather than **mí** and **ti**?

■ The pronouns used after prepositions (*for* **me,** *behind* **them,** *in front of* **us** . . .) in Spanish are the same as the subject pronouns, except **mí** is used instead of **yo** and **ti** instead of **tú**. There is an accent mark on **mí** (*me*) to distinguish it from the possessive adjective **mi** (*my*).

Prepositional Pronouns

para	mí	*for me*	para	nosotros/as	*for us*
para	ti	*for you*	para	vosotros/as	*for you*
para	usted	*for you*	para	ustedes	*for you*
para	él	*for him*	para	ellos	*for them*
para	ella	*for her*	para	ellas	*for them*

■ As with **para** in the chart, the same pronouns are used after the other prepositions you learned in *Capítulo 2*.

| ¿Quién está **detrás de ti** en la foto? | *Who is behind you in the photo?* |
| Mi familia nunca hace viajes **sin mí**. | *My family never takes trips without me.* |

■ With the preposition **con**, use **conmigo** to say *with me* and **contigo** for *with you* (sing., fam.). The other prepositional pronouns do not change after **con**.

| ¿Vas **conmigo** o **con ellos**? | *Are you going with me or with them?* |
| ¿Tienes ganas de hacer algo **con nosotros**? | *Do you feel like doing something with us?* |

■ Use the pronouns **yo** and **tú** instead of **mí** and **ti** after the prepositions **entre**, **menos** (*minus, except*), or **excepto** (*except*).

| No hay secretos **entre tú y yo**. | *There are no secrets between you and me.* |
| En mi familia, todos son altos **menos yo**. | *In my family, they are all tall except me.* |

3-31 ► Interacciones. Ask another student the following questions. He/She should answer using a prepositional pronoun.

Follow-up for 3-31.
Give students statements such as the following about yourself and have them guess to whom the pronoun refers. *Modelo: Como con ella con frecuencia.* > *¿Es su esposa? — No. — ¿Es su hija? — Sí.*

Modelo   E1: *¿Haces muchos viajes con tus padres?*
         E2: *No, no hago muchos viajes con ellos.*

1. ¿Vives con tus padres?
2. ¿Vives cerca de tu mejor amigo/a?
3. ¿Te gusta bailar con tus primos?
4. ¿Sales a comer con tus padres con frecuencia?
5. ¿Pasas mucho tiempo con tu madre?
6. ¿Asistes a clase con tu mejor amigo/a?
7. ¿Compartes el coche con tu hermano?
8. ¿Recibes correos electrónicos de tus profesores?
9. ¿Quién come contigo todos los días?
10. ¿Quién es más importante para ti?
11. ¿Quién habla mal de ti a veces?
12. ¿Quién comparte sus secretos contigo a veces?

¿Quién comparte sus secretos contigo?

3-32 ▶ ¿Qué haces con ellos? What are two things you do (or don't do) with the following people? Use a prepositional pronoun in your answer, as in the Modelo.

salir a comer / a bailar	trabajar
asistir a un concierto / a clase	limpiar la casa
hacer un viaje / una fiesta	tomar algo en un café
estudiar para los exámenes	hablar español / inglés / por
ir de compras / al cine / al parque	teléfono
ver la tele / un DVD / un partido de	. . .
fútbol americano	

Modelo   con tus abuelos
Hablo inglés con ellos. Salgo a comer con ellos. | Nunca estoy con ellos.

1. con tu madre   **3.** con tus abuelos   **5.** con tus amigos
2. con tu padre   **4.** con tus compañeros de clase   **6.** con tu mejor amigo/a

¿Y tú? Ask a partner what the preceding people do with you.

Modelo   E1: *¿Qué hacen tus abuelos contigo?*
          E2: *A veces mis abuelos van de compras conmigo. |*
              Mis abuelos nunca hacen nada conmigo.

3-33 ▶ Una foto. Mariela is describing her family in this photo. Read her statements to determine who each person is. The first answer has been given in the Modelo.

Modelo   *Su mamá es el número 1.*

Ésta es una foto de una fiesta para el cumpleaños de mi sobrino Eduardo.
Mi abuela está delante de mí y mi mamá está a mi lado.
Delante de ella está mi abuelo y mi tía Mónica está al lado de él.
Enfrente de mi tía Mónica está mi sobrino Eduardo.
A su derecha está su hermano Daniel y a su izquierda, enfrente de mi abuelo, está
    su papá, mi cuñado (*brother-in-law*) Alejandro.
Mi hermana Ximena está al lado de ellos.
Mi padre está cerca de ella, al lado de la mesa, y mi prima Aura está entre nosotros.
Mis otros primos están detrás de ella, más cerca de la casa.

Recycle: Regular -ar verbs
Activity 3-32 recycles regular -ar verbs from *Capítulo 2, Tema 2.*

Suggestion for *¿Y tú?*
Give students a few moments to prepare. Point out how to say someone *never does anything* as shown in the Modelo.

Recycle: Prepositions of place
Activity 3-33 recycles prepositions of place from *Capítulo 2, Tema 3.*

Warm-up for 3-33.
Have students prepare three sentences describing where someone in the class is, using prepositional pronouns instead of his/her name. Afterwards, have them read the sentences aloud for the class to guess who the person is. *MODELO:* E1: *Alicia está delante de ella. No hay nadie detrás de ella. David está a su izquierda y hay una pared a su derecha.* E2: *Es Nicole, ¿verdad?* E1: *Sí.*

Answers for 3-33.
Su abuelo es el número 2. Su abuela es el número 3. Su tía (Mónica) es el número 4. Su sobrino (Daniel) es el número 5. Su cuñado (Alejandro) es el número 6. Su hermana Ximena es el número 7. Su padre es el número 8. Su prima Aura es el número 9. Sus otros primos son el número 10.

Follow-up for 3-33.
Make a transparency of a photo of you with a group of friends or family members and have students ask questions identifying people with prepositions and prepositional pronouns. You may also wish to have students bring photos of their families.

📖 Vocabulario El aspecto físico y el carácter

SAM: 3-35
to 3-40

🔊 ¿Cómo es tu padre / madre? ¿Es **guapo/a?** ¿Tiene el pelo **largo** o **corto**?
CD 1
Track 61

Suggestion.
Point out that *moreno/a* generally refers to complexion color, and that *los ojos marrones* is used in some regions and *los ojos (color) café* in others. The adjective *café* is invariable.

Suggestion for *Una conversación.*
• Have students listen to the conversation first with books closed for the answers to the following questions. 1. *¿De qué color son los ojos del padre de Sonia? (Son verdes.)* 2. *¿Cuál de sus padres es chistoso y cuál es serio? (Su madre es chistosa y su padre es serio.)* Then, have them read in their books as they listen a second time.
• New words presented in the conversation include the boldfaced expressions, as well as *físicamente* and *adoptado/a*.

Audioscript for ¡A escuchar!
MARTA: *Oye Ana, tienes suerte de tener un novio como Lorenzo. Es muy guapo y elegante. Me gustan los hombres morenos como él con los ojos azules. ¡Además es tan alto y está tan delgado! ¿Por qué nunca viene con nosotras cuando salimos?*
ANA: *Siempre tiene que terminar algún trabajo. Es súper trabajador. A veces no sale de la oficina hasta casi las nueve. Además, es un poco tímido y prefiere salir en pareja.*
MARTA: *¡Debes insistir!*
ANA: *No, no quiero parecer mandona, además Lorenzo es muy terco. Es inútil insistir.*

Possible answers for ¡A escuchar!
Lorenzo es guapo, elegante, moreno, alto y delgado. Tiene los ojos azules. / Es súper trabajador, tímido y terco.

🔊 CD 1, Track 63

¡A escuchar!

Ahora escuchen otra conversación en la cual dos amigas, Marta y Ana, hablan del novio de una de ellas. ¿Cómo es su aspecto físico? ¿Y su carácter?

Es rubia. Tiene el pelo rubio.   Es moreno. Tiene el pelo **negro / castaño**.   Es pelirroja. Tiene el pelo rojo.   Es canosa. Tiene el pelo canoso.

Tiene los ojos . . .   Mi padre también tiene . . .

azules   marrones / color café

gafas

bigote

barba

verdes   grises

De carácter, ¿eres más como tu madre o más como tu padre? ¿Cómo es? ¿Es . . . ?

chistoso/a o serio/a	*funny (likes to joke around) or serious*
relajado/a o estricto/a	*easy-going or strict*
liberal o conservador/a	*liberal or conservative*
cariñoso/a o frío/a	*loving (affectionate) or cold*
generoso/a o egoísta	*generous or selfish*
tranquilo/a o temperamental	*calm or moody*
amistoso/a o presumido/a	*friendly or stuck-up*
comprensivo/a o mandón / mandona	*understanding or bossy*
flexible o terco/a	*flexible or stubborn*
realista y normal o raro/a	*down-to-earth and normal or weird*

🔊 CD 1 Track 64

Una conversación. Dos amigas, Elena y Sonia, hablan de sus padres.

ELENA: ¿Cómo son tus padres? ¿Eres más como tu madre o tu padre?
SONIA: Físicamente soy más como mi papá. Es alto y tiene el pelo castaño y los ojos verdes como yo. Mi madre tiene el pelo canoso y los ojos azules. De carácter, soy más como ella. Es chistosa, cariñosa y un poco impulsiva. **No soy nada como** mi papá. Es temperamental, muy estricto y serio. ¿Y tú? ¿Eres más como tu madre o tu padre?
ELENA: Pues, físicamente, no soy como ninguno de los dos porque soy adoptada. En el carácter, soy más como mi papá. Nosotros dos somos reservados, pero mi mamá es muy extrovertida y sociable.

el aspecto físico *physical appearance*   **guapo/a** *good-looking, handsome*   **largo/a** *long*   **corto/a** *short* (in length)   **negro/a** *black*   **castaño/a** *brown* (for hair)   **no soy nada como** *I'm not anything like*

3-34 ▶ ¿Cómo es? Complete each description with the correct form of the logical adjective from the list.

amistoso/a	mandón / mandona	sociable
comprensivo/a	*presumido/a*	temperamental
frío/a	raro/a	terco/a

Modelo   Todas mis tías por parte de mi madre creen que son mejores que nosotros. Son *presumidas*.

1. Mi madre siempre comprende todos mis problemas. Es muy ___comprensiva___.
2. A veces mi hermano está bien y luego, de pronto (*all of a sudden*) está enojado. Es ___temperamental___.
3. Mi hermano es muy ___terco___. Para él, es muy difícil admitir que no tiene razón.
4. Mi hermana habla con todo el mundo (*everyone*) y tiene muchos amigos. Es muy ___sociable___ y ___amistosa___.
5. Tengo una tía muy ___fría___. Nunca habla con nosotros y es indiferente si su familia necesita ayuda. (*help*)
6. Mi abuela por parte de mi madre insiste en controlar a todos sus hijos. Es muy ___mandona___.
7. Tengo un primo ___raro___. Es muy excéntrico.

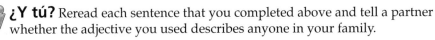 **¿Y tú?** Reread each sentence that you completed above and tell a partner whether the adjective you used describes anyone in your family.

Modelo   *Tengo un primo presumido por parte de mi madre. / No hay nadie presumido en mi familia.*

3-35 ▶ Descripciones. Describe the following people as in the Modelo.

Modelo   Mi madre *tiene el pelo castaño y los ojos verdes. De carácter es paciente y cariñosa. No es mandona. / No tengo madre.*

1. Mi padre . . .
2. La madre de mi padre . . .
3. Mi hermano/a menor . . .
4. Mi hermano/a mayor . . .
5. Mi tío/a favorito/a . . .
6. Mi mejor amigo/a . . . .

 3-36 ▶ Otra conversación. With a partner, reread *Una conversación* between Elena and Sonia. Then, change it to describe your own parents.

 3-37 ▶ Comparaciones culturales. Working in groups guess what men and women in Spain prefer in a partner, according to a survey of more than 1,300 Spaniards conducted by an online matchmaking service. Select one of the answers in italics. Afterwards, your instructor will give the correct results from this survey.

Para las españolas, el hombre ideal . . .
- es *rubio / moreno / pelirrojo*.
- tiene el pelo *largo / corto*.
- tiene los ojos *azules / marrones / verdes*.
- es *mayor / menor* que ellas.
- es *divertido / serio*.
- está *un poco musculoso / muy musculoso / delgado*.
- *comparte / no comparte* los gastos (*expenses*) al 50%.
- *trabaja para vivir / vive para trabajar*.

Para los hombres, la mujer ideal . . .
- es *rubia / morena / pelirroja*.
- tiene el pelo *largo / corto*.
- tiene los ojos *azules / marrones / verdes*.
- es *mayor / menor* que ellos.
- es *aventurera / reservada*.
- *sale con su pareja / prefiere pasar tiempo en casa*.
- *comparte / no comparte* el trabajo doméstico.
- es *económicamente independiente / no trabaja*.

Resumen de gramática

SAM: 3-41
to 3-44

Possessive Adjectives

- Possessive adjectives agree in number and gender with the object possessed, not the possessor.

- Use **el / la / los / las** + *noun* + **de** instead of *'s* to show possession in Spanish.

- Since **su(s)** can mean *your, his, her, its,* or *their,* it is often rephrased as shown here.

Possessive Adjectives

mi(s)	*my*	nuestro/a(s)	*our*
tu(s)	*your*	vuestro/a(s)	*you*
su(s)	*your, his, her, its*	su(s)	*your, their*

No es **su** casa. *It's not his house.*
Es **la** casa **de** su padre. *It's his father's house.*

su hijo
- el hijo de usted(es) *your son*
- el hijo de él *his son*
- el hijo de ella *her son*
- el hijo de ellos / ellas *their son*

¿Es el hijo **de él** o **de ella**? *Is he **his** or **her** son?*

Verbs ending in -*er* and -*ir*

- Regular **-er** and **-ir** verb endings differ only in the **nosotros/as** and **vosotros/as** forms.

-ER VERBS: aprender (a . . .) *to learn (to . . .),* **beber** *to drink,* **comer** *to eat,* **comprender** *to understand,* **correr** *to run,* **creer** *to believe,* **deber** *must, should,* **leer** *to read,* **vender** *to sell*

-IR VERBS: abrir *to open,* **asistir (a)** *to attend,* **compartir** *to share,* **escribir** *to write,* **recibir** *to receive,* **vivir** *to live*

- Use the preposition **a** before nouns following **asistir** and before infinitives following **aprender.**

- **Deber** can indicate obligation or supposition. When it indicates supposition, **deber** may be followed by **de** before the infinitive.

	leer *(to read)*	**escribir** *(to write)*
yo	leo	escribo
tú	lees	escribes
Ud., él, ella	lee	escribe
nosotros/as	leemos	escribimos
vosotros/as	leéis	escribís
Uds., ellos/as	leen	escriben

Asisto **a** muchos conciertos. *I attend a lot of concerts.*

Aprendo **a** tocar la guitarra. *I'm learning to play the guitar.*

Debemos hacer algo. *We must do something.*

Debe de estar enfermo. *He must be sick.*

The personal *a*

- Insert the preposition **a** before human direct objects, but not before things. Do not use it after **tener** to say you have friends or family members.

No comprendo **a** mi hermano. *I don't understand my brother.*

The verbs *hacer, poner, traer, salir, ver,* and *oír*

■ The verbs **hacer, poner, traer, salir,** and **ver** are like regular -er and -ir verbs in the present indicative, except for the **yo** forms. **Oír** is irregular in other forms as well.

■ Idiomatic expressions with **hacer** include: **hacer una pregunta** *to ask a question,* **hacer un viaje** *to take a trip,* and **hacer una fiesta** *to have a party.*

	hacer *(to do / to make)*	poner *(to put / to set)*	traer *(to bring)*
yo	hago	pongo	traigo
tú	haces	pones	traes
Ud., él, ella	hace	pone	trae
nosotros/as	hacemos	ponemos	traemos
vosotros/as	hacéis	ponéis	traéis
Uds., ellos/as	hacen	ponen	traen

	salir *(to go out / to leave)*	ver *(to see)*	oír *(to hear)*
yo	salgo	veo	oigo
tú	sales	ves	oyes
Ud., él, ella	sale	ve	oye
nosotros/as	salimos	vemos	oímos
vosotros/as	salís	veis	oís
Uds., ellos/as	salen	ven	oyen

El hombre que vive al lado está furioso si oye la música cuando hago una fiesta y pongo el estéreo a todo volumen.

The man who lives next door is furious if he hears the music when I have a party and I put on the stereo full blast.

The verbs *tener* and *venir*

■ The verbs **tener** and **venir** have similar forms.

■ Use **tener que** with an infinitive to say that someone *has to do* something and **tener ganas de . . .** for *to be in the mood for / to . . . , to feel like . . . .*

■ **Tener** is also used in these expressions: **tener hambre / sed / frío / calor / miedo (de) / suerte / sueño / prisa / razón / . . . años** *to be hungry / thirsty / cold / hot / afraid (of) / lucky / sleepy / in a hurry / right / . . . years old.*

	tener *(to have)*	venir *(to come)*
yo	tengo	vengo
tú	tienes	vienes
Ud., él, ella	tiene	viene
nosotros/as	tenemos	venimos
vosotros/as	tenéis	venís
Uds., ellos/as	tienen	vienen

¿Tienes hambre?

Are you hungry?

¿Tienes ganas de venir conmigo a comer o tienes que trabajar?

Do you feel like coming with me to eat or do you have to work?

Prepositional pronouns

■ The pronouns used after prepositions are the same as the subject pronouns, except **mí** and **ti** are used instead of **yo** and **tú**.

■ With the preposition **con**, use **conmigo** to say *with me* and **contigo** to say *with you* (sing., fam.).

■ After the prepositions **entre, menos** (*minus, except*), and **excepto** (*except*), use **yo** and **tú** instead of **mí** and **ti**.

sin **mí**	*without me*
cerca de **ti**	*near you*
delante de **usted**	*in front of you*
detrás de **él**	*behind him*
al lado de **ella**	*next to her*
con **nosotros/as**	*with us*
para **vosotros/as**	*for you*
entre **ustedes**	*between you*
lejos de **ellos/as**	*far from them*

SAM: 3-45 to 3-49

EN EL CENTRO DE SERVICIOS FAMILIARES

In this chapter, you learned how to describe your family and talk about your activities. Now, you will practice what you have learned in a real life simulation of working in a center providing family services to Spanish-speakers.

3-38 ► Mi familia. With a partner, imagine that the mother in this photo is describing her family. Prepare a conversation in which she says who each family member is and gives his/her age.

Modelo
E1: *¿Cómo se llama usted?*
E2: *Me llamo Isabel García Ochoa.*
E1: *¿Cuántos son ustedes en la familia?*
E2: *Somos cinco y los padres de mi esposo también viven con nosotros . . .*

Follow-up for 3-38.
Have students write a report describing the woman and her family in the third person. *Modelo: Se llama Isabel García Ochoa. Son cinco en su familia y los padres de su esposo también viven con ellos.*

3-39 ► ¿Cómo son? Another woman with whom you are talking is describing her family members' personalities. Complete the following sentences with the appropriate possessive adjectives in the shaded blanks, and the logical adjectives from the parentheses in the other blanks.

Modelo
No tengo un esposo muy *sociable. Mi* esposo es muy tímido y *reservado.* (reservado, sociable)

1. Mi esposo tiene una madre muy simpática y ____cariñosa____. ____Su____ madre no es ____mandona____. (cariñosa, mandona)
2. Mi esposo tiene hermanos egoístas y ____tercos____. ____Sus____ hermanos no son ____flexibles____. (flexibles, tercos)
3. Mi esposo y yo tenemos hijos relajados y ____tranquilos____. ____Nuestros____ hijos no son ____temperamentales____. (tranquilos, temperamentales)
4. Tengo un esposo serio y ____trabajador____. ____Mi____ esposo no es ____perezoso____. (trabajador, perezoso)
5. Tenemos una familia simpática y ____amistosa____. ____Nuestra____ familia no es ____presumida____. (presumida, amistosa)

90

3-40 ▸ En la foto. Isabel Ochoa is explaining who each person is in the photo on the previous page. Prepare sentences using prepositional pronouns to explain where each person is with respect to her and other family members.

Modelo   *Mi esposo está detrás de mí y sus padres están . . .*

3-41 ▸ Una familia perfecta. If a mother wants to give the impression that she has a perfect family life, would she say that the following people always (**siempre**), sometimes (**a veces**), or never (**nunca**) do each of the following things?

Modelo   Nuestros hijos . . . (asistir a la escuela, tener problemas en la escuela)
          Nuestros hijos siempre asisten a la escuela. Nunca tienen problemas en la escuela.

1. Yo . . . (hacer algo bueno de comer, recibir regalos de mi esposo, comprender a mi familia, creer en un futuro mejor para nosotros)
2. Mi esposo . . . (salir con sus amigos sin mí, tener ganas de estar conmigo, venir a casa después del trabajo, beber demasiado, comprender mis problemas, tener paciencia con nuestros hijos, hacer una fiesta para mi cumpleaños)
3. Mi esposo y yo . . . (comer con nuestros hijos, salir a bailar, hacer un viaje juntos, tener muchos problemas, compartir nuestros sentimientos, creer en la importancia de la comunicación, tener miedo de hablar)
4. Nuestros hijos . . . (traer a sus amigos a casa, hacer su tarea, aprender mucho en la escuela, tener sueño en clase, leer mucho, ver la tele todo el día, salir con sus amigos hasta tarde, deber estar en casa antes de las diez de la noche)

¡Hola!   **Entre profesionales**

If you work or volunteer for community organizations that provide services to Hispanic families, it is important to know how to ask about their needs and explain the services you can provide. Visit MySpanishLab for *Hoy día* to find more useful vocabulary, information, and activities such as the following one.

¿En qué puedo servirle? Here are some of the Spanish names for common types of assistance social organizations provide. Can you guess what they mean? For each statement that follows, offer the appropriate type of assistance from the list.

asistencia de empleo / cuidado de niños / ayuda alimentaria / protección contra la violencia doméstica / vivienda

Modelo   No sé qué voy a hacer. No tengo trabajo.
          ¿Necesita asistencia de empleo?

1. Tengo miedo de mi esposo cuando bebe demasiado.
2. Mi esposo está sin trabajo hasta la semana que viene y no tiene dinero para comprar comida para la familia esta semana.
3. Mis hijos y yo no tenemos donde vivir. Ahora estamos en un refugio para inmigrantes.
4. Necesito trabajar, pero tengo un hijo de tres años.

Follow up for 3-39.
Ask students: if a father believes that his son is an angel, but his daughter is very problematic, is he talking about him or her? MODELO: Nunca hay problemas con sus amigos. > Nunca hay problemas con los amigos de él. 1. Sus amigos hacen mucho para ayudar a la comunidad. 2. Sus amigos son raros y egoístas. 3. Su cuarto es un desastre. 4. En su cuarto, todo está siempre en su lugar. 5. Su música favorita tiene mucho lenguaje vulgar. 6. Me gusta su música. 7. No comprendo su actitud. 8. A veces leo sus correos electrónicos para ver con quién habla.

Follow up for 3-41.
Have students work in pairs to prepare advice for someone who wishes to improve his / her family situation. Students should mention something they must or have to do and something they should not do. 1. Usted . . . 2. Sus hijos . . . 3. Su esposo/a . . . 4. Su familia . . . MODELO: Usted . . . > Usted debe pasar más tiempo con sus hijos y tiene que compartir todo con ellos. No debe ser egoísta. No debe salir con sus amigos todo el tiempo.

Answers for *Entre profesionales.*
1. ¿Necesita protección contra la violencia doméstica? 2. ¿Necesita ayuda alimentaria? 3. ¿Necesita vivienda? 4. ¿Necesita cuidado de niños?

Publicidad en español

SAM: 3-50
to 3-52

Antes de leer

You are going to read about advertising to Hispanics. Think about the following questions before you approach the reading: *¿Qué productos o servicios crees que son más populares y venden más entre* (among) *las familias hispanas? ¿Reflejan estas preferencias valores* (values) *y tradiciones hispanas?*

> ▶ **Reading Strategy** *Skimming.* Skimming is a reading technique used for obtaining the main ideas in a text. When you skim you do not read every word; instead, you glance over the reading to seek clues that provide background information, and help you get the "gist." Look at the title, slogan, subtitle, and paragraph headings, and try to identify the main topic.

Ahora tú

3-42 ▶ **Una lista.** Look at the ads and identify the products and services offered in each. Then, make a list of the most important words and explain how they relate to the images.

Aló, ¿familia?
Cerca de ti, cerca de los tuyos

Ahora *Aló* trae a tu casa el servicio móvil *Cerca de ti.* ¿Lo oyes? Con *Cerca de ti* puedes tener hasta cinco líneas sin costo adicional y hablar los fines de semana gratis con tus familiares y amigos. Nadie te ofrece nada igual. *Aló*, diez años de servicio a las familias hispanas con tarifas competitivas.

¡En telefonía, no tenemos rival!

Secura . . . y viaja tranquilo
Porque tu familia tiene que viajar *Secura*.

Secura te trae un nuevo concepto de vehículo familiar. Robusto, seguro y cómodo. Con capacidad para ocho personas, es la alternativa ideal para las salidas de fin de semana. En viajes largos o excursiones de día, *Secura* viene a por ti.

¡Para salir en familia, *Secura*!

Casadenés, comidas con tradición
Es lo auténtico, es Casadenés.

Casadenés pone en tu mesa productos de calidad, seleccionados especialmente para satisfacer la dieta de toda tu familia. Alimentos[1] naturales perfectos para el desayuno[2], la comida y la cena de pequeños y mayores. Protege la salud[3] de tu familia, protege tus tradiciones.

¡Comer en familia es compartir Casadenés!

[1]*food* [2]*breakfast* [3]*health*

Después de leer

3-43 ► Comprensión. Answer the following questions related to the advertisements.

1. ¿Qué es *Cerca de Ti*? ¿Qué te permite (*does it allow you*) hacer?
2. ¿Crees que el anuncio de *Aló* conecta bien con las familias hispanas? ¿Por qué?
3. ¿Cómo son los productos *Casadenés*? ¿Por qué son los productos *Casadenés* atractivos para las familias hispanas?
4. ¿Por qué es *Secura* un buen automóvil para la familia?
5. ¿Qué miembros de la familia crees que están interesados en los productos y servicios que ofrecen (*offer*) los anuncios?
6. ¿Crees que estos anuncios funcionan (*these ads work*) para el público no-hispano?

3-44 ► Palabras relacionadas. Skim the ads for words related to those in the diagrams below and write them around the corresponding circle. Then, complete the diagrams with other related words or expressions you have learned in this chapter.

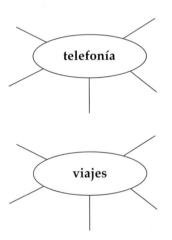

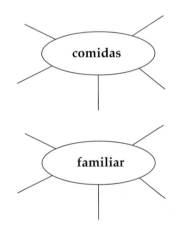

 3-45 ► Un buen automóvil. Paco is talking with his brother-in-law, Daniel, about his new automobile. Complete their conversation with the appropriate words from the list and read it with a partner.

familia	ganas	nietos	traer	suerte
fin de semana	hacer	padres	salir	ver

PACO: ¿Qué vas a (1) ___hacer___ este fin de semana?
DANIEL: Susana y yo vamos a (2) ___ver___ una película con los niños. ¿Y ustedes?
PACO: Vamos a (3) ___salir___ de excursión en mi nueva Secura.
DANIEL: ¿Vienen tus (4) ___padres___ a pasar el fin de semana con ustedes?
PACO: Sí, vienen a ver a sus (5) ___nietos___ y el sábado planeamos ir a la playa.
DANIEL: Tienes (6) ___suerte___ de tener un vehículo tan (*so*) bueno.
PACO: Sí, es un vehículo práctico y cómodo para toda la (7) ___familia___.
DANIEL: Susana y yo también tenemos (8) ___ganas___ de un auto nuevo. ¿Tienen planes para el domingo?
PACO: Sí, generalmente los domingos a los niños les gusta (9) ___traer___ a sus amigos a casa y así pasan la tarde.
DANIEL: Eso es bueno. Buen (10) ___fin de semana___.
PACO: Igualmente.

Answers for 3-43.
1. *Cerca de Ti es un servicio de telefonía móvil. Te permite tener hasta cinco líneas sin costo adicional y hablar los fines de semana gratis con tus los familiares y amigos.* 2. *Sí, porque hace énfasis en la comunicación con los familiares y amigos.* 3. *Los productos Casadenés son productos de calidad y naturales. Porque los productos Casadenés están seleccionados especialmente para satisfacer la dieta de toda la familia, pequeños y mayores.* 4. *Secura es un buen automóvil para la familia porque es robusto, seguro y cómodo, y tiene capacidad para ocho personas.* 5. & 6. *Answers will vary.*

Possible answers for 3-44.
telefonía: teléfono, llamar por teléfono, hablar por teléfono, tarifas, líneas, servicio móvil, aló; *comidas:* comer, alimentos, desayuno, comida, cena, dieta; *viajes:* viajar, hacer un viaje, excursiones, las salidas de fin de semana, vehículo; *familiar:* familia, madre, padre, hijos, hijas, abuelos, compartir, los tuyos.

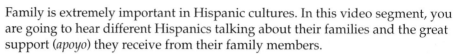

📖 Crecer en una familia hispana

SAM: 3-53 to 3-55

Antes de ver

Family is extremely important in Hispanic cultures. In this video segment, you are going to hear different Hispanics talking about their families and the great support (*apoyo*) they receive from their family members.

3-46 ► Reflexiones. Think about a typical Hispanic family and reflect on the following questions: *¿Cómo es? ¿Qué actividades crees que hacen sus miembros los fines de semana? ¿Qué rutina crees que tienen durante la semana? ¿Son las actividades similares a las que haces tú con tu familia?*

> **► Listening Strategy** *Listening for specific information.* As you listen, direct your attention to specific information you expect the speaker to mention rather than trying to understand every single word. For example, when people are talking about their family, you might listen for where they are from, how many there are in their family, or what their family is like. Try to listen for specific words that will target this information.

🎬 Ahora tú

3-47 ► Somos una familia . . . Listen attentively to Itandehui, Analissa and Edgar talk about their families. Answer the following questions about each one.

- ¿Cuál es su origen?
- ¿Cuántos son en su familia?
- ¿Cómo describe a su familia?

Después de ver

3-48 ► Una familia unida. Watch the video segment once again and answer the following questions about Rafael Escansiani and his family.

1. ¿Cuántos miembros hay en la familia Escansiani?
2. ¿Quién es el padre? ¿Y la madre?
3. Describan físicamente a los miembros de la familia Escansiani.
4. ¿Cuál crees que es la rutina diaria de los padres? ¿Y la de los hijos?
5. ¿Qué crees que hace la familia los fines de semana?

3-49 ► En sus ratos libres. Describe what you think the following people do in their free time.

1. Itandehui es estudiante de literatura y medios de comunicación. En sus ratos libres . . .
2. Rosal va a empezar (*to begin*) en la universidad y quiere ser actriz. En sus ratos libres . . .
3. Alejandro trabaja en una bodega (*food store*). En sus ratos libres . . .
4. La pasión de Analissa es la música y toca el chelo. En sus ratos libres . . .

ESCRITORES EN ACCIÓN

📖 Retrato de familia

SAM: 3-56

Antes de escribir

Think about your family and try to visualize each one of its members as you prepare your answers to the following questions: *¿Cuáles son sus características más peculiares? Piensa en cómo pasa el día tu familia y en las actividades de fin de semana. ¿Tienes una familia grande? ¿Con qué frecuencia vienen tus familiares a tu casa? ¿Qué tradiciones comparten los miembros de tu familia?*

> ▶ **Writing strategy** *Visualizing your topic.* When writing, it often helps to visualize what you are describing. To write a description of your family, start by creating a family tree to visualize your family organization. Then, think about what your family members are like and what they like to do before beginning to write.

3-50 ▶ ¡Prepárate! List any words or ideas you associate with the following four categories.

- los miembros de tu familia: su aspecto físico y su carácter
- tu rutina de la semana y la rutina de tu familia
- tus fines de semana y los fines de semana de tu familia
- las tradiciones familiares

Ahora tú

3-51 ▶ Tu retrato de familia. Now, write four paragraphs about your family using the information you prepared for each of the preceding categories.

Después de escribir

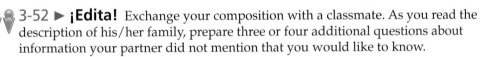

3-52 ▶ ¡Edita! Exchange your composition with a classmate. As you read the description of his/her family, prepare three or four additional questions about information your partner did not mention that you would like to know.

3-53 ▶ ¡Revisa! Revise your composition to include the answers to your partner's questions. Also make sure that your composition includes:

- ❏ appropriate vocabulary to talk about family members
- ❏ structures to express possession
- ❏ verbs to talk about daily activities
- ❏ vocabulary to talk about weekend activities

3-54 ▶ ¡Navega! Visit your online resource for *Hoy día* and use the links provided to read about famous Hispanics and their families. Compare the descriptions you find with your composition. Does it contain useful information you could include in describing your own family?

TEMA 1 TEMA 2

La familia

¿Cuántos son por parte de tu madre / padre?	How many are there on your mother's / father's side?
el/la abuelo/a (los abuelos)	grandfather / grandmother (grandparents)
el familiar	family member, relative
el/la hermano/a (los hermanos)	brother / sister (brothers and sisters)
el/la hijo/a (los hijos)	son / daughter (children)
la mascota / el perro / el gato	pet / dog / cat
el/la nieto/a (los nietos)	grandson / granddaughter (grandchildren)
el padre / la madre (los padres)	father / mother (parents)
el/la primo/a (los primos)	cousin (cousins)
el/la sobrino/a (los sobrinos)	nephew / niece (nephews and nieces)
el/la tío/a (los tíos)	uncle / aunt (aunts and uncles)

Descripciones

alto/a	tall, high
bajo/a	short (in height), low
casado/a	married
de estatura mediana	of medium height
delgado/a	thin
de mediana edad	middle-aged
divorciado/a	divorced
gordo/a	fat
joven	young
mayor	older, oldest
mejor	better, best
menor	younger, youngest
soltero/a	single

Otras palabras y expresiones

Se llama (Se llaman) . . .	His / Her name is (Their names are) . . .
tener	to have
tener . . . años	to be . . . years old
venir	to come
Vivo con . . .	I live with . . .

Adjetivos posesivos

mi(s)	my
tu(s)	your (sing., fam.)
nuestro/a(s)	our
vuestro/a(s)	your (pl., fam.)
su(s)	your (sing., form.; pl.), his, her, its, their

Medios de comunicación

un correo electrónico	e-mail
un ensayo	essay, paper
un libro de texto	textbook
un periódico	newspaper
una revista	magazine

Acciones

abrir	to open
aprender (a . . .)	to learn (to . . .)
asistir (a)	to attend
beber	to drink
compartir	to share
comprender	to understand
correr	to run
creer (en / que)	to believe (in / that)
deber	must, should
escribir	to write
leer	to read
recibir	to receive
vender	to sell

Otras palabras

el café	coffee
durante	during
ese / esa (esos / esas)	that (those)
el vino	wine

*For expressions with **tener**, see page 78.*

Lugares y eventos

el bar	*bar*
el evento deportivo	*sports event*

Expresiones verbales

hacer una fiesta	*to have a party*
hacer una pregunta	*to ask a question*
hacer un viaje	*to take a trip*
oír	*to hear*
poner	*to put, to place, to set*
poner la radio (el iPod, el CD, el DVD)	*to put on, to turn on the radio (the iPod, the CD, the DVD)*
salir	*to leave, to go out*
traer	*to bring*

Otras expresiones

un coche	*car*
contigo	*with you*
nada en especial	*nothing in particular, nothing special*

Visit MySpanishLab for *Hoy día* for links to the mnemonic dictionary online for suggestions such as the following to help you remember vocabulary from *Capítulo 3,* learn related words in Spanish, and use Spanish words to build your vocabulary in English.

EXAMPLES

beber, *to drink:* Beber is related to the English words *beverage* and *imbibe.* Related vocabulary in Spanish: una bebida, *a drink;* bebible, *drinkable;* un/a bebedor/a, *a (heavy) drinker;* un bebedero, *a drinking fountain* (in Mexico and Central America); *a drinking trough* (for animals).

comer, *to eat:* There is a little-used English word *comestible* (= *edible*) related to comer. Related vocabulary in Spanish: una comida, *a food, a meal;* un comedor, *a dining room;* comestible, *edible;* un/a comilón / comilona, *a big eater, a glutton;* un comedero, *a (bird / animal) feeder.*

El aspecto físico

Físicamente, es . . .	*Physically, he / she is . . .*
canoso/s	*gray-haired, white-haired*
guapo/a	*good-looking, handsome*
moreno/a	*dark-complexioned*
pelirrojo/a	*red-haired*
rubio/a	*blond-haired*
Tiene bigote / barba.	*He has a mustache / beard.*
Tiene gafas.	*He / She has glasses.*
Tiene el pelo . . .	*His / Her hair is . . .*
canoso	*gray*
castaño	*brown*
corto	*short*
largo	*long*
negro	*black*
rojo	*red*
rubio	*blond*
Tiene los ojos . . .	*His / Her eyes are . . .*
azules	*blue*
grises	*gray*
marrones (color café)	*brown*
verdes	*green*

El carácter

De carácter, es . . .	*Personality-wise, he / she is . . .*
amistoso/a	*friendly*
cariñoso/a	*loving, affectionate*
chistoso/a	*funny, likes to joke around*
comprensivo/a	*understanding*
conservador/a	*conservative*
egoísta	*selfish*
estricto/a	*strict*
flexible	*flexible*
frío/a	*cold*
generoso/a	*generous*
liberal	*liberal*
mandón / mandona	*bossy*
normal	*normal*
presumido/a	*stuck-up*
raro/a	*weird*
realista	*down-to-earth*
relajado/a	*easy-going*
reservado/a	*reserved*
serio/a	*serious*
sociable	*sociable*
temperamental	*moody*
terco/a	*stubborn*
tranquilo/a	*calm*

4 En casa

En este capítulo vas a aprender a hablar de la casa, el barrio (*neighborhood*) y las actividades diarias en casa.

El concepto de barrio es muy importante en las culturas hispánicas. El barrio tiene ese sentimiento de comunidad tan importante para los hispanos. Es el lugar donde las personas forman su identidad.

▶ ¿Hay un sentimiento de comunidad en tu barrio?

El hispano conserva la idea de barrio cuando emigra fuera de su país (*out of his/her country*). Los Ángeles, Nueva York, Chicago, Miami, Houston y Riverside-San Bernardino, en California, son áreas de población con más de un millón de residentes latinos.

▶ ¿Hay algún barrio hispano cerca de tu casa o universidad? ¿Cómo es?

▶ ¿Es diferente de otros barrios de la ciudad? ¿En qué es diferente?

Suggestion for chapter opener.
As students answer the questions in the culture note, you may wish to guide them with questions such as the following: 1. *Para ti, ¿es un barrio un grupo de casas, la gente que vive allí, un estilo de arquitectura, un sentimiento nostálgico o todas estas cosas? ¿Pasas mucho tiempo con tus vecinos (neighbors)? ¿Qué te gusta hacer con ellos? En el barrio donde viven tus padres, ¿hay mucho tráfico (muchas tiendas, muchos negocios [businesses] . . .) o sólo casas y apartamentos? Aquí en el barrio cerca de la universidad, ¿hay más gente (negocios, edificios grandes, eventos culturales, eventos deportivos . . .) que en el barrio de tus padres? 2. En los barrios hispanos, ¿ves casas de los mismos colores y estilos que en los otros barrios? ¿Ves mucho arte en la calle? En los parques, ¿ves más partidos de fútbol americano o de fútbol? ¿Hay más gente afuera (outside) que en otros barrios, hay menos gente afuera o es la atmósfera similar a otros barrios?*

Vocabulario   La casa y los muebles

SAM: 4-1 to 4-4

¿Prefieres vivir en el centro de **una ciudad** grande, en **las afueras** de una ciudad o en **el campo**? ¿Qué hay en tu casa?

CD 2 Track 1

¿Sabías que...?

En la mayoría de las ciudades hispanas, la gente vive en grandes edificios de apartamentos. En general, los apartamentos tienen dos o tres dormitorios, cocina, salón-comedor y uno o dos baños. Las familias están acostumbradas a convivir (*to live together*) en espacios relativamente pequeños, donde el contacto personal es más frecuente. Es común que los abuelos vivan con la familia.

¡Ojo!

In Mexico, people say **una recámara** for *a bedroom*, and in other regions, you might hear **una alcoba**. You can also use **un cuarto** or **una habitación** to say *a room*. In some regions, people say **un refrigerador** instead of **una nevera** and **rentar / la renta** instead of **alquilar / el alquiler.**

un árbol · un microondas · un comedor · un baño · una mesa · una estufa · una nevera · unas sillas · una cama · una cocina · un sofá · un dormitorio · una flor · un televisor · una sala · una piscina · una planta · un coche/un carro · un jardín

Suggestion. Point out to students that the word *televisor* refers to a television set, and that they should continue to use *televisión* to talk about viewing TV.

Suggestions for *Una conversación.*
• Have students listen to the conversation first with books closed for the answer to the following question: *¿Por qué quiere cada uno un nuevo apartamento? (Miguel quiere estar más cerca de la universidad. Diego quiere un apartamento más grande.)* Then, have them read along in their books as they listen a second time.
• Point out the new words presented in the conversation, which include the word *animales* and all glossed words.

Audioscript for ¡A escuchar!
— Aló.
— Buenas tardes, llamo por el anuncio del periódico. ¿Tiene Ud. un apartamento para alquilar?
— Sí, así es.
— ¿En qué calle está?
— En la calle Guadalupe, enfrente del parque Los Rosales.
— ¿Es grande?
— Tiene dos dormitorios pequeños, un baño, una cocina grande y la sala es grande también.
— Bueno, ¿y cuánto cuesta?
— Ochocientos noventa y cinco dólares al mes.
— Huy, ¿ochocientos noventa y cinco?
— Sí. ¿Desea ver el apartamento?
— No creo, gracias. Quiero pagar un poco menos y no necesito dos dormitorios.

 CD 2, Track 3

¡A escuchar!

Ahora, escuchen otra conversación en la cual un hombre llama por el anuncio (*ad*) de alquiler de un apartamento. ¿Dónde está el apartamento? ¿Cómo es? ¿Quiere ver el apartamento? ¿Por qué (no)?

CD 2 Track 2

Una conversación. Dos futuros compañeros de casa, Diego y Miguel, hablan.

DIEGO: ¿Dónde vives ahora, Miguel?

MIGUEL: Ahora vivo en una casa pequeña en las afueras. Mi **dirección** es calle Juárez, número 829. Me gustaría vivir en un apartamento más cerca del centro porque no me gusta trabajar en el jardín y quiero estar más cerca de la universidad. El problema es que los apartamentos en el centro son muy **caros.** Y tú, ¿dónde vives?

DIEGO: **Alquilo** un apartamento no muy lejos de aquí y no **pago** mucho de **alquiler.** Me gusta **el barrio.** Es muy **agradable** y tengo **vecinos** simpáticos, pero me gustaría tener un apartamento un poco más grande.

MIGUEL: ¿Tienes perro o gato?

DIEGO: No, no tengo animales. ¿Y tú?

MIGUEL: Tengo un perro, pero nunca está en la casa. Siempre está **afuera.**

DIEGO: ¿**Fumas**?

MIGUEL: No, ¿y tú?

DIEGO: **Yo tampoco.**

Possible answers for ¡A escuchar!
Está en la calle Guadalupe enfrente del parque Los Rosales. / Tiene dos dormitorios pequeños, un baño, una cocina grande y la sala es grande también. / No quiere ver el apartamento porque quiere pagar un poco menos y no necesita dos dormitorios.

una ciudad *a city*   **las afueras** *the outskirts*   **el campo** *the country*   **caro/a** *expensive*   **la dirección** *the address*   **alquilar** *to rent*   **pagar** *to pay*   **el alquiler** *the rent*   **el barrio** *the neighborhood*   **agradable** *pleasant, nice*   **un/a vecino/a** *a neighbor*   **afuera** *outside*   **fumar** *to smoke*   **Yo tampoco.** *Me neither.*

4-1 ▶ ¿Qué es? ¿Qué hay en estos lugares según (*according to*) la ilustración de la casa de la página anterior?

Modelo   entre la cocina y el baño
Hay un comedor entre la cocina y el baño.

1. detrás del dormitorio
2. al lado de la sala, en el jardín
3. debajo del árbol
4. entre la estufa y la nevera

5. a la izquierda del microondas
6. a la derecha del microondas
7. en el garaje, debajo del dormitorio
8. enfrente del televisor, en la sala

4-2 ▶ Entrevista. Entrevista a otro/a estudiante con estas preguntas.

1. ¿Prefieres vivir en un apartamento, una casa o un cuarto en una residencia? ¿Tienes apartamento, casa o cuarto en una residencia? ¿Está cerca de aquí? ¿En qué calle está? ¿Prefieres vivir en el centro de una ciudad grande, en las afueras o en el campo?

2. ¿Cómo es tu casa (apartamento, residencia)? ¿Es nuevo/a o viejo/a? ¿Caro/a? ¿Cuántos dormitorios hay? ¿Cuántos baños? ¿Hay piscina? ¿Qué te gusta de tu casa (apartamento, residencia)? ¿Qué no te gusta?

4-3 ▶ Otra conversación. En parejas, lean otra vez (*again*) *Una conversación* entre Diego y Miguel. Luego, usen la conversación como modelo para describir el lugar (*place*) donde viven y explicar por qué les gusta o no.

4-4 ▶ Comparaciones culturales. Lean con atención las descripciones sobre los distintos tipos de vivienda (*housing*) en los países hispanos y discutan las preguntas en grupo.

■ La arquitectura de las casas en los países hispanos es muy variada y refleja una mezcla (*mix*) de modernidad y tradicionalismo. En las ciudades es normal ver edificios altos y modernos, con muchos apartamentos, y también áreas residenciales nuevas, con viviendas unifamiliares (*single-family dwellings*) en las afueras de la ciudad. En el centro histórico de las ciudades todavía (*still*) hay casas antiguas (*old*) de arquitectura tradicional. En la ciudad donde vives, ¿hay una mezcla similar de modernidad y tradicionalismo en la arquitectura de las casas? ¿Te gustan más los edificios modernos o las casas antiguas? ¿Por qué?

■ Los colores de las casas reflejan el clima del lugar. En muchos países hispanos, los climas son tropicales y hay muchas casas de colores brillantes que repelen el calor (*heat*). En climas fríos, muchas casas están pintadas de colores oscuros (*dark*) para atraer (*to attract*) el calor. ¿Hay diferencias similares entre las casas en el norte y en el sur de Estados Unidos? ¿Reflejan las casas el clima del lugar donde están?

¡Ojo!

Starting in this chapter, instructions to activities in the textbook will be in Spanish. If you have questions about what you are to do, be sure to ask your instructor for clarification.

Suggestion.
With instructions to textbook activities now in Spanish, you may want to check for comprehension by asking for a volunteer to translate instructions to English, or you may do so yourself if needed. Instructions in the *Student Activities Manual* continue to be in English.

Recycle: Prepositions of place
Activity 4-1 recycles prepositions of place from *Capítulo 2, Tema 3.*

Answers for 4-1.
1. *Hay un baño detrás del dormitorio.* 2. *Hay una piscina al lado de la sala, en el jardín.* 3. *Hay flores debajo del árbol.* 4. *Hay un microondas entre la estufa y la nevera.* 5. *Hay una estufa a la izquierda del microondas.* 6. *Hay una nevera a la derecha del microondas.* 7. *Hay un coche / un carro en el garaje, debajo del dormitorio.* 8. *Hay un sofá enfrente del televisor, en la sala.*

Supplemental activities.
• Have students say which part of the house they associate with the following: *un sofá, una estufa, una cama, un coche / un carro, un árbol, un televisor, una nevera, una mesa, una piscina.*
• Have students say in which part of the house they generally do the following activities. *MODELO: bailar > Bailo en la sala. / Nunca bailo en casa.* (*ver la tele, hablar por teléfono, comer, usar la computadora, cocinar, hablar con tus padres, tomar el sol, pasar tiempo con los amigos, preparar la cena, descansar, hacer ejercicio, hacer tu tarea*)

Follow-ups for 4-2.
• Have students say whether they would like to have the following: *¿Te gustaría tener una casa o un apartamento más grande (más cerca / lejos del centro / de la universidad)? ¿Te gustaría tener un jardín muy grande con muchos árboles (con muchas flores)? ¿Te gustaría tener otro/a compañero/a de cuarto / casa (otros vecinos, perro, gato)? ¿Te gustaría más vivir solo/a y pagar más o tener compañero/a de casa y pagar menos? ¿Te gustaría más vivir en Nueva York o California (en México o en Canadá)? ¿Te gustaría más vivir en un apartamento en un edificio grande del centro o en una casa pequeña lejos de todo?*
• Ask the following questions. *¿Cómo es el/la compañero/a de cuarto ideal para ti? ¿Fuma o no fuma? ¿Le gustan los animales o no le gustan? ¿Es liberal o no es liberal? ¿Es más intelectual o más atlético/a? ¿Insiste en tener la casa limpia o no insiste en tener la casa limpia? ¿Le gustan las fiestas y estudia poco o no le gustan las fiestas y estudia mucho? ¿Pasa mucho tiempo contigo en casa o no pasa mucho tiempo contigo en casa?*

 Gramática 1

SAM: 4-5
to 4-9

Giving your address and other information: Numbers above 100

■ Here are the numbers from 100 to 999.

100 cien	500 quinientos/as
101 ciento uno (un/una)	600 seiscientos/as
102 ciento dos . . .	700 setecientos/as
200 doscientos/as	800 ochocientos/as
300 trescientos/as	900 novecientos/as
400 cuatrocientos/as	999 novecientos/as noventa y nueve

■ Use **cien** to say *one hundred* exactly, but use **ciento** in the numbers from 101 to 199. Do not use the word **un** before **cien** or **ciento**. Although **cien** and **ciento** do not have feminine forms in the numbers 100–199, **-cientos** changes to **-cientas** before feminine nouns in 200–999.

WITH MASCULINE NOUNS		WITH FEMININE NOUNS
100:	cien libros	cien páginas
101:	ciento un libros	ciento una páginas
200:	doscientos libros	doscientas páginas
720:	setecientos veinte libros	setecientas veinte páginas

■ In contrast to English, in Spanish a period is used to designate numbers in the thousands, and a comma is used for decimal points.

(Spanish) 1.543	mil quinientos cuarenta y tres	(English) 1,543
(Spanish) 3,25	tres coma veinticinco	(English) 3.25

■ The word for *thousand* is **mil**. **Mil** is not pluralized, nor is **un** used before it. Do not use the word **y** immediately after the words **mil** or **cien / ciento**.

1.000	mil
1.914	mil novecientos catorce
2.007	dos mil siete

■ Unlike in English, all years in Spanish are expressed using **mil,** not hundreds.

1492	mil cuatrocientos noventa y dos
2010	dos mil diez

■ When counting in the millions, say **un millón, dos millones, tres millones. . . .** Use **de** before nouns that directly follow the word **millón / millones**. If another number is between the word **millón / millones** and the noun, **de** is not used.

un millón de dólares	*one million dollars*
un millón doscientos mil dólares	*one million, two hundred thousand dollars*

4-5 ▶ El alquiler. ¿Cuánto pagas de alquiler al mes? ¿Pagas más de la cantidad indicada o menos?

Modelo $1.100
         Pago más de mil cien dólares al mes. / Pago menos de mil cien dólares al mes.

1. $150	**3.** $275	**5.** $515	**7.** $750	**9.** $1.000	**11.** $1.545
2. $199	**4.** $440	**6.** $685	**8.** $995	**10.** $1.250	**12.** $2.100

4-6 ▶ Un poco de historia. ¿En qué año ocurren estos eventos históricos? Si no estás seguro/a (*sure*), adivina (*guess*) y tu profesor/a te dirá si ocurrió (*will tell you if it happened*) **antes** o **después** hasta que selecciones el año correcto.

1492   1519   1821   1836   1846   1898   1917   1959

1. México declara su independencia de España.
2. El presidente cubano Fulgencio Batista es derrocado (*toppled*) por Fidel Castro.
3. Los puertorriqueños obtienen la nacionalidad estadounidense.
4. Cristóbal Colón llega a América por primera vez.
5. El emperador azteca, Moctezuma, se somete (*submits*) al conquistador español Hernán Cortés.
6. Texas se independiza de México.
7. Estados Unidos declara la guerra (*war*) a España.
8. Estados Unidos declara la guerra a México.

4-7 ▶ Tus preferencias. Cambia (*Change*) las siguientes oraciones para describir tu situación o tus preferencias.

1. Soy de *San Antonio*. La población es de aproximadamente *1.150.000* habitantes.
2. Prefiero vivir en una ciudad *pequeña*, de *no más de 25.000* habitantes.
3. Mi dirección es *calle Mérida, número 257*.
4. Para estudiar en esta universidad los estudiantes pagan más o menos *$3.500* al semestre.
5. Hay más de *15.000* estudiantes en esta universidad.
6. Generalmente, pago entre *$350 y $450* cada semestre por mis libros.
7. Hay muchos estudiantes en mi clase de *historia*. Hay *unos 150*.

4-8 ▶ Anuncios clasificados. Contesta las siguientes preguntas sobre estos apartamentos que se alquilan en Puerto Rico.

¿Cuántos dormitorios hay?   ¿Cuál es el número de teléfono?
¿Cuántos baños hay?   ¿Cuánto es el alquiler al mes?

1. Bonito apartamento en el segundo piso. Tres dormitorios, dos baños en excelentes condiciones. El complejo tiene piscina y cancha de tenis. $900 al mes. Teléfono: (787) 640-5823

2. Apartamento agradable y muy céntrico. 1 dormitorio/1 baño. A 5 minutos del centro. $575 al mes. Incluye agua y luz. Teléfono: (939) 644-3499

3. Precioso apartamento, 3 cuartos, 1 baño, cocina, sala, comedor, balcón. Situado en Carolina, cerca de Plaza Carolina. Acceso controlado. Precio mensual: $650. Para más información: (787) 531-7004

4. Apartamento amueblado, 2 dormitorios, 2 baños, terraza. Cerca de la piscina, cancha de tenis y playa. En excelentes condiciones. $1.200 al mes. Teléfono: (787) 864-7667

📖 Gramática 2   Negating: Indefinite and negative words

SAM: 4-10
to 4-13

Para **averiguar**

1. What are the opposites of **algo**, **alguien**, **alguno**, **también**, **y / o**, and **siempre**?
2. When a negative expression follows the verb, what must precede the verb? Is that word needed if another negative word precedes the verb?
3. What happens to **alguno** and **ninguno** before singular, masculine nouns? Do you generally use forms of **ninguno/a** in the plural?

Suggestion.
Remind students that they have already seen all of these affirmative and negative words except *alguno*.

■ Here is a list of the most common indefinite and negative words in Spanish.

Indefinite		Negative	
algo	*something*	nada	*nothing, (not) anything*
alguien, todos	*someone, everyone*	nadie	*nobody, (not) anyone*
alguno/a(s)	*some, any*	ninguno/a	*none, not any*
también	*also, too*	tampoco	*neither, not . . . either*
y, o	*and, or*	ni . . . ni . . .	*neither . . . nor . . .*
siempre, a veces	*always, sometimes*	nunca	*never*

— ¿Hablas con **alguien**?
— **No** hablo con **nadie**. Es la tele.

— *Are you talking to someone?*
— *I'm not talking with anyone. It's the TV.*

— ¿Ves **algo** interesante?

— *Are you watching something interesting?*

— No, **no** veo **nada** en especial.

— *No, I'm not watching anything in particular.*

■ Unlike English, Spanish has double negatives. When a negative expression is placed after the verb, **no** is inserted before the verb.

No salgo **nunca**.   *I never go out.*
No hago **nada**.   *I don't do anything.*

■ If any negative expression precedes the verb, **no** is not used.

Nunca salgo.   *I never go out.*
Nunca hago **nada**.   *I never do anything.*

■ **Alguno** and **ninguno** must agree in number and gender with the nouns they describe. They become **algún** and **ningún** before masculine singular nouns. **Ninguno/a** is generally used in the singular, even as a response to the plural forms **algunos/as**.

¿Hay **algunos** apartamentos disponibles?   *Are there any apartments available?*
No, no hay **ningún** apartamento disponible. *No, there is not any apartment available.*

■ Use **algún** or **ningún** directly before a singular masculine noun as in the preceding example, but use the form **alguno** or **ninguno** to replace the noun or when separated from it.

No hay **ninguno** disponible.   *There is not any available.*
Ninguno de los apartamentos está   *None of the apartments is available.*
   disponible.

Supplemental activities.
• Have students say whether they generally do the following activities with someone or don't do them with anyone. *MODELO: salir los sábados > Sí, generalmente salgo con alguien los sábados. / No, no generalmente no salgo con nadie los sábados. (estudiar, hacer la tarea de español, venir a la universidad, comer al mediodía, hacer ejercicio)*
• Have students say how often they do the following things using *algo* or *nada. MODELO: comer algo en clase. > A veces, como algo en clase. / Nunca como nada en clase. (tomar algo en clase, tomar algo con los amigos después de clase, aprender algo interesante en tus clases, hacer algo aburrido en tus clases, preparar algo de comer para tu compañero/a de cuarto, comprar algo especial para tus padres)*

Answers for 4-9.
1. No estoy con nadie. 2. No, no tengo hambre. No, no quiero comer nada. No, no tengo sed tampoco. 3. No, no va a tocar ningún grupo. 4. No prefiero ni el reggaetón ni el hip-hop. 5. No, no quiero escuchar ninguna música en especial.

Note for 4-9.
You may want to point out to students that the musical style known as *reggaetón* can also be spelled *reggetón* or *reguetón*. The authors of *Hoy día* have selected *reggaetón* as the spelling in this textbook.

4-9 ▶ En una fiesta. Alguien tiene ganas de hablar contigo en una fiesta pero tú no estás interesado/a. Primero, completa sus preguntas con una palabra lógica de la lista. Luego contesta cada pregunta con la expresión negativa que corresponda.

y	alguna	algún	alguien	o	algo	también

Modelo   ¿Te gusta bailar *y* cantar?
         No, no me gusta ni bailar ni cantar.

1. ¿Estás solo/a o estás con ___alguien___?
2. ¿Tienes hambre? ¿Quieres comer _____algo_____? ¿Tienes sed ___también___?
3. ¿Va a tocar ___algún___ grupo?
4. ¿Prefieres el reggaetón _____o_____ el hip-hop?
5. ¿Quieres escuchar ___alguna___ música en especial?

4-10 ▶ Una fiesta. ¿Son las descripciones de esta fiesta ciertas o falsas?
Corrige (*Correct*) las oraciones falsas.

Answers for 4-10.
1. *Cierto.* 2. *Cierto.* 3. *Falso. Nadie contesta el teléfono.* 4. *Cierto.* 5. *Falso. El hombre en el sofá no habla con nadie.* 6. *Cierto.* 7. *Falso. Hay un perro o un gato en la cocina.* 8. *Falso. No hay ningún niño en la fiesta.* 9. *Falso. Hay algo de comer y de beber en la fiesta.*

Follow up for 4-10.
Tell students that a husband is complaining about his mother-in-law's parties and his wife defends her mother saying the contrary. Have them give the wife's statements. MODELO: *Nadie quiere ir a sus fiestas.* > *Todos queremos ir a sus fiestas.*
1. *Nunca hay nadie interesante en las fiestas. (Siempre hay alguien interesante en las fiestas.)*
2. *Nunca hay nada bueno de comer ni de beber tampoco. (Siempre hay algo bueno de comer y de beber también.)* 3. *Nadie habla ni baila tampoco. (Todos hablan / hablamos y bailan / bailamos también.)* 4. *Siempre hay algunos problemas. (Nunca hay ningún problema.)*
5. *Alguien siempre bebe demasiado (too much). (Nadie nunca bebe demasiado.).*

Modelo   Hay alguna persona en el patio.
          Falso. No hay ninguna persona en el patio.

1. Algunos amigos salen al patio.
2. Alguien llama por teléfono.
3. Alguien contesta el teléfono.
4. Nadie oye el teléfono.
5. El hombre en el sofá habla con alguien.
6. Hay regalos para alguien.
7. No hay ni un perro ni un gato en la casa.
8. Hay algunos niños en la fiesta.
9. No hay nada de comer ni de beber en la fiesta.

4-11 ▶ ¿Es cierto? ¿Son ciertas o falsas estas oraciones para ti? Para las
oraciones ciertas, da (*give*) información más específica. Contradice (*Contradict*)
las oraciones falsas.

Modelo   Comparto cuarto con alguien.
          Cierto. Comparto cuarto con mi esposo/a. | Falso. No comparto cuarto
          con nadie.

1. Vivo con alguien.
2. Voy a salir con alguien esta noche.
3. Casi siempre hago algo con algún estudiante de la clase de español los fines de
semana.
4. Voy a estudiar con alguien de la clase de español hoy después de clase y
mañana también.
5. A veces hablo español con algún amigo o con algún familiar.
6. Generalmente, alguien hace algo especial para mi cumpleaños.

Supplemental activities.
• Have students briefly look around the room. Then, have them close their eyes and ask them questions such as the following: *¿Hay algún libro en mi escritorio / en la mesa de* (name a student)? *¿Hay alguna pregunta en la pizarra? ¿Hay algún estudiante detrás (delante) de ti? ¿Hay algún estudiante ausente* (absent) *hoy? ¿Hay algún estudiante sin libro?*
• Ask students the following questions or put them on a transparency for students to interview one another. 1. *¿Tienes planes para este fin de semana o no vas a hacer nada en especial? ¿Tienes ganas de ver alguna película? ¿Quieres comer en algún restaurante en especial? ¿Quieres ir a alguna tienda? ¿Necesitas comprar algo en particular?*
2. *¿Tienes algo que hacer el domingo o no tienes que hacer nada en especial? ¿Viene alguien a tu casa el domingo? ¿Vas a preparar algo especial de comer?*

 4-12 ▶ En nuestra clase. En grupos, usen las expresiones indefinidas y
negativas para describir a su clase. ¿Qué grupo puede (*can*) formar más oraciones?

Modelo   *Algunos estudiantes no están en clase a veces, pero casi todos estamos en*
          clase hoy.
          Casi todos los días alguien llega tarde.
          Todos trabajamos en grupo con frecuencia.

📖 Vocabulario   Los muebles y los colores

SAM: 4-14
to 4-17

🔊 ¿Qué **muebles** hay en tu cuarto? ¿Está **limpio** o **sucio** tu cuarto? ¿Está **ordenado** o
CD 2 **desordenado?** ¿Está **lleno** de cosas?
Track 4

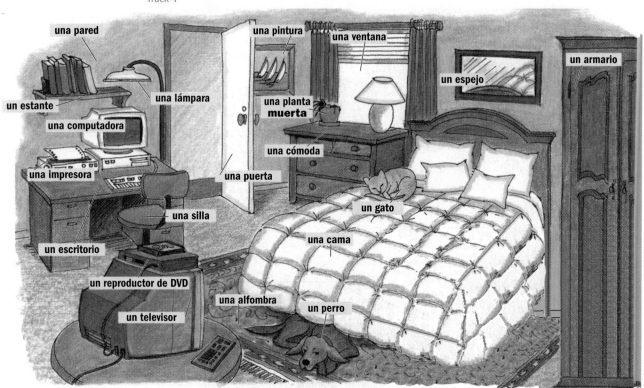

una pared · un estante · una lámpara · una computadora · un estante · una impresora · una silla · un escritorio · un reproductor de DVD · un televisor · una puerta · una pintura · una ventana · una planta muerta · una cómoda · un gato · una cama · una alfombra · un perro · un espejo · un armario

¿Sabías que...?

En países como México, el alquiler de
los apartamentos en las grandes
ciudades es caro en relación al nivel de
ingresos (*income level*) de las personas.
Por eso, es muy común para los
estudiantes alquilar un cuarto y no un
apartamento completo. En la mayoría
de los casos los cuartos se alquilan
amueblados (*furnished*), y las personas
que alquilan un cuarto tienen un baño
individual y una cocina común. Es una
buena solución para las personas que
buscan o necesitan independizarse sin
gastar mucho dinero.

¿De qué color es tu cuarto / tu sala?

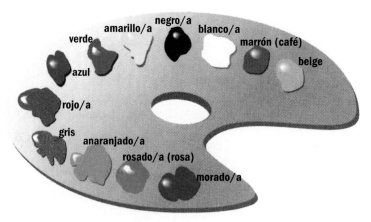

verde · amarillo/a · negro/a · blanco/a · marrón (café) · beige · azul · rojo/a · gris · anaranjado/a · rosado/a (rosa) · morado/a

---

los muebles furniture **limpio/a** clean **sucio/a** dirty **ordenado/a** neat, tidy **desordenado/a** messy
lleno/a full **muerto/a** dead

CD 2
Track 5

Una conversación. Dos amigos, Paco y Juan, hablan del compañero de casa de uno de ellos.

PACO: ¿Vives con alguien o vives solo?

JUAN: Vivo con mi compañero de casa, Mario.

PACO: ¿Te gusta vivir con él?

JUAN: Sí y no. Es simpático, pero a veces no tiene **dinero** para pagar el alquiler y es una persona un poco desordenada. Su cuarto siempre está sucio. **Deja** su ropa en **el suelo** y hay papeles y libros **por todos lados.**

PACO: ¿Limpias la casa más que él?

JUAN: Sí, mi cuarto siempre está limpio y ordenado.

PACO: ¿Comparten ustedes baño o tienes tu **propio** baño?

JUAN: **Desafortunadamente**, tenemos que usar el mismo baño.

4-13 ▶ Los colores. ¿De qué color(es) son las siguientes cosas?

Modelo la casa del presidente de Estados Unidos
Es blanca.

1. las paredes de tu cuarto
2. las paredes de tu sala
3. la alfombra de tu sala
4. tu cama
5. tu sofá
6. tu coche
7. las plantas
8. las plantas muertas
9. tu ropa hoy

4-14 ▶ ¿De quién? ¿Son estas pertenencias (*belongings*) de Juan, de Mario o de los dos?

el cuarto de Juan

el cuarto de Mario

Modelo Su alfombra es azul.
La alfombra de Juan es azul.

1. Su cuarto está ordenado.
2. Sus paredes son blancas.
3. Su escritorio está desordenado.
4. Su ropa está en el suelo.
5. Sus gatos están en su cuarto.
6. No hay pinturas en sus paredes.
7. Todos sus libros están en el estante.
8. Hay una lámpara al lado de su cama.
9. No hay nada encima de su cama.
10. La puerta de su armario está abierta.

 4-15 ▶ Otra conversación. En parejas, lean otra vez *Una conversación* entre Juan y Paco. Luego, cambien la conversación para hablar de la situación de uno/a de ustedes.

---

el dinero *money* **dejar** *to leave* **el suelo** *the ground, the floor* **por todos lados** *everywhere* **propio/a**
own **desafortunadamente** *unfortunately*

Suggestions for *Una conversación*.
• Have students listen to the conversation first with books closed for the answer to the following questions. Then, have them read along in their books as they listen a second time. 1. *¿Cómo es el compañero de casa de Juan? (Es simpático pero desordenado.)* 2. *¿Quién limpia más la casa, él o su compañero? (él)*
• Point out the new words presented in the conversation, which include only the glossed words.

CD 2, Track 6

¡A escuchar!

Ahora, escuchen otra conversación en la cual una estudiante habla de su casa y de sus compañeras. ¿Cuánto paga al mes y cómo son sus compañeras de casa? ¿Hay problemas con ellas?

Audioscript for *¡A escuchar!*
MARÍA: *Verónica, cuéntame, ¿dónde vives? Vives en una casa, ¿verdad? ¿Pagas mucho?*
VERÓNICA: *Sí, vivo en una casa que cuesta $1.725 al mes, pero comparto la casa con dos amigas. Sólo pago $575.*
MARÍA: *¿Te gusta tener dos compañeras de casa? Yo prefiero vivir sola.*
VERÓNICA: *Está bien. Son muy simpáticas y divertidas. Pasamos mucho tiempo juntas. Compartimos todo el trabajo en casa y la casa siempre está limpia.*
MARÍA: *¿Cuántos baños hay?*
VERÓNICA: *Ése es el único problema. Sólo hay un baño para las tres.*

Possible answers for *¡A escuchar!*
La casa cuesta $1.725 y ella paga $575. Sus compañeras son simpáticas y divertidas. / El único problema es que sólo hay un baño.

Answers for 4-14.
1. *El cuarto de Juan está ordenado.* 2. *Las paredes de los dos son blancas.* 3. *El escritorio de Mario está desordenado.* 4. *La ropa de Mario está en el suelo.* 5. *Los gatos de Mario están en su cuarto.*
6. *No hay pinturas en las paredes de Juan.*
7. *Todos los libros de Juan están en el estante.*
8. *Hay una lámpara al lado de la cama de Juan.*
9. *No hay nada encima de la cama de Juan.*
10. *La puerta del armario de Juan está abierta.*

📖 Gramática 1 — Describing: Using *ser* and *estar*

SAM: 4-18
to 4-21

Para averiguar

1. What are two uses of **estar**?
2. What are five uses of **ser**?
3. What types of adjectives do you use with **ser** to describe someone or something? What types of adjectives do you use with **estar**? What are some adjectives that can change meaning, depending on whether they are used with **ser** or **estar**?
4. In English, how would you translate **¿Cómo están tus padres?** How would you translate **¿Cómo son tus padres?**

Suggestions
Tell students to remember the two uses of *estar*, and by process of elimination use *ser* elsewhere.

Suggestions.
• You may wish to point out that *casado/a* and *divorciado/a* may be used with either *ser* or *estar*. However, when saying to whom someone is married or from whom someone is divorced, you must use *estar* (*estar casado con / estar divorciado de*).
• Have students describe the current condition / status of the following people or places using a word from the list of adjectives used with *estar*: *tu madre / tu padre, tus compañeros de clase, tú, tu cuarto, tu sala*. Then, have students think of an adjective that describes a non-changing characteristic of each of these people or places and describe them using *ser*.
• Have students describe how they feel generally when they are in the following places or with the following people. *MODELO: en la clase de matemáticas > Generalmente, estoy contento/a cuando estoy en la clase de matemáticas. (en la clase de español, en un examen muy difícil, solo/a en tu cuarto el sábado por la noche, en un restaurante con tus padres, en una fiesta con mucha gente desconocida, en un club nocturno lleno de gente, en un concierto de música hip-hop, en un concierto de música clásica, en un museo de arte abstracto, en un parque solo/a por la noche, en el trabajo todo el día)*

■ Although **ser** and **estar** both mean *to be*, the two verbs are not interchangeable.

Use **estar**:

1) to describe changeable conditions, physical states, or current status with adjectives.
   — **¿Está** limpio o sucio tu cuarto?
   — Mi cuarto casi siempre **está** desordenado.

2) to say where or with whom someone or something is.
   — ¿Dónde **está** tu compañero de casa?
   — **Está** en el patio con sus amigos.

Use **ser**:

1) to describe general traits or characteristics with adjectives.
   — ¿Cómo **es** la residencia donde vives?
   — **Es** agradable y mi compañero de cuarto **es** simpático.

2) to say where someone is from.
   — ¿De dónde **es** tu compañero de cuarto?
   — **Es** de Puerto Rico.

3) to identify people and things or describe them using a noun.
   — ¿Quién **es** ese muchacho?
   — **Es** mi vecino. **Es** un buen amigo.

4) to talk about time.
   — Mis clases **son** a las diez y a la una.

5) to say *It's (good / bad / important . . .)* when making generalizations.
   — **Es** importante pagar el alquiler a tiempo.

■ Here are the adjectives you have seen that are used with **estar**.

abierto/a *open*	**enfermo/a** *sick, ill*	**nervioso/a** *nervous*
aburrido/a *bored*	**enojado/a** *angry*	**ocupado/a** *busy*
cansado/a *tired*	**juntos/as** *together*	**ordenado/a** *neat, tidy*
casado/a *married*	**limpio/a** *clean*	**solo/a** *alone*
confundido/a *confused*	**listo/a** *ready*	**sorprendido/a** *surprised*
contento/a *glad, happy*	**lleno/a** *full*	**sucio/a** *dirty*
desordenado/a *messy*	**molesto/a** *upset, bothered*	**triste** *sad*
divorciado/a *divorced*	**muerto/a** *dead*	

■ Some adjectives can be used with either **ser** or **estar**, but have different meanings with each verb. Compare the uses of **ser** and **estar** below and in the sentences that follow.

estar aburrido/a	*to be bored*	**ser aburrido/a**	*to be boring*
estar listo/a	*to be ready*	**ser listo/a**	*to be smart, clever*

Tu novia **está** bonita.	*Your girlfriend is / looks pretty.*	(on a specific occasion)
Tu novia **es** bonita.	*Your girlfriend is pretty.*	(in general)

■ Also compare their use in the following questions.

¿Cómo **está** tu padre?	*How is your father doing?*
¿Cómo **es** tu padre?	*What is your father like?*

4-16 ▶ Mi casa. Un joven habla de su casa y su familia. ¿Se usa **ser** o **estar** en las siguientes oraciones?

Mi casa (1) ___está___ (es / está) en las afueras y (2) ___es___ (es / está) muy bonita. Tengo una familia grande y cuando todos (3) ___estamos___ (somos / estamos) juntos en la casa, hay nueve personas. Comparto cuarto con mi hermano mayor y nuestro dormitorio siempre (4) ___está___ (es / está) desordenado. Mi hermano (5) ___es___ (es / está) muy perezoso y su ropa siempre (6) ___está___ (es / está) en el suelo y sus cosas (7) ___están___ (son /están) por todos lados. (8) ___Es___ (Es / Está) difícil (9) ___estar___ (ser / estar) en el cuarto con mi hermano todo el tiempo porque nunca (10) ___está___ (es / está) contento. (11) ___Es___ (Es / Está) una persona muy temperamental y siempre (12) ___está___ (es / está) molesto por algo. Por eso, generalmente (13) ___estoy___ (soy / estoy) en la sala. Nuestra sala (14) ___es___ (es / está) muy grande y agradable y siempre (15) ___está___ (es / está) limpia. Mis padres (16) ___son___ (son / están) muy trabajadores y limpian la sala y la cocina todos los días. (17) ___Es___ (Es / Está) bueno tener padres como ellos.

4-17 ▶ Descripciones. El muchacho de la actividad anterior contesta preguntas acerca de (*about*) su hermano. Completa las siguientes preguntas con la forma correcta del verbo **ser** o **estar**. Luego, contesta las preguntas según (*according to*) la ilustración.

Modelo   ¿Quién *es*? ¿Tu hermano o tu hermana?
            Es mi hermano.

1. ¿Cómo ___es___? ¿Moreno o rubio? ¿Guapo o feo?
2. ¿___Es___ joven or viejo?
3. ¿Dónde ___está___? ¿En casa? ¿En clase? ¿En el trabajo?
4. ¿Con quién ___está___? ¿Con sus amigos? ¿Solo?
5. ¿Cómo ___está___? ¿Contento de estar solo? ¿Molesto? ¿Aburrido?
6. ¿___Está___ ocupado?
7. ¿___Está___ en la sala o en su cuarto?
8. ¿De qué color ___es___ el sillón (*armchair*)?

4-18 ▶ Entrevista. Completa las siguientes preguntas con la forma correcta del verbo **ser** o **estar**.

1. ¿___Estás___ (tú) muy cansado/a los fines de semana? ¿___Estás___ (tú) muy ocupado/a los fines de semana? ¿Dónde ___estás___ (tú) generalmente los sábados por la noche? ¿en casa? ¿con los amigos? ¿Cuál ___es___ tu día de la semana favorito?
2. ¿Quién ___es___ tu mejor amigo/a? ¿De dónde ___es___ (él/ella)? ¿___Es___ estudiante? ¿___Son___ ustedes muy parecidos/as (*alike*)? ¿___Están___ (Uds.) juntos/as con frecuencia? ¿Dónde ___está___ el apartamento / la casa de tu mejor amigo/a? Generalmente, ¿___está___ limpio/a o sucio/a su apartamento / casa?
3. ¿Cuál ___es___ tu restaurante favorito? ¿___Está___ cerca de aquí? ¿En qué calle ___está___? ¿___Es___ un restaurante mexicano? ¿Cuándo ___está___ abierto?

👣 **¿Y tú?** Entrevista a un/a compañero/a de clase con las preguntas anteriores.

Warm-ups for 4-16.
• Refer students to the drawing of Mario's room on page 107 and tell them: *Usa el verbo es o está con las siguientes palabras para describir el cuarto de Mario: bonito (Su cuarto no es bonito.); blanco (Su cuarto es blanco.); desordenado (Su cuarto está desordenado.); limpio (Su cuarto no está limpio.); lleno de libros (Su cuarto está lleno de libros.); un desastre (Su cuarto es un desastre.)* Then, ask students whether the same words describe their own room.
• Remind students that *estar* is used to say where things are located, and have them say where the following things are in Mario's room on page 107: *los gatos, los libros, la ropa, las pinturas, la silla, la computadora.*

Suggestion for 4-16.
• Have students explain why they use *ser* or *estar* in each case by picking use 1 or 2 of *estar* or use 1, 2, 3, 4, or 5 of *ser* from the preceding page.
• Have students write a similar paragraph about themselves.

Follow-ups for 4-16.
• Have students say whether the following words or phrases describe their house: *Mi casa (no) es / está . . . (grande, en el campo, en las afueras, limpia, cerca de la universidad, blanca, agradable, en la calle* [name a street near the university], *la casa más bonita de la calle)*
• Have students choose between *(no) soy* and *(no) estoy* to say whether these adjectives describe them: *cansado/a, trabajador/a, triste, tímido/a, intelectual, confundido/a, enojado/a, responsable, mexicano/a, enfermo/a, impulsivo/a.* Continue with the following nouns or phrases: *estudiante, en clase todos los días, de California, el / la novio/a de otro/a estudiante de la clase, cerca de la puerta.*

Recycle: Interrogative words
Activity 4-14 recycles interrogative words from *Capítulo 2, Tema 2.*

Possible answers for 4-17.
1. *Es moreno y guapo.* 2. *Es joven.* 3. *Está en casa.* 4. *Está solo.* 5. *Está molesto y aburrido.* 6. *No, no está ocupado.* 7. *Está en la sala.* 8. *Es rojo.*

Supplemental activity.
Ask students how they would translate the verb *to be* in the following sentences: 1. Today is Wednesday. *(Hoy es miércoles.)* 2. I'm very busy on Wednesdays. *(Estoy muy ocupado/a los miércoles.)* 3. I'm at the university in the morning. *(Estoy en la universidad por la mañana.)* 4. My biology class is at eleven o'clock. *(Mi clase de biología es a las once.)* 5. My work is very difficult. *(Mi trabajo es muy difícil.)* 6. Sometimes I'm bored at work. *(A veces estoy aburrido/a en el trabajo.)* 7. I'm very tired after work. *(Estoy muy cansado/a después del trabajo.)* 8. My apartment is very far from my work. *(Mi apartamento está muy lejos de mi trabajo.)* 9. It's not very big. *(No es muy grande.)* 10. It's almost never at home. *(Casi nunca estoy en casa.)*

📖 Gramática 2 Making comparisons: Comparatives

SAM: 4-22
to 4-26

Para averiguar

1. How can **más . . . que** and **menos . . . que** be translated in English?
2. What does **tan . . . como** mean? And **tanto . . . como**? When does **tanto** change forms?
3. What are four adjectives and two adverbs with irregular comparatives?

Suggestions.
• Point out in the sample sentences that the word order of these comparative expressions is generally similar to that in English.
• Remind students that they saw the irregular comparatives *mayor* and *menor* in *Capítulo 3* when talking about their family.
• Point out to students that the agreement of *tanto* is parallel to the agreement of *mucho* and *poco* when it is used as an adjective or an adverb.

■ Use the following expressions to compare people or things.

más . . . que	*more . . . than, -er . . . than*
menos . . . que	*less . . . than, fewer . . . than*
tan . . . como	*as . . . as*
tanto/a/os/as . . . como	*as much . . . as, as many . . . as*

Tu baño es **más** grande **que** mi cocina.
Your bathroom is bigger than my kitchen.

Paso **menos** tiempo en casa **que** tú.
I spend less time at home than you.

Mi apartamento es **tan** grande **como** tu casa.
My apartment is as big as your house.

Limpio **tanto como** tú.
I clean as much as you.

■ The following adjectives and adverbs have irregular comparatives and do not use **más**.

bueno/a	*good*	}	**mejor**	*better*
bien	*well*			
malo/a	*bad*	}	**peor**	*worse*
mal	*badly*			
joven	*young*		**menor**	*younger*
viejo/a	*old*		**mayor**	*older*

Mi hermana **mayor** cocina **mejor** que yo.
My older sister cooks better than I do.

■ **Tanto** (*as much, as many*) can be an adjective or an adverb. As an adjective, it must agree in number and gender with the noun that follows. As an adverb, it always ends with **-o**.

ADJECTIVE: Tengo **tantas** ventanas en mi cuarto **como** tú.
I have as many windows in my room as you.

ADVERB: Cocino **tanto como** tú.
I cook as much as you do.

4-19 ▶ Comparaciones.

¿Estás de acuerdo (*Do you agree*) con las siguientes oraciones? Cambia cada oración si es necesario para expresar tu opinión.

Modelo Los coches rojos son tan bonitos como los coches azules.
Estoy de acuerdo. Los coches rojos son tan bonitos como los coches azules. /
No estoy de acuerdo. Los coches rojos son más (menos) bonitos que los coches azules.

Continuation for 4-19.
Have students say whether the following statements are true about their home. 1. *Mi cuarto es tan grande como la sala.* 2. *Paso tanto tiempo en casa los lunes como los domingos.* 3. *Vivo tan cerca de la universidad como mi mejor amigo/a.* 4. *Estudio tanto en la biblioteca como en mi casa.* 5. *Hay tantos muebles en mi cuarto como en la sala.* 6. *Por lo general, mi cuarto está tan ordenado como la sala.*

1. Generalmente, un sofá es tan caro como un coche.
2. Para mí, las paredes amarillas son tan bonitas como las paredes rosadas.
3. Los gatos son tan inteligentes como los perros.
4. Generalmente, los apartamentos son tan caros como las casas.
5. Un televisor es tan útil (*useful*) como una computadora.
6. El precio (*price*) de una casa nueva es tan importante como el barrio.
7. Las ciudades grandes son tan interesantes como el campo.
8. Generalmente, el centro de la ciudad es tan tranquilo como las afueras.

4-20 ► ¿En la ciudad o en el campo? ¿Prefieres vivir en el centro de una ciudad, en las afueras o en el campo? En grupos, preparen comparaciones de los tres ambientes (*environments*). Pueden (*You can*) usar las ideas de la lista o sus propias ideas.

actividades al aire libre	jardines grandes	restaurantes
actividades culturales	oportunidades de	tráfico
árboles	empleo (*employment*)	tranquilidad
casas	plantas	. . .
gente	problemas	

Modelo   *Hay menos tráfico en las afueras de una ciudad que en el centro, pero hay más tráfico que en el campo.*

4-21 ► Comparaciones culturales. El estilo de vida (*lifestyle*) urbano es bastante diferente entre las ciudades hispanas y las norteamericanas. Lee la siguiente información y contesta las preguntas, utilizando las estructuras para expresar comparación en español.

1. El metro (*subway*) de Madrid y de la ciudad de México son modelos de transporte público que millones de personas usan todos los días. En la ciudad de México no está permitido circular en coche todos los días para prevenir el aumento de la contaminación (*pollution*). ¿Crees que tanta gente tiene coche en México o España como en Estados Unidos? ¿Crees que la gente usa más el transporte público que en Estados Unidos?

2. La concentración mayor (*major*) de población en las ciudades hispanas está en los centros urbanos y no en las afueras. Y en Estados Unidos, ¿viven tantas personas en el centro de la ciudad como en las afueras?

3. La casa típica del centro de una ciudad hispana no tiene jardín ni piscina. Generalmente, ¿tienen jardín las casas en Estados Unidos? ¿Son las casas del centro tan grandes como las casas de las afueras en las ciudades norteamericanas?

4. En general, las ciudades tienen muchas zonas verdes, como parques y bosques (*wooded areas*). Son famosos el Parque del Retiro en Madrid y el Bosque de Chapultepec en México DF. La gente pasa mucho tiempo fuera de casa, al aire libre o de paseo (*strolling*) por las calles con la familia y los amigos. En Estados Unidos, ¿pasa la gente tanto tiempo fuera de casa como en los países hispanos?

El Parque del Retiro en Madrid, España.

📖 **Vocabulario**   Más actividades diarias

SAM: 4-27
to 4-28

🔊 ¿Qué quieres hacer mañana por la mañana?
CD 2
Track 7

¡Ojo!

Although the verb **almorzar** means *to eat lunch* in most Spanish-speaking areas, Mexican speakers often use it to refer to a late breakfast.

Suggestions for *Una conversación*.
• Have students listen to the conversation first with books closed for the answer to the following questions: 1. *¿Qué van a hacer juntos y cuándo?* (*Van a jugar al tenis el sábado a las siete.*) 2. *¿Qué necesita hacer uno de ellos el viernes por la noche?* (*Tiene que trabajar.*) Then, have them read along in their books as they listen a second time.
• Point out the new words presented in the conversation, which include only the glossed words.

Audioscript for *¡A escuchar!*
AURA: *¿Aló?*
SILVIA: *Aló, Aura, ¿cómo estás? Soy yo, Silvia.*
AURA: *Hola, Silvia. Estoy bien, gracias. Y tú, ¿qué tal?*
SILVIA: *Estoy muy bien. Oye, voy a almorzar con mi madre en el centro hoy. ¿Quieres venir con nosotras? Después vamos a ir de compras.*
AURA: *¿A qué hora? No puedo hasta la una de la tarde. Ahora estoy en la casa de mi hermana y necesito volver primero a mi apartamento.*
SILVIA: *No hay problema. Podemos comer a la una. ¿Te gusta el restaurante Jardín Mediterráneo?*
AURA: *Me gusta mucho. Entonces nos vemos a la una en el restaurante Jardín Mediterráneo.*
SILVIA: *Sí, perfecto. Hasta luego.*
AURA: *Ciao.*

🔊 CD 2, Track 9

¡A escuchar!

Ahora, escuchen otra conversación en la cual dos amigas hablan por teléfono de sus planes para esta tarde. ¿Qué van a hacer juntas? ¿A qué hora y dónde?

Possible answers for *¡A escuchar!*
Van a almorzar juntas a la una de la tarde en el restaurante Jardín Mediterráneo.

dormir hasta tarde

desayunar en casa / **empezar** el día con un buen desayuno

¿Qué prefieres hacer por la tarde?

almorzar en el parque

jugar a los videojuegos

¿Por la noche vas a . . . ?

cenar con unos amigos

volver temprano a casa después de cenar

Una conversación. Dos amigos hacen planes para este fin de semana.

🔊 CD 2 Track 8

ESTELA: Manuel, ¿quieres jugar al tenis conmigo este viernes por la noche?
MANUEL: **Lo siento, no puedo** este viernes. Tengo que trabajar.
ESTELA: ¿Puedes jugar el sábado?
MANUEL: No sé. **Vuelvo a** trabajar el sábado por la tarde. ¿A qué hora quieres jugar?
ESTELA: ¿A qué hora vas a volver del trabajo?
MANUEL: A las seis.
ESTELA: Entonces, ¿a las siete o las siete y media en el parque?
MANUEL: Puedo jugar a las siete.

---

desayunar *to eat / have breakfast*   **empezar** *to begin, to start*   **almorzar** *to eat / have lunch*   **cenar** *to eat / have dinner*   **volver** *to return*   **temprano** *early*   **Lo siento.** *I'm sorry.*   **no puedo** *I can't*   **vuelvo a** (+ infinitive) *I (verb) again*

4-22 ▶ Mañana. Cambia las palabras en letra cursiva para describir tus planes para mañana.

1. Mañana, voy a dormir hasta *las nueve.*
2. Voy a dormir *seis o siete horas.*
3. Voy a desayunar *en The Golden Omelet.*
4. Voy a almorzar *con mi novio.*
5. Por la tarde, voy a *ir al parque y voy a jugar al tenis.*
6. Voy a volver a casa *a las cinco y media.*
7. Voy a cenar *en casa a las siete y media.*
8. Después de cenar, voy a *jugar a los videojuegos.*

4-23 ▶ Excusas. Utiliza el primer grupo de expresiones para invitar a un/a compañero/a de clase a hacer algo contigo esta noche, mañana y el domingo por la tarde. Tu compañero/a debe dar excusas, utilizando el segundo grupo de expresiones.

Modelo   E1: *¿Quieres volver a la biblioteca esta noche para estudiar conmigo?*
            E2: *No puedo esta noche. Tengo que lavar la ropa.*
            E1: *¿Puedes practicar español conmigo mañana por la mañana?*
            E2: *Lo siento . . .*

Invitaciones

¿Quieres . . . conmigo?
¿Puedes . . . ?
¿Tienes ganas de . . . ?
¿Te gustaría . . . ?

cenar	**desayunar**	**volver a la**
jugar a los	**ir al cine**	**biblioteca**
videojuegos	**tomar algo**	**para estudiar**
almorzar	**practicar español**	**. . .**

Excusas

No puedo. Tengo que . . .
Lo siento. Necesito . . .
Lo siento. No tengo ganas, prefiero . . .

trabajar	**volver a casa**
ir a clase	**ir al supermercado**
dormir la siesta	**cenar con mi hermano**
estudiar	**descansar**
ir a la casa de . . .	**lavar (*to wash*) la ropa**
limpiar la casa	**. . .**

4-24 ▶ Entrevista. Entrevista a un/a compañero/a de clase con estas preguntas.

1. ¿Qué días puedes dormir hasta tarde? ¿Hasta qué hora prefieres dormir los sábados? ¿Cuántas horas necesitas dormir para no estar cansado/a al día siguiente? ¿Tienes sueño a veces en tus clases?

2. ¿Desayunas todos los días? ¿Desayunas en un restaurante con frecuencia? Generalmente, ¿desayunas con alguien o desayunas solo/a? ¿Cuál es el mejor restaurante para desayunar cerca de la universidad? ¿Desayunas en la cama a veces? ¿Tienes hambre por la mañana si no desayunas o no necesitas desayunar?

3. ¿A qué hora prefieres almorzar? Generalmente, ¿traes comida para almorzar en la universidad? ¿Puedes volver a tu casa para almorzar? ¿Te gusta almorzar a veces en el parque? ¿Te gusta almorzar a veces en el patio de tu casa?

4. ¿Cenas temprano o tarde generalmente? Generalmente en casa, ¿cenas en el comedor, en la cocina o enfrente de la tele? ¿En qué restaurante cenas con más frecuencia? ¿Prefieres desayunar, almorzar o cenar en un restaurante? ¿Dónde vas a cenar esta noche?

4-25 ▶ Otra conversación. En parejas, lean otra vez *Una conversación* entre Estela y Manuel. Luego, preparen una conversación en la cual ustedes hacen planes para cenar, almorzar o desayunar juntos/as.

Recycle activities.
• Remind students of the verb form *quiero* from *Capítulo 2, Tema 4* and have them say whether they want to do the following things. *¿Quieres . . . (desayunar en un restaurante este sábado, almorzar en el parque este sábado, volver a casa después de clase hoy, jugar a los videojuegos esta tarde)?*
• Remind students of the verb form *prefiero* from *Capítulo 2, Tema 2* and have them say which of the following they prefer. *¿Prefieres . . . (dormir hasta tarde o empezar el día temprano, almorzar en casa o almorzar en un restaurante, jugar a los videojuegos o ver la televisión, dormir la siesta (to take a nap) en el sofá o dormir la siesta en la cama, cenar antes de las siete o cenar más tarde, volver a casa hoy después de clase o ir a la biblioteca)?*

Warm-ups for 4-23.
• Practice turning down invitations by having students complete sentences such as the following: 1. *No puedo ir al cine hoy porque mis padres vienen a mi casa esta noche y está muy sucia. Tengo que . . .* 2. *No puedo ir al café ahora. Voy al gimnasio. Tengo que . . .* 3. *No puedo ir al parque ahora. Estoy muy cansado/a. Tengo que . . .*
• Have students use *(no) puedo* to say whether they can do the following things tomorrow. If they cannot, have them give a reason why using *tengo que . . .* or similar expressions. *Modelo: dormir hasta tarde > Sí, puedo dormir hasta tarde mañana. / No, no puedo dormir hasta tarde mañana porque tengo que ir a una clase a las ocho.* (dormir hasta las diez, almorzar en tu restaurante favorito, jugar a los videojuegos todo el día, cenar con tus padres, salir con tus amigos por la noche, volver a casa muy tarde)

Continuation for 4-24.
Ask students: 1. *¿A qué hora vas a volver a casa hoy? ¿Vas a volver a la universidad esta noche?* 2. *¿Te gusta jugar al fútbol (tenis, básquetbol)? ¿Prefieres jugar o ver un partido en la tele? ¿Te gusta jugar a los videojuegos? ¿Prefieres jugar a los videojuegos solo/a o con otra persona?*

 **Gramática 1** Talking about daily activities:
Stem-changing verbs

SAM: 4-29
to 4-31

■ Some verbs have vowel changes in the stem when they are conjugated in the
present tense. The last **e** of the stem becomes **ie** or **i**, and the last **o** of the stem
becomes **ue** in all of the forms except **nosotros** and **vosotros**.

empezar (e → ie) *(to begin)*	
yo empiezo	nosotros/as empezamos
tú empiezas	vosotros/as empezáis
Ud., él, ella empieza	Uds., ellos/as empiezan

poder (o → ue) *(to be able, can, may)*	
yo puedo	nosotros/as podemos
tú puedes	vosotros/as podéis
Ud., él, ella puede	Uds., ellos/as pueden

pedir (e → i) *(to ask for, to order)*	
yo pido	nosotros/as pedimos
tú pides	vosotros/as pedís
Ud., él, ella pide	Uds., ellos/as piden

Other verbs that follow these patterns are:

e → ie		**o (u) → ue**		**e → i**	
cerrar	*to close*	**almorzar**	*to eat lunch*	**decir**	*to say, to tell*
entender	*to understand*	**contar**	*to count, to tell*	**repetir**	*to repeat*
pensar (en)	*to think (about)*	**dormir**	*to sleep*	**servir**	*to serve*
perder	*to lose, to miss*	**encontrar**	*to find*		
preferir	*to prefer*	**jugar (u → ue)**	*to play*		
querer	*to want*	**recordar**	*to remember*		
		volver	*to return*		

■ **Decir** has an irregular form for **yo** (**yo digo** *I say*). Use **decir** for *to tell* when
telling a piece of information, but **contar** when recounting a story (**una
historia**) or telling a joke (**un chiste**). **Contar con** also means *to count on*.

Siempre **digo** la verdad.	*I always tell the truth.*
Mi padre siempre **cuenta** chistes.	*My father always tells jokes.*

■ Use **pensar** followed by an infinitive to say what you *intend* or *plan to do*.
Volver is used with infinitives to say one redoes something or does something
again. Use the preposition **a** before infinitives after **volver**, and also after
empezar when saying what someone is beginning to do.

Pienso estudiar francés también.	*I intend to study French too.*
Vuelvo a leer las preguntas.	*I reread the questions.*
Empiezo a entender.	*I'm beginning to understand.*

4-26 ▶ ¿Sí o no? Explica si en la clase de español las siguientes personas
hacen cada actividad entre paréntesis.

Modelo   Yo . . . (encontrar los exámenes de español difíciles)
          Yo (no) encuentro los exámenes de español difíciles.

1. Yo . . . (dormir en clase, entender bien, recordar todo el vocabulario, querer
   más tarea, pensar en español)
2. El/La profesor/a . . . (decir muchas cosas en español, preferir hablar español,
   repetir mucho, querer buenos estudiantes, recordar mi nombre)
3. Nosotros . . . (poder hacer preguntas en inglés, volver a clase mañana, querer
   exámenes más difíciles, repetir muchas palabras)

4-27 ► ¡Yo también! Dos amigos describen su rutina diaria (*daily*). ¿Haces lo mismo que ellos? Cambia la forma del verbo y las palabras en letra cursiva (si es necesario) para describir lo que tú haces.

Modelo   Dormimos hasta *las nueve todos los días.*
Yo también duermo hasta las nueve todos los días. |
Yo duermo hasta las seis y media o las siete todos los días.

1. Por lo general, almorzamos *en McDonalds.*
2. Jugamos al tenis *todos los días.*
3. Hoy volvemos a casa a *las tres de la tarde.*
4. Generalmente, empezamos nuestra tarea a *las cuatro y media de la tarde.*
5. Preferimos cenar a *las ocho o las nueve.*
6. Pedimos una pizza *dos o tres veces a la semana.*
7. Dormimos *nueve* horas todas las noches.
8. Repetimos la misma rutina *de lunes a viernes, pero podemos hacer otras cosas los fines de semana.*

4-28 ► En mi familia. Usa uno de los verbos de la página anterior con cada expresión para describir quiénes en tu familia hacen estas cosas.

Modelo   **a.** muy tarde
A veces todos volvemos muy tarde a casa.
b. primero
Mi padre vuelve primero a casa.
c. antes de las tres
Nadie de mi familia vuelve a casa antes de las tres.

1. a. hasta tarde
   b. poco
   c. más

2. a. en el trabajo
   b. en la universidad
   c. solo/a

3. a. bien
   b. todos los días
   c. a veces

 4-29 ► Entrevista. Entrevista a un/a compañero/a de clase con estas preguntas.

1. ¿Prefieres almorzar en casa, en un restaurante o en la cafetería? ¿A qué hora almuerzas? ¿Duermes la siesta a veces después de almorzar?
2. ¿Juegas al tenis? ¿al fútbol? ¿al básquetbol? ¿a los videojuegos? ¿Con quién juegas? ¿Quién pierde generalmente? ¿Pierdes la paciencia a veces cuando juegas?
3. ¿A qué hora vuelves hoy a casa? ¿Dónde piensas cenar esta noche? ¿Qué quieres hacer después de la cena? ¿Vuelves a la universidad mañana?

📖 Gramática 2 Describing how you do things: Adverbs

SAM: 4-32
to 4-34

Note for adverbs.
You may want to point out to students that when a string of adverbs with *-mente* are placed one after another, *-mente* is attached only to the last one. The others are the same as the feminine form of the corresponding adjective: *Duermo tranquila y fácilmente.*

Possible answers for 4-30.
1. Por lo general, duermo tranquilamente hasta las siete.; 2. Desayuno regularmente.; 3. Juego excesivamente a los videojuegos.; 4. Vuelvo considerablemente más tarde a casa los fines de semana.; 5. Limpio completamente la casa al menos una vez a la semana.; 6. Pienso constantemente en mis problemas.; 7. Entiendo perfectamente todos los problemas de mi mejor amigo/a.; 8. Pierdo fácilmente la paciencia con la gente.

Follow-up for 4-30.
Point out to students that adverbs can often be replaced with prepositional phrases. Have them say which adverb from the activity could be replaced with the following phrases: *con frecuencia, con tranquilidad, a la perfección, en exceso, con regularidad, por completo.*

■ Adverbs are used to say *how, where, when,* or *how much* someone does something. Just as adverbs can be formed from adjectives in English by adding the ending *-ly* (*perfect > perfectly, easy > easily*), adverbs are formed from adjectives in Spanish by adding the ending **-mente** to the end of the feminine form of the adjective. If an adjective has a written accent mark, it will be maintained on the adverb.

lógico/a → lógica**mente**
independiente → independiente**mente**
fácil → fácil**mente**

■ As a general rule, adverbs are placed just after a verb they modify.

Limpio **constantemente** la casa.	*I clean the house constantly.*
Vuelvo **tarde** a casa los sábados.	*I return home late on Saturdays.*

■ Adverbs may also modify adjectives or other adverbs. In that case, adverbs are placed before the adjective or other adverb that they modify.

Tienes una casa **perfectamente** situada.	*You have a perfectly situated house.*
Juego **muy** mal al tenis.	*I play tennis very badly.*

4-30 ▶ En casa. Completa cada oración con el adverbio formado del adjetivo entre paréntesis e indica si la oración te describe a ti (*describes you*).

Modelo   Duermo hasta tarde los sábados. (frecuente)
Sí, duermo frecuentemente hasta tarde los sábados. |
No, no duermo frecuentemente hasta tarde los sábados.

1. Por lo general, duermo hasta las siete. (tranquilo/a)
2. Desayuno. (regular)
3. Juego a los videojuegos. (excesivo/a)
4. Vuelvo más tarde a casa los fines de semana. (considerable)
5. Limpio la casa al menos una vez a la semana. (completo/a)
6. Pienso en mis problemas. (constante)
7. Entiendo todos los problemas de mi mejor amigo/a. (perfecto/a)
8. Pierdo la paciencia con la gente. (fácil)

Generalmente, ¿desayunas en casa o en un café?

4-31 ▶ Un/a buen/a compañero/a de cuarto. Completa las siguientes oraciones lógicamente con los adverbios entre paréntesis para describir un/a buen/a compañero/a de cuarto.

Modelo   Escucha cuando hablo de problemas entre nosotros/as. No contesta sin escuchar. (rápidamente, pacientemente)
Escucha pacientemente cuando hablo de problemas entre nosotros/as. No contesta rápidamente sin escuchar.

1. Siempre reacciona (*reacts*) cuando hay problemas. Nunca reacciona sin pensar en lo que hace. (tranquilamente, emocionalmente)
2. Comparte el trabajo de la casa. No deja sus cosas por todos lados. (perezosamente, voluntariamente)
3. Siempre cumple (*keeps, carries out*) con su palabra. Nunca promete (*promises*) cosas que no va a cumplir. (falsamente, completamente)
4. Respeta la privacidad. No habla de mis problemas personales con todo el mundo (*everyone*). (consideradamente, públicamente)
5. No bebe en casa. Sólo bebe de vez en cuando. (socialmente, excesivamente)

4-32 ▶ Comparaciones culturales. Lee con atención el siguiente texto sobre la situación de muchos jóvenes en España y Latinoamérica.

En España y otros países de Latinoamérica, es realmente difícil encontrar un trabajo con un buen salario después de la universidad, y los padres hispanos entienden que deben mantener[1] a sus hijos. Por eso, los jóvenes viven en casa generalmente hasta los veinticinco o treinta años.

La dinámica familiar también es menos tradicional que en el pasado. Los padres son más permisivos, y los hijos respetan las normas familiares consideradamente. Así, padres e hijos conviven[2] armoniosamente en la casa de los padres.

A muchos jóvenes les gustaría independizarse[3] de sus padres después de terminar la universidad, pero viven en la casa de sus padres para ahorrar[4] un poco de dinero, y para poder después casarse[5] y comprar una casa.

[1]*support* [2]*live together* [3]*to become independent* [4]*to save* [5]*to get married*

Ahora, compara esta información con la situación de la gente joven donde vives. Utiliza **más . . . que, menos . . . que** o **tan . . . como** con el adverbio formado del adjetivo entre paréntesis.

Modelo   Los jóvenes viven. (independiente)
En muchos países hispanos los jóvenes viven menos independientemente que aquí. | Aquí los jóvenes viven más independientemente que en muchos países hispanos.

1. Los jóvenes encuentran trabajo. (fácil)
2. Los jóvenes se independizan de sus padres. (rápido)
3. Los jóvenes viven con sus padres. (tranquilo)
4. Los jóvenes ahorran dinero antes de independizarse. (paciente)
5. Los padres mantienen (*support*) a sus hijos. (voluntario)
6. Los padres aceptan la privacidad de sus hijos. (comprensivo)

📖 Vocabulario El barrio y los vecinos

SAM: 4-35
to 4-38

🔊 CD 2 Track 10 ¿Prefieres vivir en el centro **animado** de una ciudad donde hay más actividades culturales, pero también hay más gente, tráfico y **ruido?** ¿Te gusta . . .?

¿Sabías que...?

Hay una tendencia cada vez más popular en los países hispanos a vivir en las afueras. En muchas ciudades proliferan complejos residenciales muy similares a las zonas suburbanas de Estados Unidos. Muchas personas prefieren vivir allí porque es más seguro para la familia y las casas también son más grandes y más modernas que los apartamentos del centro. Muchos de estos complejos residenciales tienen seguridad (*security*) privada, y todos los servicios básicos: escuelas, supermercados, centros comerciales.

estacionar el coche en un estacionamiento

sacar la basura a la calle

lavar la ropa en una lavandería

usar el transporte público / tomar el autobús al trabajo

esperar en la parada de autobús

¿Prefieres vivir en una casa en las afueras con más espacio para las actividades al aire libre, pero también con más **quehaceres domésticos**? ¿Te gusta . . .?

arreglar cosas que no **funcionan**

cortar el césped

trabajar en el jardín

pagar **el recibo de la luz** (del agua, del gas)

ir a la escuela en bicicleta

🔊 CD 2, Track 12

¡A escuchar!

Ahora, escuchen otra conversación en la cual Daniel encuentra a un amigo, Rafael, que vive en su edificio de apartamentos. ¿Qué aspectos le gustan a Rafael? ¿Cuáles no? ¿En qué apartamento vive cada uno? ¿Cuánto cuesta el alquiler?

🔊 CD 2 Track 11

Una conversación. Sara habla de su nuevo barrio con Isabel.

ISABEL: ¿Te gusta tu nueva casa? ¿Cómo es el barrio?
SARA: Me gusta mucho. La calle donde vivo es muy tranquila y el barrio es **seguro** y agradable, pero está lejos de la oficina y la luz y el agua **cuestan** casi trescientos dólares al mes.
ISABEL: Y tus vecinos, ¿cómo son?
SARA: El vecino que vive al lado es muy **hablador** y **chismoso**. Siempre está afuera en el patio y es un poco **ruidoso**. En la casa de enfrente vive una familia **bastante callada**. Los dos niños siempre juegan y **andan** por la calle **en bicicleta**.

---

animado/a *lively* **el ruido** *noise* **los quehaceres domésticos** *chores* **arreglar** *to fix, to straighten out* (a problem), *to straighten up* (a room) **funcionar** *to work* (describing a machine, system, plan) **el recibo de la luz** *the light bill, the electric bill* **seguro/a** *safe* **costar (o > ue)** *to cost* **hablador/a** *talkative, chatty* **chismoso/a** *gossipy* **ruidoso/a** *noisy* **bastante** *rather, quite* **callado/a** *quiet* **andar en bicicleta** *to ride a bicycle*

4-33 ▶ Vecinos. Indica si los siguientes adjetivos describen más a los vecinos de Carlos o a los de David.

Modelo   amistosos
Los vecinos de Carlos son más amistosos que los vecinos de David.

1. sociables
2. callados
3. habladores
4. tranquilos
5. ruidosos
6. animados
7. aburridos
8. divertidos

Answers for 4-33.
Los vecinos de Carlos son más sociables, habladores, ruidosos, animados y divertidos. Los vecinos de David son más callados, tranquilos y aburridos.

4-34 ▶ ¿En el centro o en las afueras? Cambia las siguientes comparaciones para expresar tu opinión de la vida (*life*) en una ciudad y en las afueras.

Modelo   Hay tanto tráfico en las afueras como en el centro.
Hay menos tráfico en las afueras que en el centro.

1. Cuesta tanto comprar una casa en las afueras como en el centro.
2. Hay tantos edificios de apartamentos en las afueras como en el centro.
3. Hay tanto espacio para estacionar los coches en las afueras como en el centro.
4. El alquiler es tan alto en las afueras como en el centro.
5. Es tan seguro jugar afuera o andar en bicicleta en las afueras como en el centro.
6. Los vecinos son tan chismosos en las afueras como en el centro.

 4-35 ▶ Otra conversación. En parejas, vuelvan a leer *Una conversación* entre Isabel y Sara. Luego, cambien la conversación para hablar de su barrio.

 4-36 ▶ Comparaciones culturales. Lee la siguiente información sobre las escuelas en los países hispanos y discute las preguntas con un/a compañero/a.

La educación pública en los países hispanos

En España y Latinoamérica la educación primaria o educación general básica (5–14 años) es obligatoria y gratuita¹ y la calidad de la educación pública es muy buena. La mayoría de los niños que asisten a escuelas públicas reciben una preparación académica excelente. Las escuelas privadas son generalmente católicas y los estudiantes toman la asignatura² de religión además de³ las otras asignaturas.

Generalmente, cada barrio tiene su propia escuela o colegio público donde los niños completan su educación primaria. Sin embargo, la pobreza⁴ que afecta a muchos barrios urbanos o zonas rurales de América Latina hace a muchos niños abandonar la escuela antes de completar su educación primaria. Es el caso de Bolivia, la República Dominicana, El Salvador, Guatemala, Nicaragua y Venezuela donde entre el 40 y el 80 por ciento de los estudiantes dejan de asistir⁵ a la escuela antes de completar la educación primaria. Todos los miembros de la familia, incluyendo los niños, tienen que trabajar para sobrevivir⁶.

¹*mandatory and free* ²*subject* ³*besides* ⁴*poverty* ⁵*stop attending* ⁶*to survive*

1. En Estados Unidos, ¿creen que la calidad de la educación pública es mejor o peor que la de la educación privada? ¿Son diferentes las escuelas públicas de las afueras y las de las zonas urbanas?
2. En la educación primaria, ¿creen que el abandono escolar (*school drop-out*) es tan alto en algunos barrios de Estados Unidos como en Bolivia o Guatemala?

Recycle: Comparatives
Activities 4-33 and 4-34 recycle comparatives from *Tema 2*.

Follow-up for 4-34.
Have students work in groups to prepare lists of advantages (*ventajas*) and disadvantages (*desventajas*) of living in an apartment in the center of town vs. in a house in the outskirts. See which group can make the most complete list.

Supplemental activity.
Preguntas personales. 1. ¿Prefieres vivir en un edificio de apartamentos en el centro o en una casa en las afueras? ¿Alquilas una casa o un apartamento? 2. ¿Hay buen transporte público donde vives? ¿Hay mucho tráfico en tu calle? ¿Hay mucho espacio para estacionar tu coche? 3. ¿Lavas la ropa en tu casa o en una lavandería pública? ¿Hay lavandería en tu edificio de apartamentos? 4. ¿Con qué frecuencia sacas la basura? 5. ¿Tienes que cortar el césped donde vives? ¿Te gusta trabajar en el jardín? 6. ¿Tienes que pagar la luz? ¿el agua? ¿el gas?

Resumen de gramática

SAM: 4-39
to 4-44

Numbers above 100

- Use **cien** for 100 exactly, but **ciento** in 101–199.

- Numbers 200 through 999 agree in gender with the nouns they modify, but **cien / ciento** does not in 100 through 199.

- **Mil** does not change in the plural forms.

- Use **un** in **un millón** (*one million*), but not with **cien / ciento** (*one hundred*) or **mil** (*one thousand*).

- Use **de** before nouns directly after **millón / millones**.

- Do not use **y** (*and*) immediately after the words **cien / ciento, mil,** or **millón**.

- Years are expressed using **mil**, not hundreds.

- Use a period to designate thousands, and a comma for decimals.

MASCULINE NOUNS	FEMININE NOUNS
100: cien libros	cien páginas
101: ciento un libros	ciento un páginas
200: doscientos libros	doscientas páginas
710: setecientos diez libros	setecientas diez páginas
3.100 tres mil cien	*three thousand one hundred*
1.000 mil	*one thousand*
un millón de dólares	*one million dollars*
un millón doscientos mil dólares	*one million two hundred thousand dollars*
1999 mil novecientos noventa y nueve	*nineteen ninety-nine*
2011 dos mil once	*twenty eleven*
1.500 mil quinientos	*one thousand five hundred*
3,25 tres coma veinticinco	*three point twenty-five*

Indefinite and negative words

- Spanish uses multiple negatives. When the negative expressions **nada, nadie, nunca, ninguno/a, ni,** and **tampoco** are placed after the verb, **no** is inserted before it, unless another negative expression already precedes the verb.

- **Alguno/a** and **ninguno/a** become **algún** and **ningún** directly before masculine singular nouns. **Ninguno/a** is generally used in the singular.

—¿Necesitas **algo** para tu nuevo apartamento?
—No, **no** necesito **nada**.
—¿Tienes **algunos** vecinos antipáticos?
—No, **no** tengo **ningún** vecino así. / No, **no** tengo **ninguno** así. / No, **ninguno** de mis vecinos es antipático.

Do you need anything for your new apartment?
No, I don't need anything.
Do you have any unpleasant neighbors?
No, I don't have any neighbors like that. / No, I don't have any like that. / No, none of my neighbors is unpleasant.

Using ser and estar

Use **estar** to say *to be* when talking about:

1) conditions or current status with adjectives.

2) where or with whom.

Use **ser** to say *to be* when talking about:

1) traits or characteristics with adjectives.

2) where someone / something is from.

3) who or what someone or something is.

4) when.

5) generalized judgements (*It's . . .*).

1) **Estoy** contento/a con mi casa nueva.

2) ¿En qué calle **está**?

1) Mi casa **es** muy agradable.

2) Mis vecinos **son** de Perú.

3) **Son** maestros bilingües.

4) **Es** tarde cuando vuelven.

5) **Es** malo trabajar tanto.

I am happy with my new house.

On what street is it?

My house is very pleasant.

My neighbors are from Peru.

They are bilingual teachers.

It's late when they return.

It's bad to work so much.

Comparatives

- Use the following expressions to make comparisons. As an adjective, **tanto** agrees with nouns for gender and number. As an adverb, it always ends with **-o**.

más . . . que	*more / -er . . . than*
menos . . . que	*less / fewer . . . than*
tan . . . como	*as . . . as*
tanto/a/os/as . . . como	*as much / many . . . as*

- The following comparisons are irregular.

mejor *better*		**menor** *younger*	
peor *worse*		**mayor** *older*	

Hay **tantas** bicicletas **como** coches en la calle.
There are as many bicycles as cars in the street.

Mi vecina no está afuera **tanto como** yo.
My neighbor is not outside as much as me.

Vivo **más** cerca **que** tú.
I live closer than you.

Mi apartamento es **menos** caro **que** tu casa.
My apartment is less expensive than your house.

El baño es casi **tan** grande **como** la cocina.
The bathroom is almost as big as the kitchen.

No pago **tanto como** tú.
I don't pay as much as you.

Uno de mis vecinos es **mayor** que yo y el otro es **menor**.
One of my neighbors is older than me and the other one is younger.

Stem-changing verbs

- In the following stem-changing verbs, the last vowel of the stem changes in all forms except **nosotros** and **vosotros**.

  - e > ie verbs: **cerrar** *to close;* **empezar (a)** *to begin (to);* **entender** *to understand;* **pensar (en)** *to think (about);* **perder** *to lose, to miss;* **preferir** *to prefer;* **querer** *to want*
  - o > ue verbs: **almorzar** *to eat lunch;* **contar (con)** *to count (on), to tell* (stories, jokes); **dormir** *to sleep;* **encontrar** *to find;* **jugar (u > ue)** *to play;* **poder** *can, may, to be able;* **recordar** *to remember;* **volver (a)** *to return (to), to . . . again*
  - e > i verbs: **decir (yo digo)** *to say, to tell* (information); **pedir** *to ask for, to order;* **repetir** *to repeat;* **servir** *to serve*

empezar (e → ie) *(to begin)*

yo	empiezo	nosotros/as	empezamos
tú	empiezas	vosotros/as	empezáis
Ud., él, ella	empieza	Uds., ellos/as	empiezan

poder (o → ue) *(to be able, can, may)*

yo	puedo	nosotros/as	podemos
tú	puedes	vosotros/as	podéis
Ud., él, ella	puede	Uds., ellos/as	pueden

pedir (e → i) *(to ask for, to order)*

yo	pido	nosotros/as	pedimos
tú	pides	vosotros/as	pedís
Ud., él, ella	pide	Uds., ellos/as	piden

Mi vecino no **dice** mucho, pero **empieza** a hablar más.
My neighbor doesn't say much, but he's starting to talk more.

Su esposa siempre **cuenta** chistes.
His wife always tells jokes.

Empezamos a pasar más tiempo juntos.
We are starting to spend more time together.

A veces ceno con él el viernes, y luego **vuelvo** a cenar con él el sábado.
Sometimes I have dinner with him on Friday, and then I have dinner with him again on Saturday.

Adverbs

- Add **-mente** (*-ly*) to the end of the feminine form of adjectives to turn them into adverbs, maintaining any accent marks from the adjectives.

discreto/a → discretamente
emocional → emocionalmente

discreet → discreetly
emotional → emotionally

- As a general rule, place adverbs just after verbs or before adjectives or other adverbs they modify.

Tengo una vecina chismosa que habla **constantemente**.
I have a gossipy neighbor who is constantly talking.

Está **completamente** loca.
She's completely crazy.

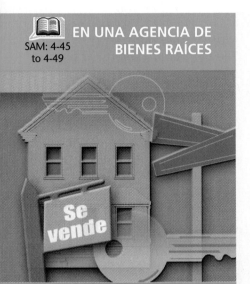

SAM: 4-45
to 4-49

EN UNA AGENCIA DE BIENES RAÍCES

En este capítulo, aprendiste (*you learned*) a hablar de la casa y el barrio. Ahora vas a repasar lo que aprendiste con una simulación de la vida real trabajando como agente de bienes raíces (*real estate agent*) con clientes hispanos.

4-37 ▸ Se vende. Lee los siguientes anuncios de casas. ¿Cuál es el precio (*price*) de cada una? ¿De cuántos pies cuadrados (*square feet*) es cada una? ¿Cuáles son los números de teléfono?

La Mejor Revista Inmobiliaria　　　　　*Verano* | **VENTA CASA 21**　**87**

1. VENTA CASA. Se vende casa parcialmente renovada con 3 cuartos, 2 baños, sala y comedor. La casa tiene 1.084 pies cuadrados y el patio aproximadamente 1.900. Necesita reparaciones generales. No pierda esta oportunidad de vivir prácticamente en el centro del área metropolitana cerca de centros comerciales, restaurantes, escuelas, etc. con mucho terreno. Llamar al 990-7565, 990-4567, 635-2912. Precio: $211.500,00.

2. Casa de 2.280 pies cuadrados localizada en las afueras, 4 dormitorios, clóset grande en cuarto matrimonial, 2 baños, cocina recientemente renovada, sala, comedor, balcón y garaje para dos autos. $175.000 o mejor oferta, venta por dueños. Para más información o para visitar la propiedad, llamar al 793-7989 ó 545-5404.

3. Casa céntricamente localizada de 1.600 pies cuadrados y de reciente construcción, 3 cuartos y un baño, 2 cuartos con aire acondicionado y sistema de purificación por ósmosis. Relativamente cerca de centros comerciales, hospitales y campo de golf. Todo por $165.000,00. Para más información, llamar al 223-2992 ó 214-1112.

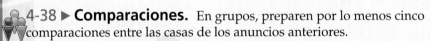

4-38 ▸ Comparaciones. En grupos, preparen por lo menos cinco comparaciones entre las casas de los anuncios anteriores.

Modelo　　*La casa número uno tiene menos dormitorios que la casa dos, pero tiene tantos dormitorios como la casa tres.*

4-39 ▸ En otras palabras. Vuelve a leer los anuncios y haz (*make*) una lista de todos los adverbios con la terminación **-mente**.

Answers for 4-39.
parcialmente, aproximadamente, prácticamente, recientemente, céntricamente, relativamente.

4-40 ▸ Este barrio. Completa esta descripción de un barrio donde se vende una casa. Utiliza **hay** o formas de **ser** o **estar**.

Las casas (1) ___son___ nuevas y las calles (2) ___están___ limpias. (3) ___Es___ un barrio seguro y las escuelas (4) ___son___ buenas. El barrio (5) ___está___ cerca de la universidad y las calles (6) ___están___ llenas de coches los días de clase, pero no (7) ___hay___ mucho tráfico los fines de semana. (8) ___Hay___ muchos restaurantes y (9) ___están___ abiertos hasta tarde.

4-41 ▶ Algunas preguntas. Una familia piensa comprar una casa en el barrio donde vives. Completa cada pregunta con la forma correcta del verbo lógico entre paréntesis.

1. ¿ _Pueden_ jugar los niños afuera en la calle o en los parques sin problema? ¿ _Juegan_ muchos niños afuera? ¿ _Duermen_ a veces vagabundos (*vagrants*) en los parques? (jugar, dormir, poder)

2. ¿ _Sirven_ los autobuses el barrio? ¿A qué hora _empiezan_ a circular los autobuses? ¿Cuánto _cuesta_ el autobús? (costar, servir, empezar)

3. Generalmente, ¿ _almuerzan_ los niños en la escuela o _pueden_ (ellos) volver a casa para comer? ¿A qué hora _vuelven_ (ellos) de la escuela primaria al final del día? (almorzar, poder, volver)

¿Y tú? Ahora entrevista a otro/a estudiante con las preguntas anteriores sobre (*about*) el barrio donde vive.

4-42 ▶ Ventajas y desventajas. Hablas con un cliente de las ventajas y desventajas (*advantages and disadvantages*) de alquilar un apartamento en vez de (*instead of*) tener su propia casa. Prepara oraciones con el opuesto (*opposite*) de las palabras en letra cursiva.

Modelo   Si tiene su propia casa, tiene que pagar la luz *y* el agua.
          Si alquila un apartamento, a veces no tiene que pagar ni la luz ni el agua.

1. Si tiene su propia casa, tiene que cortar el césped *y* trabajar en el jardín.
2. Si tiene su propia casa, puede hacer *algunos* cambios (*changes*).
3. Si tiene su propia casa, casi *siempre* tiene la responsabilidad de reparar *algo*.
4. Si tiene su propia casa, *nunca* depende de *nadie* para arreglar *ningún* problema.

¡Hola! **Entre profesionales**

Whether you work in real estate here or you need to find lodging for a stay in a Spanish-speaking country, you will need to know the vocabulary to describe the housing options that are available and regional differences in terminology. Visit MySpanishLab for *Hoy día* to find more useful vocabulary, information, and activities such as the following one.

Más anuncios. Lee estos anuncios clasificados de viviendas en España, México y Puerto Rico. ¿Qué palabras se usan en cada anuncio para decir: *for rent, an apartment, a bedroom, parking, refrigerator*?

Se alquila piso, 3 dormitorios, 2 baños, sala, comedor y cocina, totalmente equipado con frigorífico y lavadora. Párquing incluido. 900€ con agua y luz. Teléfono: 91 377 51 07   (Barcelona, España)

Se renta departamento céntrico. Tres recámaras, dos baños, cuarto de estudio, comedor, cocina con refrigerador nuevo, estacionamiento para dos autos. $9.000 Teléfono: (55) 56 73 64 29   (Distrito Federal, México)

Se alquila: Apartamento, dos habitaciones, un baño, un estacionamiento, en buenas condiciones. Incluye agua y luz. Excelentes áreas recreativas con piscina, gimnasio y gacebo. Equipo: Estufa eléctrica, nevera, aire de ventana. 900$ Teléfono: 787 735 8991   (San Juan, Puerto Rico)

La música, ¿símbolo de identidad?

SAM: 4-50
to 4-52

Antes de leer

¿Cómo es el barrio donde vives? ¿Tiene la palabra *barrio* alguna connotación para ti en inglés? ¿Asocias tu barrio con algún ritmo musical? ¿Conoces (*Are you familiar with*) el ritmo musical del reggaetón? ¿Con qué ideas asocias este tipo de música?

> ▶ **Reading Strategy** *Predicting content*. Sometimes, the title of a reading or visuals that accompany it will trigger personal associations with the topic that allow you to think ahead about the information that will likely be discussed in the passage. Predicting the content of readings will allow you to anticipate new vocabulary you encounter in Spanish.

Ahora tú

4-43 ▶ **Relaciones.** Lee el título del artículo que aparece a continuación. ¿Qué palabras o ideas relacionadas con el tema crees que van a aparecer? ¿Crees que se van a mencionar distintos tipos de música? ¿La vida de los artistas? ¿Los temas y mensajes (*messages*) de las canciones? ¿Preferencias musicales?

Suggestion for *La música, ¿símbolo de identidad?*
Discuss what *barrio* means in English to your students. Point out that although in the United States the term *el barrio* can have negative connotations, generally in Spanish, it just means *the neighborhood*.

Note. *Reggaetón* (also spelled *reggetón* and *reguetón*) combines reggae music with influences from Latin America and rapping. Originating in Panama, it spread throughout the Hispanic world starting in the late nineties.

Suggestion.
You may want to have students search online for a video or recording of Daddy Yankee performing the song "*Barrio fino.*"

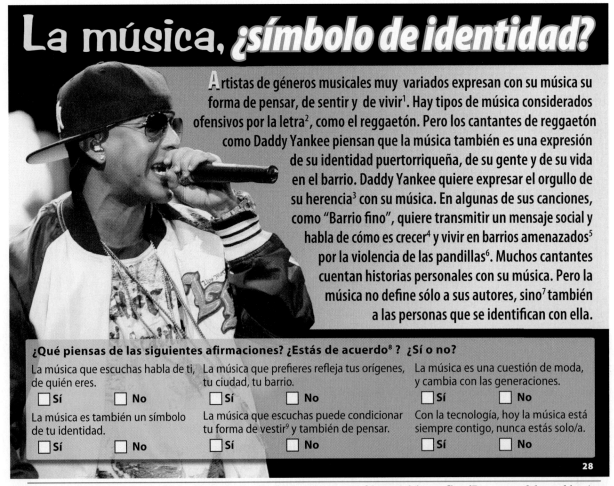

La música, ¿símbolo de identidad?

Artistas de géneros musicales muy variados expresan con su música su forma de pensar, de sentir y de vivir[1]. Hay tipos de música considerados ofensivos por la letra[2], como el reggaetón. Pero los cantantes de reggaetón como Daddy Yankee piensan que la música también es una expresión de su identidad puertorriqueña, de su gente y de su vida en el barrio. Daddy Yankee quiere expresar el orgullo de su herencia[3] con su música. En algunas de sus canciones, como "Barrio fino", quiere transmitir un mensaje social y habla de cómo es crecer[4] y vivir en barrios amenazados[5] por la violencia de las pandillas[6]. Muchos cantantes cuentan historias personales con su música. Pero la música no define sólo a sus autores, sino[7] también a las personas que se identifican con ella.

¿Qué piensas de las siguientes afirmaciones? ¿Estás de acuerdo[8]? ¿Sí o no?

La música que escuchas habla de ti, de quién eres.
☐ Sí ☐ No

La música que prefieres refleja tus orígenes, tu ciudad, tu barrio.
☐ Sí ☐ No

La música es una cuestión de moda, y cambia con las generaciones.
☐ Sí ☐ No

La música es también un símbolo de tu identidad.
☐ Sí ☐ No

La música que escuchas puede condicionar tu forma de vestir[9] y también de pensar.
☐ Sí ☐ No

Con la tecnología, hoy la música está siempre contigo, nunca estás solo/a.
☐ Sí ☐ No

28

[1]*their way of thinking, feeling, and living* [2]*lyrics* [3]*pride of his heritage* [4]*to grow up* [5]*threatened* [6]*gangs* [7]*but* [8]*Do you agree?* [9]*way of dressing*

Después de leer

 4-44 ▶ Tus opiniones. Comenta con un/a compañero/a tus respuestas a las afirmaciones del artículo. Explica por qué estás de acuerdo o no. Después entrevista a tu compañero/a con las siguientes preguntas.

1. ¿Qué música o canciones asocias con tu barrio?
2. ¿Hay algún tipo de música ofensivo para ti? ¿Cuál? ¿Por qué?
3. ¿Te gustan las canciones que tienen un mensaje social? ¿Por qué?
4. ¿Qué cantantes conoces (*do you know*) que hablen en sus canciones de su barrio o de sus orígenes?

4-45 ▶ Las pandillas. En muchas canciones de reggaetón, se habla de la influencia de las pandillas (*gangs*) en los barrios. Completa el siguiente texto con la forma correcta de **ser** o **estar**.

Recycle: *Ser* and *estar*
Activity 4-45 recycles *ser* and *estar* from *Tema 2*.

La violencia (1) _____es_____ un problema grande en algunos barrios marginales. Muchos jóvenes (2) _____están_____ solos, sin sus padres, todo el día, y no (3) _____están_____ listos para tomar grandes responsabilidades o defenderse. El ambiente (*environment*) del barrio no siempre (4) _____es_____ bueno para los jóvenes que no saben (*know*) muy bien qué destino seguir (*to follow*) y (5) _____están_____ confundidos sobre su futuro. En algunos casos, sobrevivir (*to survive*) (6) _____es_____ más importante que ir a clase y estudiar. Las pandillas (7) _____son_____ grupos de jóvenes de barrios urbanos que, generalmente, (8) _____están_____ juntos para ofrecerse protección. Pero sus actividades no (9) _____son_____ siempre legales. La vida en muchos barrios no (10) _____es_____ fácil.

4-46 ▶ Un concierto de Daddy Yankee. Teresa quiere ir a un concierto de Daddy Yankee y le pide a su amigo Ángel que la acompañe (*to accompany her*). Completa cada parte de su conversación con el verbo adecuado de la lista.

Recycle: Stem-changing verbs
Activity 4-46 recycles stem-changing verbs from *Tema 3*.

cerrar	volver	querer	contar	poder

TERESA: Hay un concierto de Daddy Yankee el próximo sábado. ¿(1) _____Quieres_____ ir?
ÁNGEL: Ay, Teresa, no (2) _____puedo_____. Tengo que trabajar el sábado y no (3) _____vuelvo_____ a casa hasta la medianoche.
TERESA: ¿La medianoche?
ÁNGEL: Sí, el restaurante donde trabajo (4) _____cierra_____ a las diez y después, mi jefe (*boss*) siempre (5) _____cuenta_____ conmigo para limpiar el lugar.

dormir	jugar	querer	pensar	almorzar

TERESA: Y el domingo, ¿qué (6) _____piensas_____ hacer?
ÁNGEL: Sabes que normalmente, los domingos (7) _____duermo_____ hasta tarde, y a las tres (8) _____juego_____ en el parque con mi equipo de béisbol.
TERESA: Oh, sí, es cierto. Y el lunes, ¿(9) _____almuerzas_____ con alguien en la universidad?
ÁNGEL: No, el lunes no almuerzo con nadie, ¿(10) _____quieres_____ almorzar en la cafetería?
TERESA: Sí, en la cafetería está bien.
ÁNGEL: Perfecto, hasta el lunes. Diviértete (*Have fun*) en el concierto.

📖 Educadores de hoy

SAM: 4-53 to 4-55

Antes de ver

La educación es una parte esencial del desarrollo (*development*) del individuo. El apoyo familiar (*family support*) y la educación que los jóvenes reciben en la escuela son la base para un buen futuro. Por eso, las escuelas son tan importantes para el barrio y pueden hacer una gran diferencia. En el video les presentamos a Pietro González y Bárbara Bonilla, dos maestros hispanos en Estados Unidos.

4-47 ▶ Reflexiones. ¿Crees que las minorías están bien representadas en las universidades norteamericanas? ¿Están bien representadas entre (*among*) los profesores y administradores también? ¿Qué porcentaje del alumnado (*student body*) en tu universidad es de origen hispano?

> ▶ **Listening Strategy** *Anticipating what people say*. To improve comprehension, think of specific questions that you think might be answered in the audio segment. These questions will help you stay focused during the listening process, and the responses you obtain will often correspond to the main ideas of the audio segment.

Ahora tú

🎬 **4-48 ▶ Somos maestros.** En el video Bárbara y Pietro hablan de sus experiencias como maestros de español en escuelas públicas. Prepara unas preguntas que piensas que vas a poder contestar después de ver el video. Utiliza **quién, qué, cuándo, cómo, dónde** o **por qué** para crear las preguntas.

Modelo *¿Qué enseña Bárbara?*
¿Qué enseña Pietro?

Después de ver

4-49 ▶ ¿Quién es quién? Indica si las descripciones se refieren (*refer*) a Bárbara o a Pietro.

1. Es de origen chileno.
2. Es de origen cubano.
3. Enseña en una escuela pública bilingüe para niños hispanos.
4. Enseña todos los niveles (*levels*) de español, de Español 1 a Español 5.
5. Sus estudiantes hablan poco inglés.
6. Sus estudiantes estudian español.
7. Quiere enseñar a sus estudiantes que hay diferentes latinos.
8. Enseña porque hace algo importante por los jóvenes.

Answers for 4-49.
1. *Pietro;* 2. *Bárbara;* 3. *Pietro;* 4. *Bárbara;*
5. *Pietro;* 6. *Bárbara;* 7. *Bárbara;* 8. *Pietro*

 4-50 ▶ El futuro del español. Escuchen otra vez las palabras del maestro Pietro al final de su testimonio y expliquen cuál es, según él (*according to him*), el futuro del español en Estados Unidos. Después, en grupos de tres, contesten las siguientes preguntas desde (*from*) su perspectiva personal.

1. En Estados Unidos, ¿crees que es más importante aprender español o alemán? ¿Por qué?
2. ¿Por qué estudias español? ¿Te gustaría estudiar otras lenguas? ¿Cuáles? ¿Por qué?
3. ¿Crees que está mejor preparada para el mercado de trabajo (*job market*) una persona que habla una lengua o una persona que habla varias? ¿Por qué?

📖 Un correo electrónico informal

AM: 4-56

Antes de escribir

Un estudiante hispano va a estudiar en tu universidad y vivir contigo. Tienes que escribirle (*to write him*) un correo electrónico con información sobre dónde vives y cómo es tu casa (apartamento o residencia). Lee la estrategia antes de escribir.

> ► **Writing strategy** *Using conventional phrases and logical organization*.
> It is common to use a casual style with a cordial tone when sharing personal information by e-mail. Your e-mail should also be organized logically. Before you begin to write, prepare some notes and organize them in a sequence that will add coherence to your message.
>
> Here are some conventional greetings and farewells you can use in Spanish to open and close e-mail messages.
>
> For opening your e-mail:
>
> **Hola . . . , ¿qué tal?** *Hi . . . , how are you?*
> **Querido/a . . .** *(Dear . . .)*
>
> For closing your e-mail:
>
> **Adiós** *Good-bye*
> **Hasta pronto** *See you soon*
> **Un saludo** *Greetings*
> **Un abrazo** *A hug*
> **Besos** *Kisses*

4-51 ► **¡Prepárate!** Antes de empezar a escribir, anota ideas relacionadas con las cuatro categorías siguientes:

- tu dirección y las partes de tu casa / apartamento / residencia
- tu cuarto
- el barrio y los vecinos
- tu carácter y tus actividades en casa

Ahora tú

4-52 ► **Tu correo electrónico informal.** Escribe ahora tu correo electrónico en cuatro párrafos correspondientes a las categorías mencionadas.

Después de escribir

 4-53 ► **¡Edita!** Intercambia (*Exchange*) tu correo electrónico con un/a compañero/a y revisa su texto. ¿Aparece toda la información relevante? Piensa en sugerencias para mejorar (*to improve*) la gramática y la organización del texto.

4-54 ► **¡Revisa!** Revisa tu correo electrónico y asegúrate que contenga (*make sure it contains*) los siguientes elementos:

- ❏ el vocabulario apropiado para hablar de las partes de la casa
- ❏ los adjetivos para describir tu cuarto, tu barrio y tus vecinos
- ❏ el verbo **ser** para describir cómo son tu casa, tu cuarto, tu barrio y tus vecinos
- ❏ el verbo **estar** para indicar dónde está tu casa y cómo está normalmente tu cuarto
- ❏ los verbos para hablar de tus actividades en casa

 4-55 ► **¡Navega!** Busca programas para estudiar español en un país hispano y lee la descripción del alojamiento (*lodging*). ¿Hay más información para incorporar en tu correo? Visita la página web de *Hoy día* y usa los enlaces (*links*) sugeridos para esta actividad.

En casa

las afueras	outskirts
el alquiler	rent
el animal	animal
el árbol	tree
el armario	wardrobe, closet
el baño	bathroom
el barrio	neighborhood
el campo	country
el centro	center, downtown
el coche (el carro)	car
la cocina	kitchen
el comedor	dining room
la dirección	address
el dormitorio	bedroom
la estufa	stove
la flor	flower
el garaje	garage
el jardín	garden, yard
el microondas	microwave oven
la nevera	refrigerator
la sala	living room
el sofá	sofa
el televisor	television set
el/la vecino/a	neighbor

Acciones

alquilar	to rent
fumar	to smoke
pagar	to pay

Otras palabras y expresiones

afuera	outside
agradable	pleasant, nice
caro/a	expensive
Me gustaría(n) . . .	I would like . . .

For numbers above 100, see page 102.
For indefinite and negative words, see page 104.

El cuarto, los muebles y los accesorios

la alfombra	rug
la cómoda	chest (of drawers)
el espejo	mirror
la impresora	printer
la lámpara	lamp
los muebles	furniture
la pared	wall
la pintura	painting
el reproductor de DVD	DVD player
el suelo	ground, floor

Descripciones

desordenado/a	messy
limpio/a	clean
listo/a	ready
lleno/a	full
muerto/a	dead
ordenado/a	neat, straightened up
propio/a	own
sucio/a	dirty

Los colores

amarillo/a	yellow
anaranjado/a	orange
azul	blue
beige	beige
blanco/a	white
gris	gray
marrón (café)	brown
morado/a	purple
negro/a	black
rojo/a	red
rosado/a (rosa)	pink
verde	green

Otras palabras y expresiones

dejar	to leave (something somewhere)
desafortunadamente	unfortunately
el dinero	money
la persona	person
por todos lados	everywhere

For a list of adjectives used with estar, see page 108.

Acciones

almorzar (ue)	to eat / have lunch
cenar	to eat / have dinner
cerrar (ie)	to close
contar (ue)	to count, to tell
decir (i, yo digo)	to say, to tell
desayunar	to eat / have breakfast
dormir (ue)	to sleep
dormir (ue) la siesta	to take a nap
empezar (ie)	to begin
encontrar (ue)	to find
entender (ie)	to understand
jugar (ue) (a los videojuegos)	to play (video games)
pedir (i)	to ask for, to order
pensar (ie)	to think, to intend
perder (ie)	to lose, to miss
poder (ue)	to be able, can, may
preferir (ie)	to prefer
querer (ie)	to want
recordar (ue)	to remember
repetir (i)	to repeat
servir (i)	to serve
volver (ue) (a)	to return, to . . . again

Otras palabras y expresiones

el desayuno	breakfast
Lo siento.	I'm sorry.

En la calle

el autobús	bus
la basura	trash
el ruido	noise
el tráfico	traffic
el transporte público	public transportation

Los lugares

la escuela	school
el estacionamiento	parking lot
la lavandería	laundromat
la parada de autobús	bus stop

Otros sustantivos

el espacio	space
la privacidad	privacy
el quehacer doméstico	chore
el recibo de la luz (del agua, del gas)	light / electric (water, gas) bill
la responsabilidad	responsibility

Expresiones verbales

andar en bicicleta	to ride a bicycle
arreglar	to fix, to straighten out / up
cortar el césped	to cut the grass
costar (ue)	to cost
esperar	to wait (for)
estacionar	to park
funcionar	to work (for machines, plans, or systems)
lavar	to wash
No conozco a	I don't know (a person)
sacar	to take out

Descripciones

animado/a	lively
callado/a	quiet
chismoso/a	gossipy
cultural	cultural
hablador/a	talkative, chatty
práctico/a	practical
ruidoso/a	noisy
seguro/a	safe

 ▶ Visit MySpanishLab for *Hoy día* for links to the mnemonic dictionary online for suggestions such as the following to help you remember vocabulary from this chapter, learn related words in Spanish, and use Spanish words to build your vocabulary in English.

EXAMPLES

pensar, *to think:* The English adjective *pensive* means *deep in thought.* Related words: **el pensamiento,** *thought, thinking* and **pensativo/a,** *pensive.*

lavar, *to wash:* In English, you wash up in a *lavatory,* and you might use *Lava* soap. Related words: **un lavabo,** *a washbasin, a bathroom sink;* **un lavadero,** *a laundry room;* **una lavadora,** *a washing machine;* **un lavaplatos,** *a dishwasher;* **la lavandería,** *laundry, the laundromat.*

5 Los fines de semana

En el este capítulo, vas a aprender a hablar más de la rutina diaria, las actividades de tiempo libre y las fiestas.

Los españoles son en general gente activa, feliz y sociable, según un estudio del Centro de Investigaciones Sociales sobre relaciones interpersonales. Los jóvenes de 18 a 24 años prefieren divertirse (*to have fun*) con sus amigos para desconectar de la rutina diaria. Pero, los españoles de 35 a 44 años prefieren divertirse con su familia en su tiempo libre.

▶ ¿Prefieres divertirte con tu familia o con tus amigos?

▶ ¿Necesitas estar solo/a veces para desconectar?

Los españoles creen todavía en el matrimonio. Un 72,6% de los entrevistados no está de acuerdo con la frase, "El matrimonio es una institución pasada de moda (*outdated*)". Aproximadamente un 98% de los españoles cree que la fidelidad (*faithfulness*) y la tolerancia son factores muy importantes para el buen funcionamiento de un matrimonio.

▶ ¿Estás de acuerdo con la frase "el matrimonio es una institución pasada de moda"?

▶ ¿Cuáles crees que son los factores más importantes para el buen funcionamiento de un matrimonio?

Suggestion for chapter opener.
Expand the discussion of the questions presented in the book by asking questions such as the following. First section: *¿Prefieres hablar de tus problemas con tus amigos o con algún familiar, o depende del problema? ¿Con qué familiar hablas más de tus problemas? ¿Puedes hablar de todo con tus padres? ¿Con tu mejor amigo/a?* Second section: *¿Vives en un barrio multicultural u homogéneo? Para ti, ¿es importante tener una pareja* (life partner) *de la misma cultura que la tuya* (yours)? *¿Crees que es importante para la pareja tener la misma religión?* Third section: *¿Qué es más importante en un matrimonio o en una pareja: la atracción física, la fidelidad, la diversión, la estabilidad económica, la paciencia, el respeto mutuo? ¿Crees que es necesario en un matrimonio tener los mismos intereses o la misma religión? ¿Es importante tener hijos? ¿Cuántos hijos te gustaría tener? ¿Te gustaría pasar toda la vida con la misma persona? ¿Crees que el amor es para siempre?*

Note for chapter opener.
See the IRM for source information relating to the statistical data presented.

Vocabulario La rutina diaria

SAM: 5-1
to 5-4

CD 2
Track 26

Duermo hasta tarde.
Me despierto a las diez.

Me quedo un poco en la cama y
me levanto a las diez y media.

¿Sabías que...?

La siesta es una costumbre muy extendida en los países hispanos. Muchas personas vuelven a casa a la una y media o dos de la tarde para almorzar y descansan un rato (*a while*) después de comer. La siesta, según médicos especialistas, tiene muchos beneficios: aumenta la productividad y la creatividad y el trabajador se siente más predispuesto (*inclined*) a trabajar. También es beneficiosa para los estudiantes. Después de dormir una hora de siesta, los chicos y chicas se levantan más descansados y concentrados para aprender.

 ¡Ojo!

The verbs presented on this page have reflexive pronouns (**me, te . . .**) before them. In the following grammar explanation, you will learn when to include such pronouns. In this vocabulary presentation use them where they appear and focus on the meaning of the verbs.

Me baño o **me ducho** por la mañana
y me lavo el pelo todos los días.

Me lavo los dientes.

Me lavo la cara, me maquillo y
me visto para salir.

Me relajo en casa por la tarde.

Me encuentro con mis amigos en
el centro. **Me divierto** mucho.

Cuando **me siento** cansada,
vuelvo a casa y **me acuesto**.

---

me quedo *I stay*　**me levanto** *I get up*　**me baño** *I bathe*　**me ducho** *I shower*　**me lavo la cara** *I wash my face*　**me visto** *I get dressed*　**me encuentro con** *I meet up with, I get together with*　**me divierto** *I have fun*　**me siento** *I feel*　**me acuesto** *I go to bed*

Una conversación. Dos amigos, Adán y Maite, hablan de su rutina de los sábados.

ADÁN: ¿Te despiertas tarde los sábados?

MAITE: No, me levanto a las seis y media. Trabajo a las ocho los sábados y me ducho antes de salir.

ADÁN: ¿Trabajas todo el día?

MAITE: No, vuelvo a casa a las dos.

ADÁN: ¿Qué haces por la tarde?

MAITE: Generalmente, me quedo en casa y me relajo. A veces duermo la siesta.

ADÁN: ¿Te quedas en casa por la noche también?

MAITE: Los sábados por la noche, prefiero salir con mis amigos a cenar o a bailar.

ADÁN: ¿Te acuestas tarde?

MAITE: Sí, casi siempre me acuesto tarde los sábados porque puedo dormir hasta tarde los domingos.

5-1 ▶ ¿Qué se hace primero? Una estudiante habla de su rutina diaria. ¿En qué orden dice que hace las siguientes cosas?

Modelo   Me levanto. / Me despierto. / Desayuno.
Me despierto, me levanto y luego desayuno.

1. Me visto. / Me maquillo. / Me lavo la cara.
2. Me levanto. / Voy a la universidad. / Me visto.
3. Ceno. / Vuelvo a la casa. / Me acuesto después de estudiar.
4. Me levanto después de quince minutos. / Me despierto. / Me quedo un poco en la cama.
5. Me lavo los dientes. / Desayuno. / Me despierto.
6. Nos relajamos un poco después de comer. / Mis amigos y yo nos encontramos en la cafetería. / Almorzamos.

5-2 ▶ Mi rutina. Selecciona las palabras en letra cursiva que mejor describan tu rutina de los sábados o utiliza otra expresión para completar las oraciones.

1. Me despierto a *las ocho / las nueve / las diez* / . . . y me levanto *inmediatamente / después de quince minutos* / . . .
2. Me despierto *fácilmente / con dificultad*.
3. Me baño *por la mañana / por la tarde / por la noche*.
4. Me visto en *mi cuarto / el baño*.
5. Para relajarme, me gusta *escuchar música / leer una revista* / . . .
6. Generalmente, me quedo en casa *los sábados por la noche / los domingos por la tarde / todo el fin de semana* / . . .
7. Me divierto mucho cuando mis amigos y yo *vamos a bailar / vamos al café / jugamos al vóleibol* / . . .
8. No me divierto mucho cuando mis amigos y yo *vamos al centro comercial / hablamos de política* / . . .
9. Los sábados me acuesto a *las diez / las once* / . . .

5-3 ▶ Otra conversación. En parejas, vuelvan a leer *Una conversación* entre Adán y Maite. Luego, cambien la conversación para hablar de su rutina de los sábados.

 CD 2, Track 28

¡A escuchar!

Escuchen otra conversación en la cual dos amigos, Blanca y Gustavo, hablan de su rutina de los lunes. ¿Quién se levanta más temprano, él o ella? ¿Quién vuelve a casa primero? ¿A qué hora se acuesta cada uno?

Gramática 1 Describing your routine: Reflexive verbs

SAM: 5-5
to 5-8

Para averiguar

1. What is a reflexive verb?
2. What are two types of verbs that are often reflexive in Spanish, but not in English?
3. Which reflexive pronoun is used with each subject?
4. Where do you place reflexive pronouns with verbs conjugated in the present tense? Where do you place them with an infinitive after **antes de** or **después de**?
5. Will infinitives used after **antes de** or **después de** be translated by an infinitive in English?

Suggestions.
• Point out that *ir* means *to go*, but *irse* means *to go away* or *to leave*.
• Use the illustrations of Adela to explain the difference between reflexive and non-reflexive use of verbs. Then, give students the following sentences, asking if the verb would be reflexive or not in Spanish. 1. I wake up at 6:00 in the morning. 2. I wake my children up at 6:45. 3. I bathe every morning. 4. I have to bathe my youngest son, too. 5. I wash clothes three times a week. 6. I wash my hair every day. 7. My children get dressed before breakfast. 8. I get dressed after breakfast. 9. I always sit down with my children to eat breakfast. 10. I put my children to bed at 8:30. (After having students decide whether the verbs are reflexive, you may wish to remind them of the use of the personal *a* and have them translate some of the preceding sentences.)
• Point out that any action that can be done to someone else can generally be done to oneself, and many verbs students have already seen can be made reflexive. Ask students what the following reflexive verbs mean: *limpiarse, mirarse (en el espejo), comprarse algo, arreglarse, prepararse, cortarse, servirse, perderse.*

¡Ojo!

Generally, the definite article (**el, la, los, las**) is used instead of possessive adjectives (**mi, tu, su, nuestro/a**) with nouns naming a part of the body or clothing after a reflexive verb.

Me lavo **la** cara   I wash *my* face.

■ Use reflexive verbs to describe actions that people do to or for themselves.

REFLEXIVE: Adela se baña.
Adela is bathing (herself).

NON-REFLEXIVE: Adela baña al perro.
Adela is bathing the dog.

■ When conjugating reflexive verbs, remove the **se** from the infinitive and place the reflexive pronoun corresponding to the subject before the verb: **me** (*myself*), **te** (*yourself*), **nos** (*ourselves*), **os** (*yourselves*), **se** (*himself, herself, oneself, yourself, yourselves, themselves*).

lavarse *(to wash oneself)*

yo	**me**	lavo	nosotros/as	**nos**	lavamos
tú	**te**	lavas	vosotros/as	**os**	laváis
Ud., él, ella	**se**	lava	Uds., ellos/as	**se**	lavan

■ Verbs used with reflexive pronouns in English (*myself, . . .*) are generally reflexive in Spanish (*to look at oneself* > **mirarse**). Verbs describing a change in mental or physical state or people doing something to their own body, including changing its position such as sitting down or standing up, are also generally reflexive in Spanish.

■ Some common reflexive verbs include the following. Note the stem-changing verbs indicated by **(ie)**, **(i)**, or **(ue)**.

aburrirse	*to get bored*	**maquillarse**	*to put on make-up*
acostarse (ue)	*to lie down, to go to bed*	**ponerse (la ropa)**	*to put on (one's clothes)*
bañarse	*to bathe, to take a bath*		
despertarse (ie)	*to wake up*	**presentarse**	*to introduce oneself*
divertirse (ie)	*to have fun*	**quedarse**	*to stay*
ducharse	*to take a shower*	**relajarse**	*to relax*
enojarse	*to get angry*	**sentarse (ie)**	*to sit down*
irse	*to go away, to leave*	**sentirse (ie)**	*to feel*
lavarse (el pelo)	*to wash (one's hair)*	**vestirse (i)**	*to get dressed*
levantarse	*to get up*		

— ¿A qué hora **te acuestas**?
— **Me acuesto** a la medianoche y **me despierto** a las cinco y media.
— ¿No **te sientes** cansado?
— Sí, necesito dormir más.

— *What time do you go to bed?*
— *I go to bed at midnight and I wake up at five thirty.*
— *Don't you feel tired?*
— *Yes, I need to sleep more.*

■ After prepositions like **para** (*in order to*), **después de** (*after*), or **antes de** (*before*), use the infinitive form of verbs, changing the reflexive pronoun to match the subject of the sentence. Note that in English, a different structure is used.

Me levanto inmediatamente **después de despertarme**.

{ *I get up immediately **after waking up**. / I get up immediately **after I wake up**.*

5-4 ▶ La rutina diaria. Completa las oraciones con la forma correcta de los verbos entre paréntesis en el orden lógico para describir la rutina diaria de Alejandro los lunes.

Modelo   Alejandro casi siempre *se despierta* a las seis, pero no *se levanta* inmediatamente. *Se queda* cinco o diez minutos en la cama después de despertarse. (quedarse, despertarse, levantarse)

1. Todas las mañanas __se ducha__ y __se viste__ rápidamente en el baño. Luego, va a la cocina y __se sienta__ a la mesa a desayunar. (vestirse, ducharse, sentarse)
2. Después de desayunar, __se lava__ los dientes, __se pone__ la mochila y __se va__ para la universidad a las siete. (lavarse, ponerse, irse)
3. Alejandro siempre __se sienta__ cerca del profesor en todas sus clases. __Se divierte__ con frecuencia en sus clases de música y francés, pero casi siempre __se aburre__ en su clase de historia porque el profesor es monótono. (divertirse, aburrirse, sentarse)
4. Los lunes, Alejandro __se queda__ en la universidad siete horas y __se va__ del campus a las cuatro. Después de sus clases, __se divierte__ un poco con los amigos en un café. (quedarse, irse, divertirse)
5. Generalmente, Alejandro __se siente__ cansado alrededor de (*around*) las once de la noche. Entonces, __se pone__ el pijama y __se acuesta__. (acostarse, ponerse, sentirse)

¿Y tú? Ahora, cambia las oraciones anteriores para describir tu rutina los días de clase y comparte la información con un/a compañero/a.

Modelo   *Casi siempre me despierto a las siete y media y me levanto inmediatamente. Casi nunca me quedo en la cama después de despertarme.*

5-5 ▶ Mi rutina los fines de semana. Expresa la misma idea sustituyendo un verbo de la lista por las palabras en letra cursiva en cada pregunta.

aburrirse	irse	ponerse	relajarse
despertarse (ie)	levantarse	quedarse	sentirse (ie)

Modelo   *¿Te levantas* tempranos los sábados? *¿Te despiertas tempranos los sábados?*

1. ¿A qué hora *te despiertas* los sábados?
2. ¿*Descansas* los sábados o tienes que trabajar?
3. Los sábados, ¿*sales* temprano de casa o *estás* en casa por la mañana?
4. ¿*Estás aburrido/a* o te diviertes cuando juegas a los videojuegos?
5. Normalmente, ¿*te vistes con* ropa elegante o ropa informal para salir con los amigos?
6. ¿*Estás* cansado/a los domingos por la mañana?

¿Y tú? Ahora, entrevista a un/a compañero/a de clase con las nuevas preguntas.

5-6 ▶ En mi familia. ¿Quién de tu familia hace las siguientes cosas?

Modelo   despertarse más temprano
Yo me despierto más temprano. / Todos nos despertamos a la misma hora.

1. despertarse primero
2. levantarse más tarde
3. acostarse más tarde
4. bañarse por la mañana
5. quedarse más en casa
6. divertirse más

📖 Gramática 2

SAM: 5-9 to 5-11

Saying what you do for each other: Reciprocal verbs

Para **averiguar**

1. What is a reciprocal verb?
2. Do reciprocal verbs in Spanish look different or have a different word order from reflexive verbs?
3. How would you say: My friends and I see (need, understand) each other?

Supplemental activities.
• Ask students: *¿Se llevan bien o se llevan mal dos personas si hacen las siguientes cosas en un matrimonio?* 1. *Se pelean todos los días.* 2. *Se abrazan todo el tiempo.* 3. *Nunca se hablan.* 4. *Se quieren mucho.* 5. *Se encuentran todos los días para almorzar.* 6. *Nunca se besan.* 7. *Se compran muchos regalos.* 8. *Se dicen cosas feas.* 9. *Se escriben poemas.* 10. *Nunca se miran a los ojos.* 11. *Siempre se ayudan en casa.* 12. *Se hablan de todo.* 13. *Con frecuencia se dicen que se quieren.* 14. *Se divorcian.*
• Ask students: *¿Describen estas oraciones una relación ideal con tu compañero/a de cuarto?* Respuestas posibles: *Está bien. / No me gusta. / No me importa.* (It doesn't matter to me.)
1. *Tu compañero/a de cuarto siempre se acuesta en el sofá de la sala.* 2. *Uds. se ven poco.* 3. *Él/Ella se enoja contigo todo el tiempo.* 4. *Siempre se divierten juntos/as.* 5. *Él/Ella se lava los dientes en la cocina.* 6. *Él/Ella se queda en casa todo el tiempo.* 7. *Él/Ella nunca se viste cuando pasa el día en casa.* 8. *Él/Ella se sienta en el suelo para hacer su tarea.*
• Have students say whom these sentences might describe. *MODELO: Nos hablamos mucho por teléfono.* > *Mi madre y yo nos hablamos mucho por teléfono.* 1. *Nos comunicamos con frecuencia por Internet.* 2. *Nos vemos todos los días.* 3. *Nos abrazamos con frecuencia.* 4. *Nos llevamos bien.* 5. *Nos peleamos con frecuencia.* 6. *Nos ayudamos con el español.*

■ Whereas reflexive verbs indicate that someone does something to or for one-self, reciprocal verbs indicate that two or more people do something to or for one another or each other.

■ Reciprocal verbs have the same pronouns (**nos, os, se**) and the same word order as reflexive verbs. Many verbs that you have already seen can be made reciprocal by adding the reciprocal pronouns.

Mis vecinos nunca **se hablan**.   *My neighbors never talk to each other.*
Nos vemos con frecuencia.   *We see one another frequently.*

■ Here are some reciprocal and reflexive verbs that are useful when describing relationships.

abrazarse	*to hug each other*	**enamorarse (de)**	*to fall in love (with)*
ayudarse	*to help each other*		
besarse	*to kiss each other*	**encontrarse (ue)**	*to meet up with each other*
casarse (con)	*to marry, to get married (to)*		
		llevarse bien (con)	*to get along well (with)*
comunicarse	*to communicate with each other*		
		pelearse	*to fight*
divorciarse (de)	*to divorce, to get divorced (from)*	**quererse (ie)**	*to love each other*

Mi novio/a y yo **nos hablamos** por teléfono o **nos comunicamos** por correo electrónico varias veces al día.

Nos vemos casi todos los días. **Nos encontramos** en un café después del trabajo.

Nos queremos mucho y **nos vamos a casar** algún día.

5-7 ▶ Mi mejor amigo y yo. ¿Describen las siguientes oraciones tu relación con tu mejor amigo/a? Contesta **cierto** o **falso** y corrige las oraciones falsas.

1. Nos hablamos por teléfono todos los días.
2. Nos comunicamos más por correo electrónico que por teléfono.
3. Nos vemos todos los días.
4. Nos encontramos a veces en un café.
5. Nos encontramos todos los días después de esta clase.
6. Nos abrazamos cuando nos vemos.
7. Nos ayudamos cuando hay problemas.
8. Nunca nos peleamos.

5-8 ▶ Una pareja feliz. Usen los verbos de la lista para contar una historia de amor entre Pablo y Felicia. Trabajen en grupos e incluyan todos los detalles (*details*) posibles. Luego, intercambien (*exchange*) su descripción con la de otro grupo para ver cuál es más completa e interesante.

Modelo   *Pablo y Felicia se ven por primera vez en un café. Se miran y Pablo se sienta en la mesa de al lado . . .*

verse por primera vez	no separarse hasta tarde	enamorarse
mirarse a los ojos	pedirse los números de teléfono	besarse
levantarse	abrazarse antes de irse	nunca pelearse
presentarse	hablarse por teléfono todos los días	quererse
hablarse por horas	encontrarse todos los días	casarse

Follow-up for 5-8.
Preguntas personales. 1. Cuando sales con tu mejor amigo/a, generalmente ¿dónde se encuentran? ¿Se abrazan Uds. cuando se ven? ¿Con qué frecuencia se ven Uds.? 2. ¿Se llevan bien todos tus amigos? ¿Todos tus familiares? ¿Se abrazan todos tus tíos y primos cuando se ven? 3. ¿Con quién de tu familia te enojas a veces? ¿Por qué? ¿Se pelean Uds. con frecuencia? 4. ¿Con quién de tu familia te llevas mejor? ¿Se cuentan ustedes todo? ¿Se ayudan si tienen problemas? ¿Siempre se divierten juntos/as o se aburren a veces? 5. ¿Te sientes cómodo/a cuando dos personas se pelean enfrente de todos en público? ¿Te sientes cómodo/a cuando dos personas se besan enfrente de todos en público? Para ti, ¿es romántico o es tonto si dos novios se miran románticamente a los ojos por mucho tiempo sin hablar? 6. ¿Crees que es importante casarse? ¿Es importante quedarse con la misma persona por toda la vida (life)? ¿Es posible vivir toda la vida con la misma persona sin aburrirse? ¿Te aburres fácilmente en las relaciones? ¿Es malo divorciarse o es mejor divorciarse si dos personas con hijos pequeños se aburren y ya no se quieren?

5-9 ▶ Comparaciones culturales. Lee el siguiente artículo sobre el rol de las mujeres en la sociedad hispana y contesta las preguntas.

Answers for 5-9.
1. se casan (casarse), se quedan (quedarse), se ocupan (ocuparse), se preocupan (preocuparse), relajarse, se siente (sentirse), prepararse, realizarse; 2. la familia y la crianza de los hijos; Answers will vary. 3. Se casan entre los 20 y los 25 años; Answers will vary. 4. Answers will vary.

Aunque (*Although*) la situación está cambiando en las nuevas generaciones, la mentalidad de muchas mujeres hispanas es diferente a la percepción que tiene la mujer norteamericana sobre el equilibrio laboral y familiar (*balance between work and family*). En muchos países de Latinoamérica la familia y la crianza (*raising*) de los hijos son prioridades para el individuo, y la mujer tiene un rol fundamental en estas sociedades. Las mujeres hispanas que optan por el matrimonio se casan generalmente entre los 20 y los 25 años. Las familias hispanas son a veces numerosas, y las responsabilidades de la mujer son muy grandes. Algunas mujeres hispanas son madres y esposas, se quedan en casa, se ocupan de (*take care of*) todos los quehaceres domésticos y se preocupan por el bienestar (*well-being*) de la familia. No hay tiempo para relajarse. El hombre generalmente trabaja fuera de la casa y se siente responsable de la economía familiar. El machismo es un estereotipo extendido en el mundo hispano, pero en realidad la mujer tiene un rol muy importante en la sociedad. Las mujeres hispanas entienden que ser madre es importante, pero también valoran (*value*) mucho prepararse en la escuela y en la universidad, y realizarse profesionalmente.

1. Identifica los verbos reflexivos en el texto e indica cuál es el infinitivo en cada caso.
2. ¿Cuáles son las prioridades del individuo en muchos países de Latinoamérica? ¿Son similares a las prioridades de la sociedad norteamericana?
3. Las mujeres hispanas que deciden casarse, ¿a qué edad se casan generalmente? ¿Tiene la mujer norteamericana responsabilidades similares a la mujer hispana? ¿Comparte estas responsabilidades con su pareja (*partner*)?
4. ¿Crees que la mujer norteamericana media (*average*) tiene tiempo para relajarse? ¿Qué hace la mujer norteamericana media para relajarse?

Vocabulario   La ropa

SAM: 5-12 to 5-19

¿En qué tienda prefieres comprar ropa? ¿Es cara, **barata** o tiene **precios** razonables? **¿Gastas** mucho en ropa? ¿Qué **llevas** cuando vas a la playa? ¿Qué te pones para salir con los amigos?

CD 2
Track 29

¿Sabías que...?

En muchos países hispanos el sistema de tallas (*sizes*) en la ropa es diferente al de Estados Unidos. En España, por ejemplo, la talla más pequeña en ropa de mujer, equivalente a la talla 0 norteamericana, es la 34. También las tallas aumentan de dos en dos, así la talla 2 equivale a la 36, y así sucesivamente. Los números de los zapatos también cambian. En muchos países hispanos, el sistema que se usa también incluye dos dígitos.

 ## ¡Ojo!

Other commonly used words for **los tenis** include **los zapatos de tenis** and **las zapatillas de tenis**.

la camisa
el suéter
las botas
la corbata
los pantalones
la chaqueta
el traje
las sandalias
el impermeable
el abrigo
el sombrero
la gorra
el cinturón
el vestido
la camiseta
la blusa
los zapatos
los calcetines
la falda
los pantalones cortos
los jeans
la sudadera
el pijama
los tenis
el traje de baño
la bolsa

CD 2
Track 30

Una conversación. Una mujer compra un traje de baño.

DEPENDIENTA: ¿En qué puedo servirle?

CLIENTA: **Busco** un traje de baño.

DEPENDIENTA: ¿Qué color prefiere usted?

CLIENTA: Algo en amarillo o rosado si tiene. Llevo la **talla** 36.

DEPENDIENTA: ¿Le gustan éstos? **Están de moda.** Cuestan 415 pesos. ¿Es demasiado?

CLIENTA: No, es un buen precio. **¿Me** puedo **probar ese** traje de baño amarillo?

DEPENDIENTA: Sí, **cómo no. Los probadores** están **por acá.** *Después de probarse el traje de baño . . .*

DEPENDIENTA: ¿Le gusta ese traje de baño o desea probarse otro?

CLIENTA: **Me** voy a **llevar** éste.

DEPENDIENTA: ¿Cómo desea pagar, **en efectivo,** con cheque o con **tarjeta de débito o de crédito?**

CLIENTA: Con mi tarjeta de crédito.

CD 2, Track 31

¡A escuchar!

Escuchen otra conversación en la cual un hombre compra ropa. ¿Qué busca? ¿De qué color es la que compra? ¿Cuánto cuesta?

---

barato/a *cheap*   **el precio** *the price*   **gastar** *to spend*   **llevar** *to wear, to carry, to take*   **el dependiente / la dependienta** *the salesclerk*   **el cliente / la clienta** *the customer*   **buscar** *to look for*   **la talla** *size*   **estar de moda** *to be in fashion*   **probarse** *to try on*   **ese / esa (esos / esas)** *that (those)*   **cómo no** *of course*   **los probadores** *the fitting rooms*   **por acá** *over / through here*   **llevarse** *to take (away)*   **en efectivo** *in cash*   **una tarjeta** *a card*

5-10 ▶ ¿Quién habla? ¿Quién dice las siguientes cosas en una tienda, el cliente o el dependiente?

Modelo ¿En qué puedo servirle?
el dependiente

1. No quiero nada muy caro.
2. ¿Cuánto desea gastar?
3. ¿Tiene algo más barato?
4. ¿Qué talla lleva usted?
5. Quiero algo en azul o blanco.
6. ¿Me puedo probar esta camisa?
7. Los probadores están por acá.
8. ¿Necesita algo más o eso es todo?

5-11 ▶ ¿Qué te pones? ¿Qué ropa te pones en estas situaciones?

Modelo Vas a la playa.
Me pongo un traje de baño.

1. Vas a la montaña a esquiar.
2. Vas al lago a nadar.
3. Vas al parque a correr.
4. Sales a bailar con tus amigos.
5. Vas a una entrevista (*interview*) importante.
6. Te quedas en casa todo el día para relajarte.
7. Vas a la clase de español.
8. Vas a una boda (*wedding*).

5-12 ▶ Entrevista. Entrevista a otro/a estudiante con estas preguntas.

1. ¿Qué tienda cerca de aquí tiene ropa cara / barata / bonita? ¿En qué tiendas compras mucha ropa?
2. Para ti, ¿qué es más importante, el precio o la calidad? ¿Cuál es tu tienda favorita?
3. Cuando sales con los amigos los sábados, ¿prefieres usar jeans o pantalones más elegantes? ¿En qué ocasiones te pones un traje / un vestido?

5-13 ▶ Otra conversación. En parejas, vuelvan a leer *Una conversación* y preparen otra conversación lógica donde uno/a de ustedes quiere comprar un traje o un vestido en una tienda.

5-14 ▶ Comparaciones culturales. La moda es un aspecto muy importante de las culturas hispanas. Lee la siguiente información y contesta las preguntas.

En general, la mujer hispana se arregla mucho (*dresses up*) tanto para ir al trabajo como para salir de fiesta. Dependiendo de los países, hay una preferencia en la ropa por colores más vivos (*bright*) como en el Caribe, o colores más sobrios (*muted*) como en España y Argentina. La ropa de diseñadores hispanos como Isabel Toledo, Oscar de la Renta o Adolfo Domínguez se ve hoy también en las tiendas elegantes de Estados Unidos. ¿Cuál es tu color favorito para la ropa? ¿Qué tipo de ropa llevas para ir a clase o al trabajo? ¿Y para salir de fiesta?

Los hombres hispanos, en general, son bastante clásicos en la ropa que usan. En los países del Caribe, donde el clima es muy caliente (*hot*), la ropa preferida por los hombres es de lino (*linen*) y la guayabera es muy típica de estos lugares, una camisa de lino que se lleva por fuera del (*untucked*) pantalón. Normalmente, los hombres no llevan pantalones cortos por la calle, sólo si van a la playa o de excursión. En Estados Unidos, ¿llevan los hombres pantalones cortos por la calle?

📖 Gramática 1

SAM: 5-20 to 5-21

Pointing out people and things: Demonstrative adjectives and pronouns

Para averiguar

1. How do you say *this / these* in Spanish?
2. How do you say *that / those*? What is the difference between **ese** and **aquel**?
3. How do you say *this one* instead of *this shirt*? Which may have a written accent mark, *this one* or *this shirt*?
4. When do you use the forms **esto, eso,** and **aquello**?

Note.
You may wish to point out to students that the accents on demonstrative pronouns are now considered optional by the *Real Academia Española*. Since students will see them used in numerous texts, they are used throughout *Hoy día*.

Suggestions.
• Remind students that they have already seen *este / esta* in time expressions: *este semestre, este fin de semana, esta noche, esta semana.*
• Bring three examples of various types of clothing (three shirts, three ties, three pairs of socks, etc.) to class. Keep one of each yourself, and give the other two to students. Use *este / ese / aquel* to ask students whether they prefer the one you have, the one they have, or the one the other student has: *¿Prefieres esta camisa que yo tengo, esa camisa que tú tienes o aquélla que tiene . . . ?*

Supplemental activity.
Discuss the use of the neuter forms *esto, eso,* and *aquello.* Put the phrases *Eso es posible (imposible, normal, absurdo, tonto, buena idea, mala idea . . .)* on the board, and have students use them to react to the following situations. 1. *En una tienda no aceptan efectivo. Todos tienen que pagar con tarjeta de crédito o tarjeta de débito.* 2. *Tu mejor amigo/a ya tiene nueve tarjetas de crédito y quiere otra.* 3. *Tu amigo/a siempre se prueba la ropa antes de comprar algo.* 4. *Gastas más de diez mil dólares al año en ropa.* 5. *En una tienda los clientes tienen que pagar por usar los probadores.* 6. *En una tienda, la ropa cuesta menos si los clientes pagan en efectivo.* 7. *En la universidad, todos los estudiantes tienen que llevar traje o vestido.* 8. *Muchos estudiantes vienen a clase en jeans y camiseta.* 9. *Tu profesor de matemáticas viene a clase en traje de baño.*

■ Use the following demonstrative adjectives to say *this / these* or *that / those*. There are two ways to say *that / those* in Spanish: **ese / esa / esos / esas** and **aquel / aquella / aquellos / aquellas**. **Aquel** is generally used to describe something at a greater distance than **ese**.

este (this / these)		**ese** (that / those)		**aquel** (that / those)	
este sombrero	*this hat*	ese sombrero	*that hat*	aquel sombrero	*that hat*
esta falda	*this skirt*	esa falda	*that skirt*	aquella falda	*that skirt*
estos zapatos	*these shoes*	esos zapatos	*those shoes*	aquellos zapatos	*those shoes*
estas botas	*these boots*	esas botas	*those boots*	aquellas botas	*those boots*

¿Te gustan **estos** zapatos?	*Do you like these shoes?*
Me gusta **esa** blusa con **esa** falda.	*I like that blouse with that skirt.*
¿Puedo probarme **aquel** traje?	*May I try on that suit (over there)?*

■ The demonstrative pronouns look just like the demonstrative adjectives, except that the noun is omitted. Pronouns may have an optional accent mark on the stressed **e** to distinguish them from adjectives.

¿Te gustan estos zapatos?	*Do you like these shoes?*
No, prefiero **éstos**.	*No, I prefer these.*
Este reloj es más barato que **ése**.	*This watch is cheaper than that one.*

■ Use the neuter form of the demonstratives: **esto, eso,** or **aquello** to say *this* or *that* when referring to a general idea or a situation rather than to a specific noun, or when referring to a noun that has not yet been identified.

Eso es imposible.	*That is impossible.*
Esto es muy importante.	*This is very important.*
¿Qué es **aquello**?	*What is that (over there)?*

👥 5-15 ▶ **Preferencias.** Imagina que estás de compras con un/a amigo/a. Usando la forma correcta de los adjetivos demostrativos, pregúntale a un/a compañero/a de clase cuál de los artículos de ropa prefiere. Tu compañero/a debe contestar según sus gustos (*according to his/her tastes*).

Modelo

ESTE/A/OS/AS	ESE/A/OS/AS	AQUEL/AQUELLA/OS/AS
pantalones negros	jeans	pantalones blancos

E1: *¿Prefieres estos pantalones negros, esos jeans o aquellos pantalones blancos?*
E2: *Prefiero los jeans.*

ESTE/A/OS/AS	ESE/A/OS/AS	AQUEL/AQUELLA/OS/AS
1. corbata roja	corbata azul	corbata verde
2. camisa rosada	camisa negra	camisa blanca
3. sandalias	tenis	botas
4. falda corta	falda larga	vestido
5. traje gris	traje negro	traje blanco
6. camiseta de la universidad	camiseta multicolor	camiseta blanca o de un solo color
7. blusa sin mangas (*sleeveless*)	blusa de manga larga	blusa de manga corta

5-16 ▶ De compras. Estás en una tienda con una amiga que busca ropa nueva. Completa cada pregunta con **este / esta / estos / estas** y hazle la pregunta a otro/a estudiante. Tu compañero/a de clase debe contestar que es lo opuesto (*the opposite*) de lo que tú crees.

Modelo   E1: ¿Es demasiado largo *este* vestido?
          E2: *No, es demasiado corto.*

1. ¿Son demasiado grandes ___*estos*___ zapatos?
2. ¿Es muy cara ___*esta*___ camisa?
3. ¿Es demasiado larga ___*esta*___ falda?
4. ¿Es feo ___*este*___ traje?
5. ¿Es demasiado corto ___*este*___ cinturón?
6. ¿Son muy caros ___*estos*___ suéteres?
7. ¿Son de buena calidad (*quality*) ___*estas*___ botas?
8. ¿Son muy altos ___*estos*___ precios?

5-17 ▶ Cumplidos. En parejas, utilicen **ese / esa / esos / esas** con estos adjetivos para hacerles cumplidos (*to compliment*) a sus compañeros de clase. Pueden usar **parecer** para decir *to seem* o *to look* o **ser** (*to be*).

agradable	cómodo	de última moda	nuevo
bonito	de buena calidad	elegante	práctico
caro	de un color bonito	fácil de lavar	versátil

Modelos   *Mario, esos zapatos parecen muy cómodos.*
           Anita, esa camiseta es muy bonita.

5-18 ▶ Mis favoritos. Entrevista a tu compañero/a sobre sus cosas y personas favoritas. Después, reacciona a su respuesta con una de las expresiones de la lista y explica por qué te gusta o no.

> **Ese / Esa . . . también me gusta.**
> **Ese / Esa . . . no me gusta.**
> **No conozco (*I'm not familiar with*) ese / esa . . .**

Modelo   tu tienda favorita
          E1: *¿Cuál es tu tienda favorita?*
          E2: *Mi tienda favorita es Macy's.*
          E1: *Esa tienda también me gusta. Tiene ropa bonita. /*
              Esa tienda no me gusta. Tiene precios altos. /
              No conozco esa tienda.

1. tu restaurante favorito
2. tu película favorita
3. tu color favorito
4. tu actor favorito
5. tu actriz favorita
6. tu ciudad favorita
7. tu programa de televisión favorito
8. tu canción (*song*) favorita

5-19 ▶ ¿Cuál prefieres? En parejas, inventen una conversación entre estas amigas, Alicia y Elena.

Modelo   E1: *Alicia, ¿me debo comprar este vestido?*
          E2: *Ese vestido no me gusta mucho, Elena.*
              Prefiero esta falda y cuesta menos.
              ¿Te gusta esta falda anaranjada y negra?. . .

📖 Gramática 2
SAM: 5-22
to 5-25

Saying what you intend to do: Using reflexive and reciprocal verbs in the infinitive

■ When a conjugated verb is followed by a reflexive / reciprocal verb in the infinitive, the reflexive / reciprocal pronoun may be placed either before the conjugated verb or attached to the end of the infinitive without changing the meaning of the sentence. The pronoun must correspond to the subject of the conjugated verb.

Me voy a levantar temprano.
Voy a levantar**me** temprano.   } *I'm going to get up early.*

■ To say what someone just did, use **acabar de** followed by an infinitive. **Acabar** is conjugated as a regular -**ar** verb.

Acabamos de comer.   *We just ate.*
Acabo de levantarme.
Me **acabo de** levantar.   } *I just got up.*

5-20 ▶ ¿Y el sábado? ¿Van a hacer estas personas las actividades indicadas entre paréntesis este sábado? Utiliza el pronombre reflexivo o recíproco lógico.

Este sábado . . .

Modelo   (Yo) . . . (levantarse antes de las seis de la mañana)
(No) Voy a levantarme antes de las seis de la mañana. /
(No) Me voy a levantar antes de las seis de la mañana.

1. (Yo) . . . (levantarse tarde, quedarse en casa por la mañana, relajarse por la tarde, ponerse un traje, casarse, acostarse después de la dos de la mañana)
2. Mi mejor amigo/a y yo . . . (verse, encontrarse en el centro, divertirse juntos/as, quedarse en el centro hasta muy tarde, relajarse juntos/as en mi casa)
3. Mi madre . . . (despertarse temprano, quedarse todo el día en casa, levantarse tarde, maquillarse, ponerse ropa formal para salir por la noche, relajarse por la noche)

5-21 ▶ ¿Qué van a hacer? Un hombre habla con su esposa sobre la familia y el trabajo. Completa cada oración con un infinitivo lógico de la lista. Cambia el pronombre reflexivo si es necesario.

acostarse	divertirse	*levantarse*	ponerse	relajarse
despertarse	lavarse	maquillarse	quedarse	

Modelo   Acabo de despertarme pero no quiero *levantarme* inmediatamente.

1. ¿Acabas de bañarte? ¿Vas a ___maquillarte___ antes de vestirte o después?
2. Los niños acaban de desayunar. Ahora, necesitan ___lavarse___ los dientes antes de irse a la escuela.
3. Acabo de ponerme la camisa pero todavía (*still*) necesito ___ponerme___ la corbata.
4. Son las diez y acabo de llegar a la oficina. Voy a ___quedarme___ aquí hasta las seis.
5. Son las seis y acabo de salir del trabajo pero voy a ___divertirme___ un poco con mis compañeros de trabajo en un café antes de volver a casa.
6. Los niños acaban de ponerse el pijama y tienen sueño. Van a ___acostarse___.
7. Acabamos de trabajar todo el día. Ahora necesitamos ___relajarnos___. ¿Quieres ver un DVD?
8. Acabas de terminar una semana difícil. Mañana es sábado y puedes ___despertarte___ tarde.

5-22 ▶ Vacaciones de primavera (*Spring break*). Vas a pasar las vacaciones con un/a compañero/a de clase y quieres saber si tiene la misma rutina diaria. Traduce el verbo entre paréntesis para completar las siguientes preguntas.

Cuando estás de vacaciones . . .

1. ¿Te gusta ___levantarte___ (*to get up*) temprano o tarde?
2. ¿Necesitas café para ___despertarte___ (*to wake up*) por la mañana?
3. ¿Prefieres ___bañarte___ (*to bathe*) o ___ducharte___ (*to shower*) por la mañana o por la noche?
4. ¿Cuánto tiempo necesitas para ___vestirte___ (*to get dressed*) por la mañana?
5. ¿Qué te gusta hacer para ___divertirte___ (*to have fun*)?
6. ¿Te gusta ___acostarte___ (*to go to bed*) tarde?

 ¿Y tú? Ahora, usa las preguntas para entrevistar a otro/a estudiante sobre su rutina típica durante las vacaciones de primavera.

 5-23 ▶ Mis amigos y yo. Pregúntale a un/a compañero/a de clase cuál es la rutina de las personas indicadas.

Modelo   (Tú) . . . poder / levantarse tarde / todos los días
          E1: *¿Puedes levantarte tarde todos los días? | ¿Te puedes levantar tarde todos los días?*
          E2: *Puedo levantarme tarde sólo los sábados. | Me puedo levantar tarde sólo los sábados. ¿Y tú?*
          E1: *Yo puedo levantarme tarde todos los días menos los martes y jueves. | Yo me puedo levantar tarde todos los días menos los martes y jueves.*

Tú . . .

1. preferir / vestirse antes de desayunar o después
2. tener que / levantarse temprano los sábados
3. poder / relajarse hoy después de clase

Tus padres . . .

4. tener que / levantarse temprano los sábados
5. preferir / acostarse tarde o temprano los sábados
6. preferir / quedarse en casa los domingos

Tu mejor amigo/a y tú . . .

7. preferir / encontrarse en un café o en la casa de uno/a de ustedes
8. ir a / verse mañana
9. preferir / comunicarse por correo electrónico, por SMS (*text messaging*) o por teléfono

 5-24 ▶ Entrevista. Entrevista a otro/a estudiante con estas preguntas.

1. ¿A qué hora te vas a acostar esta noche? ¿Tienes que levantarte temprano mañana? ¿Vas a quedarte en casa mañana por la mañana? ¿A qué hora vas a irte de casa mañana?
2. ¿Puedes relajarte esta noche o tienes que estudiar o trabajar? ¿Qué haces para relajarte? ¿Escuchas música? ¿Lees un libro? ¿Ves la televisión?
3. ¿Qué haces para divertirte con los amigos? ¿Dónde prefieren encontrarse tus amigos y tú generalmente cuando salen? ¿Siempre se besan cuando se ven?

Note for 5-23.
In item 9 point out that *SMS* (*text messaging*) comes from the English words *Short Message Service* and is also known in Spanish as *Servicio de mensajes cortos*. You may wish to give students some common ways of texting words in Spanish: +*(más)*, *tb* (también), *k* (que), *nd* (nada), *tp* (tampoco), *x* (por), *xq* (porque). You may also wish to discuss whether students think texting could eventually affect spelling in a language or alter it in any other way.

Follow-up for 5-23.
Remind students of the use of the infinitive and the placement of reflexive pronouns after *antes de* and *después de*. Then, tell them: *Estás cuidando* (You are taking care of) *a dos niños. ¿Necesitan hacer los niños la primera actividad antes o después de la segunda?* Modelo: *lavarse los dientes / acostarse > Necesitan lavarse los dientes antes de acostarse.* 1. *levantarse inmediatamente / despertarse* 2. *desayunar / levantarse* 3. *lavarse los dientes / desayunar* 4. *bañarse / vestirse* 5. *ponerse el cinturón / ponerse los pantalones* 6. *salir para la escuela / vestirse* 7. *irse rápido para la escuela / llegar tarde* 8. *hacer su tarea / divertirse con los videojuegos* 9. *lavarse los dientes / acostarse* 10. *quedarse en la cama y dormir / acostarse*

Vocabulario Una fiesta

¿Qué están haciendo en la fiesta?
¿Se están divirtiendo **los invitados**?

CD 2
Track 32

¿Sabías que...?

Hay distintas maneras de brindar (*to toast*) en español. Algunos de los brindis (*toasts*) más tradicionales son **¡Salud!** (*To your health!*) y **¡Chinchín!** (*Cheers!*). Otros brindis populares son: **Arriba, abajo, al centro y adentro,** donde la persona hace los gestos indicados con la copa en la mano, y también **Salud, dinero, amor y tiempo para gozarlos** (*to enjoy them*).

¡Ojo!

In this *Tema*, you will learn a new verb form ending with **-ando** or **-iendo** (*-ing*). Note how it is used here to say what someone is do*ing* at the moment. You will learn more about using this verb form in the next grammar section.

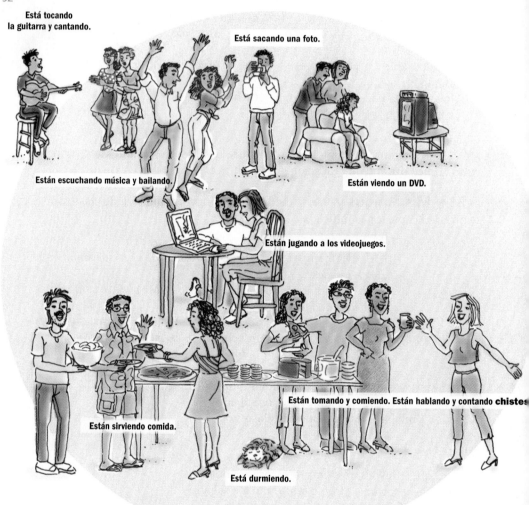

Está tocando la guitarra y cantando.

Está sacando una foto.

Están escuchando música y bailando.

Están viendo un DVD.

Están jugando a los videojuegos.

Están tomando y comiendo. Están hablando y contando **chistes**

Están sirviendo comida.

Está durmiendo.

Suggestions for *Una conversación.*
• Have students listen to the conversation first with books closed for the answers to the following questions. Then, have them read along in their books as they listen a second time. 1. ¿Qué está haciendo María? (*nada en especial*) 2. ¿Adónde va a ir María con Carlos y sus amigos? (*a una fiesta a la casa del primo de Carlos*)
• The only new word presented in the conversation is *chau*.

Possible answers for *¡A escuchar!*
Javier está en el parque. / Delia está limpiando la casa. (See facing page for Audioscript.)

CD 2, Track 34

¡A escuchar!

Ahora, escuchen otra conversación telefónica entre dos amigos, Delia y Javier. ¿Dónde está Javier? ¿Qué está haciendo Delia?

CD 2
Track 33

Una conversación. Dos amigos hablan por teléfono.

MARÍA: ¿Aló?
CARLOS: ¿Puedo hablar con María, por favor?
MARÍA: Soy yo. ¿Eres tú, Carlos?
CARLOS: Hola, María. ¿Cómo estás?
MARÍA: Bien, Carlos. ¿Y tú?
CARLOS: Bien. ¿Estás ocupada? ¿Qué estás haciendo?
MARÍA: Nada en especial. ¿Por qué?
CARLOS: Mis amigos y yo estamos en el café El Rincón y después vamos a una fiesta a la casa de mi primo. ¿Quieres ir con nosotros?
MARÍA: Sí, cómo no. Llego en veinte minutos.
CARLOS: Está bien. Hasta luego.
MARÍA: Chau.

---

los invitados *the guests* **un chiste** *a joke*

5-25 ▶ ¿Qué tal la fiesta? ¿Es una fiesta divertida o aburrida si los invitados están haciendo estas cosas?

Modelo   Todos están hablando.
          Es una fiesta divertida.

1. Están hablando de política.
2. Están escuchando música hip-hop.
3. Todos están jugando a los videojuegos.
4. Están viendo videos de las vacaciones de tu mejor amigo/a.
5. Todos están contando chistes.
6. Están viendo el Superbowl en la tele.
7. Todos están bailando.
8. Todos están divirtiéndose.

5-26 ▶ Una fiesta. Estás en una fiesta en la casa de un amigo. ¿Qué están haciendo todos? Completa las oraciones con un verbo lógico de la lista.

abrazándose	cantando	jugando	tomando
bailando	comiendo	*sirviendo*	viendo
besándose	durmiendo	tocando	

Modelo   Mi amigo está *sirviendo* la comida.

1. Unos amigos y yo estamos ___viendo___ un video.
2. Yo estoy ___tomando___ limonada.
3. Dos novios están ___bailando___ un tango.
4. Alguien está ___durmiendo___ una siesta en el sofá.
5. Alguien está ___tocando___ el piano y ___cantando___ canciones.
6. El gato está ___comiendo___ la comida de un invitado.
7. Unos invitados están ___jugando___ a los videojuegos.
8. Dos novios están ___abrazándose___ y ___besándose___ enfrente de todos.

5-27 ▶ Otra conversación. En parejas, vuelvan a leer *Una conversación* entre Carlos y María. Luego, cambien la conversación para invitar a su compañero/a de clase a hacer algo.

5-28 ▶ Comparaciones culturales. En los países hispanos, la música es un elemento esencial de su cultura y la variedad de ritmos es excepcionalmente rica (*rich*). Lee la información y contesta las preguntas.

■ La música del Caribe representa una combinación exuberante de ritmos africanos, europeos e indígenas. Una gran parte de los ritmos caribeños tiene su origen en la música de los esclavos traídos (*slaves brought*) de África. La salsa, el merengue, el danzón y el mambo son bailes típicos de Cuba, Puerto Rico, la República Dominicana y la costa de Colombia y Venezuela. En tu región, ¿hay música con influencias africanas, europeas o indígenas?

■ La música de mariachi es una representación del folklore mexicano. Los grupos de mariachis están formados generalmente por violines, trompetas y guitarras. Generalmente la música de mariachi expresa sentimientos de amor o describe la vida rural de México. En Estados Unidos y Canadá, ¿qué ritmos musicales representan el folklore o describen la vida rural de las distintas partes del país?

■ El tango, creado por los inmigrantes pobres de Buenos Aires entre 1850 y 1890, es un baile típicamente argentino lleno de pasión y con mucho contacto físico. Esto escandaliza a la sociedad conservadora de la época y el tango es prohibido. Pero la gente continúa bailando en secreto. En tu cultura, ¿hay música o bailes escandalosos para algunas personas? ¿Por qué son escandalosos?

Tango en el Barrio de San Telmo.

 Gramática 1

SAM: 5-28
to 5-31

Describing what people are doing at the moment: The present progressive

Para averiguar

1. What is the ending of the present participle of -**ar** verbs in Spanish? What is the ending of -**er** and -**ir** verbs? These endings correspond to what verb ending in English?
2. Which verb meaning *to be* do you use with present participles to say what is happening?
3. When does the **i** of the -**iendo** ending change to **y**?
4. Which category of verbs has stem changes in present participles: -**ar**, -**er**, or -**ir**? What do **o** and **e** become?
5. In the present progressive, what are the two possible placements of the reflexive pronoun? When the pronoun is attached to the end of the present participle, what do you write on the stressed syllable of the verb?
6. What are two cases in which the present progressive is used in English, but not in Spanish?

Suggestion.
The present participles of *preferir* (*prefiriendo*) and *venir* (*viniendo*) are not included in the list of stem-changing -*ir* verbs, because they are generally not used in the present progressive. You may wish to present them as well, and point out that they are generally used only in sentences such as: *Prefiriendo descansar, mi esposo nunca quiere salir los sábados.*

Suggestion.
You may wish to point out to students that present participles cannot be used as nouns in Spanish, and that you use infinitives instead: *Ver es creer.* (Seeing is believing.)

Supplemental activities.
• Ask students: *¿Dónde está tu amigo si está haciendo estas cosas?* MODELO: *Está comprando un libro. > Está en la librería.* 1. *Está levantando pesas.* 2. *Está nadando.* 3. *Está durmiendo.* 4. *Está asistiendo a clase.* 5. *Está tomando el sol.* 6. *Está viendo una película.*
• Ask students: *¿Qué hora es si estás haciendo estas cosas los días de clase?* MODELO: *Estás desayunando. > Son entre las siete y media y las ocho de la mañana. / Nunca desayuno los días de clase.* 1. *Estás almorzando.* 2. *Estás haciendo tu tarea.* 3. *Estás trabajando.* 4. *Estás viendo la televisión.* 5. *Estás cenando.*
• Ask students: *¿Quién está haciendo estas cosas ahora en nuestra clase?* MODELO: *comiendo > Mónica y Lisa están comiendo. Nadie está comiendo.* (*hablando, durmiendo, escuchando las preguntas, escribiendo, comiendo, tomando café, buscando algo, leyendo, fumando, mirando al / a la profesor/a, haciendo este ejercicio*)

■ Use the present progressive to say what someone is in the process of doing at a particular moment.

■ The present progressive is composed of a conjugated form of **estar** followed by the present participle, which is the equivalent of the -*ing* form of the verb in English. The present participle is formed by replacing the -**ar** ending of infinitives with -**ando,** and -**er** or -**ir** with -**iendo.**

hablar	→	**hablando**	¿Quién **está hablando**?	*Who is talking?*
comer	→	**comiendo**	**Estamos comiendo.**	*We're eating.*
escribir	→	**escribiendo**	¿Qué **estás escribiendo**?	*What are you writing?*

■ The initial **i** of the -**iendo** ending changes to **y** when it falls between two vowels. This occurs with **leer (leyendo), oír (oyendo),** and **creer (creyendo).**

leer	→	**leyendo**	¿Qué **estás leyendo**?	*What are you reading?*

■ There is no stem change in the present participle of -**ar** and -**er** stem-changing verbs.

almorzar	→	**almorzando**	¿Estás **almorzando**?	*Are you having lunch?*
perder	→	**perdiendo**	Estamos **perdiendo.**	*We're losing.*

■ Stem-changing -**ir** verbs have the following changes in the present participle.

o → u:	dormir → **durmiendo**	Todos **están durmiendo.**	*Everyone is sleeping.*
e → i:	servir → **sirviendo**	**Están sirviendo** la cena.	*They're serving dinner.*

Other stem-changing -**ir** verbs you have seen include: **decir (diciendo), pedir (pidendo), repetir (repitiendo), vestir (vistiendo),** and **divertir (divirtiendo).**

■ In the present progressive, reflexive pronouns may be placed either before the conjugated form of **estar** or attached to the end of the present participle. When attached to the end of the present participle, there is a written accent mark over the **a** or **e** of the -**ando** or -**iendo** ending.

Se están divirtiendo. / Están divirtié**ndo**se.	*They are having fun.*
Me estoy sirviendo café. / Estoy sirvié**ndo**me café.	*I'm serving myself some coffee.*

■ In Spanish, the present progressive is rarely used with verbs that indicate coming and going. The simple present tense is used instead.

Vamos con ustedes.	*We're going with you.*
Vienen ahora.	*They're coming now.*

■ Do not use the present progressive to express future actions as you do in English. Use the immediate future (**ir a** + infinitive) instead.

Voy a trabajar este fin de semana.	*I'm working this weekend.*

■ Remember to use infinitives instead of present participles after **antes de** and **después de**.

antes de **dormir**	*before sleeping*
después de **levantarse**	*after getting up*

5-29 ▶ ¿Dónde estás? Estás en los siguientes lugares y alguien te llama (*calls you*) al celular. En parejas, preparen conversaciones para decir dónde estás y qué estás haciendo allí utilizando una actividad lógica de la lista.

bailar con mis amigos	*dormir la siesta*	*tomar un café*
buscar unos zapatos nuevos	**estudiar**	**ver una exposición**
cenar	**hacer ejercicio**	**ver un partido de fútbol**
comprar un libro	**jugar al fútbol**	**americano**
divertirse con los amigos	**nadar**	

Modelo   en un club nocturno
E1: *¿Dónde estás?*
E2: *Estoy en un club nocturno.*
E1: *¿Qué estás haciendo?*
E2: *Estoy bailando con mis amigos.*

1. en un café
2. en la playa
3. en la biblioteca
4. en el parque

5. en una fiesta
6. en el centro comercial
7. en casa
8. en el gimnasio

9. en una librería
10. en un restaurante
11. en el estadio
12. en el museo

5-30 ▶ ¿Qué está haciendo?
¿Qué está haciendo Adela?

Modelo   *Está levantándose.*
Se está levantando.

1.

2.

3.

4.

5.

6.

5-31 ▶ ¿En qué orden? Un padre habla de lo que (*what*) acaba de hacer y lo que está haciendo ahora su familia. ¿Cuál es el orden lógico?

Modelo   yo (vestirse / bañarse)
Acabo de bañarme. Ahora estoy vistiéndome.
(Me acabo de bañar. Ahora me estoy vistiendo.)

1. yo (despertarse / preparar el desayuno)
2. mi esposa (bañarse / levantarse)
3. nosotros (almorzar / sentarse a comer)
4. mi esposa y yo (lavar los platos / comer)
5. mi esposa (sentarse en el sofá / dormir la siesta)
6. nuestra hija mayor (maquillarse para salir / bañarse)
7. nuestra hija mayor (salir para una fiesta / divertirse con los amigos)
8. nuestros hijos menores (acostarse / dormir)

📖 Gramática 2

SAM: 5-32 to 5-35

Making plans and setting the date: Months and dates

¡Ojo!

When referring to today's date, Spanish speakers will often omit **el** before the number: **Hoy es nueve de abril.** Note that it is never omitted when referring to when an event will take place: **El próximo examen es el veinte de abril.**

Answers for 5-32.
1. *el 16 de septiembre;* 2. *el 5 de mayo;* 3. *el 2 de noviembre;* 4. *el 4 de julio;* 5. *el 12 de octubre;* 6. *el 15 de septiembre;* 7. *el 27 de febrero;* 8. *el 28 de julio;* 9. *el 5 de julio;* 10. *el 9 de julio*

■ To give the date, use the ordinal number **primero** for the first of a month, but use the cardinal numbers (**dos, tres, cuatro . . . treinta y uno**) for the other days. The names of months are not capitalized in Spanish. As with days of the week, use **el** to say *on* a date.

El primero / dos / tres . . . de . . .

enero	*January*	**mayo**	*May*	**septiembre**	*September*
febrero	*February*	**junio**	*June*	**octubre**	*October*
marzo	*March*	**julio**	*July*	**noviembre**	*November*
abril	*April*	**agosto**	*August*	**diciembre**	*December*

— ¿Qué fecha es hoy? — *What's the date today?*
— Es el veinte de diciembre. — *It's December twentieth.*
— ¿Qué vas a hacer para la Navidad? — *What are you going to do for Christmas?*
— Voy a estar en México. Voy a volver el primero de enero. — *I'm going to be in Mexico. I'm going to return on January first.*

■ When talking about a period of several days or more, you can use **desde** to give the starting date and **hasta** to say *until when.*

Voy a estar de vacaciones **desde** el veintitrés de diciembre **hasta** el dos de enero.

I'm going to be on vacation (starting) from the twenty-third of December until January second.

5-32 ▶ ¿Cuál es la fecha? ¿Con qué fecha de la lista asocias cada celebración? Adivina (*Guess*) si no estás seguro/a y tu profesor/a te dirá (*will tell you*) si la fecha correcta es antes o después hasta que tu respuesta sea correcta.

En Dolores (ahora Dolores Hidalgo), México, el cura (*priest*) Miguel Hidalgo inició la Guerra de Independencia en el año 1810 con el Grito de Dolores (*Cry from Dolores*). Cada 15 de septiembre un poco antes de la medianoche el presidente mexicano sale al balcón del Palacio Nacional para conmemorar este evento.

el 27 de febrero	el 28 de julio
el 5 de mayo	el 15 de septiembre
el 4 de julio	el 16 de septiembre
el 5 de julio	el 12 de octubre
el 9 de julio	el 2 de noviembre

1. el Día de la Independencia de México
2. la conmemoración de la victoria de los mexicanos contra los franceses en la batalla de Puebla
3. el Día de los Muertos en México
4. la Fiesta Nacional de Puerto Rico
5. la Fiesta Nacional de España
6. el Día de la Independencia de Costa Rica, El Salvador, Guatemala, Honduras y Nicaragua
7. el Día de la Independencia de la República Dominicana
8. el Día de la Independencia de Perú
9. el Día de la Independencia de Venezuela
10. el Día de la Independencia de Argentina

Originalmente creada para representar la clase social alta después de la revolución mexicana, la catrina es símbolo del Día de los Muerto, celebrado cada año el dos de noviembre.

5-33 ▶ ¿Qué vas a hacer? Pregúntale a otro/a estudiante si generalmente hace estas cosas en las fechas indicadas.

Modelo   el 31 de octubre / disfrazarse (*to dress up, to put on a costume*)
E1: *Generalmente, ¿te disfrazas el treinta y uno de octubre?*
E2: *A veces me disfrazo, pero otras veces no. ¿Y tú?*
E1: *Yo casi siempre me disfrazo.*

1. el 17 de marzo / ponerse ropa verde
2. el 25 de diciembre / pasar el día con la familia
3. el 31 de diciembre / salir con los amigos
4. el 1° de enero / levantarse temprano o tarde
5. el 14 de febrero / hacer algo especial
6. el 4 de julio / ver los fuegos artificiales (*fireworks*)

5-34 ▶ Un calendario. ¿Qué planes tiene esta persona para este mes?

Modelo   *Va a visitar a su abuelita el primero de mayo.*

Mayo

lunes	martes	miércoles	jueves	viernes	sábado	domingo
				1 visitar a abuelita	2	3 fiesta en San Antonio
4	5	6	7	8 ESTUDIAR	9	10
11	12	13	14	15 playa	16	17 viaje a México
	exámenes					
18	19	20	21	22 regresar de México	23 trabajo →	24
25 trabajo	26	27	28 →	29 exposición de arte	30	31

5-35 ▶ Una fiesta. En parejas, hablen de una fiesta imaginaria que van a hacer para el cumpleaños de uno/a de ustedes. ¿Cuándo y dónde van a hacer la fiesta? ¿A quiénes van a invitar y qué van a hacer para divertirse? Preparen una conversación lógica.

Recycle: Numbers from 0-100
Activities 5-33 and 5-34 recycle numbers from 0-100 from *Capítulo 1, Tema 2.*

Supplemental activities.
• Have students take turns guessing your birthday. Indicate whether your birthday is before or after the guessed date by saying *antes* or *después* after each guess until they narrow it down to the correct date. Repeat the activity having the class guess other students' birthdays.
• Have students refer to their syllabus and answer questions such as the following. 1. *¿En qué fecha vamos a hacer el examen sobre este capítulo?* 2. *¿En qué fecha vamos a hacer el examen final?* 3. *¿Vamos a hacer un examen oral este mes?* 4. *¿Cuál es la fecha del próximo examen oral?*

• Write the Spanish names of zodiac signs on the board. Read each sign's dates in random order and have students say what sign it is: *Acuario (20 de enero – 19 de febrero), Piscis (20 de febrero – 20 de marzo), Aries (21 de marzo – 19 de abril), Tauro (20 de abril – 20 de mayo), Géminis (21 de mayo – 21 de junio), Cáncer (22 de junio – 22 de julio), Leo (23 de julio – 22 de agosto), Virgo (23 de agosto – 21 de septiembre), Libra (22 de septiembre – 22 de octubre), Escorpión (23 de octubre – 21 de noviembre), Sagitario (22 de noviembre – 21 de diciembre), Capricornio (22 de diciembre – 19 de enero).* Print out current horoscopes from the Internet by searching *horóscopos* and have students summarize theirs using the immediate future.

Recycle: Ir a + infinitive
Activity 5-35 recycles *ir a* + infinitive from *Capítulo 2, Tema 3.*

Vocabulario — El tiempo y las estaciones

SAM: 5-36 to 5-42

¿Sabías que...?

En los países de habla hispana, las temperaturas aparecen en grados centígrados y no en grados Fahrenheit. Para convertir los grados centígrados a grados Fahrenheit, multiplica por 9/5 y suma (*add*) 32.

¡Ojo!

The progressive forms **está lloviendo** (*it is raining*) and **está nevando** (*it is snowing*) are commonly used to say how the weather is at a particular moment. Use the infinitives **llover** and **nevar** to say how the weather is going to be in the near future: **Va a llover / nevar.** (*It's going to rain / snow.*)

Suggestion for *Una conversación.*
Have students listen to the conversation first with books closed for the answers to the following questions. 1. *¿Qué van a hacer si hace buen tiempo mañana? (Carlos va a trabajar e ir al parque. Lupe va a ir de compras.)* 2. *¿Qué van a hacer si llueve? (Carlos va a estudiar y Lupe va a pasar el día en casa.)* Then, have them read along in their books as they listen a second time.

Possible answers for ¡A escuchar!
Va a llegar el lunes a las dos y media de la tarde. / Esta semana no hace frío pero llueve casi todos los días. / Si hace mal tiempo van a ir al museo, a un concierto y al teatro. (See facing page for Audioscript.)

CD 2, Track 37

¡A escuchar!

Ahora, escuchen otra conversación en la cual Sonia va a visitar a Cristina, una amiga que vive muy lejos. ¿Cuándo va a llegar? ¿Qué tiempo hace esta semana? ¿Qué van a hacer si hace mal tiempo?

CD 2 Track 35

¿Cuál es tu **estación** favorita?

la primavera (20 de marzo – 21 de junio)
el verano (21 de junio – 22 de septiembre)
el otoño (22 de septiembre – 21 de diciembre)
el invierno (21 de diciembre – 20 de marzo)

¿Qué tiempo hace?

Hace sol. **El cielo** está **despejado**. Hace buen tiempo.

Hace (mucho) viento.

El cielo está nublado.

Llueve.

Nieva.

Hace (mucho) frío.

Hace fresco.

Hace (mucho) calor.

CD 2 Track 36

Una conversación. Dos amigos, Lupe y Carlos, hablan de sus planes para mañana.

LUPE: ¿Qué vas a hacer mañana?
CARLOS: Tengo que trabajar por la mañana. Por la tarde, quiero ir al parque si hace buen tiempo. Si llueve, voy a estudiar. ¿Y tú? ¿Qué vas a hacer?
LUPE: Nada en especial. Si hace mal tiempo, voy a pasar el día en casa. Quiero dormir hasta tarde. Si hace buen tiempo, tengo ganas de ir de compras.

la estación *season*   **¿Qué tiempo hace?** *What's the weather like?*   **el cielo** *the sky*   **despejado/a** *clear*

5-36 ▶ ¿Es lógico? Completa cada oración con la terminación lógica.

Modelo   Hace frío y *nieva* (hace calor, nieva).

En Taxco, México, cada día es como un día de primavera.

1. Hace calor y ___*hace sol*___. (hace fresco, hace sol).
2. Llueve y *hace mal tiempo*. (hace mal tiempo, hace sol).
3. El cielo está nublado y ___*llueve*___. (llueve, hace sol).
4. El cielo está despejado y ___*hace sol*___. (llueve, hace sol).
5. Hace sol y *hace buen tiempo*. (hace buen tiempo, nieva).

5-37 ▶ Cuando . . . ¿Qué te gusta hacer cuando hace el tiempo indicado?

comer en el patio	ir de compras	leer
dormir	ir al cine / lago / parque	nadar
esquiar	jugar a los videojuegos	quedarse en casa
ir a la playa	jugar al tenis	. . .

Modelo   Cuando hace fresco, *me gusta correr por el parque.*

1. Cuando llueve . . .
2. Cuando nieva . . .
3. Cuando hace mucho frío . . .
4. Cuando hace mucho calor . . .
5. Cuando hace buen tiempo . . .

5-38 ▶ ¿Qué te pones? Describe la ropa que te pones cuando hace el tiempo indicado en la actividad anterior.

Modelo   Cuando hace fresco, *me pongo una camisa, un suéter y jeans.*

5-39 ▶ Otra conversación. En parejas, vuelvan a leer *Una conversación* entre Carlos y Lupe. Luego, preparen una conversación en la cual hablen de sus planes para este sábado si hace buen tiempo y si hace mal tiempo.

5-40 ▶ Comparaciones culturales. El clima afecta en cierta forma la personalidad de la gente y sus rutinas. Lee la siguiente información y contesta las preguntas.

El Caribe hispano, Cuba, Puerto Rico y la República Dominicana es un claro ejemplo de cómo el clima soleado (*sunny*) de todo el año influye en el carácter alegre (*joyful*) de las personas. Los caribeños tienen, en general, una actitud positiva ante la vida. Les gusta disfrutar de (*enjoy*) la vida y relajarse sin estrés ni prisas. El clima también afecta la actividad diaria de la gente. En climas cálidos (*warm*), como el Caribe, las personas socializan con frecuencia en la calle, porque hace buen tiempo y es agradable pasar tiempo al aire libre, en parques, plazas o junto (*by*) al mar. La luz del sol es fuente (*sunlight is a source*) de energía y vitalidad, y según los expertos, las personas que viven en climas cálidos son más sociables y abiertas que las personas que viven en climas fríos que son, generalmente, más reservadas.

1. ¿Crees que en las zonas cálidas de Estados Unidos la gente es más sociable y menos reservada que en las regiones más frías? ¿Crees que el clima es un factor en las diferencias de carácter?
2. ¿Cómo crees que influye el clima en la rutina y las diversiones de una persona que vive en Boston y una persona que vive en Miami?

Resumen de gramática

SAM: 5-43
to 5-46

Reflexive verbs

- Reflexive verbs describe actions that people do to or for themselves.

- In Spanish, verbs are also often reflexive when describing a change in mental or physical state: **aburrirse, despertarse (ie), divertirse (ie), enojarse, relajarse, sentirse (ie).**

  Reflexive verbs are also used when saying people do something to their own body: **acostarse (ue), bañarse, ducharse, lavarse (el pelo), levantarse, maquillarse, ponerse (la ropa), sentarse (ie), vestirse (i).**

- After reflexive verbs, the definite article (**el, la, los, las**) is used instead of possessive adjectives (*my, your, . . .*) with parts of the body or items of clothing.

- Reflexive pronouns are placed before the conjugated verb.

- With infinitives and present participles, they may be placed before the conjugated verb or attached to end of the infinitive or **-ando** / **-iendo** form of the verb.

- Note that after **antes de, después de,** or **para,** the reflexive pronoun must be placed at the end of an infinitive.

Reflexive Pronouns

me	*myself*		**nos**	*ourselves*
te	*yourself*		**os**	*yourselves*
se	*yourself, oneself, himself, herself,*		**se**	*yourselves, themselves*

bañarse *to bathe (oneself)*

yo	**me**	baño		nosotros/as	**nos**	bañamos
tú	**te**	bañas		vosotros/as	**os**	bañáis
Ud., él, ella	**se**	baña		Uds., ellos/as	**se**	bañan

—Generalmente, ¿dónde **te sientas** en clase?
—**Me siento** cerca del profesor.
—¿**Te aburres** en tus clases?

—**Me aburro** a veces, pero normalmente **me divierto**.

—*Generally, where do you sit in class?*
—*I sit near the professor.*
—*Do you get bored in your classes?*

—*I get bored sometimes, but normally I have fun.*

Me lavo **el** pelo todos los días. — *I wash **my** hair every day.*

Me visto en quince minutos. — *I get dressed in fifteen minutes.*

Me estoy visitiendo ahora. / Estoy vistiéndo**me** ahora. — *I'm getting dressed now.*

Me voy a vestir en el baño. / Voy a vestir**me** en el baño. — *I'm going to dress in the bathroom.*

Me maquillo después de vestir**me**. — *I put on my make-up after getting dressed.*

Reciprocal verbs

- Reciprocal verbs indicate that two or more people do something to or for one another or each other. Reciprocal verbs have the same pronouns (**nos, os, se**) and the same placement rules as reflexive verbs.

—¿**Se** ven tu novia y tú todos los días?
—Sí, **nos** encontramos después del trabajo para cenar.

—*Do you and your girlfriend see each other every day?*
—*Yes, we meet each other after work for dinner.*

Acabar de

- To say what someone just did, use **acabar de** + an infinitive. **Acabar** is a regular **-ar** verb.

Acabamos de levantarnos.
Acabo de lavarme el pelo.
¿**Acabas de** llegar?

We just got up.
I just washed my hair.
Did you just arrive?

Demonstrative adjectives and pronouns

- Use the demonstrative adjectives to say *this / these* or *that / those*. There are two ways to say *that / those*, **ese** and **aquel**. **Aquel** is generally used to describe something at a greater distance than **ese**.

- Demonstrative pronouns look like demonstrative adjectives, but they may have a written accent on the stressed **e**, and the noun is omitted.

- Use the neuter forms: **esto, eso**, and **aquello** to refer to an idea or a situation rather than to a specific noun, or to refer to an unidentified noun.

este *(this / these)*	**ese** *(that / those)*	**aquel** *(that / those)*
este sombrero	ese sombrero	aquel sombrero
esta falda	esa falda	aquella falda
estos zapatos	esos zapatos	aquellos zapatos
estas botas	esas botas	aquellas botas

¿Te gusta **este** traje o prefieres **ése** detrás de ti?

Do you like this suit or do you prefer that one behind you?

Eso es imposible.
Esto es muy importante.

That is impossible.
This is very important.

Present progressive

- Use the present progressive to describe actions in progress at a particular moment. It is composed of a conjugated form of **estar** and the present participle (**-ando / -iendo** form of the verb). The **i** of **-iendo** changes to **y** between vowels.

- Stem changes occur only with **-ir** verbs in the present progressive. With these verbs **o** changes to **u** and **e** changes to **i**. There is no stem change for **-ar** and **-er** stem-changing verbs.

- In Spanish, the present progressive is rarely used with **ir** or **venir**. The simple present tense is used instead.

- Do not use the present progressive to express future actions as you do in English. Use the immediate future (**ir a** + infinitive) instead.

hablar → **hablando**   ¿Quién está hablando?   *Who is talking?*
comer → **comiendo**   Estamos comiendo.   *We are eating.*
escribir → **escribiendo**   ¿Qué estás escribiendo?   *What are you writing?*

leer → le**y**endo   ¿Qué estás leyendo?   *What are you reading?*

dormir → d**u**rmiendo   ¿Está durmiendo el bebé?   *Is the baby sleeping?*
servir → s**i**rviendo   ¿Qué estás sirviendo?   *What are you serving?*
almorzar → almorzando   ¿Estás almorzando?   *Are you having lunch?*
perder → perdiendo   Estamos perdiendo.   *We are losing.*

¿Adónde vas?   *Where are you going?*
¿Vienen hoy?   *Are they coming today?*

¿Qué vas a hacer esta noche?   *What are you doing tonight?*
Voy a quedarme en casa.   *I'm staying home.*

Dates

- To give the date, use **primero** for the first of a month, but use the cardinal numbers (**dos, tres . . . treinta y uno**) for the other days. Months are not capitalized in Spanish.

- When giving a range of dates, use **desde** to give the starting date and **hasta** to say *until* when.

Siempre voy a muchas fiestas **el treinta y uno de diciembre** y duermo todo el día **el primero de enero**.

I always go to many parties on December thirty-first and sleep all day on January first.

Voy a estar de vacaciones **desde** el quince de agosto **hasta** el primero de septiembre.

I'm going to be on vacation from August fifteenth until September first.

SAM: 5-47 to 5-50

📖 **EN EL SERVICIO DE PROTECCIÓN AL MENOR**

En este capítulo, aprendiste (*you learned*) a hablar de la rutina diaria. Ahora vas a repasar lo que aprendiste con una simulación de la vida real trabajando para el Servicio de Protección al Menor (*Child Protective Services*).

5-41 ▶ Custodia temporal. Estás a cargo de (*in charge of*) dos hermanos, Diego y Lorenzo. Si se portan (*behave*) bien, ¿hacen las siguientes cosas o no?

Modelos llevarse bien irritarse todo el tiempo
Sí, se llevan bien. *No, no se irritan todo el tiempo.*

1. decirse cosas feas
2. hablarse con respeto
3. insultarse
4. pelearse
5. enojarse todo el tiempo
6. ayudarse

5-42 ▶ ¿Ángel o diablito? Lorenzo, el hermano mayor, se describe como un niño casi perfecto, pero dice que su hermano menor, Diego, tiene muchos problemas. ¿Qué dice Lorenzo que hace cada uno?

Modelo levantarse de mal humor (*mood*) / levantarse de buen humor
Diego se levanta de mal humor pero yo me levanto de buen humor.

1. despertarse muy poco durante la noche / despertarse mucho
2. enojarse con frecuencia / casi nunca enojarse
3. quedarse en la cama hasta muy tarde / casi siempre levantarse temprano
4. siempre lavarse los dientes / nunca lavarse los dientes
5. ponerse ropa sucia con frecuencia / siempre ponerse ropa limpia
6. acostarse temprano si hay clase al día siguiente / acostarse muy tarde

👥 **¿Y tú?** Ahora pregúntale a otro/a estudiante si es más como Lorenzo o más como su hermano menor Diego.

Modelo levantarse de mal humor (*mood*) / levantarse de buen humor
E1: *¿Te levantas de mal humor o te levantas de buen humor?*
E2: *Generalmente me levanto de buen humor.*

5-43 ▶ ¿Qué están haciendo? ¿Qué acaban de hacer los niños? ¿Qué están haciendo ahora? Utiliza los verbos en el orden lógico.

Modelo desayunar / levantarse
Los niños acaban de levantarse. Ahora están desayunando.

1. desayunar / lavarse los dientes
2. vestirse / bañarse
3. ponerse la chaqueta / vestirse
4. volver de la escuela / hacer su tarea
5. relajarse / terminar su tarea
6. enojarse / pelearse
7. acostarse / ponerse el pijama
8. acostarse / dormir

5-44 ▶ ¿Qué tiempo hace? Diles a los niños qué tiempo hace y qué ropa necesitan ponerse.

Modelo *Hace mucho frío. Necesitan ponerse un abrigo y botas.*

1.
2.
3.
4.

5-45 ▸ De compras. Estás buscando ropa para los niños en el centro comercial. En grupos de tres, preparen una conversación en la cual hablan de varias prendas (*articles of clothing*). Utilicen **este / esta / estos / estas, ese / esa / esos / esas** y **aquel / aquella / aquellos / aquellas** en la conversación.

5-46 ▸ Días feriados. Utiliza las fechas de la lista y explica cuando hay vacaciones en la escuela de los niños. ¡Ojo! En español se escribe el día antes del mes.

Modelo   *Las vacaciones de Navidad son desde el dieciocho de diciembre hasta el primero de enero.*

| 15/1 | 16/2 | 13/3–22/3 | 26/5 | 1/9 | 21/11–26/11 | 18/12–1/1 |

las vacaciones de Navidad
el Día del Trabajo
el Día de los Presidentes
las vacaciones de primavera

el Día de Conmemoración
(*Memorial Day*)
el cumpleaños de Martin Luther King
las vacaciones de Acción de Gracias

Entre profesionales

If you enjoy working with children, you might consider working in bilingual education. Visit MySpanishLab for *Hoy día* to find more useful vocabulary, information, and activities such as the following related to this field of work.

5-47 ▸ Una junta con la directora. La directora (*principal*) de una escuela bilingüe habla con un grupo de padres. Completa sus oraciones con el infinitivo lógico.

| ponerse | ofrecerse | familiarizarse | sentirse |
| comunicarse | reunirse (*to meet*) | presentarse | |

1. Para los padres es muy importante ___*sentirse*___ parte de la escuela de sus hijos. Una buena manera de ___*familiarizarse*___ con las actividades de la escuela y sus programas es ___*ofrecerse*___ como voluntario.
2. Los padres deben ___*reunirse*___ con los maestros varias veces al año para hablar sobre los progresos de sus hijos. Si vienen durante las horas de instrucción, es necesario ___*presentarse*___ en la oficina para firmar (*to sign*) el registro.
3. Si tienen preguntas, deben ___*comunicarse*___ con el maestro de su hijo o ___*ponerse*___ en contacto con el personal de la oficina.

Answers for 5-41.
1. *No, no se dicen cosas feas.* 2. *Sí, se hablan con respeto.* 3. *No, no se insultan.* 4. *No, no se pelean.* 5. *No, no se enojan todo el tiempo.* 6. *Sí, se ayudan.*

Follow-up for 5-41.
In pairs, have students prepare exchanges where they tell the children whether they need to do or should not do each thing listed in the activity. Their partner plays the role of the children saying what they are or are not going to do to behave. *MODELOS:* 1. — *Uds. necesitan llevarse bien.* — *Nos vamos a llevar bien.* 2. — *No deben irritarse todo el tiempo.* — *No vamos a irritarnos más.*

Answers for 5-42.
1. *Yo me despierto muy poco durante la noche, pero Diego se despierta mucho.* 2. *Diego se enoja con frecuencia, pero yo casi nunca me enojo.* 3. *Diego se queda en la cama hasta muy tarde, pero yo casi siempre me levanto temprano.* 4. *Yo siempre me lavo los dientes, pero Diego nunca se lava los dientes.* 5. *Diego se pone ropa sucia con frecuencia, pero yo siempre me pongo ropa limpia.* 6. *Yo me acuesto temprano si hay clase al día siguiente, pero Diego se acuesta muy tarde.*

Possible answers for 5-43.
1. *Los niños acaban de desayunar. Ahora se están lavando los dientes.* 2. *Los niños se acaban de bañar. Ahora se están vistiendo.* 3. *Los niños se acaban de vestir. Ahora se están poniendo la chaqueta.* 4. *Los niños acaban de volver de la escuela. Ahora están haciendo su tarea.* 5. *Los niños acaban de terminar su tarea. Ahora se están relajando.* 6. *Los niños se acaban de enojar. Ahora se están peleando.* 7. *Los niños se acaban de poner el pijama. Ahora se están acostando.* 8. *Los niños se acaban de acostar. Ahora están durmiendo.*

Possible answers for 5-44.
1. *Está lloviendo. Necesitan ponerse un impermeable.* 2. *Hace frío. Necesitan ponerse un abrigo y botas.* 3. *Hace fresco. Necesitan ponerse un suéter o una sudadera.* 4. *Hace calor. Necesitan ponerse pantalones cortos y una camiseta.*

Suggestion for 5-45.
Give students the following words and see how many they can include in a logical way in their conversations: *te gusta(n), preferir, barato, caro, razonable, desmasiado, bonito, feo, probarse, gastar, llevar, ponerse, buscar, costar, estar de moda.*

Possible answers for 5-46
El Día del Trabajo es el primero de septiembre. / El Día de los Presidentes es el dieciséis de febrero. / Las vacaciones de primavera son desde el trece hasta el veintidós de marzo. / El Día de Conmemoración es el veintiséis de mayo. / El cumpleaños de Martin Luther King es el quince de enero. / Las vacaciones de Acción de Gracias son desde el veintiuno al veintiséis de noviembre.

Pronóstico del tiempo

SAM: 5-51
to 5-52

Antes de leer

¿Cómo es el clima en tu ciudad? ¿Miras el pronóstico del tiempo normalmente? ¿Te vistes de acuerdo con (*according to*) las predicciones del tiempo?

> ▶ **Reading Strategy** *Using standard formats.* Standard formats, like the weather forecast and other visual materials, facilitate the reading of certain texts when learning a foreign language. For example, when you look at a weather forecast, there are certain details accompanied by visuals that are used universally, no matter what the language is. When reading in a foreign language, take into account the non-textual information to help you gather information.

Ahora tú

5-48 ▶ Pronóstico semanal. Observa con atención el gráfico del pronóstico del tiempo en Santiago, Chile. ¿Qué tiempo va a hacer cada día?

Modelo   *El lunes, dos de agosto va a hacer viento y va a hacer fresco.*

DISFRUTA CHILE.COM

El tiempo en Chile

Chile es un país de grandes contrastes y el clima refleja su variedad geográfica. El clima de Santiago, la capital, es mediterráneo. Las estaciones no están muy definidas y en realidad Santiago tiene una estación de lluvias y una estación seca[1]. Durante los meses de invierno, de mayo a septiembre, llueve bastante, pero generalmente no nieva mucho. El resto del año hace buen tiempo y las temperaturas son agradables. La temperatura media durante el invierno es de 8 grados centígrados aproximadamente, y la temperatura media durante el verano es de 19 grados centígrados.

Destinos
Vuelos
Hoteles
Ocio
Guía de restaurantes

Pronóstico semanal de Santiago de Chile

	jueves	viernes	sábado	domingo	lunes	martes	miércoles
	29 de julio	30 de julio	31 de julio	1 de agosto	2 de agosto	3 de agosto	4 de agosto
Mínima	3° C	0° C	2° C	6° C	5° C	4° C	3° C
Máxima	9° C	5° C	12° C	13° C	12° C	11° C	9° C

[1]*dry*

Después de leer

5-49 ▶ Un viaje a Santiago. Contesta las siguientes preguntas relacionadas con la lectura.

1. En Santiago, ¿están las estaciones del año bien definidas? ¿Cuántas estaciones hay?
2. ¿Cuándo es la estación de lluvias en Santiago? ¿Nieva también en la capital? Y en tu ciudad, ¿en qué estación llueve mucho? ¿Nieva algunas veces?
3. ¿Qué tiempo hace generalmente en agosto en tu ciudad? ¿Hace más frío o más calor que en Santiago, Chile?
4. Imagina que tus amigos y tú van a visitar Santiago de Chile, ¿en qué mes del año van a ir? ¿Por qué?
5. ¿Qué crees que hace la gente en Santiago durante los meses de julio y agosto? ¿Haces las mismas actividades en julio y agosto?

Possible answers for 5-49.
1. *No, las estaciones del año no están bien definidas. Hay dos estaciones, una estación de lluvias y una estación seca.* 2. *La estación de lluvias es de mayo a septiembre. No, no nieva generalmente en la capital.* For the remaining parts of 2. and for 3. 4. & 5. answers will vary.

5-50 ▶ ¿Qué tiempo está haciendo? Contesta las siguientes preguntas utilizando el presente progresivo cuando sea apropiado.

1. ¿Cuál es tu estación favorita? ¿Qué tiempo está haciendo ahora en tu ciudad?
2. ¿Influye el clima en las actividades que tú y tus amigos están planeando? ¿Cómo?
3. ¿Crees que está cambiando el clima en tu ciudad a causa del calentamiento global (*global warming*)? Si crees que sí, ¿cómo está cambiando?
4. ¿Qué efectos notas que está teniendo el calentamiento global en Estados Unidos o en el mundo (*the world*)?

5-51 ▶ Planes. Completa la conversación de estas dos amigas con el verbo adecuado de la lista. Atención a los pronombres reflexivos.

Recycle: Reflexive verbs
Activity 5-51 recycles reflexive verbs from *Tema 1*.

acostarse	encontrarse	llevarse	relajarse
divertirse	levantarse	quedarse	sentirse

FÁTIMA: Lola, ¿qué vas a hacer durante las vacaciones de primavera?

LOLA: No sé, acabo de terminar los exámenes, y prefiero (1) _quedarme_ en casa y (2) _relajarme_. Estoy muy cansada. ¿Y tú?

FÁTIMA: Voy a (3) _encontrarme_ con mi hermana que está estudiando en Santiago, Chile.

LOLA: ¡Qué bueno! Ustedes van a (4) _divertirse_ mucho.

FÁTIMA: Sí, pero no voy a descansar nada. Mi hermana es muy activa, y seguro que vamos a (5) _levantarnos_ todos los días temprano para ir de excursión, y vamos a (6) _acostarnos_ tarde porque a ella le gusta mucho salir por la noche a bailar.

LOLA: Sí, pero ella va a (7) _sentirse_ muy contenta con tu visita.

FÁTIMA: Hmmm . . . eso es si podemos (8) _llevarnos_ bien, porque cuando está aquí en casa, nos peleamos con frecuencia.

5-52 ▶ Más pronósticos del tiempo. Prepara un pronóstico del tiempo de tu ciudad para los próximos siete días. Utiliza como modelo el formato de las predicciones del tiempo en Santiago de Chile. Incluye las temperaturas en grados centígrados y en grados Fahrenheit.

Suggestion for 5-53.
Some examples of different ethnic groups that live in the United States: *alemanes, árabes, chinos, franceses, indios, irlandeses, italianos, japoneses, vietnamitas.*

Answers for 5-55.
1. *Sí, se sienten muy orgullosos de su herencia hispana.* 2. *Analissa e Itandehui se encuentran con muchos mexicanos en Nueva York, y Jorge y Rosal se encuentran con muchos puertorriqueños. Pero, Edgar no se encuentra con muchos paraguayos*

Answers for 5-55. (continued)
3. *Sí, se divierten viviendo su herencia en su vida diaria. Analissa escucha música mexicana y lee mucho en español. Jorge trabaja en una compañía de teatro en el Bronx que representa obras en español. Itandehui trabaja con la Academia de Mariachi de Nueva York. Edgar habla en guaraní con algunos amigos paraguayos y toma su hierba mate. Rosal no va a Puerto Rico con frecuencia y vive su herencia hispana en la ciudad.* 4. *Se sienten felices viviendo en Nueva York, porque la cultura hispana es muy accesible en la ciudad, en los restaurantes, el mundo de la música, las artes y la educación.*

📖 Mi gente, mi herencia

SAM: 5-53
to 5-55

Antes de ver

Cada vez más las tradiciones y las culturas del mundo se encuentran y la identidad es cada vez más global. Pero todavía las personas se sienten orgullosas (*proud*) de sus raíces (*roots*) y viven su herencia (*heritage*) de una manera especial. Escucha los testimonios de varios hispanos en el video que describen cómo viven su herencia.

5-53 ▶ Reflexiones. Piensa en los distintos grupos étnicos que viven en Estados Unidos. ¿Cómo crees que viven su herencia en su rutina diaria? Y tú, ¿cómo vives tu herencia familiar?

> **▶ Listening strategy** *Listening for words of the same family.* Adjectives that describe nationality derive from the name of the country of origin. In English, adjectives that describe nationality usually end in *-an*, *-ian*, *-n*. In Spanish, the most common endings for these adjectives are **-ano/a**, **-eño/a**, **-ino/a**, **-ol/a**, **-ayo/a**.
>
> de Perú → peru**ano/a**
> de Honduras → hondur**eño/a**
> de Argentina → argent**ino/a**
> de España → españ**ol/a**
> de Paraguay → paragu**ayo/a**

Ahora tú

🎬 **5-54 ▶ Soy de . . .** Escucha a las personas en el video e identifica su país o región de origen y su nacionalidad como en el Modelo.

Modelo   *Héctor es de Costa Rica. Es costarricense.*

1. Analissa   **2.** Jorge   **3.** Itandehui   **4.** Edgar   **5.** Rosal

Answers for 5-54.
1. *Analissa es de Texas. Es texana.* 2. *Jorge es de Puerto Rico. Es puertorriqueño.* 3. *Itandehui es de México. Es mexicana.* 4. *Edgar es de Paraguay. Es paraguayo.* 5. *Rosal es de Puerto Rico. Es puertorriqueña.*

Después de ver

5-55 ▶ ¿Se sienten orgullosos? Vuelve a escuchar con atención las palabras de las personas en el video que hablan sobre su herencia y sus raíces y responde de manera general a las siguientes preguntas.

1. ¿Se sienten orgullosos (*proud*) de su herencia?
2. ¿Se encuentran con gente de su mismo origen en la ciudad donde viven?
3. ¿Se divierten viviendo su herencia en su vida diaria? ¿Cómo se divierten?
4. ¿Cómo se sienten viviendo en Nueva York?

5-56 ▶ Descripciones. Describe a las siguientes personas del video e imaginen cómo es su rutina diaria y qué hacen cuando están con su familia y amigos.

1. Analissa Martínez, músico
2. Edgar Alcaraz, estudiante de administración de empresas
3. Hector Marín, pintor

Follow-up for 5-56.
Ask students to listen again to Itandehui's testimonial, and compare her leisure time activities with the activities that they and their friends do in their free time.

Confirmación de una visita

SAM: 5-56

Antes de escribir

Un/a amigo/a va a visitarte (*to visit you*) el próximo fin de semana. Vas a escribirle para confirmar las fechas de su visita, y contarle qué van a hacer, qué tiempo va a hacer y la ropa que debe traer.

> ▶ **Writing strategies** *Sequencing actions.* When talking about your plans, you will generally need to sequence events and activities using words and expressions that will provide order to your text and make it flow more smoothly. Here are some examples:
>
> | | | | |
> |---|---|---|---|
> | **primero** | *first* | **durante** | *during* |
> | **luego** | *then, next, later* | **mientras tanto** | *meanwhile* |
> | **más tarde** | *later* | **en seguida** | *right away* |
> | **pronto** | *soon* | **desde . . . hasta** | *(starting)* |
> | **después** | *afterwards* | | *from . . . until* |

¡Ojo!

Remember to use infinitives instead of the *-ing* form or a conjugated form of a verb after **antes de** and **después de**.

Vamos a relajarnos un poco **antes de salir**.
We are going to relax a little before going out.
We are going to relax a little before we go out.

5-57 ▶ **¡Prepárate!** Antes de escribir tu nota de confirmación, anota ideas relacionadas con las cuatro categorías siguientes:

■ las fechas de la visita de tu amigo/a
■ las actividades que van a realizar durante su visita
■ el tiempo que va a hacer
■ la ropa que él/ella debe traer

Ahora tú

5-58 ▶ **Tu nota de confirmación.** Escribe ahora tu nota de confirmación incluyendo ideas de las categorías mencionadas y un saludo (*greeting*) y una despedida (*farewell*) de la página 127.

Después de escribir

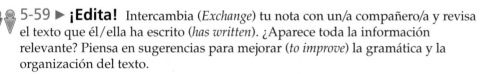

5-59 ▶ **¡Edita!** Intercambia (*Exchange*) tu nota con un/a compañero/a y revisa el texto que él/ella ha escrito (*has written*). ¿Aparece toda la información relevante? Piensa en sugerencias para mejorar (*to improve*) la gramática y la organización del texto.

5-60 ▶ **¡Revisa!** Revisa tu nota y asegúrate (*make sure*) que contenga los siguientes elementos:

❏ los verbos para hablar de actividades diarias
❏ el vocabulario para hablar del clima
❏ el vocabulario para hablar de la ropa
❏ las palabras y estructuras para indicar la secuencia de los eventos

5-61 ▶ **¡Navega!** Visita la página web de *Hoy día* para encontrar enlaces de buscadores (*links for search engines*) en español. Selecciona uno e introduce el nombre de tu ciudad, el estado y la palabra "turismo". ¿Hay sitios en español con información sobre el turismo en tu ciudad? ¿Describen actividades o lugares interesantes para incluir en tus planes de visita de tu amigo/a? ¿Qué otra información útil aparece?

5 Vocabulario

La rutina diaria

aburrirse	to get bored
acostarse (ue)	to lie down, to go to bed
bañarse	to bathe, to take a bath
despertarse (ie)	to wake up
divertirse (ie, i)	to have fun, to amuse yourself
ducharse	to shower, to take a shower
irse	to leave, to go away
lavarse el pelo / la cara	to wash your hair / your face
lavarse los dientes	to brush your teeth
levantarse	to get up
maquillarse	to put on make-up
ponerse (la ropa)	to put on (your clothes)
quedarse	to stay
relajarse	to relax
sentarse (ie)	to sit down
sentirse (ie, i)	to feel
vestirse (i, i)	to get dressed

Las interacciones personales

abrazar(se)	to hug (each other)
ayudar(se)	to help (each other)
besar(se)	to kiss (each other)
casarse (con)	to marry, to get married (to)
comunicar (se)	to communicate (with each other)
divorciarse (de)	to divorce, to get divorced (from)
enamorarse (de)	to fall in love (with)
encontrarse (ue) (con)	to get together (with), meet up (with)
enojarse	to get angry
llevarse bien (con)	to get along well (with)
pelearse	to fight
presentarse	to introduce yourself
querer(se) (ie)	to love (each other)

La ropa

el abrigo	overcoat
la blusa	blouse
la bolsa	purse
las botas	boots
los calcetines	socks
la camisa	shirt
la camiseta	T-shirt
la chaqueta	jacket
el cinturón	belt
la corbata	necktie
la falda	skirt
la gorra	cap
el impermeable	raincoat
los jeans	jeans
los pantalones	pants
los pantalones cortos	shorts
el pijama	pajamas
las sandalias	sandals
el sombrero	hat
la sudadera	sweatshirt
el suéter	sweater
los tenis	sneakers
el traje	suit
el traje de baño	swimsuit
el vestido	dress
los zapatos	shoes

De compras

el cliente / la clienta	customer
el dependiente / la dependienta	salesclerk
el precio	price
los probadores	fitting rooms
la talla	size

Acciones

buscar	to look for
gastar	to spend (money)
llevar	to take, to carry, to wear
llevarse	to take away
probarse (ue)	to try on

Descripciones

aquel / aquella (aquellos/as)	that (those) (over there)
barato/a	cheap
ese / esa (esos/as)	that (those)
este / esta (estos/as)	this (these)
razonable	reasonable

Otras palabras y expresiones

cómo no	of course
con cheque	with a check
con tarjeta de crédito / débito	with a credit / debit card
en efectivo	in cash
¿En qué puedo servirle?	How may I help you?
estar de moda	to be in fashion
por acá	over / through here

La fecha

¿Qué fecha es?	What is the date?
Es (el) primero (dos, tres . . .) de . . .	It's the first (second, third . . .) of . . .
enero	January
febrero	February
marzo	March
abril	April
mayo	May
junio	June
julio	July
agosto	August
septiembre	September
octubre	October
noviembre	November
diciembre	December

Otras palabras

¿Aló?	Hello? (on the telephone)
Chau.	Ciao., Bye.
el chiste	joke
el/la invitado/a	guest
sacar una foto	to take a picture

El tiempo

¿Qué tiempo hace?	What's the weather like?
El cielo está despejado / nublado.	The sky's clear / cloudy.
Hace buen / mal tiempo.	The weather's good / bad.
Hace (mucho) calor.	It's (very) hot.
Hace fresco.	It's cool.
Hace (mucho) frío.	It's (very) cold.
Hace sol.	It's sunny.
Hace viento.	It's windy.
Llueve.	It rains. It's raining.
Nieva.	It snows. It's snowing.
Va a llover / nevar.	It's going to rain / to snow.

Las estaciones del año

la primavera	spring
el verano	summer
el otoño	autumn, fall
el invierno	winter

 ▶ Visit MySpanishLab for *Hoy día* for links to the mnemonic dictionary online for suggestions such as the following to help you remember vocabulary from this chapter, learn related words in Spanish, and use Spanish words to build your vocabulary in English.

EXAMPLES

hacer calor, *to be hot:* The body burns **calor,**ies for heat. Related words in Spanish: **calentar (ie),** *to heat;* **calentarse (ie),** *to get hot, to warm up;* **un clima cálido,** *a warm climate;* **un día caluroso,** *a hot day;* **un plato caliente,** *a hot plate.*

hacer sol, *to be sunny:* **Sol**ar energy comes from the sun and a **sol**stice refers to a shifting in the position of the sun with respect to the northern and southern hemispheres. Related words in Spanish: **solar,** *solar;* **un día soleado,** *a sunny day;* **el solsticio,** *the solstice.*

6 En Internet

En este capítulo, vas a hablar de las computadoras y los usos de Internet y repasar (*review*) el vocabulario y la gramática de los capítulos anteriores.

Terra Networks es el proveedor (*provider*) de servicios de Internet número uno en Latinoamérica y España y produce más contenido original digital para los hispanos en Estados Unidos que cualquier (*any*) otra compañía. Según un estudio de Terra Networks, el 75% de los internautas (*Internet users*) hispanos en Estados Unidos utiliza frecuentemente Internet y ve la televisión al mismo tiempo. El 44% de este 75% envía (*sends*) mensajes instantáneos o por correo electrónico sobre el programa que está mirando. El 40% dice que busca información en Internet de productos anunciados en televisión y el 35% visita el sitio web del programa que está viendo.

- ▶ ¿Ves la tele mientras navegas en la web?
- ▶ ¿Envías mensajes sobre los programas que ves?
- ▶ ¿Buscas información en Internet de los productos que ves anunciados en televisión?

How to use the review chapter.
This review chapter has been designed to provide instructors with the flexibility to do all or part of it as a review in class or to have students do it using MySpanishLab at home. Communicative activities have been designed for interactive media so that students can complete them and receive feedback at home, and expansion activities are suggested in the teacher's notes for more open-ended communication in class.

Suggestion for chapter opener.
As students answer the questions in the culture note, you may wish to guide them with additional questions such as the following: *¿A qué hora usas más Internet? ¿A qué hora ves más la tele? ¿Con qué frecuencia envías mensajes sobre programas de televisión? ¿De qué programas hablas más con tus amigos? ¿Con qué frecuencia buscas información sobre actores por Internet? ¿Quiénes son los actores más buscados* (searched) *por Internet en este momento? ¿Haces más búsquedas* (searches) *sobre programas de televisión, sobre actores o sobre productos que ves en la tele?*

Note for statistical data.
See the IRM for source information relating to the statistical data presented.

Vocabulario Los procesadores de texto

SAM: 6-1
to 6-2

¿Sabías que...?

Con frecuencia se usan términos ingleses en español para hablar de las computadoras:

la web = la red
el email = el correo electrónico
el spam = el correo no deseado
el software = la aplicación informática / el programa informático
el hardware = los componentes físicos de una computadora
el comando = la orden

¡Ojo!

Comprehension strategies. Many words related to technology are cognates, and you can often guess the meanings of other words by basing them on the formats of similar software in English with which you are already familiar. You may wish to review the comprehension strategies *Recognizing cognates* and *Using standard formats* on pages 28 and 156.

Note for vocabulary.
New words in this review chapter are not considered active vocabulary and do not appear on the final exam or in subsequent chapters. New vocabulary is included in order to review the learning / comprehension strategies presented in preceding chapters of *Hoy día*. There is no end-of-chapter vocabulary list.

Suggestion for *Una conversación.*
Have students think of the four most common things they do using a computer. Then, have students listen with books closed jotting down four uses of computers mentioned in the conversation (*comunicarse por email, usar un procesador de texto navegar por Internet, participar en una red social*). Finally, have students open their books and listen again as they read along.

Answers for *¡A escuchar!*
Quiere aprender a vender cosas en Internet. / Ya sabe usar el correo electrónico. / Necesita aprender a subir fotos en Internet. (See facing page for Audioscript.)

 CD 2, Track 51

¡A escuchar!

Ahora escuchen otra conversación en la cual un hombre mayor habla de por qué quiere aprender a navegar por la red. ¿Qué quiere aprender a hacer en Internet? ¿Qué sabe hacer ya (*already know how to do*)? ¿Qué necesita aprender a subir (*upload*)?

En este capítulo vas a repasar el vocabulario y las estructuras gramaticales de los *Capítulos 1–5* en una simulación de la vida real dando clases de computación para mayores (*senior citizens*) en español en un centro comunitario. No se presenta gramática nueva.

 CD 2, Track 49

¿Qué procesador de texto usas? ¿Qué se ve en la pantalla (*screen*) al abrir el programa?

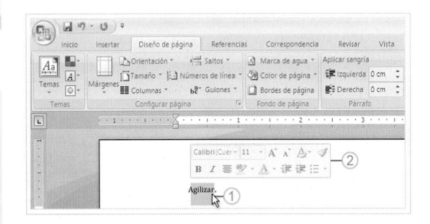

Una conversación. Un voluntario de un centro comunitario habla con una señora mayor que no sabe (*doesn't know how*) usar la computadora pero quiere aprender.

EL VOLUNTARIO: ¿Qué desea aprender a hacer con la computadora?

LA SEÑORA: Sobre todo, quiero entender a mis hijos y a mis nietos cuando hablan de las computadoras y la tecnología, pues cuando estoy con ellos, no entiendo nada. Además, quiero comunicarme con ellos por email.

EL VOLUNTARIO: ¿Sabe usar un procesador de texto como *Microsoft Word*?

LA SEÑORA: No, no sé nada de computadoras, pero quiero aprender a navegar por Internet y usar el correo electrónico. Tengo una amiga que habla de sus viajes y otras experiencias virtuales. Tiene muchos amigos virtuales, ¡hasta un novio! No sé exactamente qué son los viajes ni los novios virtuales, pero me parecen interesantes para una persona mayor que vive sola como yo.

EL VOLUNTARIO: ¿Le gustaría crear una página o participar en una red social como *Facebook* o *MySpace*?

LA SEÑORA: No quiero mi propia página, pero me gustaría ver las páginas de mis nietos.

6-1 ▶ Comandos. Explícale a una persona con quien estás trabajando en qué menú de Microsoft Word (**Inicio, Insertar, Diseño de página** o **el botón de *Microsoft Office*)** debe hacer clic para realizar (*perform*) las siguientes acciones.

Modelo   Para crear un nuevo documento, se hace clic en *el botón de Microsoft Office*.

1. Para cambiar la fuente de cursiva a negrita (*bold*) se hace clic en . . .
2. Para encontrar formas como círculos o triángulos, se hace clic en . . .
3. Para insertar una tabla, se hace clic en . . .
4. Para cambiar la orientación de la página, se hace clic en . . .
5. Para insertar o cambiar un encabezado (*heading*) o un pie de página (*footer*), se hace clic en . . .
6. Para abrir un archivo (*file*), se hace clic en . . .
7. Para cambiar los márgenes de la página, se hace clic en . . .
8. Para copiar, cortar o pegar (*paste*) texto, se hace clic en . . .
9. Para insertar números de páginas, se hace clic en . . .
10. Para cambiar el número de columnas, se hace clic en . . .

6-2 ▶ Comparaciones culturales. Lee el siguiente artículo basado en un informe de la UNESCO sobre la brecha digital (*digital divide*) en el mundo y prepara una lista de los cognados que encuentres agrupados en las siguientes categorías: adjetivos, sustantivos (*nouns*) y verbos. Luego, contesta las preguntas que siguen al artículo.

Modelos   ADJETIVOS: *titulado*
         SUSTANTIVOS: *sociedades*
         VERBOS: *alerta*

En un informe titulado "Hacia las sociedades del conocimiento", la Organización de las Naciones Unidas para la Educación, la Ciencia y la Cultura (UNESCO) alerta que el uso de Internet puede resultar en la desaparición de la mayoría de las 6.000 lenguas que se hablan hoy en el planeta. El documento mantiene que las nuevas tecnologías favorecen la homogeneización de la cultura y disminuyen la diversidad, señalando que "tres de cada cuatro páginas en Internet están escritas en inglés".

La organización reconoce que las nuevas tecnologías ofrecen muchos beneficios para las sociedades, pero también afirma que la disparidad en el acceso a las tecnologías de la información, la llamada "brecha digital", es un obstáculo entre los habitantes de muchas partes del mundo y los servicios ofrecidos por Internet. El 90% de la gente conectada a Internet vive en los países industrializados y usa un "club selecto" de lenguas vehiculares.

1. ¿Cuántas lenguas se hablan ahora en el planeta?
2. ¿Crees que es importante conservar esas lenguas?
3. De cada cuatro páginas web en Internet, ¿cuántas están escritas en inglés?
4. ¿Cómo se dice "la brecha digital" en inglés?
5. ¿Qué porcentaje de la gente que usa Internet vive en los países industrializados?

📖 Repaso 1

SAM: 6-3
to 6-4

Expressing the verb to be:
Ser, estar, and hay

Para averiguar

In the activities on this page, you will be reviewing the verbs *ser, estar,* and *hay.* Do you remember . . .

■ whether you use the forms of **ser** or **estar** to say who people are? where they are from? where they are now? what they are like? how they are doing?

■ how you say *there is, there are, is there,* and *are there?*

■ what types of adjectives you use with **ser** to describe someone or something? what types of adjectives you use with **estar**?

See pages 12, 20, 40, and 108 or refer to the verb charts in the appendix or in *MySpanishLab* for review.

6-3 ▶ Ansiedades. Varias personas mayores hablan de su deseo y su miedo de aprender a usar una computadora. Empieza cada oración con **Somos . . .** o **Estamos . . .**

Modelo   poco acostumbrados (*accustomed*) a las nuevas tecnologías
Estamos poco acostumbrados a las nuevas tecnologías.

1. listos para aprender
2. mayores
3. como el loro (*parrot*) viejo que no aprende a hablar
4. interesados en la tecnología
5. nerviosos con las computadoras
6. estudiantes dedicados
7. preparados para la lección

6-4 ▶ Primeros pasos. Estás explicándole a alguien cómo se usa un procesador de texto. Completa las siguientes oraciones con **hay** o la forma correcta de **ser** o **estar**. Utiliza cada verbo sólo una vez en cada explicación.

Modelo   No *hay* por qué *estar* nervioso. *Es* fácil aprender a usar una computadora.

1. No ____es____ difícil usar este procesador de texto. ____Hay____ varios menús y los más importantes ____están____ en la barra de herramientas (*tool bar*).
2. La barra de herramientas ____está____ en la parte superior de la pantalla (*screen*). ____Es____ la barra donde ____hay____ varios iconos.
3. ____Hay____ algunos iconos que no ____están____ siempre visibles en la barra de herramientas porque ____son____ menos útiles.
4. ____Es____ posible mover una selección de texto de una parte de un documento a otra, utilizando los dos botones "cortar" y "pegar" (*paste*) que ____están____ en la parte izquierda de la barra de herramientas. También ____hay____ un botón para copiar texto.
5. Una fuente ____es____ un estilo de letra. ____Hay____ varias opciones como *Ariel* o *Tahoma* y la selección de fuentes ____está____ en este menú.
6. El comando "Ortografía y gramática" ____es____ útil si quiere ver si ____hay____ errores gramaticales o errores de ortografía. ____Está____ en el menú "Revisar".
7. ____Es____ fácil crear un documento, ¿verdad? ¿ ____Hay____ preguntas o ____está____ todo claro por el momento?

6-5 ▶ ¿Por qué vender por Internet? Durante una lección sobre Internet, los participantes hablan de las tiendas en línea. Completa las siguientes oraciones con **hay** o con la forma correcta de **ser** o **estar**.

Modelo   *Hay* muchos beneficios de tener una tienda en Internet.

1. No ____es____ necesario tener mucho dinero para establecer una tienda en línea.
2. No ____hay____ límite de posibilidades si su tienda ____está____ en Internet.
3. Sus productos ____están____ disponibles (*available*) para todo el mundo y no solamente en un área limitada.
4. La tienda puede ____estar____ abierta las veinticuatro horas del día.
5. No ____hay____ gastos (*expenses*) de alquiler ni de servicios públicos.
6. El correo electrónico ____es____ la mejor manera de promocionar los productos y no cuesta nada.
7. Las tiendas en Internet ____son____ muy competitivas y el servicio al cliente ____es____ muy importante.
8. Si los clientes no ____están____ satisfechos (*satisfied*), siempre ____hay____ otras opciones para comprar por Internet.

Answers for 6-3.
1. *Estamos . . .* ; 2. *Somos . . .* ; 3. *Somos . . .* ;
4. *Estamos . . .* ; 5. *Estamos . . .* ; 6. *Somos . . .* ;
7. *Estamos . . .*

Suggestions for 6-3.
• Point out to students that the expression in item #3 refers to a common saying in Spanish, *¡El loro viejo no aprende a hablar!*. Ask students to translate the saying and if they can think of a similar expression in English. ("You can't teach an old dog new tricks.")
• After each statement, ask students: *¿Indica esta oración el deseo o el miedo de aprender a usar una computadora?*
• Have students use *(No) Soy . . . / (No) Estoy . . .* to make similar statements about themselves as Spanish students with the following cues: Modelo: *acostumbrado/a a la pronunciación del español > Estoy / No estoy acostumbrado/a a la pronunciación del español.* 1. *listo/a para aprender;* 2. *una persona mayor;* 3. *interesado/a en la cultura hispana;* 4. *nervioso/a en clase;* 5. *un/a estudiante dedicado/a;* 6. *preparado/a para la lección de hoy*

📖 Repaso 2   Naming and describing people and things: Articles, nouns, and adjectives

SAM: 6-5
to 6-6

6-6 ▶ Términos. Completa las siguientes definiciones relacionadas con las computadoras con las formas correctas del artículo definido (**el, la, los, las**). Luego, indica qué expresión de la lista se explica en cada definición.

la compresión de archivos	la extensión	la piratería
la placa madre	la informática	

Modelo   Es *la* placa (*board*) principal de circuitos de *la* computadora.
              Es *la placa madre.*

1. Es _____el_____ grupo de tres letras que identifican _____la_____ categoría de un archivo (*file*) como .doc para _____los_____ documentos de *Microsoft Word* o .pdf para _____los_____ archivos de *Adobe*.
2. Es _____la_____ reducción del tamaño (*size*) de archivos para su transmisión vía Internet.
3. Es _____el_____ tratamiento automático de _____la_____ información por medio de computadoras.
4. Es _____el_____ robo o _____la_____ destrucción de un programa informático o de otro material protegido.

6-7 ▶ Más términos. Completa las siguientes definiciones con las formas correctas del artículo indefinido (**un, una**). Luego, indica qué expresión de la lista se explica en cada definición.

una aplicación	un chat	un icono
un avatar	*una descarga*	un emoticono

Modelo   Es *una* transferencia de datos por Internet.
              Es *una descarga.*

1. Es _____una_____ conversación en tiempo real por Internet.
2. Es _____un_____ pequeño símbolo en la pantalla de _____una_____ computadora que representa _____un_____ programa.
3. Es _____un_____ programa usado para realizar _____una_____ tarea específica.
4. Es _____un_____ símbolo como :-) o :-(que representa las emociones o los sentimientos de _____una_____ persona en comunicaciones vía Internet.
5. Es _____una_____ representación gráfica de _____un_____ participante en _____una_____ sala de chat o _____un_____ foro.

6-8 ▶ Emoticonos. Dos amigas usan los siguientes emoticonos en lugar de adjetivos o sustantivos (*nouns*) en sus mensajes instantáneos. Cambia los emoticonos por la palabra española en la forma correcta.

-_-	normal	:-(	triste	$-$	rico/a
OwO	sorprendido/a	:-\	disgustado/a	:-x	callado/a
<3	enamorado/a	:-O	asustado/a (*scared*)	0:-)	santo/a
:-)	feliz	:-m	pensativo/a	ò-ó	enojado/a

DANIELA: Hola, Mónica. ¿Cómo estás?
MÓNICA: Estoy muy :-). Estoy <3 de un chico.
DANIELA: Estoy OwO. ¿Quién es? ¿Cómo es?
MÓNICA: Es un 0:-). Es un chico :-m y :-x pero muy guapo y tiene padres $-$.
        ¿Y tú? ¿Cómo estás?
DANIELA: Estoy un poco :-(y :-O. Mi novio está ò-ó conmigo.
MÓNICA: Es -_- tener problemas de vez en cuando, aún en las relaciones :-).

Para averiguar

In the activities on this page, you will be reviewing definite and indefinite articles, nouns, and adjectives. Do you remember . . .
- what the two forms of the word for *a/an* in Spanish are? for *some*?
- what the four forms of the word for *the* are?
- what endings generally indicate that a noun or adjective is masculine? feminine?
- when you add **-s** to nouns and adjectives to make them plural? when you add **-es?**
- where you place adjectives with respect to the noun they describe? how adjectives and articles agree with the nouns they modify?

See pages 12 and 18 for review.

Answers for 6-6.
1. *Es la extensión.* 2. *Es la compresión de archivos.* 3. *Es la informática.* 4. *Es la piratería*

Answers for 6-7.
1. *Es un chat.* 2. *Es un icono.* 3. *Es una aplicación.* 4. *Es un emoticono.* 5. *Es un avatar.*

Answers for 6-8.
feliz, enamorada, sorprendida, santo, pensativo, callado, ricos, triste, asustada, enojado, normal, felices

📖 Repaso 3 Saying how many: Numbers

SAM: 6-7
to 6-8

Para **averiguar**

In the activities on this page, you will be reviewing numbers. Do you remember . . .

- which numbers between 16 and 99 are written as single words? which must be written as three separate words?
- when you use **cien** to say *one hundred*? when you use **ciento**?
- which of these numbers does not change in plural forms: **cien/ciento, mil, un millón**? which has feminine plural forms?
- when you use a period with numbers in Spanish? a comma?

See pages 14 and 102 for review.

6-9 ▶ **Los bloggers hispanos.** Completa las siguientes estadísticas de una encuesta (*survey*) de bitacoras.com sobre los bloggers hispanos con los números indicados.

Modelo   El *ochenta y uno* (81) por ciento de los bloggers son hombres y el *diecinueve* (19) por ciento son mujeres.

1. El _____ (38) por ciento de los bloggers tiene entre _____ (25) y _____ (34) años y el _____ (80) por ciento tiene entre _____ (19) y _____ (44) años.

2. El _____ (51) por ciento de los bloggers hispanos son españoles, el _____ (12) por ciento son argentinos, el _____ (9) por ciento mexicanos, el _____ (7) por ciento chilenos y el _____ (21) por ciento es de otras regiones hispanas.

3. El _____ (34) por ciento de los blogs tiene temas personales o autobiográficos, el _____ (11) por ciento es sobre las noticias (*news*) y la actualidad (*current issues*), el _____ (10) por ciento sobre cultura y sociedad, el _____ (6) por ciento sobre los medios de comunicación, el _____ (5) por ciento sobre historia, literatura y arte y el _____ (3) por ciento sobre tecnología.

4. El momento de la semana más activo en los blogs son los miércoles de _____ (16) a _____ (20) horas, es decir entre las _____ (4) y las _____ (8) de la tarde. El domingo es el día menos activo.

6-10 ▶ **¿Cuál se usa más?** Compara el número de impactos (*hits*) en búsquedas por Internet para averiguar qué terminos son más comunes en español. Indica los números en español.

Modelo   "un sitio web" (14.800.000), "un sitio de Internet" (433.000)
Hay catorce millones ochocientos mil para "un sitio web" y cuatrocientos treinta y tres mil para "un sitio de Internet".

1. "página web" (145.000.000), "página de Internet" (546.000.000)
2. "navegar en la red" (69.100), "navegar en la web" (46.100)
3. "un buscador de Internet" (55.000), "un motor de búsqueda de Internet" (2.100.000)
4. "escribir un email" (46.800), "escribir un correo electrónico" (41.700)
5. "recibir spam" (40.400), "recibir correos no deseados" (212)
6. "una aplicación informática" (221.000), "un programa informático" (617.000)
7. "abrir un archivo" (188.000), "abrir un documento" (88.000)
8. "cargar una foto" (59.700), "subir una foto" (823.000)

📖 Repaso 4   Making comparisons: Comparatives

SAM: 6-9
to 6-10

6-11 ▶ Más sobre los blogs. Lee la siguiente información sobre los blogs y completa las oraciones con **más . . . que, menos . . . que** o **tanto . . . como.**

Modelo   El 86% de los bloggers escribe blogs en casa, el 38% en el trabajo, el 8% en un centro de estudios y el 7% en cibercafés. Los bloggers escriben *más* en casa *que* en el trabajo y casi *tantos* bloggers escriben donde estudian *como* en un cibercafé.

1. El 5% de los bloggers hispanos son peruanos, el 4% son colombianos y, el 3% son venezolanos. Hay ____*más*____ bloggers colombianos ____*que*____ venezolanos, pero hay ____*menos*____ colombianos ____*que*____ peruanos.

2. El 22% dedica más de una hora todos los días a los blogs, el 24% una hora y el 23% media hora. Casi ____*tantas*____ personas pasan más de una hora en los blogs ____*como*____ las que pasan una hora o media hora en los blogs.

3. El 35% de los bloggers hispanos lee blogs en otras lenguas y un 65% lo hace sólo en español. ____*Más*____ bloggers hispanos prefieren leer blogs sólo en español ____*que*____ en otras lenguas.

4. El 2% de los blogs es sobre temas humorísticos, el 1,9% sobre fotografía, el 1,9% sobre diseño y moda (*fashion*), el 1,8% sobre empleo y el 1,8% sobre música. Hay ____*tantos*____ blogs sobre fotografía ____*como*____ sobre diseño y moda, y hay ____*tantos*____ blogs sobre empleo ____*como*____ sobre música, pero hay ____*más*____ blogs sobre temas humorísticos ____*que*____ sobre cada uno de estos temas.

5. El 19% de los bloggers prefiere escribir por la noche, el 8% por la mañana y el 8% por la tarde. El 60% de los bloggers no tiene una hora preferida para escribir. ____*Tantos*____ bloggers prefieren escribir por la mañana ____*como*____ por la tarde, pero ____*menos*____ bloggers prefieren la mañana o la tarde ____*que*____ la noche.

6-12 ▶ Correcciones. Corrige las siguientes afirmaciones incorrectas usando **más . . . que** o **menos . . . que** en lugar de (*in place of*) **tan / tanto . . . como.**

Modelo   En Estados Unidos los adultos pasan *tanto* tiempo navegando en Internet *como* viendo la televisión.
    En Estados Unidos los adultos pasan más tiempo navegando en Internet que viendo la televisión.

1. Las redes (*networks*) sociales son *tan* populares entre las personas mayores (*senior citizens*) *como* entre los jóvenes.
2. Internet es *tan* popular *como* los periódicos para informarse de las noticias (*news*).
3. Generalmente, la información publicada en Internet es *tan* fidedigna (*trustworthy*) *como* la información publicada en los libros.
4. Generalmente, se puede encontrar información *tan* reciente en Internet *como* en los libros.
5. Es *tan* fácil expresar su opinión en un blog *como* en la página editorial de un periódico.
6. Hay *tantas* páginas web en otras lenguas *como* en inglés.
7. La distribución de publicidad por televisión es *tan* cara *como* por email.
8. Las conexiones a Internet vía línea telefónica normal son *tan* rápidas *como* las conexiones vía fibra óptica.

Para **averiguar**

In the activities on this page, you will be reviewing comparatives. Do you remember . . .
■ how **más . . . que** and **menos . . . que** can be translated in English?
■ what **tan . . . como** means?
■ what **tanto . . . como** means? when **tanto** changes forms?
See page 110 for review.

Note for statistical data.
See the IRM for source information relating to the statistical data presented.

Follow-ups for 6-11.
• For each of the items in 6-11 *Más sobre los blogs*, have students who participate in blogs say what is true for them, or have them say what they think would be true for bloggers here.
• Have students review the statistics in 6-9 *Los bloggers hispanos*, and ask: 1. ¿Hay más o menos hombres que mujeres que participan en blogs hispanos? 2. ¿Hay más o menos mexicanos que españoles? 3. ¿Hay más o menos argentinos que chilenos? 4. ¿Hay más o menos blogs sobre tecnología que sobre noticias y actualidad? 5. ¿Escriben los hispanos en blogs más o menos los domingos que los miércoles?
• Have students say whether the first term listed for each item in 6-10 *Términos* is used more or less than the second term. Modelo: *Se usa "página web" menos que "página de Internet".*

Answers for 6-12.
1. menos . . . que; 2. más . . . que; 3. menos . . . que; 4. más . . . que; 5. más . . . que; 6. menos . . . que; 7. más . . . que; 8. menos . . . que

📖 **Vocabulario** Los sitios web y las búsquedas

SAM: 6-11
to 6-12

¿Sabías que...?

El código de país de una URL de una página web indica su país de origen. Por ejemplo, la extensión **.ar** indica que una página es de Argentina o **.bo** representa Bolivia. ¿Puedes adivinar que países hispanos tienen los siguientes códigos: **.cl**, **.co**, **.cr**, **.cu**, **.do**, **.ec**, **.es**, **.gt**, **.hn**, **.mx**, **.ni**, **.pa**, **.pe**, **.py**, **.sv**, **.uy**, **.ve**?

Answers for ¿Sabías que . . . ?
.cl Chile, **.co** Colombia, **.cr** Costa Rica, **.cu** Cuba, **.do** la República Dominicana, **.ec** Ecuador, **.es** España, **.gt** Guatemala, **.hn** Honduras, **.mx** México, **.ni** Nicaragua, **.pa** Panamá, **.pe** Perú, **.py** Paraguay, **.sv** El Salvador, **.uy** Uruguay, **.ve** Venezuela

CD 2
Track 52

Generalmente se pueden clasificar los sitios web en las siguientes categorías:

sitio buscador
sitio de comercio electrónico
sitio weblog (blog)
sitio de información
sitio de noticias
sitio de comunidad virtual

¿A qué categoría pertenece la página web que sigue?

👁 ¡Ojo!

Comprehension strategy. In order to find information efficiently on the Internet, it is necessary to skim web pages quickly to see whether they contain the information you are looking for. Skim the web page shown here to determine whether it is the homepage for a blog site, a company site, or a news site. What types of products does it offer? If you were looking for language textbooks, should you look further on this site or search for another one? See page 92 to review the comprehension strategy *Skimming*.

el encabezado

el punto central que llama más la atención

los menús de enlaces

el pie de página

CD 2
Track 53

Una conversación. Un voluntario que enseña diseño de páginas de Internet habla con un señor sobre el diseño de una página web.

EL VOLUNTARIO: ¿Qué tipo de página web le gustaría crear?

EL SEÑOR: Mi hijo es carpintero y quiero hacer una página para su compañía con información básica.

EL VOLUNTARIO: Bueno, primero vamos a hablar de la organización de la página principal. Normalmente hay cuatro secciones básicas en la página inicial. El encabezado tiene el nombre y el logo de la compañía. ¿Ya tienen un logo?

EL SEÑOR: Sí, es el nombre de la compañía, *Carpintería Reyes*, con dibujos de varias herramientas de carpintería.

EL VOLUNTARIO: Debajo del encabezado viene el contenido principal. Con frecuencia aquí hay una foto o una imagen como punto central para llamar la atención. A la derecha o a la izquierda del contenido principal está el menú de enlaces para navegar por otras páginas del sitio.

EL SEÑOR: ¿Como páginas con más fotos y una lista de precios?

EL VOLUNTARIO: Sí, así es. Finalmente está el pie de página. Frecuentemente contiene información como la dirección, el teléfono y la dirección de correo electrónico de la compañía.

Suggestion for *Una conversación*.
Set the scene for *Una conversación* and have students listen with books closed for the four basic sections of a typical home page (*la página inicial*): *el encabezado, el contenido principal, el menú de enlaces, el pie de la página.* Then, have students open their books and listen again as they read along.

Follow-up for *Una conversación*.
• Ask students to use context to guess the meaning of the following words: *la página principal / inicial, el encabezado, dibujos, herramientas de carpintería, el contenido, enlaces, el pie de página.*

CD 2, Track 54

¡A escuchar!

Ahora escuchen otra conversación en la cual dos personas hablan de una página de Internet de una agencia de viajes. ¿Cuáles son los aspectos positivos y cuáles los negativos del sitio?

6-13 ▶ Comparaciones culturales. Lee el siguiente artículo sobre el comercio electrónico en Latinoamérica. Luego indica si las afirmaciones que siguen el texto son ciertas o falsas. Corrige las oraciones falsas.

El comercio electrónico en Latinoamérica

Hay varios obstáculos para el comercio electrónico en Latinoamérica: la baja conectividad, la desconfianza[1] de los consumidores y la poca disposición[2] al uso de tarjetas de crédito, pero las tiendas en línea empiezan a establecerse. Actualmente, el comercio electrónico crece[3] un 40% anualmente y las posibilidades de mantener esta expansión son buenas.

Chile es el país de Latinoamérica más activo en comercio electrónico y el 77% de los internautas[4] dice comprar en línea. Así mismo, los residentes de la capital chilena, Santiago, poseen más tarjetas de crédito que los de cualquier otra región de Latinoamérica. Argentina es el segundo país más activo con el 74% y México el tercero con el 71%. Los productos que más se venden por Internet son equipos electrónicos (50%), teléfonos u otros equipos de comunicación (28%) y libros (18%).

[1]*mistrust* [2]*willingness* [3]*is growing* [4]*Internet users*

1. El uso de tarjetas de crédito es bajo en Latinoamérica y esto afecta al comercio electrónico de la región.
2. Menos consumidores compran en línea en Chile que en otras regiones de Latinoamérica.
3. Se gasta tanto en libros en línea como en equipos electrónicos.

Audioscript for *¡A escuchar!*
EL AMIGO: *¡Qué bonitas fotos! ¿Piensas hacer un viaje?*
EL USUARIO: *Sí, esta agencia de viajes de Internet es muy popular y ofrece muchos viajes interesantes. Tiene un sitio bonito, pero es un poco difícil de navegar.*
EL AMIGO: *¿Por qué?*
EL USUARIO: *El sitio no es muy rápido. Las fotos y los gráficos tardan mucho tiempo en cargar.*
EL AMIGO: *¿Es fácil encontrar la información que buscas?*
EL USUARIO: *No, ése es otro problema del sitio. Tengo que regresar a la página principal para iniciar cada búsqueda.*
EL AMIGO: *Así van a perder clientes.*

Answers for *¡A escuchar!*
Positivo: Es un sitio bonito. / Negativo: Es un poco difícil de navegar. El sitio no es muy rápido. Las fotos y los gráficos tardan mucho tiempo en cargar. El usuario tiene que regresar a la página principal para iniciar cada búsqueda.

Answers for 6-13.
1. cierto; 2. falso; Más consumidores compran en línea en Chile que en otras regiones de Latinoamérica; 3. falso; Se gasta menos en libros en línea que en equipos electrónicos.

Follow-up for 6-13.
Ask students about their online purchases: *¿Compras mucho por Internet? ¿Cómo pagas generalmente, con tarjeta de crédito o con un servicio como PayPal? ¿Qué compras más en línea, ¿equipos electrónicos o libros? ¿Música o libros? ¿Ropa o música? ¿Descargas (Do you download) mucha música?*

📖 **Repaso 1**

SAM: 6-13 to 6-14

Saying what people do: Conjugations of **-ar, -er,** and **-ir** verbs

Para **averiguar**

In the activities on this page, you will be reviewing the **-ar, -er,** and **-ir** verbs. Do you remember . . .

- what the endings of regular **-ar** verbs that go with each of the subject pronouns are?
- what the endings of regular **-er** verbs are?
- in what two forms **-ir** verb endings differ from those of **-er** verbs?

See pages 44 and 76 or refer to the verb charts in the appendix or in *MySpanishLab* for review.

6-14 ▶ La generación multitarea (*multitasking*). En el mundo moderno, todos tenemos que hacer varias cosas a la vez. Completa el siguiente artículo sobre la multitarea con las formas correctas de los verbos entre paréntesis.

Se dice que los jóvenes de hoy (1) _pertenecen_ (pertenecer) a la "generación multitarea". (Ellos) (2) _Escuchan_ (escuchar) música en su iPod, (3) _participan_ (participar) en un chat y (4) _responden_ (responder) a mensajes en su celular, todo mientras (5) _estudian_ (estudiar) o (6) _intentan_ (intentar [*to attempt*]) estudiar para un examen al día siguiente. La tecnología (7) _permite_ (permitir) hacer varias actividades a la vez, pero muchos expertos (8) _creen_ (creer) que la multitarea (9) _reduce_ (reducir) la capacidad de aprendizaje y memoria. Según algunos estudios, una persona que (10) _hace_ (hacer) varias tareas a la vez, (11) _comprende_ (comprender) menos porque no (12) _entra_ (entrar) profundamente en la materia. Esto (13) _limita_ (limitar) la capacidad de aprender en detalle porque no (14) _deja_ (dejar) suficiente tiempo para la consolidación de la materia en la memoria. Según un estudio de la Universidad de California, Los Ángeles, "las personas que (15) _aprenden_ (aprender) cosas utilizando la multitarea (16) _utilizan_ (utilizar) una parte diferente del cerebro que las personas que (17) _están_ (estar) concentradas en una sola cosa." Además de causar problemas de aprendizaje, las investigaciones (18) _indican_ (indicar) que la multitarea (19) _produce_ (producir) más estrés y a veces (20) _causa_ (causar) problemas de salud (*health*).

6-15 ▶ Cómo evitar la multitarea en la oficina. La multitarea puede causar mucho estrés en la oficina. Aquí hay una descripción de cómo una empleada combate el estrés de la multitarea en el trabajo. Completa las descripciones de manera lógica con los verbos entre paréntesis en la forma **ella**.

Modelo *Crea* listas organizadas de las cosas que *necesita* hacer. (crear, necesitar)

1. _Organiza_ los papeles en su escritorio en bandejas (*trays*) con el nombre del proyecto y así nunca _busca_ cosas perdidas en un escritorio desordenado. (buscar, organizar)
2. Cuando _llega_ a la oficina empieza con las tareas más difíciles. Dice que se siente más tranquila el resto del día si _termina_ ese trabajo primero. (llegar, terminar)
3. _Lee_ y _responde_ a los correos electrónicos a intervalos predeterminados. (leer, responder)
4. _Mira_ su correo electrónico a las nueve de la mañana, a la una y a las cinco de la tarde y siempre _escribe_ respuestas a los correos electrónicos inmediatamente para no perder tiempo. (escribir, mirar)
5. _Descansa_ a intervalos regulares y _usa_ el tiempo para levantarse y hacer un poco de ejercicio. (usar, descansar)
6. Si es posible, no _pasa_ todo el día enfrente de la computadora. _Limita_ el trabajo en la computadora a tres horas seguidas (*in a row*). (limitar, pasar)
7. Cuando _regresa_ a su casa, _deja_ el trabajo en la oficina. (dejar, regresar)

📖 Repaso 2   Requesting information: Question formation

SAM: 6-15
to 6-16

6-16 ▶ Cuestionario. Estás preparando un cuestionario para los participantes en cursos de informática de un centro comunitario. Completa las siguientes preguntas con la palabra interrogativa lógica.

Modelo   *¿Qué* desea aprender a hacer con la computadora? ¿Comunicarse por correo electrónico? ¿Navegar por Internet? ¿Usar un procesador de texto?

1. ¿ __Por qué__ quiere aprender a usar Internet? ¿Quiere buscar información? ¿Desea vender o comprar por Internet? ¿Quiere participar en una comunidad virtual?

2. ¿ __Qué__ tipo de computadora prefiere usted? ¿Un Mac o un PC?

3. ¿ __Cuánta__ experiencia tiene con las computadoras? ¿Ninguna? ¿Poca? ¿Mucha?

4. ¿ __Dónde__ va a usar la computadora? ¿En casa? ¿En casa de otra persona? ¿En la biblioteca municipal?

5. ¿ __Quién__ puede ayudarle con la computadora en casa? ¿Un hijo? ¿Un nieto? ¿Un amigo? ¿Un vecino? ¿Nadie?

6. ¿ __Cuántas__ horas a la semana puede usted dedicar a las lecciones de informática? ¿Dos o tres horas? ¿Cinco horas? ¿Más de cinco horas?

7. ¿ __Cuándo__ es mejor ofrecer las lecciones en el centro comunitario? ¿Por la mañana? ¿Por la tarde? ¿Por la noche?

8. ¿ __Cuál__ es el mejor número de teléfono para comunicarnos con usted durante el día?

6-17 ▶ Preguntas frecuentes. Aquí hay una lista de respuestas a las preguntas más frecuentes sobre Internet. Escribe la pregunta lógica para cada respuesta usando las palabras subrayadas (*underlined*) con la palabra interrogativa lógica.

Modelo   <u>Una cookie es</u> un pequeño archivo de texto que un sitio web deja en la computadora de los visitantes.
       ¿Qué es una cookie?

1. <u>La diferencia entre Internet y una Intranet es</u> que Internet se refiere a la conexión de computadoras a través de todo el mundo (*across the whole world*) y una Intranet es una conexión entre las computadoras de una sola organización.

2. <u>Un dominio es</u> el nombre de un sitio web.

3. Generalmente, <u>la inscripción (*registration*) de un dominio lleva (*takes*)</u> de 2 a 4 <u>días</u>.

4. <u>Es posible determinar si un dominio está disponible (*available*)</u> buscando el nombre en la base de datos *Whois* en Internet.

5. <u>La inscripción de un dominio cuesta</u> más o menos diez dólares al año.

6. <u>Hay</u> más de 100.000.000 <u>sitios web en el mundo</u>.

7. <u>Hay más páginas web que sitios de Internet</u> porque un sitio web puede contener miles de páginas.

8. <u>Un motor de búsqueda es</u> un software que busca texto según criterios determinados por el usuario.

9. <u>Los motores de búsqueda más populares son</u> *Google* y *Yahoo*.

10. <u>Las oficinas centrales de *Google* y *Yahoo* están</u> en California.

Para **averiguar**

In the activities on this page, you will be reviewing question formation. Do you remember . . .
- where you generally place the subject with respect to the verb in a question?
- how you say *who, what, which, where, when, why, how, how much, how many,* and *how often* in Spanish?
- whether you use **qué** or **cuál** to translate *What is . . .?* or *What are . . .?* when asking for a definition? when asking for a selection out of a group of possibilities?

See page 46 for review.

Follow-up for 6-16.
Ask students similar questions about themselves: *¿Qué te gusta hacer con la computadora? ¿Qué tipo de computadora prefieres? ¿Dónde usas más la computadora? ¿Cuánta experiencia tienes con el programa informático Excel? ¿Con Adobe? ¿Con Dreamweaver? ¿Cuántas horas al día usas la computadora? ¿Cuánto tiempo dedicas a diversiones en la computadora? ¿Cuándo estás más en línea? ¿Por la mañana, por la tarde o por la noche? Generalmente, ¿cuál es el mejor número para comunicarme contigo, el de tu celular o el de tu casa? ¿Tienes dos teléfonos o sólo un teléfono celular o un teléfono fijo (*landline*) en casa?*

Answers for 6-17.
1. *¿Cuál es la diferencia entre Internet y una Intranet?* 2. *¿Qué es un dominio?* 3. *¿Cuántos días lleva la inscripción de un dominio?* 4. *¿Cómo es posible determinar si un dominio está disponible?* 5. *¿Cuánto cuesta la inscripción de un dominio?* 6. *¿Cuántos sitios web hay en el mundo?* 7. *¿Por qué hay más páginas web que sitios de Internet?* 8. *¿Qué es un motor de búsqueda?* 9. *¿Cuáles son los motores de búsqueda más populares?* 10. *¿Dónde están las oficinas centrales de Google y Yahoo?*

📖 Repaso 3

SAM: 6-17
to 6-18

Saying what people have: Tener and tener expressions

Answers for 6-18.
1. Mi novio tiene; 2. Yo tengo; 3. El café tiene; 4. Yo tengo; 5. Todos tenemos / Yo tengo / Mi novio tiene; 6. Todos tenemos / Yo tengo / Mi novio tiene

Answers for 6-19.
1. tengo miedo; 2. tenemos ansiedad; 3. tener confianza; 4. tiene razón; 5. tener paciencia; 6. tienen la capacidad; 7. Tenemos acceso; 8. tener amigos; 9. tiene ganas de; 10. tener precaución; 11. tienen malas intenciones; 12. Tengo ochenta años; 13. tengo mucha experiencia

6-18 ▶ En un café. La mujer con la blusa morada describe a las personas en esta foto y el café donde pasa mucho tiempo. Completa las siguientes oraciones con el sujeto correcto de la lista y la forma correcta de **tener**.

Yo	Mi novio	Todos	El café

Modelo   *Yo tengo* un a blusa morada.

1. _____ una camisa gris.
2. _____ una computadora portátil.
3. _____ *WiFi*.
4. _____ mucha sed.
5. _____ entre veinte y treinta años.
6. _____ mucho trabajo.

6-19 ▶ ¿Qué tiene? Una voluntaria que enseña una clase de informática habla con un señor mayor. Completa las oraciones de manera lógica con la forma correcta de **tener** en las expresiones entre paréntesis.

EL SEÑOR: (Yo) (Modelo) *Tengo curiosidad* de aprender a usar la computadora pero (1) _____ de arruinar algo. (tener curiosidad, tener miedo)

LA VOLUNTARIA: Todos (nosotros) (2) _____ cuando usamos una computadora por primera vez, pero usted necesita (3) _____ en sí mismo (*yourself*). ¿Con qué frecuencia ve usted a una persona arruinar una computadora? Nunca, ¿verdad? (tener ansiedad, tener confianza)

EL SEÑOR: Sí, usted (4) _____. No es lógico. Necesita (5) _____ conmigo. No estoy acostumbrado a las nuevas tecnologías. (tener paciencia, tener razón)

LA VOLUNTARIA: Le va a gustar mucho. Hoy día las computadoras (6) _____ de hacer cosas increíbles. (Nosotros) (7) _____ al mundo entero por Internet. (tener acceso, tener la capacidad)

EL SEÑOR: Por fin voy a (8) _____ con quienes hablar. Mi esposa no (9) _____ hablar y prefiere ver la televisión. (tener amigos, tener ganas de)

LA VOLUNTARIA: Pero, es importante (10) _____ en las relaciones en línea. Nunca debe dar información personal como su número de seguridad social ni información sobre sus cuentas bancarias porque algunas personas (11) _____. (tener precaución, tener malas intenciones)

EL SEÑOR: (Yo) (12) _____ y (13) _____ con gente deshonesta. (tener mucha experiencia, tener ochenta años)

📖 Repaso 4   Saying what people do: Verbs with irregular **yo** forms

SAM: 6-19 to 6-20

6-20 ▶ Costumbres. Uno de los voluntarios del centro explica para qué usa Internet. Combina las frases de manera lógica usando la conjunción **cuando** con la primera o segunda parte de la oración y los verbos en la forma **yo**.

Modelos   verificar los horarios de las películas por Internet / salir al cine
*Verifico los horarios de las películas por Internet **cuando** salgo al cine.*

salir para el aeropuerto / verificar el estatus del vuelo (*flight*) en la web
***Cuando** salgo para el aeropuerto, verifico el estatus del vuelo en la web.*

1. oír una canción (*song*) que me gusta / descargar (*download*) la canción de *iTunes*
2. ver algo interesante en la tele / buscar más información por Internet sobre el tema del programa
3. hacer un viaje / reservar el hotel por Internet
4. subir mis fotos a mi álbum de fotos en línea / venir de vacaciones

6-21 ▶ Tiendas en línea. Estás hablando de los beneficios de las tiendas en línea. Completa las oraciones de manera lógica con la forma correcta de los verbos entre paréntesis.

Modelo   Si (yo) *oigo* un anuncio (*ad*) sobre un producto nuevo, *hago* una búsqueda por Internet para informarme sobre el producto. (hacer, oír)

1. Yo nunca ___salgo___ de casa para ir de compras. Siempre ___hago___ todas mis compras por Internet. (hacer, salir)
2. Las tiendas virtuales ___ponen___ a su disposición toda clase de productos y generalmente ___tienen___ los mejores precios. (poner, tener)
3. (Yo) ___Veo___ productos en tiendas virtuales por todo el país antes de comprar y generalmente los productos ___tienen___ la misma garantía que en una tienda normal. (tener, ver)
4. En varios blogs, los clientes ___dicen___ qué productos y tiendas son los mejores y ___hacen___ recomendaciones. (decir, hacer)
5. Cuando los productos ___salen___ de una tienda virtual, generalmente los clientes reciben un correo electrónico que ___dice___ cuando van a llegar. (decir, salir)
6. Un servicio de entrega (*delivery*) ___trae___ las compras a casa y (yo) no ___tengo___ que perder tiempo manejando (*driving*) ni gastar gasolina. (tener, traer)

Para **averiguar**

In the activities on this page, you will be reviewing verbs with irregular **yo** forms. Do you remember . . .
- what the **yo** forms of the verbs **hacer, poner, traer, salir, venir,** and **ver** are?
- what the forms of the verb **oír** are? what **oír** means?
- what three idiomatic expressions with **hacer** are?
- which verb can be used to say that you *turn on* something?
See pages 72 and 82 or refer to the verb charts in the appendix or in *MySpanishLab* for review.

Answers for 6-20.
1. *Cuando oigo una canción que me gusta, descargo la canción de iTunes.* 2. *Cuando veo algo interesante en la tele, busco más información por Internet sobre el tema del programa.* 3. *Cuando hago un viaje, reservo el hotel por Internet.* 4. *Subo mis fotos a mi álbum de fotos en línea cuando vengo de vacaciones.*

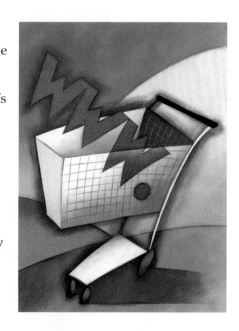

📖 **Vocabulario** Usos de Internet

SAM: 6-21
to 6-22

¿Sabías que...?

Según un estudio de *SophosLabs,* Estados Unidos es el líder mundial en producción de spam y genera el 28.4 del spam enviado por Internet. Entre los países hispanos, México es el número 1, produciendo un 1,9% de correo no deseado.

escribir y recibir correos electrónicos

CorreoHD

Redactar
Recibidos (12)
Destacados
Chat
Enviados
Borradores
Spam
Papelera
Contactos
Tareas

buscar información o leer noticias

chatear o participar en redes sociales

descargar música

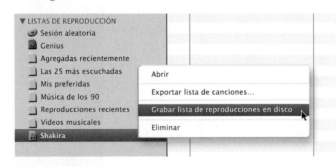

ver videos o jugar a los videojuegos

CD 2
Track 56

Una conversación. Una voluntaria está explicándole a un novato (*beginner*) cómo hacer un CD de música descargada.

EL NOVATO: Tengo varias canciones descargadas que quiero grabar en un CD, pero no entiendo lo que tengo que hacer.

LA VOLUNTARIA: Bueno, es muy fácil. En el menú *Archivo* se selecciona "Nueva lista de reproducción" para crear una carpeta nueva con el nombre del CD que quiere grabar. Así es... muy bien... Ahora, con el ratón, puede arrastrar las canciones que quiere a esa lista de reproducción.

EL NOVATO: ¡Es muy fácil!

LA VOLUNTARIA: Sí, y rápido. Después de arrastrar todas las canciones, necesita hacer clic con el botón derecho sobre la lista de reproducción. En la ventana que aparece, puede configurar la grabación. Es mejor seleccionar la velocidad de grabación mínima, y yo prefiero dejar dos segundos entre las canciones.

 CD 2, Track 57

¡A escuchar!

Ahora escuchen otra conversación en la cual un voluntario está explicándole a un novato como enviar un mensaje. ¿Qué palabras se usan para expresar *To, Subject, Attach* y *Send*?

6-22 ▶ Correo electrónico.
Explica cómo se dice cada palabra en negrita (*boldface*) en los programas de correo electrónico de inglés.

Modelo Se hace clic en **Redactar** para escribir un correo nuevo.
Redactar significa "Write" o "Compose" en inglés.

1. Se hace clic en **Recibidos** para ver los correos enviados a tu dirección de correo electrónico.
2. Se hace clic en **Destacados** para ver correos anteriores marcados como importantes.
3. Se hace clic en **Enviados** para ver correos enviados a otras personas.
4. Se hace clic en **Borradores** para ver correos anteriores no enviados.
5. Se hace clic en **Papelera** para ver los correos recientemente eliminados.

6-23 ▶ Comparaciones culturales.
Lee el siguiente texto sobre el uso de Internet en Latinoamérica. Luego, selecciona las palabras correctas entre paréntesis para completar las oraciones que siguen al artículo.

Según un estudio de *Tendenciasdigitales.com,* los usos principales de Internet en Latinoamérica son en orden de importancia: enviar (*to send*) y recibir correos electrónicos (86% de los usuarios), buscar información (82%), chatear (69%), descargar archivos, software o música (57%), ver videos (53%), visitar redes sociales (52%), leer noticias (35%), realizar operaciones bancarias (34%), comprar productos o servicios (34%), realizar cursos o estudios (33%). Actualmente, los usos de Internet que crecen (*are growing*) más rápidamente son las redes sociales. La expansión reciente de las redes sociales es todo un fenómeno de masas. Entre sus usuarios el 71,2% participa en comunidades vituales para comunicarse, el 47,5% para ver fotos y el 35,3% para saber qué hacen sus amigos. Uno de los atractivos de las redes sociales es que facilita interacciones con terceras personas a través de (*third parties through*) una segunda porque los contactos de cada uno son visibles para todos los demás.

1. Los latinoamericanos usan Internet (*más, menos, tanto*) para descargar música (*que, como*) para buscar información.
2. Los latinoamericanos usan Internet (*más, menos, tanto*) para realizar operaciones bancarias (*que, como*) para comprar productos o servicios.
3. Los latinoamericanos usan redes sociales (*más, menos, tanto*) para hablar con la gente (*que, como*) para ver fotos.

¡Ojo!

Comprehension strategies. In *Comparaciones culturales,* you are going to read about the most common uses of the Internet in Latin America and the growing importance of social networks (*redes sociales*). Begin to guess some of the information in the report by jotting down in English the ten most common things that you and others do on the Internet. Then, as you read, see which ones are mentioned. You can review the comprehension strategies *Anticipating content* and *Guessing meaning from context* on pages 30 and 60.

📖 Repaso 1

SAM: 6-23
to 6-24

Saying where you go and what you are going to do: **Ir, ir a** + infinitive

Para averiguar

In the activities on this page, you will be reviewing the verb **ir** and **ir a** + infinitive. Do you remember . . .

■ what the forms of the verb **ir** are?
■ how you say *I go*? how you say *I am going*?
■ what expression you use to say what someone is going to do?

See page 52 or refer to the verb charts in the appendix or in *MySpanishLab* for review.

6-24 ▶ Tecnologías del futuro. ¿Crees que las siguientes tecnologías van a ser comunes en el futuro o que nunca van a existir? Completa cada oración con la forma correcta de **ir** para expresar tu opinión. Luego di (*say*) si crees que **es probable, es posible** o **es imposible**.

Modelo   Micrófonos conectados a computadoras *van* a traducir perfectamente de una lengua a otra en tiempo real.
Es posible.

1. Procesadores de texto ____van____ a escribir nuestros pensamientos (*thoughts*) directamente en un documento sin la necesidad de usar un teclado (*keyboard*).
2. En las tiendas, los clientes ____van____ a poder obtener información sobre productos y comparar precios usando el código de barras (*bar code*) y su teléfono celular conectado a Internet.
3. (Nosotros) ____Vamos____ a sentirnos cómodos sin calor ni frío en todo momento gracias a ropa con computadoras ligeras (*light*), invisibles y flexibles.
4. Los doctores del futuro ____van____ a ser computadoras capaces (*capable*) de diagnosticar las enfermedades (*illnesses*) en segundos.
5. Los virus informáticos ____van____ a mutarse para poder infectar a los humanos.
6. (Nosotros) ____Vamos____ a vivir en casas inteligentes sin la necesidad de hacer tareas domésticas.
7. Televisores inteligentes ____van____ a apagarse (*turn themselves off*) automáticamente si el televidente (*viewer*) se duerme durante un programa.
8. Papel inteligente en las paredes de los cuartos de una casa ____va____ a cambiar de color o diseño al pulsar (*upon pushing*) un botón.

6-25 ▶ ¿Qué se hace primero? ¿En qué orden dice alguien que va a hacer las siguientes cosas? Haz oraciones lógicas con **ir a** + infinitivo en la forma **yo**.

Modelo   consultar los sitios más interesantes / hacer una búsqueda
Voy a hacer una búsqueda y voy a consultar los sitios más interesantes.

1. comparar los precios / visitar varias tiendas en línea
2. comprar una nueva computadora / buscar la tienda más barata
3. abrir el procesador de texto / escribir un documento
4. escribir el texto / usar el corrector ortográfico (*spellcheck*)
5. corregir los errores / enviar el documento por correo electrónico
6. cerrar mi correo electrónico / leer los mensajes
7. descargar (*download*) varias canciones / hacer un CD
8. abrir una tienda en línea / comprar un dominio para un sitio web

📖 Repaso 2   Indicating whose it is: Possessive adjectives

SAM: 6-25
to 6-26

6-26 ▶ Explicaciones. Combina los elementos de cada columna para explicar las siguientes cosas. Usa la forma correcta del verbo **ser** y la palabra **de** como en el Modelo.

Modelo   *Un dominio es el nombre de un sitio web.*

un dominio	el código de país (*country*)	un documento
la terminación ".doc"	una placa de circuitos	*un sitio web*
una URL	el sistema operativo	una organización
las letras "mx"	la extensión	la página inicial de un sitio
un dominio con ".org"	*el nombre*	una computadora
la placa (*board*) madre	un sitio	un sitio web mexicano
Windows	la dirección	muchas computadoras personales

Para averiguar

In the activities on this page, you will be reviewing the possessive adjectives. Do you remember . . .

■ how you say *my, your, his, her, its, our,* and *their* in Spanish?
■ whether the ending of a possessive adjective agrees with the number and gender of the owner or of the object possessed?
■ what you use in Spanish instead of 's to show possession?

See page 70 for review.

6-27 ▶ Mensajes. Completa los siguientes mensajes dejados en la página de una red social con los adjetivos posesivos indicados.

La Bella

29 jul   02:29 a.m.

Me gusta (1) ___*tu*___ (*your*) página.
(2) ___*Mis*___ (*My*) amigos y yo estamos interesados en el arte y la fotografía como tú. Todos los miembros de (3) ___*nuestra*___ (*our*) comunidad tenemos páginas muy bonitas.
(4) ___*Mis*___ (*My*) amigos son todos muy creativos y (5) ___*sus*___ (*their*) páginas siempre tienen fotos nuevas e interesantes.

Picasso

30 jul   11:41 a.m.

Eres muy interesante y (6) ___*tu*___ (*your*) página es sensacional. Me gustaría ser (7) ___*tu*___ (*your*) amigo y chatear contigo. (8) ___*Nuestros*___ (*Our*) perfiles son muy parecidos. (9) ___*Mis*___ (*My*) intereses principales también son el arte y la fotografía. Chateo con (10) ___*tu*___ (*your*) amigo Daniel B. con frecuencia. ¡(11) ___*Su*___ (*His*) página es increíble! También me gustan (12) ___*sus*___ (*his*) videos.

6-28 ▶ Nuestro sitio web. Estás preparando el texto para un sitio web de una nueva tienda electrónica. Completa las siguientes oraciones de manera lógica con la forma correcta de **nuestro/a/os/as** en uno de los espacios en blanco y **su/s** en el otro.

Modelo   Bienvenidos a _*nuestro*_ sitio web. Somos _*su*_ mejor opción para comprar equipos electrónicos.

1. Ofrecemos mejor selección que todos ___*nuestros*___ competidores y ___*sus*___ precios son más altos.
2. Estamos a ___*su*___ servicio y garantizamos todos ___*nuestros*___ productos.
3. ¡___*Nuestro*___ objetivo es ___*su*___ satisfacción!
4. ___*Nuestros*___ técnicos bilingües están listos para responder a todas ___*sus*___ preguntas.
5. ___*Nuestro*___ departamento de servicio al cliente está abierto las veinticuatro horas del día para ajustarse a ___*su*___ horario.
6. ___*Su*___ información personal está segura con nosotros. Nunca compartimos información de ___*nuestros*___ clientes con terceros (*third parties*).
7. ___*Su*___ opinión es importante para nosotros. ___*Nuestra*___ dirección de correo electrónico es Servicio@Electrogigante.com.
8. Gracias por ___*su*___ visita a ___*nuestro*___ sitio web.

Warm-up for 6-26.
Have students complete the following sentences with a logical noun. You may wish to provide a list on the board. Answers are given in parentheses. *MODELO: Hotmail es el nombre de . . . > Hotmail es el nombre de un servicio de correo electrónico.* 1. *Macintosh es el nombre de . . . (una computadora).* 2. *Google es es nombre de . . . (un motor de búsqueda / un buscador).* 3. *Facebook es el nombre de . . . (una red social).* 4. *Microsoft Word es el nombre de . . . (un procesador de texto).* 5. *MySpace es el nombre de . . . (una red social).* 6. *Dell es el nombre de . . . (una computadora).* 7. *Gmail es el nombre de . . . (un servicio de correo electrónico).*

Answers for 6-26.
La terminación ".doc" es la extensión de un documento. / Una URL es la dirección de la página inicial de un sitio. / Las letras "mx" son el código de país de un sitio web mexicano. / Un dominio con ".org" es un sitio de una organización. / La placa madre es una placa de circuitos de una computadora. / Windows es el sistema operativo de muchas computadoras personales.

📖 **Repaso 3**   Pointing out which one: Demonstratives

SAM: 6-27
to 6-28

Para averiguar

In the activities on this page, you will be reviewing the demonstrative adjectives. Do you remember . . .
- how you say *this / these* in Spanish?
- how you say *that / those*?
- what the difference between **ese** and **aquel** is?

See page 140 for review.

6-29 ▶ ¿Este botón o aquel botón? Completa las siguientes explicaciones con la forma correcta de **este / esta / estos / estas** en el primer espacio en blanco y **aquel / aquella / aquellos / aquellas** en el segundo.

Modelo   *Este* botón con **B** es para cambiar la fuente a negrita y *aquel* botón con *I* es para letra cursiva.

1. ___Estos___ botones con muchas líneas son para alinear o centrar el texto y ___aquellos___ botones con puntos o números y líneas son para insertar viñetas (*bullets*) o números.
2. ___Este___ botón con U es para subrayar texto y ___aquel___ botón con **abc** es para usar el corrector ortográfico.
3. ___Estas___ palabras subrayadas con rojo tienen errores ortográficos y ___aquellas___ palabras subrayadas con verde tienen errores de gramática.
4. ___Esta___ hoja en blanco es para crear un documento nuevo y ___aquella___ carpeta (*folder*) abierta es para abrir un archivo que ya existe.
5. ___Este___ icono con tijeras (*scissors*) es para cortar texto y ___aquel___ icono con dos hojas es para copiar texto.
6. ___Esta___ letra X^2 es para el superíndice (*superscript*) y ___aquella___ letra X_2 es para el subíndice.

6-30 ▶ Más mensajes. Completa los siguientes mensajes de una red social con los adjetivos demostrativos indicados.

La Bella

30 oct   01:41 a.m.

¡Hola! Me gusta mucho tu página nueva con
(1) ___estos___ (*these*) gráficos tan bonitos y
(2) ___estas___ (*these*) fotos con todos. ¿Quién es (3) ___ese / aquel___ (*that*) hombre tan guapo contigo en la primera foto? Voy a cambiar mi página uno de
(4) ___estos___ (*these*) días también.

Picasso

03 nov   10:12 a.m.

¡Qué sorpresa ver
(5) ___esa / aquella___ (*that*) foto de todos nosotros en tu página! Recuerdo
(6) ___ese / aquel___ (*that*) día con nuestros amigos en
(7) ___esa / aquella___ (*that*) playa. ¿Quieres volver
(8) ___este___ (*this*) fin de semana? No tengo que trabajar (9) ___este___ (*this*) sábado.

Repaso 4

SAM: 6-29
to 6-30

Saying what people do: Stem-changing verbs

6-31 ▶ ¿Un usuario (*user*) o un motor de búsqueda?

Explica quién hace las siguientes cosas, un usuario o un motor de búsqueda.

Modelo   servir para buscar texto en sitios web
Un motor de búsqueda sirve para buscar texto en sitios web.

1. querer buscar algo
2. encontrar páginas web con el texto buscado
3. perder la concentración a veces
4. contar millones de sitios web en unos segundos
5. repetir la misma acción millones de veces en segundos
6. perder la paciencia con problemas técnicos
7. jugar a los videojuegos en la computadora para descansar
8. recordar la URL de millones de sitios web
9. entender los errores ortográficos
10. dormir si está cansado
11. servir a millones de usuarios
12. cerrar el motor de búsqueda después de terminar

Para averiguar

In the activities on this page, you will be reviewing stem-changing verbs. Do you remember . . .

■ in what forms of stem-changing verbs **e** becomes **ie** or **i**, and **o** or **u** becomes **ue**?
■ in what two forms there is no stem change?
■ which **-ar**, **-er**, and **-ir** verbs have stem changes?
■ what the irregular **yo** form of **decir** is?

See page 114 or refer to the verb charts in the appendix or in *MySpanishLab* for review.

Answers for 6-31.
1. Un usuario quiere buscar algo. 2. Un motor de búsqueda encuentra páginas web con el texto buscado. 3. Un usuario pierde la concentración a veces. 4. Un motor de búsqueda cuenta millones de sitios web en unos segundos. 5. Un motor de búsqueda repite la misma acción millones de veces en segundos. 6. Un usuario pierde la paciencia con problemas técnicos. 7. Un usuario juega a los videojuegos en la computadora para descansar. 8. Un motor de búsqueda recuerda la URL de millones de sitios web. 9. Un usuario entiende los errores ortográficos. 10. Un usuario duerme si está cansado. 11. Un motor de búsqueda sirve a millones de usuarios. 12. Un usuario cierra el motor de búsqueda después de terminar.

6-32 ▶ Bienvenido.

Estás preparando texto para un sitio web de una nueva tienda electrónica. Completa las siguientes oraciones con la forma correcta del verbo lógico entre paréntesis.

Modelo   (Nosotros) *Entendemos* que nuestros clientes *cuentan* con el mejor servicio. (contar, entender)

1. (Nosotros) __Tenemos__ los productos que usted __quiere__ a los mejores precios. (querer, tener)
2. (Nosotros) __Servimos__ a nuestros clientes con rapidez y dedicación. Usted nunca __pierde__ su tiempo con nosotros. (perder, servir)
3. (Nosotros) __Pedimos__ disculpas (*pardon*) a nuestros clientes si no __encuentran__ algo que buscan. (encontrar, pedir)
4. Si usted no __encuentra__ el producto que busca, (nosotros) __podemos__ ayudarlo. (encontrar, poder)
5. (Nosotros) __Entendemos__ que usted __puede__ tener preguntas. (entender, poder)
6. Usted __puede__ comprar las veinticuatro horas del día porque nuestra tienda en línea nunca __cierra__. (cerrar, poder)
7. Nuestros clientes siempre __vuelven__ porque (nosotros) __pensamos__ en ellos como amigos. (pensar, volver)
8. Siempre escuchamos y __recordamos__ lo que nuestros clientes __dicen__. (decir, recordar)

 **Vocabulario** Las comunidades en línea, los blogs y los foros

SAM: 6-31
to 6-32

Aquí hay unos comentarios de blogs.
CD 2
Track 58 ¿De qué tipo de blog son?

un blog personal o autobiográfico

un blog sobre noticias y actualidad

un blog sobre sociedad

un blog sobre deportes

un blog sobre cine o televisión

un blog sobre tecnología

un blog humorístico

un blog sobre juegos

¿Sabías que...?

Además de *MySpace* y *Facebook*, las redes sociales *Hi5* y *Sonico* son muy populares in Latinoamérica. *Sonico* es una red social basada en Argentina.

¡Ojo!

Comprehension strategy. In order to read blogs efficiently, it is necessary to be able to focus on the main idea of an entry or an opinion. See page 62 to review the comprehension strategy *Identifying the main idea.*

Debes visitar este sitio si quieres divertirte con juegos de Bob Esponja. Me gusta mucho. Hay un juego en el cual Bob maneja un bus a Atlantis y tienes que usar el cursor para guiar el bus entre las medusas y las algas. En otro juego puedes vestir a Bob, poniéndole ropa de diferentes estilos. ¡Es muy divertido!

Eres adicto a Internet cuando . . .

Dices que te llamas jgarcia@correo.com.
Tus hijos se llaman *Google* y *Yahoo*.
Tu perro tiene su propia página web.
Tu esposa pone su foto al lado del monitor para recordarte que existe.
Compras una casa de *Adobe*.
Le dices al taxista que tu dirección es: http://www.calleToledo.com/apto18.htm.

Tanto en el aspecto tenístico como en el mental, las capacidades del "Gran Roger" son fuera de lo común. Es un genio, un virtuoso, sin puntos débiles, que nació para ser el mejor tenista de la historia. Tiene un extraordinario talento bajo presión, con una excelente tolerancia a la frustración y una incomparable capacidad de adaptación a todo tipo de situaciones.

Algunos nunca leen blogs. Para otros los blogs son profetas de una nueva revolución de la información. Para mí, son una formidable herramienta para la libertad de expresión. En las sociedades donde existe censura y los medios de comunicación tradicionales están controlados por el gobierno, frecuentemente los bloggers son los auténticos periodistas.

CD 2
Track 59

Una conversación. Un hombre y una mujer recién casados están mirando un blog juntos y hacen comentarios sobre las entradas.

EL ESPOSO: Me gusta este sitio. Siempre tiene los mejores chistes. Vamos a leer los chistes sobre parejas. Escucha éste, "No desayuno porque pienso en ti. No almuerzo porque pienso en ti. No ceno porque pienso en ti. No duermo porque tengo hambre."

LA ESPOSA: Ah, mira ése, "Un anuncio en Match.com dice: Hombre invisible busca a mujer transparente para hacer cosas nunca vistas" . . . ¿Qué puede significar "cosas nunca vistas"? . . . Voy a leer el siguiente: "¿Por qué se casan las mujeres? Por falta de experiencia. ¿Por qué se divorcian? Por falta de paciencia. ¿Por qué se vuelven a casar? Por falta de memoria." . . . Pues yo tengo mucha paciencia, ¿verdad?

EL ESPOSO: ¡Claro que sí! Eres muy paciente . . . Bueno, vamos a leer el próximo chiste: "Tres hombres están en un bar y uno dice: De todas las películas de Disney mi esposa prefiere *Blancanieves y los siete enanitos,* y tenemos siete hijos. Otro hombre dice: Mi esposa prefiere *Los tres caballeros,* y tenemos tres hijos. El tercer hombre se levanta para irse y los otros le preguntan: ¿Por qué te vas? Y él contesta: Es que la película favorita de mi esposa es *101 Dálmatas.*"

LA ESPOSA: Ahh . . . Me gusta esa película. ¡Es mi favorita de todas!

EL ESPOSO: ¿De verdad?

Suggestion for *Una conversación.*
Set the scene for *Una conversación* and have students listen with books closed for the answer to the following questions. *¿De qué tipo de blog hablan?* (un blog humorístico), *¿Cuál es la película favorita de la esposa?* (101 Dálmatas). Then, have students open their books and listen again as they read along.

 CD 2, Track 60

¡A escuchar!

Ahora escuchen otra conversación en la cual una pareja habla de un blog. ¿Qué tipo de blog es? ¿De qué personas hablan?

6-33 ▶ **Comparaciones culturales.** Aquí hay tres respuestas a la pregunta "¿Son las redes sociales una pérdida de tiempo?" de un blog español. ¿Estás de acuerdo?

Yo estoy a favor de las redes sociales. Soy miembro de una red social y gracias a este sitio me comunico con amigos que viven muy lejos. También se encuentran grupos con intereses en común y el usuario tiene acceso a muchos foros que pueden ser educativos. Pero, entiendo que para muchos es una pérdida de tiempo. El factor determinante es el usuario.

En general las redes sociales no tienen ningún valor educativo. O por lo menos yo nunca aprendo nada viendo fotos de mis amigos y los amigos de los amigos de . . . o contestando cuestionarios de personalidad. Su propósito no es para educar sino que sirven para socializar, tal como lo indica su nombre. Sí, es verdad que pueden llegar a ser una pérdida de tiempo si se usan en exceso, pero no entiendo por qué hay que estar "a favor o en contra".

Tienen su utilidad, sobre todo para encontrarse o contactar con amigos. Incluso se usan para los negocios. Sin embargo, a mí no me gustan demasiado.

Audioscript for *¡A escuchar!*
EL ESPOSO: *¿Qué DVD vamos a ver esta noche? Voy a ir a la tienda a alquilar uno.*
LA ESPOSA: *A mí, me gustaría ver esa película con Penélope Cruz de hace unos años, Volver.*
EL ESPOSO: *Es una película del director español Almodóvar, ¿no? Vamos a ver que dicen en el blog Rodando.com. A veces me gustan sus películas y a veces no. A ver . . . A esta primera persona le gusta mucho. Escucha: "Esta película no tiene defectos. Su color, su estética, su música . . . cada detalle tiene su significado. Volver es una película conmovedora. Es un placer visual y auditivo".*
LA ESPOSA: *También me gusta este comentario. Escucha: "Me gusta la visión de las mujeres en las películas de Almodóvar. Es lo mejor que hace . . . hablar de nosotras y no precisamente 'hablar con ellas'".*
EL ESPOSO: *Bueno, si quieres, voy a buscar esa película.*

Answers for *¡A escuchar!*
Es un blog sobre cine. / Hablan de Penélope Cruz y el director español Almodóvar.

Follow-up for *Comparaciones culturales.*
Have students write their own entry to the blog, answering the question: *¿Son las redes sociales una pérdida de tiempo?*

 **Repaso 1**

SAM: 6-33
to 6-34

Saying what people do for themselves: Reflexive verbs

6-34 ▶ Adicción a Internet. Una esposa se queja (*is complaining*) porque su esposo es adicto a Internet y nunca pasa tiempo con ella. Completa sus oraciones para decir si hacen las cosas indicadas **siempre** o **nunca**.

Modelo   Mi esposo y yo . . . (divertirse juntos)
Mi esposo y yo nunca nos divertimos juntos.

1. Mi esposo . . . (quedarse toda la noche frente a la computadora)
2. Mi esposo . . . (acostarse hasta muy tarde)
3. Yo . . . (acostarse sola)
4. Mi esposo y yo . . . (comunicarse)
5. Mi esposo . . . (comunicarse con otras personas en línea)
6. Mi esposo . . . (enojarse si yo quiero usar la computadora)
7. Mi esposo y yo . . . (pelearse por la computadora)
8. Yo . . . (aburrirse sola)
9. Nosotros . . . (llevarse bien)
10. Un esposo y una esposa que . . . (divertirse juntos) . . . (divorciarse)

6-35 ▶ Relaciones cibernéticas. Completa cada sección del siguiente artículo sobre la infidelidad cibernética de manera lógica con la forma correcta de los verbos reflexivos entre paréntesis.

Modelo   El número de infieles *se multiplica* cada día en Internet. Millones de personas casadas *se inician* en relaciones sentimentales o románticas con desconocidos en sitios de conversación en Internet. (iniciarse, multiplicarse)

1. Usan el anonimato de sus computadoras para ___*convertirse*___ en otra persona de otra edad y estado civil (*age and marital status*). ___*Se divierten*___ con conquistas virtuales, con la ayuda de cámaras de video, servicios de mensajería instantánea y mensajes electrónicos. (convertirse, divertirse)
2. Este tipo de relaciones es una adicción para algunas personas que ___*se conectan*___ para ver quién está en línea después de que su pareja ___*se acuesta*___. (acostarse, conectarse)
3. Es el caso de Eduardo, ingeniero de 39 años. Todas las noches sigue la misma rutina: cena con su esposa y sus dos hijos, mira la televisión un rato y, a eso de las nueve ___*se sienta*___ frente a la computadora y ___*se transforma*___ en Don Juan, alias que usa para navegar por sitios de chat. (sentarse, transformarse)
4. Eduardo admite, "A veces, (yo) ___*me quedo*___ en línea varias horas y no ___*me acuesto*___ hasta las dos o tres de la mañana". (acostarse, quedarse)
5. "(Yo) ___*Me siento*___ como un jóven de veinte años cuando estoy chateando en línea," confiesa, "pero es díficil ___*levantarme*___ al día siguiente". (levantarse, sentirse)

📖 Repaso 2   Saying what people do for each other: Reciprocal verbs

SAM: 6-35 to 6-36

6-36 ▶ En una red social. Un miembro de una red social habla de lo que hace con sus amigos virtuales. Forma oraciones con los verbos en la forma **nosotros** y la terminación lógica de la lista.

grupos de discusión	nuestra red social
mensajería instantánea	auriculares (*headsets*) y micrófonos
el anonimato en Internet	una cámara web

Modelo   hacerse amigos virtuales con . . .
          Nos hacemos amigos virtuales con nuestra red social.

1. escribirse mensajes en tiempo real con . . .
2. verse con . . .
3. comunicarse sobre temas específicos con . . .
4. hablarse con chat de voz (*voice*) con . . .
5. protegerse de predadores en línea con . . .

6-37 ▶ Chistes. Encuentras los siguientes chistes en un blog humorístico. Completa cada chiste con la forma correcta de los verbos recíprocos o reflexivos de la lista correspondiente.

acostarse   despertarse   escribirse   *hablarse*   levantarse   pelearse

En este matrimonio el esposo y la esposa no *se hablan* (Modelo) después de (1) ___pelearse___ , sino que (*but instead*) (2) ___se escriben___ una nota para comunicarse. Una tarde después de una pelea, los dos se enojan y el esposo le escribe a su esposa, "¿Cuándo vamos a cenar?" y ella le escribe "La cena ya está lista". A la medianoche, todavía están enojados cuando (3) ___se acuestan___ . Él le escribe "Quiero despertarme a las 7:00" y ella le escribe "Está bien". Pasa la noche y cuando él (4) ___se despierta___ al día siguiente, ve que son las 10:30. Luego encuentra a su lado un papel que dice "Son las 7:00. Tienes que (5) ___levantarte___ ."

afeitarse	levantarse	ponerse	sentirse
casarse (3 veces)	mantenerse	quejarse (*to complain*)	

Una chica (6) ___se siente___ indecisa, porque no sabe (*know*) con cuál de sus dos pretendientes debe (7) ___casarse___ . Uno es doctor, y el otro es militar. Le pregunta a su madre: ¿Con cuál de los dos debo (8) ___casarme___ , mamá?
— Inmediatamente su madre reponde: Debes (9) ___casarte___ con el militar, con él vas a ser más feliz.
— ¿Por qué dices eso, mamá?
— Mira, ellos (10) ___se levantan___ temprano, (11) ___se afeitan___ todas las mañanas, (12) ___se ponen___ ropa limpia que lavan ellos mismos y (13) ___se mantienen___ en forma (*shape*). Además reciben órdenes sin (14) ___quejarse___ .

acostarse	mirarse	preguntarse

Dos pulgas (*fleas*) (15) ___se acuestan___ en el pelo de un perro, ven las estrellas (*the stars*), luego (16) ___se miran___ y (17) ___se preguntan___ : ¿crees que hay vida en otro perro?

Para **averiguar**

In the activities on this page, you will be reviewing reciprocal verbs. Do you remember . . .
■ what a reciprocal verb is?
■ whether reciprocal verbs in Spanish look different or have different word order from reflexive verbs?
■ where you place reciprocal pronouns with verbs conjugated in the present tense? where you place them with an infinitive after **antes de** or **después de**?
■ what the two possible placements of the reciprocal pronoun are when you use a reciprocal verb in the infinitive following a conjugated verb? whether the reciprocal pronoun with infinitives changes to correspond to the subject of the conjugated verb?
See pages 136 and 142 or refer to the verb charts in the appendix or in *MySpanishLab* for review.

Suggestion for 6-36 and 6-37.
Point out that some of the verbs are reciprocal and others are reflexive in these activities. Ask students to sort the verbs according to type.

Answers for 6-36.
1. *Nos escribimos mensajes en tiempo real con mensajería instantánea.* 2. *Nos vemos con una cámara web.* 3. *Nos comunicamos sobre temas específicos con grupos de discusión.* 4. *Nos hablamos con chat de voz con auriculares y micrófonos.* 5. *Nos protegemos de predadores en línea con el anonimato en Internet.*

Follow-up for 6-37.
As homework, have students search "*chistes cortos en español*" to find a joke to share with the class.

📖 Repaso 3

SAM: 6-37
to 6-38

Describing what is happening: The present progressive

Suggestion for 6-38.
Have students look at live web cams from sites in Hispanic countries around the world.

Answers for 6-38.
1. *Hace buen tiempo. No está lloviendo.* 2. *Todos están paseando tranquilamente por la calle.*
3. *Nadie está corriendo.* 4. *Nadie está comiendo.*
5. *Una mujer está hablando por teléfono.* 6. *Una mujer con un abrigo marrón está mirando hacia la cámara.* 7. *Un hombre con gafas de sol está acompañando al hombre con la chaqueta gris.*
8. *Los dos hombres están observando algo a la derecha.*

Answers for 6-39.
1. *estoy hablando, Estoy leyendo;* 2. *estás divirtiéndote / te estás divirtiendo, Estás saliendo;*
3. *estamos celebrando, estamos abrazándonos / nos estamos abrazando;* 4. *está viendo, está durmiendo*

6-38 ▶ Por cámara web. Estás viendo una calle peatonal en Buenos Aires, Argentina, mediante una cámara web en vivo. Escoge (*Choose*) la descripción que mejor describa lo que está pasando y complétala con el presente progresivo del verbo entre paréntesis.

Modelo   Mucha gente . . . / Nadie . . . (entrar y salir de tiendas)
          Mucha gente está entrando y saliendo de tiendas.

1. Hace buen tiempo. No . . . / Hace mal tiempo y . . . (llover)
2. Todos . . . / Nadie . . . (pasear tranquilamente por la calle)
3. Dos niños . . . / Nadie . . . (correr)
4. Varias personas . . . / Nadie . . . (comer)
5. Un hombre . . . / Una mujer . . . (hablar por teléfono)
6. Un hombre con una chaqueta gris . . . / Una mujer con un abrigo marrón . . . (mirar hacia [*towards*] la cámara)
7. Un hombre con gafas de sol . . . / Una mujer con gafas de sol . . . (acompañar al hombre con la chaqueta gris)
8. Los dos hombres . . . / Sólo el hombre con las gafas del sol . . . (observar algo a la derecha)

6-39 ▶ Chateando. Dos amigos virtuales, Picasso y La Bella, están chateando en una red social. Completa su conversación de manera lógica con los verbos entre paréntesis en el presente progresivo.

Modelo   BELLA: Hola, Picasso. ¿Qué *estás haciendo* (tú)? *¿Estás chateando* con alguien? (chatear, hacer)

1. PICASSO: Hola, Bella. No, (yo) no _____ con nadie en particular. _____ los perfiles de los amigos de mis amigos. (hablar, leer)
2. BELLA: Escucha, Picasso, ¡parece que (tú) _____ en grande en las fotos nuevas del parque de atracciones que tienes en tu página! ¿Quiénes son esas muchachas contigo? ¿ _____ con una de ellas? (divertirse, salir)
3. PICASSO: Son mis primas. En las fotos (nosotros) _____ el cumpleaños de mi prima. Ella y yo _____ en la primera foto . . . Oye Bella, ¿por qué nunca estás conectada recientemente? (abrazarse, celebrar)
4. BELLA: Es que mis padres dicen que pierdo demasiado tiempo en línea, pero esta noche mi madre _____ la tele y mi padre ya _____. (dormir, ver)

📖Repaso 4 Describing how: Adverbs

SAM: 6-39
to 6-40

6-40 ▶ Test de personalidad. Estás preparando un test de personalidad llamado *¿Eres obsesivo compulsivo?* para un sitio web. En las siguientes preguntas, forma un adverbio sinónimo de las palabras en letra cursiva usando uno de los adjetivos entre paréntesis.

Modelo   ¿Haces ciertos gestos *una y otra vez*? (voluntario, repetitivo)
¿Haces ciertos gestos *repetitivamente*?

1. ¿Limpias *demasiado* las cosas? (excesivo, completo)
2. *¿Siempre* te lavas las manos? (activo, constante)
3. ¿Revisas *varias veces* el gas, el agua, las luces y las cerraduras (*the lights and locks*) cuando sales de casa? (repetido, regular)
4. ¿Organizas *minuciosamente* tus viajes antes de salir? (breve, detallado)
5. ¿Sigues rutinas *sistemáticamente*? (metódico, relajado)
6. ¿Completas *escrupulosamente* todo tu trabajo? (meticuloso, rápido)
7. ¿Te vistes siempre *con ropa elegante* para salir con los amigos? (impecable, casual)
8. ¿Evitas (*Do you avoid*) *sin razón* ciertas cosas porque crees que traen mala suerte? (periódico, supersticioso)
9. ¿Piensas *con frecuencia* en problemas sin poder pensar en otra cosa? (frecuente, ilógico)
10. ¿Te sientes frustrado/a *con facilidad*? (fácil, reciente)

6-41 ▶ Seguridad en Internet. Aquí hay unas reglas importantes para proteger a los hijos en Internet. Completa cada una de manera lógica con adverbios formados a partir de los adjetivos entre paréntesis.

Es importante . . .

Modelo   vigilar *constantemente* los acciones de los hijos y hablar *abiertamente* con ellos. (abierto, constante)

1. estar _____ informado de los riesgos (*risks*) en Internet para hablar _____ con los hijos. (claro, suficiente)
2. usar seudónimos en vez de identificarse _____ porque los predadores buscan _____ víctimas inocentes en Internet. (constante, personal)
3. hablar _____ con los hijos de situaciones _____ peligrosas (*dangerous*) en Internet. (franco, potencial)
4. seleccionar una contraseña (*password*) _____ recordable por el usuario pero _____ descifrable por otros. (difícil, fácil)
5. cerrar _____ los sistemas de correo electrónico en computadoras de uso público después de terminar porque no se cierran _____ al abrir otra página. (automático, regular)
6. hacer preguntas si los hijos cambian _____ de pantalla (*screen*) cuando entras en su cuarto o si están _____ molestos por tus interrupciones. (inusual, rápido)
7. hablar _____ de problemas con los hijos sin reaccionar _____. (calmado, exagerado)
8. recordar que no se debe descargar _____ música o películas aun (*even*) navegando _____ en la web. (anónimo, ilegal)

Follow-up for 6-41.
Have students work in groups to prepare two or three sentences describing someone addicted to the Internet using adverbs based on some of the following adjectives or others of their choice. *Modelo: constante > Abre constantemente su correo electrónico para ver si hay mensajes nuevos. (excesivo, regular, completo, principal, aproximado, simple, normal, real, repetido, total, entero, perfecto, persistente, incesante)*

Para **averiguar**

In the activities on this page, you will be reviewing the formation and use of adverbs. Do you remember . . .

■ what ending you use to form an adverb from an adjective in Spanish? whether you attach this ending to the masculine or feminine form of the adjective?

■ where you generally place adverbs with respect to verbs they modify? where you place them if they modify a whole sentence? if they modify an adjective?

See page 116 for review.

Answers for 6-40.
1. *¿Limpias excesivamente las cosas?* 2. *¿Te lavas constantemente las manos?* 3. *¿Revisas repetidamente el gas, el agua, las luces y las cerraduras cuando sales de casa?* 4. *¿Organizas detalladamente tus viajes antes de salir?* 5. *¿Sigues rutinas metódicamente?* 6. *¿Completas meticulosamente todo tu trabajo?* 7. *¿Te vistes siempre impecablemente para salir con los amigos?* 8. *¿Evitas supersticiosamente ciertas cosas porque crees que traen mala suerte?* 9. *¿Piensas frecuentemente en problemas sin poder pensar en otra cosa?* 10. *¿Te sientes fácilmente frustrado/a?*

Follow-up for 6-40.
Have students answer each question.

Answers for 6-41.
1. *estar suficientemente informado de los riesgos en Internet para hablar claramente con los hijos.* 2. *usar seudónimos en vez de identificarte personalmente porque los predadores buscan constantemente víctimas inocentes en Internet.* 3. *hablar francamente con los hijos de situaciones potencialmente peligrosas en Internet.* 4. *seleccionar una contraseña fácilmente recordable por el usuario pero difícilmente descifrable por otros.* 5. *cerrar regularmente los sistemas de correo electrónico en computadoras de uso público después de terminar, porque no se cierran automáticamente al abrir otra página.* 6. *hacer preguntas si los hijos cambian rápidamente de pantalla cuando entras en su cuarto o si están inusualmente molestos por tus interrupciones.* 7. *hablar calmadamente de problemas con los hijos sin reaccionar exageradamente.* 8. *recordar que no se debe descargar ilegalmente música o películas aun navegando anónimamente en la web.*

Verb Charts

Regular Verbs: Simple Tenses

Infinitive / Present Participle / Past Participle	Indicative					Subjunctive		Imperative
	Present	Imperfect	Preterit	Future	Conditional	Present	Imperfect	Commands
hablar hablando hablado	hablo hablas habla hablamos habláis hablan	hablaba hablabas hablaba hablábamos hablabais hablaban	hablé hablaste habló hablamos hablasteis hablaron	hablaré hablarás hablará hablaremos hablaréis hablarán	hablaría hablarías hablaría hablaríamos hablaríais hablarían	hable hables hable hablemos habléis hablen	hablara hablaras hablara habláramos hablarais hablaran	habla (tú), no hables hable (usted) hablemos hablad (vosotros), no habléis hablen (Uds.)
comer comiendo comido	como comes come comemos coméis comen	comía comías comía comíamos comíais comían	comí comiste comió comimos comisteis comieron	comeré comerás comerá comeremos comeréis comerán	comería comerías comería comeríamos comeríais comerían	coma comas coma comamos comáis coman	comiera comieras comiera comiéramos comierais comieran	come (tú), no comas coma (usted) comamos comed (vosotros), no comáis coman (Uds.)
vivir viviendo vivido	vivo vives vive vivimos vivís viven	vivía vivías vivía vivíamos vivíais vivían	viví viviste vivió vivimos vivisteis vivieron	viviré vivirás vivirá viviremos viviréis vivirán	viviría vivirías viviría viviríamos viviríais vivirían	viva vivas viva vivamos viváis vivan	viviera vivieras viviera viviéramos vivierais vivieran	vive (tú), no vivas viva (usted) vivamos vivid (vosotros), no viváis vivan (Uds.)

Regular Verbs: Perfect Tenses

Indicative					Subjunctive	
Present Perfect	**Past Perfect**	**Preterit Perfect**	**Future Perfect**	**Conditional Perfect**	**Present Perfect**	**Past Perfect**
he	había	hube	habré	habría	haya	hubiera
has	habías	hubiste	habrás	habrías	hayas	hubieras
ha hablado	había hablado	hubo hablado	habrá hablado	habría hablado	haya hablado	hubiera hablado
hemos comido	habíamos comido	hubimos comido	habremos comido	habríamos comido	hayamos comido	hubiéramos comido
habéis vivido	habíais vivido	hubisteis vivido	habréis vivido	habríais vivido	hayáis vivido	hubierais vivido
han	habían	hubieron	habrán	habrían	hayan	hubieran

Irregular Verbs

Infinitive / Present Participle / Past Participle	Indicative					Subjunctive		Imperative
	Present	**Imperfect**	**Preterit**	**Future**	**Conditional**	**Present**	**Imperfect**	**Commands**
andar	ando	andaba	anduve	andaré	andaría	ande	anduviera	anda (tú),
andando	andas	andabas	anduviste	andarás	andarías	andes	anduvieras	no andes
andado	anda	andaba	anduvo	andará	andaría	ande	anduviera	ande (usted)
	andamos	andábamos	anduvimos	andaremos	andaríamos	andemos	anduviéramos	andemos
	andáis	andabais	anduvisteis	andaréis	andaríais	andéis	anduvierais	andad (vosotros),
	andan	andaban	anduvieron	andarán	andarían	anden	anduvieran	no andéis
								anden (Uds.)
caer	caigo	caía	caí	caeré	caería	caiga	cayera	cae (tú),
cayendo	caes	caías	caíste	caerás	caerías	caigas	cayeras	no caigas
caído	cae	caía	cayó	caerá	caería	caiga	cayera	caiga (usted)
	caemos	caíamos	caímos	caeremos	caeríamos	caigamos	cayéramos	caigamos
	caéis	caíais	caísteis	caeréis	caeríais	caigáis	cayerais	caed (vosotros),
	caen	caían	cayeron	caerán	caerían	caigan	cayeran	no caigáis
								caigan (Uds.)
dar	doy	daba	di	daré	daría	dé	diera	da (tú),
dando	das	dabas	diste	darás	darías	des	dieras	no des
dado	da	daba	dio	dará	daría	dé	diera	dé (usted)
	damos	dábamos	dimos	daremos	daríamos	demos	diéramos	demos
	dais	dabais	disteis	daréis	daríais	deis	dierais	dad (vosotros),
	dan	daban	dieron	darán	darían	den	dieran	no deis
								den (Uds.)
decir	digo	decía	dije	diré	diría	diga	dijera	di (tú),
diciendo	dices	decías	dijiste	dirás	dirías	digas	dijeras	no digas
dicho	dice	decía	dijo	dirá	diría	diga	dijera	diga (usted)
	decimos	decíamos	dijimos	diremos	diríamos	digamos	dijéramos	digamos
	decís	decíais	dijisteis	diréis	diríais	digáis	dijerais	decid (vosotros),
	dicen	decían	dijeron	dirán	dirían	digan	dijeran	no digáis
								digan (Uds.)

Irregular Verbs (continued)

Infinitive / Present Participle / Past Participle	Indicative					Subjunctive		Imperative
	Present	Imperfect	Preterit	Future	Conditional	Present	Imperfect	Commands
estar estando estado	estoy estás está estamos estáis están	estaba estabas estaba estábamos estabais estaban	estuve estuviste estuvo estuvimos estuvisteis estuvieron	estaré estarás estará estaremos estaréis estarán	estaría estarías estaría estaríamos estaríais estarían	esté estés esté estemos estéis estén	estuviera estuvieras estuviera estuviéramos estuvierais estuvieran	está (tú), no estés esté (usted) estemos estad (vosotros), no estéis estén (Uds.)
haber habiendo habido	he has ha hemos habéis han	había habías había habíamos habíais habían	hube hubiste hubo hubimos hubisteis hubieron	habré habrás habrá habremos habréis habrán	habría habrías habría habríamos habríais habrían	haya hayas haya hayamos hayáis hayan	hubiera hubieras hubiera hubiéramos hubierais hubieran	
hacer haciendo hecho	hago haces hace hacemos hacéis hacen	hacía hacías hacía hacíamos hacíais hacían	hice hiciste hizo hicimos hicisteis hicieron	haré harás hará haremos haréis harán	haría harías haría haríamos haríais harían	haga hagas haga hagamos hagáis hagan	hiciera hicieras hiciera hiciéramos hicierais hicieran	haz (tú), no hagas haga (usted) hagamos haced (vosotros), no hagáis hagan (Uds.)
ir yendo ido	voy vas va vamos vais van	iba ibas iba íbamos ibais iban	fui fuiste fue fuimos fuisteis fueron	iré irás irá iremos iréis irán	iría irías iría iríamos iríais irían	vaya vayas vaya vayamos vayáis vayan	fuera fueras fuera fuéramos fuerais fueran	ve (tú), no vayas vaya (usted) vamos, no vayamos id (vosotros), no vayáis vayan (Uds.)
oír oyendo oído	oigo oyes oye oímos oís oyen	oía oías oía oíamos oíais oían	oí oíste oyó oímos oísteis oyeron	oiré oirás oirá oiremos oiréis oirán	oiría oirías oiría oiríamos oiríais oirían	oiga oigas oiga oigamos oigáis oigan	oyera oyeras oyera oyéramos oyerais oyeran	oye (tú), no oigas oiga (usted) oigamos oíd (vosotros), no oigáis oigan (Uds.)

Irregular Verbs (continued)

Infinitive Present Participle Past Participle	Indicative					Subjunctive		Imperative
	Present	Imperfect	Preterit	Future	Conditional	Present	Imperfect	Commands
poder pudiendo podido	puedo puedes puede podemos podéis pueden	podía podías podía podíamos podíais podían	pude pudiste pudo pudimos pudisteis pudieron	podré podrás podrá podremos podréis podrán	podría podrías podría podríamos podríais podrían	pueda puedas pueda podamos podáis puedan	pudiera pudieras pudiera pudiéramos pudierais pudieran	
poner poniendo puesto	pongo pones pone ponemos ponéis ponen	ponía ponías ponía poníamos poníais ponían	puse pusiste puso pusimos pusisteis pusieron	pondré pondrás pondrá pondremos pondréis pondrán	pondría pondrías pondría pondríamos pondríais pondrían	ponga pongas ponga pongamos pongáis pongan	pusiera pusieras pusiera pusiéramos pusierais pusieran	pon (tú), no pongas ponga (usted) pongamos poned (vosotros), no pongáis pongan (Uds.)
querer queriendo querido	quiero quieres quiere queremos queréis quieren	quería querías quería queríamos queríais querían	quise quisiste quiso quisimos quisisteis quisieron	querré querrás querrá querremos querréis querrán	querría querrías querría querríamos querríais querrían	quiera quieras quiera queramos queráis quieran	quisiera quisieras quisiera quisiéramos quisierais quisieran	quiere (tú), no quieras quiera (usted) queramos quered (vosotros), no queráis quieran (Uds.)
saber sabiendo sabido	sé sabes sabe sabemos sabéis saben	sabía sabías sabía sabíamos sabíais sabían	supe supiste supo supimos supisteis supieron	sabré sabrás sabrá sabremos sabréis sabrán	sabría sabrías sabría sabríamos sabríais sabrían	sepa sepas sepa sepamos sepáis sepan	supiera supieras supiera supiéramos supierais supieran	sabe (tú), no sepas sepa (usted) sepamos sabed (vosotros), no sepáis sepan (Uds.)
salir saliendo salido	salgo sales sale salimos salís salen	salía salías salía salíamos salíais salían	salí saliste salió salimos salisteis salieron	saldré saldrás saldrá saldremos saldréis saldrán	saldría saldrías saldría saldríamos saldríais saldrían	salga salgas salga salgamos salgáis salgan	saliera salieras saliera saliéramos salierais salieran	sal (tú), no salgas salga (usted) salgamos salid (vosotros), no salgáis salgan (Uds.)

Irregular Verbs (continued)

Infinitive / Present Participle / Past Participle	Indicative						Subjunctive		Imperative
	Present	Imperfect	Preterit	Future	Conditional		Present	Imperfect	Commands
ser siendo sido	soy eres es somos sois son	era eras era éramos erais eran	fui fuiste fue fuimos fuisteis fueron	seré serás será seremos seréis serán	sería serías sería seríamos seríais serían		sea seas sea seamos seáis sean	fuera fueras fuera fuéramos fuerais fueran	sé (tú), no seas sea (usted) seamos sed (vosotros), no seáis sean (Uds.)
tener teniendo tenido	tengo tienes tiene tenemos tenéis tienen	tenía tenías tenía teníamos teníais tenían	tuve tuviste tuvo tuvimos tuvisteis tuvieron	tendré tendrás tendrá tendremos tendréis tendrán	tendría tendrías tendría tendríamos tendríais tendrían		tenga tengas tenga tengamos tengáis tengan	tuviera tuvieras tuviera tuviéramos tuvierais tuvieran	ten (tú), no tengas tenga (usted) tengamos tened (vosotros), no tengáis tengan (Uds.)
traer trayendo traído	traigo traes trae traemos traéis traen	traía traías traía traíamos traíais traían	traje trajiste trajo trajimos trajisteis trajeron	traeré traerás traerá traeremos traeréis traerán	traería traerías traería traeríamos traeríais traerían		traiga traigas traiga traigamos traigáis traigan	trajera trajeras trajera trajéramos trajerais trajeran	trae (tú), no traigas traiga (usted) traigamos traed (vosotros), no traigáis traigan (Uds.)
venir viniendo venido	vengo vienes viene venimos venís vienen	venía venías venía veníamos veníais venían	vine viniste vino vinimos vinisteis vinieron	vendré vendrás vendrá vendremos vendréis vendrán	vendría vendrías vendría vendríamos vendríais vendrían		venga vengas venga vengamos vengáis vengan	viniera vinieras viniera viniéramos vinierais vinieran	ven (tú), no vengas venga (usted) vengamos venid (vosotros), no vengáis vengan (Uds.)
ver viendo visto	veo ves ve vemos veis ven	veía veías veía veíamos veíais veían	vi viste vio vimos visteis vieron	veré verás verá veremos veréis verán	vería verías vería veríamos veríais verían		vea veas vea veamos veáis vean	viera vieras viera viéramos vierais vieran	ve (tú), no veas vea (usted) veamos ved (vosotros), no veáis vean (Uds.)

Stem-Changing and Orthographic-Changing Verbs

Infinitive / Present Participle / Past Participle	Indicative					Subjunctive		Imperative
	Present	Imperfect	Preterit	Future	Conditional	Present	Imperfect	Commands
almorzar (z, c) almorzando almorzado	almuerzo almuerzas almuerza almorzamos almorzáis almuerzan	almorzaba almorzabas almorzaba almorzábamos almorzabais almorzaban	almorcé almorzaste almorzó almorzamos almorzasteis almorzaron	almorzaré almorzarás almorzará almorzaremos almorzaréis almorzarán	almorzaría almorzarías almorzaría almorzaríamos almorzaríais almorzarían	almuerce almuerces almuerce almorcemos almorcéis almuercen	almorzara almorzaras almorzara almorzáramos almorzarais almorzaran	almuerza (tú) no almuerces almuerce (usted) almorcemos almorzad (vosotros) no almorcéis almuercen (Uds.)
buscar (c, qu) buscando buscado	busco buscas busca buscamos buscáis buscan	buscaba buscabas buscaba buscábamos buscabais buscaban	busqué buscaste buscó buscamos buscasteis buscaron	buscaré buscarás buscará buscaremos buscaréis buscarán	buscaría buscarías buscaría buscaríamos buscaríais buscarían	busque busques busque busquemos busquéis busquen	buscara buscaras buscara buscáramos buscarais buscaran	busca (tú) no busques busque (usted) busquemos buscad (vosotros) no busquéis busquen (Uds.)
corregir (g, j) corrigiendo corregido	corrijo corriges corrige corregimos corregís corrigen	corregía corregías corregía corregíamos corregíais corregían	corregí corregiste corrigió corregimos corregisteis corrigieron	corregiré corregirás corregirá corregiremos corregiréis corregirán	corregiría corregirías corregiría corregiríamos corregiríais corregirían	corrija corrijas corrija corrijamos corrijáis corrijan	corrigiera corrigieras corrigiera corrigiéramos corrigierais corrigieran	corrige (tú) no corrijas corrija (usted) corrijamos corregid (vosotros) no corrijáis corrijan (Uds.)
dormir (ue, u) durmiendo dormido	duermo duermes duerme dormimos dormís duermen	dormía dormías dormía dormíamos dormíais dormían	dormí dormiste durmió dormimos dormisteis durmieron	dormiré dormirás dormirá dormiremos dormiréis dormirán	dormiría dormirías dormiría dormiríamos dormiríais dormirían	duerma duermas duerma durmamos durmáis duerman	durmiera durmieras durmiera durmiéramos durmierais durmieran	duerme (tú) no duermas duerma (usted) durmamos dormid (vosotros) no durmáis duerman (Uds.)
incluir (y) incluyendo incluido	incluyo incluyes incluye incluimos incluís incluyen	incluía incluías incluía incluíamos incluíais incluían	incluí incluiste incluyó incluimos incluisteis incluyeron	incluiré incluirás incluirá incluiremos incluiréis incluirán	incluiría incluirías incluiría incluiríamos incluiríais incluirían	incluya incluyas incluya incluyamos incluyáis incluyan	incluyera incluyeras incluyera incluyéramos incluyerais incluyeran	incluye (tú), no incluyas incluya (usted) incluyamos incluid (vosotros), no incluyáis incluyan (Uds.)

Stem-Changing and Orthographic-Changing Verbs (continued)

Infinitive / Present Participle / Past Participle	Indicative					Subjunctive		Imperative
	Present	Imperfect	Preterit	Future	Conditional	Present	Imperfect	Commands
llegar (g, gu) llegando llegado	llego llegas llega llegamos llegáis llegan	llegaba llegabas llegaba llegábamos llegabais llegaban	llegué llegaste llegó llegamos llegasteis llegaron	llegaré llegarás llegará llegaremos llegaréis llegarán	llegaría llegarías llegaría llegaríamos llegaríais llegarían	llegue llegues llegue lleguemos lleguéis lleguen	llegara llegaras llegara llegáramos llegarais llegaran	llega (tú) no llegues llegue (usted) lleguemos llegad (vosotros) no lleguéis lleguen (Uds.)
pedir (i, i) pidiendo pedido	pido pides pide pedimos pedís piden	pedía pedías pedía pedíamos pedíais pedían	pedí pediste pidió pedimos pedisteis pidieron	pediré pedirás pedirá pediremos pediréis pedirán	pediría pedirías pediría pediríamos pediríais pedirían	pida pidas pida pidamos pidáis pidan	pidiera pidieras pidiera pidiéramos pidierais pidieran	pide (tú), no pidas pida (usted) pidamos pedid (vosotros), no pidáis pidan (Uds.)
pensar (ie) pensando pensado	pienso piensas piensa pensamos pensáis piensan	pensaba pensabas pensaba pensábamos pensabais pensaban	pensé pensaste pensó pensamos pensasteis pensaron	pensaré pensarás pensará pensaremos pensaréis pensarán	pensaría pensarías pensaría pensaríamos pensaríais pensarían	piense pienses piense pensemos penséis piensen	pensara pensaras pensara pensáramos pensarais pensaran	piensa (tú), no pienses piense (usted) pensemos pensad (vosotros), no penséis piensen (Uds.)
producir (zc) produciendo producido	produzco produces produce producimos producís producen	producía producías producía producíamos producíais producían	produje produjiste produjo produjimos produjisteis produjeron	produciré producirás producirá produciremos produciréis producirán	produciría producirías produciría produciríamos produciríais producirían	produzca produzcas produzca produzcamos produzcáis produzcan	produjera produjeras produjera produjéramos produjerais produjeran	produce (tú), no produzcas produzca (usted) produzcamos producid (vosotros), no produzcáis produzcan (Uds.)
reír (i, i) riendo reído	río ríes ríe reímos reís ríen	reía reías reía reíamos reíais reían	reí reíste rio reímos reísteis rieron	reiré reirás reirá reiremos reiréis reirán	reiría reirías reiría reiríamos reiríais reirían	ría rías ría riamos riáis rían	riera rieras riera riéramos rierais rieran	ríe (tú), no rías ría (usted) riamos reíd (vosotros), no riáis rían (Uds.)

Stem-Changing and Orthographic-Changing Verbs (continued)

Infinitive Present Participle Past Participle	Indicative					Subjunctive		Imperative
	Present	Imperfect	Preterit	Future	Conditional	Present	Imperfect	Commands
seguir (i, i) (ga) siguiendo seguido	sigo sigues sigue seguimos seguís siguen	seguía seguías seguía seguíamos seguíais seguían	seguí seguiste siguió seguimos seguisteis siguieron	seguiré seguirás seguirá seguiremos seguiréis seguirán	seguiría seguirías seguiría seguiríamos seguiríais seguirían	siga sigas siga sigamos sigáis sigan	siguiera siguieras siguiera siguiéramos siguierais siguieran	sigue (tú), no sigas siga (usted) sigamos seguid (vosotros), no sigáis sigan (Uds.)
sentir (ie, i) sintiendo sentido	siento sientes siente sentimos sentís sienten	sentía sentías sentía sentíamos sentíais sentían	sentí sentiste sintió sentimos sentisteis sintieron	sentiré sentirás sentirá sentiremos sentiréis sentirán	sentiría sentirías sentiría sentiríamos sentiríais sentirían	sienta sientas sienta sintamos sintáis sientan	sintiera sintieras sintiera sintiéramos sintierais sintieran	siente (tú), no sientas sienta (usted) sintamos sentid (vosotros), no sintáis sientan (Uds.)
volver (ue) volviendo vuelto	vuelvo vuelves vuelve volvemos volvéis vuelven	volvía volvías volvía volvíamos volvíais volvían	volví volviste volvió volvimos volvisteis volvieron	volveré volverás volverá volveremos volveréis volverán	volvería volverías volvería volveríamos volveríais volverían	vuelva vuelvas vuelva volvamos volváis vuelvan	volviera volvieras volviera volviéramos volvierais volvieran	vuelve (tú), no vuelvas vuelva (usted) volvamos volved (vosotros), no volváis vuelvan (Uds.)

Spanish-English Glossary

The **Spanish-English Glossary** presents all active vocabulary presented in *Hoy día*, as well as all words used in the readings, except for exact cognates. Numbers following entries indicate the chapter where words are introduced. All translations separated by commas before a number are considered active in that chapter. Gender of nouns in Spanish is indicated by *(m)* for masculine and *(f)* for feminine. Nouns referring to people that have both masculine and feminine forms are indicated by *(m/f)*, and those that are generally used in the prural are followed by *(pl)*.

A

a to; **a causa de** because of; **a continuación** next; **a la derecha de** to the right of 2; **a la izquierda de** to the left of 2; **a la parrilla** grilled; **a la una, a las dos** at one o'clock, at two o'clock 2; **a pesar de que** despite, in spite of; **a petición** upon request 11; **A qué hora?** At what time? 2; **a través de** across; **a veces** sometimes 4; at times 2; **al** + *infinitivo* as soon as you + verb 7; **al** + *infinitivo* upon verb + *-ing* 7; **al aire libre** outdoors 2; **al este de** east of 2; **al fondo de** at the end of, at the back of 7; **al horno** baked; **al lado de** next to 2; **al norte de** north of 2; **al oeste de** west of 2; **al principio** at the beginning 8; **al sur de** south of 2; **al vapor** steamed
abajo down
abandonar abandon
abierto/a open 2, 4
abogado/a *(m/f)* lawyer 8
abono *(m)* fertilizer
abordar board 7
abrazar(se) hug (each other) 5
abrazo *(m)* hug
abrigo *(m)* coat; overcoat 5
abril April 5
abrir open 3
abrocharse el cinturón buckle your seatbelt 7
absolutamente absolutely
absurdo/a absurd 10
abuela *(f)* grandmother 3
abuelo *(m)* grandfather 3
abuelos *(mpl)* grandparents 3
aburrido/a bored 2, 4; boring 1
aburrirse get bored 5
abuso *(m)* abuse
acá here 5; **por acá** over / through here 5
acabar de have just
acampar camp 7
acceder accede
acceso *(m)* access 11

accesorio *(m)* accessory 4
accidente *(m)* accident 10
acción *(f)* action
acelerar accelerate, speed up
aceptar accept
acerca de about 8
aclarar clarify
acompañar accompany
aconsejar advise 10
acontecimiento *(m)* event 8
acostarse (ue) lie down, go to bed 5
acostumbrado/a accustomed
acostumbrar accustom
actitud *(f)* attitude
actividad *(f)* activity 2
activista *(m/f)* activist
activo/a active
actor *(m)* actor 8
actriz *(f)* actress 8
actualidad *(f)* current event
actualmente currently, presently
actuar act
acusación *(f)* accusation
adaptación *(f)* adaptation
adaptar adapt
adecuado/a appropriate
además besides 11
adentro inside
adicción *(f)* addiction
adicional additional
adicto/a *(m/f)* addict
Adiós. Good-bye. 1
adivinar guess
adjetivo *(m)* adjective
administración *(f)* administration; **administración de empresas** *(f)* business administration
administrador/a *(m/f)* administrator
admirador/a *(m/f)* admirer
admirar admire
admitir admit
adobado/a marinated
adolescencia *(f)* adolescence
adónde (to) where 2
adoptar adopt
adquisitivo/a purchasing

adulto/a *(m/f)* adult
adverbio *(m)* adverb
advertencia *(f)* warning
advertir warn
aerolínea *(f)* airline 7
aeropuerto *(m)* airport 7
afectar affect
afeitarse shave
afirmación *(f)* affirmation
africano/a African
afuera outside 4
afueras *(fpl)* outskirts 4
agencia *(f)* agency
agencia de viajes *(f)* travel agency 7
agente *(m/f)* agent
agitación *(f)* agitation 12
agosto August 5
agradable agreeable; pleasant, nice 4
agresivo/a aggressive
agrícolo/a agricultural
agricultor/a *(m/f)* farmer 8
agricultura *(f)* agriculture
agua *(f, el)* water 4
ahora now
ahorrar save 11
ahumado/a smoked
aire *(m)* air; **aire acondicionado** air conditioning; **al aire libre** outdoors 2
ajustarse a adjust to
alarma *(f)* alarm
alarmado/a alarmed
alcoba *(f)* bedroom
alcohólico/a alcoholic
aldredor de around
alegrarse de que be happy that 11
alemán *(m)* German
alergia *(f)* allergy 10
alertar alert
alfombra *(f)* rug 3, 4
alga *(f)* seaweed
álgebra *(f)* algebra
algo something 4
alguien someone 4
alguno/a(s) some, any 4
alimenticio/a nourishing
alimento *(m)* food

alinear align
aliviar alleviate
allí there
almorzar (ue) eat / have lunch 4
almuerzo (ligero) (m) (light) lunch 9
Aló. Hello. (on the telephone) 5
alojamiento (m) lodging
alojarse en stay at (on a trip), lodge at 7
alquilar rent 4
alquiler (m) rent 4
alternativo/a alternative
alto/a tall, high 3
alumno/a (m/f) pupil, student 8
ama de casa (f, el) housewife 8
amable lovable
amarillo/a yellow 4
ambiente (m) atmosphere;
    environment 11
amigo/a (m/f) friend; mejor amigo/a (m/f)
    best friend 1
amistoso/a friendly 3
amor (m) love
amueblado/a furnished
analgésico (m) analgesic
anaranjado/a orange 4
andar en bicicleta ride a bicycle 4
ángel (m) angel
animación (f) animation
animado/a lively 4
animal (m) animal 4
ánimo (m) courage; dar ánimo a alguien
    cheer someone up 10; levantarle el
    ánimo lift someone's spirits 10
anoche last night 7
anonimato (m) anonymity
anónimo/a anonymous
anotar note, write down
ansiedad (f) anxiety
antes before; antes de before 2; lo antes
    posible as soon as possible
antibióticos (mpl) antibiotics 10
anticipar anticipate
antidepresivo (m) antidepressant
antiguo/a old
antiinflamatorio (m) anti-inflammatory
antipático/a unpleasant 1
antónimo (m) antonym
anual annual
anualmente annually
anunciante (m/f) advertiser
anunciar announce, advertise
anuncio (m) advertisement
anuncio clasificado (m) classified ad
año (m) year 1; al año per year 1;
    tener . . . años be . . . years old 3
apagar turn off 11
aparecer appear
apartamento (m) apartment

apasionado/a passionate
apellido (m) last name 11
aplicación informática (f) software 6
aplicar apply
apoyo (m) support
apreciar appreciate
aprender learn (to) 3
aprendizaje (m) learning
apropriado/a appropriate
aproximadamente approximately
aproximar approximate
aquel / aquella (aquellos as) that (those)
    (over there) 5
aquí here 1
árbol (m) tree 4
archivador (m) filing cabinet 11
archivar file 11
archivero (m) filing cabinet
archivo (m) archive 6
área (f) area
área recreativa (f) recreation area
argentino/a (m/f) Argentine
armario (m) wardrobe, closet 4
armas (fpl) arms (military)
armoniosamente harmoniously
arqueológico/a archeological
arquitectura (f) architecture
arrastrar drag
arreglar fix, straighten out / up 4
arrestar arrest
arriba up
arroz (m) rice 9
arruinar ruin
arte (m) art
artículo (m) article; artículos de oficina
    (mpl) office supplies 11
artista (m/f) artist
artritis (f) arthritis 10
arvejas (fpl) peas
asado/a roasted
asalto (m) assault
ascender go up, climb
ascensor (m) elevator 7
asco (m) disgust, revulsion 9; dar asco
    be revolting, be unable to stand 9
asegurar assure
asesinar murder
así thus; ¡Así es! that's right 9
asiento (m) seat 7
asignar assign
asistencia (f) assistance
asistente de vuelo (m/f) flight attendant 7
asistir (a) attend 3
asma (f) asthma
asociar associate
aspecto (m) aspect 11
aspecto físico physical appearance 3
aspirina (f) aspirin 10

asunto (m) matter, subject
asustado/a frightened, scared 8
ataque (m) attack
atención (f) attention
atender (ie) attend to, wait on 11
atentamente sincerely
aterrizar land 7
atlántico/a Atlantic
atleta (m/f) athlete
atmósfera (f) atmosphere
atracción (f) attraction
atractivo/a attractive
atraer attract
atún (m) tuna
audiencia (f) audience
aumentar increase
aumento (m) increase; raise 11
aún even
aunque although
ausente absent
autenticidad (f) authenticity
auténtico/a authentic
auto (m) automobile, auto, car
autobiográfico/a autobiographical
autobús (m) bus 4
autodisciplina (f) self-discipline
automáticamente automatically
automático/a automatic
automedicación (f) self-medication
automedicarse self-medicate
automóvil (m) automobile, auto, car
autor/a (m/f) author
autoridad (f) authority
autorretrato (m) self-portrait
avance (m) advance
aventurero/a adventurous
averiguar investigate
avión (m) airplane 7
ayer yesterday 7
ayuda (f) help; ayuda alimentaria (f)
    food assistance; ayuda humanitaria
    (f) humanitarian aid 12
ayudar(se) help (each other) 5
azúcar (m) sugar 9
azul blue 3, 4

B

bailar dance 2
baile (m) dance
bajar de get off / out of, get down from 7
bajar de peso lose weight 9
bajo/a short (in height), low 3
balcón (m) balcony 7
banana (f) banana
banano (m) banana
banca (f) banking 11
banco (m) bank 7

banquete *(m)* banquet
bañarse bathe, take a bath 5
baño *(m)* bathroom 4
bar *(m)* bar
barato/a inexpensive, cheap 5
barba *(f)* beard 3
barra de herramientas *(f)* tool bar
barrio *(m)* neighborhood 4
basar base
base de datos *(f)* database 11
básico/a basic
básquetbol *(m)* basketball
bastante enough
basura *(f)* trash 4
bebé *(m)* baby
bebedero *(m)* drinking fountain
beber drink 3
bebible drinkable
bebida *(f)* drink 9; **bebida alcohólica** *(f)* alcoholic drink 9
beige beige 4
béisbol *(m)* baseball 8
beisbolista *(m/f)* baseball player 8
bellas artes *(fpl)* fine arts
belleza *(f)* beautiful
bello/a beautiful
beneficiar benefit
beneficio *(m)* benefit 11
beneficioso/a beneficial
besar(se) kiss (each other) 5
beso *(m)* kiss
biblioteca *(f)* library 1
bicicleta *(f)* bicycle 4; **andar en bicicleta** ride a bicycle 4
bien well 1, 4; **muy bien** very well 1
bienes raíces *(mpl)* real estate
bienestar *(m)* well-being
bienvenido/a welcome 7
bigote *(m)* mustache 3
bilingüe bilingual
billete *(m)* bill 11; ticket 7
biología *(f)* biology
bistec *(m)* steak 9
blanco *(m)* space
blanco/a white 4
bloqueador solar *(m)* sunblock
blusa *(f)* blouse 5
boca *(f)* mouth 10
boda *(f)* wedding 8
bodega *(f)* wine shop
boleto *(m)* ticket 7
bolígrafo *(m)* pen
bolsa *(f)* purse 5
bombero/a *(m/f)* firefighter 8
bonito/a handsome / pretty 1
borrador eraser; delete button
bosque *(m)* woods, forest 7
botánico/a *(m/f)* herbalist
botas *(fpl)* boots 5

botella *(f)* bottle 9
botón button 6
botones *(m)* bellboy
Brasil Brazil
brazada *(f)* stroke (swimming)
brazo *(m)* arm 10
breve brief
brillante brilliant
brócoli *(m)* broccoli 9
bronquitis *(f)* bronchitis
brusco/a brusque
Buenas noches. Good evening. Good night. 1
Buenas tardes. Good afternoon. 1
bueno/a good 1
Buenos días. Good morning. 1
buscador *(m)* search engine
buscar look for 5; search
búsqueda *(f)* search; **motor de búsqueda** *(m)* search engine
buzón de voz *(m)* voice mailbox 11

C

cabeza *(f)* head 10
cada each 1
cada vez every time
cadena *(f)* chain; channel, chain
caer a fall into 8; **caerse** fall 10
café *(adj.)* brown 3
café *(m)* coffee 2; **café solo** *(m)* black coffee 9
cafeína *(f)* caffeine 9
cafetería *(f)* cafeteria 1
cajero/a *(m/f)* teller, cashier 11; **cajero automático** *(m)* ATM machine 11
cajón *(m)* drawer 11
calabacín *(m)* squash 9
calabaza *(f)* pumpkin, gourd
calcetines *(mpl)* socks 5
calculadora *(f)* calculator 1
calcular calculate 11
calendario *(m)* calendar
calentar(se) (ie) heat; *refl* get hot, warm up
calidad *(f)* quality
cálido/a warm
caliente hot
calificado/a qualified
callado/a quiet 4; silent 6
calle *(f)* street 4
calmado/a calm
calor *(m)* heat; **Hace (mucho) calor.** It's (very) hot. 5; **tener calor** be hot 3
calorías *(fpl)* calories 9
caluroso/a warm
cama *(f)* bed 1; **cama doble** *(f)* double bed 7

cámara *(f)* room; **cámara de comercio** *(f)* chamber of commerce
camarero/a *(m/f)* waiter
camarones *(mpl)* shrimp 9
cambiar change / exchange 7
cambio *(m)* change; **cambios climáticos** *(m)* climate change
camello *(m)* camel
caminar walk 10
camisa *(f)* shirt 5
camiseta *(f)* T-shirt 5
campaña *(f)* campaign
campeonato *(m)* championship 8
campo *(m)* country 4
campus *(m)* campus
Canadá Canada
canal *(m)* channel
cancelar cancel
cancha de tenis *(f)* tennis court
canción *(f)* song
candidato/a *(m/f)* candidate
canoso/a gray-haired, white-haired 3
cansado/a tired 4
cantante *(m/f)* singer 8
cantar sing 2
cantidad *(f)* quantity
capacidad *(f)* capacity
capítulo *(m)* chapter
captar capture
cara *(f)* face 10
carácter *(m)* character 3
característica *(f)* characteristics
carbohidratos *(mpl)* carbohydrates 9
cárcel *(f)* prison
cargar fotos take photographs
cargo *(m)* charge 11
Caribe Caribbean
caribeño/a Caribbean
cariñoso/a loving, affectionate 3
carne *(f)* meat 9
carne de cerdo *(m)* pork
caro/a expensive 4
carpeta *(f)* file (folder) 11
carpintería *(f)* carpentry
carpintero/a *(m/f)* carpenter
carrera *(f)* career; **hacer la carrera de . . .** get a degree in . . . 8
carretera *(f)* highway
carro *(m)* car 4
carta *(f)* letter; menu 9
casa *(f)* house; **en casa** at home 4
casado/a married 3, 4
casarse (con) marry, get married (to) 5
casi almost 2
caso *(m)* case
castaño brown 3
catarata *(f)* cataract; waterfall
catarro *(m)* cold 10
catedral *(f)* cathedral

categoría (f) category
católico/a Catholic
causar cause
cebolla (f) onion 9
celebración (f) celebration
celebrar celebrate
celular (m) cell phone
cena (f) dinner 2
cenar eat / have dinner 4
censo (m) census
censura (f) censure
centavo (m) cent 9
centígrado (m) centigrade
centralizado/a centralized
centrar center
céntrico/a central
centro (m) center, downtown 4; centro comercial (m) shopping center, mall 2; centro comunitario (m) community center
Centroamérica Central America
centroamericano/a (m/f) Central American
cerca (de) near 2
cercana/o close, near
cerdo/a (m/f) pig
cereales (mpl) cereal 9
cerebro (m) brain 10
ceremonia (f) ceremony
cerrado/a closed 2
cerrar (ie) close 4
cerveza (f) beer 9
césped (m) grass, lawn 4
chaqueta (f) jacket 5
chatear chat 6
Chau. Ciao, Bye. 5
chau see you later
chelo (m) cello
cheque de viaje (m) traveler's check 7
chequeo (m) checkup
chequera (f) checkbook 11
chica (f) girl
chícharos (mpl) peas 9
chico (m) boy
chile (m) chile pepper 9; chile relleno (m) stuffed pepper 9
chileno/a Chilean
chino (m) Chinese
chisme (m) gossip
chismoso/a gossipy 4
chiste (m) joke 5
chistoso/a funny, likes to joke around 3
choclo (m) corn
chuleta de cerdo (f) pork chop 9
cibercafé (m) cybercafé
cibernético/a cybernetic
cien(to) hundred
ciencia (f) science
ciencias políticas (fpl) political science

ciencias sociales (fpl) social sciences
científico/a (m/f) scientist 8
cierto/a certain; true
cifra (f) number, figure
cigarrillo (m) cigarette
cine (m) cinema 2
cinturón (m) belt 5; seat belt
circuito (m) circuit
circulación (f) circulation
circular circulate, drive
círculo (m) circle
circunstancia (f) circumstance
cirugía (f) surgery 10
cirujano/a (m/f) surgeon 10
cita (f) appointment 10; date
ciudad (f) city 2; ciudad natal (f) hometown
civilización (f) civilization
claramente clearly
claro/a clear
clase (f) class 1; clase (de español) (f) (Spanish) class 1; compañero/a de clase (m/f) classmate 1; ¿Qué clases tienes? What classes do you have? 1; salón de clase (m) classroom 1
clásico/a classical 2
clasificados (mpl) classified ads
clasificar classify
claúsula (f) clause
cliente / clienta (m/f) customer 5
clientela (f) clientele
clima (m) climate
clóset (m) closet
club nocturno (m) night club 2
cobrar cash (a check), charge (a fee) 11
coche (m) car, automobile 3
cocina (f) kitchen 4
cocinar cook 2
código (m) code
cognado (m) cognate
coherente coherent
colapsar collapse
colega (m/f) colleague 11
colegio (m) college, school; high school 8
colesterol (m) cholesterol 9, 10
coliflor (m) cauliflower 9
colocar place, put
colombiano/a Colombian
colonizador/a (m/f) colonizer
coloquial colloquial
color (m) 4
columna (f) column
comando (m) order 6
combatir combat
combinación (f) combination
combinar combine
comedero (m) bird / animal feeder
comedia (f) comedy
comedor (m) dining room 4

comentar comment
comentario (m) commentary 6
comenzar (ie) begin, start 10
comer eat 2; comer fuerte eat heavily 9
comercial commercial
comercio (m) commerce
comestible edible
cometer commit
cómico/a comic
comida (f) food 1; meal 9; comida basura (f) junk food 9
comienzo (m) beginning
comisión (f) commission
comité (f) committee
¿cómo? how? 2; ¿Cómo es . . . ? How is . . . ?, What's . . . like? 1; ¿Cómo está usted? How are you? (form.) 1; ¿Cómo estás? How are you? (fam.) 1; cómo no of course 5; ¿Cómo se dice . . . en inglés? How do you say . . . in English? 1; ¿Cómo se escribe? How is that written? 1; ¿Cómo se llama usted? What is your name? (form.) 1; ¿Cómo te llamas? What is your name? (fam.) 1
como like, as 1; tan . . . como as . . . as 4; tan pronto como as soon as 11; tanto/a/os/as . . . como as much . . . as, as many . . . as 4
cómoda (f) chest (of drawers) 4
cómodo/a comfortable
compañero/a (m/f) companion 1; compañero/a de casa (m/f) housemate; compañero/a de clase (m/f) classmate 1; compañero/a de cuarto (m/f) roommate 1
compañía (f) company 11
comparación (f) comparison
comparar compare
compartimento (m) compartment
compartir share 3
compatibilidad (f) compatibility 11
compatriota (m/f) compatriot 12
competición (f) competition
competir compete
competitivo/a competitive
complejo (m) complex
complementar complement
complemento directo / indirecto (m) direct / indirect object
completamente completely
completar complete
completo/a full, complete 11
complicado/a complicated
cómplice (m/f) accomplice
componentes físicos (m) hardware 6
comprar buy 2
comprender understand 3; No comprendo. I don't understand. 1

comprensivo/a understanding 3
compresión (f) compression 6
comprometer commit
computación (f) computing
computador (m) computer
computadora (f) computer 1
común common 10
comunicación communication
comunicar(se) communicate (with each other) 5
comunidad (f) community; **centro comunitario** (m) community center
comunitario/a community (adj.)
con with 2; **con / sin acento** with / without an accent 1; **con antelación** in advance 7; **con atención** with attention 8; **con cheque** with a check 5; **con frecuencia** frequently 2; **¿con qué frecuencia?** how often? 2; **con regularidad** regularly 10; **con retraso** with a delay, late 7; **con tarjeta de crédito / débito** with a credit / debit card 5; **con vistas a . . .** with a view of . . . , overlooking 7
concentración (f) concentration
concentrado/a concentrated
concentrarse concentrate 10
concepto (m) concept
concientización pública (f) public awareness
concierto (m) (classical music) concert 2
conciso/a concise
concreto/a concrete
concursante (m/f) contestant, competitor
concurso (m) game show, competition
condado (m) county
condenar condemn
condición (f) condition
condicional conditional
condicionar condition
condimento (m) condiment
conducir drive
conectar connect 8
conectividad (f) connectivity
conexión (f) connection
conferencia (f) conference
confesar confess
confianza (f) confidence
confiar have confidence in, trust
configurar configure
confirmación (f) confirmation
confirmar confirm
confundido/a confused 2, 4
confusión (f) confusion
congestión (f) congestion 10
congestionado/a congested 10
congresista (m/f) congressman/woman
Congreso (m) Congress 12
conjunción (f) conjunction

conmemorar commemorate
conmigo with me 2
connotación (f) connotation
conocer know, be familiar with, be acquainted with, meet 7; **conocido/a** known; **No conozco a . . .** I don't know . . . (a person) 4
conocimiento (m) knowledge
conquista (f) conquest
conquistar conquer
consecuencia (f) consequence
consejero/a (m/f) counselor 8
consejo (m) advice, counsel
conservador/a conservative 3
conservar conserve
consideradamente considerately
consistir consist
consonante (f) consonant
constantemente constantly
construcción (f) construction 8
consulado (m) consulate
consulta (f) consultation
consultar consult
consumerismo (m) consumerism
consumidor/a (m/f) consumer
consumo (m) consumption
contabilidad (f) accounting
contactar contact
contacto (m) contact
contador/a (m/f) accountant 8, 11
contaminación (f) contamination
contaminar contaminate
contar (ue) count, tell 4
contenedor (m) container
contener contain
contenido (m) content
contento/a happy, glad 2; **estar contento/a de que** be happy that 11
contestar answer 2
contexto (m) context
contigo with you 3
continuar continue
contra against
contrario (m) contrary
contraseña (f) password
contraste (m) contrast
contratar hire 11
contribución (f) contribution
contribuir contribute
control de seguridad (m) security check 7
controlar control 10
conversación (f) conversation
convertir convert
cooperación (f) cooperation
copa (f) stemmed glass, wine glass 9
copia (f) copy; **sacar una copia** make a copy 11
copiar copy

corazón (m) heart 10
corbata (f) necktie 5
cordialmente cordially
corrección (f) correction
correcto/a right, correct 7
corregir correct
correo (m) mail; **correo electrónico** (m) e-mail 3; **correo no deseado** (m) spam 6; **oficina de correos** (f) post office 7
correr run 3
corresponder correspond
correspondiente corresponding
corriente running
corrupción (f) corruption
cortar(se) cut (oneself) 10; **cortar el césped** cut the grass 4; **cortarse el pelo** cut one's hair 7
corte (f) court
Corte Suprema (f) Supreme Court
cortesía (f) courtesy
corto/a short 3
cosa (f) thing 1
cosmopolito/a cosmopolitan
costa (f) coast
costar (ue) cost 4
costarricense Costa Rican
costo (m) cost
costo de vida (m) cost of living
costoso/a costly
costumbre (f) custom
crear create
creatividad (f) creativity
crecer grow
creciente growing
crédito (m) credit
creer (en / que) believe (in / that) 3
crema (f) cream 9
crimen (m) crime
criminalidad (f) crime (in general) 12
cristal crystal
criterios (mpl) criteria
criticar criticize
crítico/a (m/f) critic
cruce (m) intersection
cuaderno (m) notebook 1; **cuaderno de ejercicios** (m) workbook 1
cuadra (f) (city) block 7
cuál(es) which, what 2
cualidad (f) quality
cualquier any
¿cuándo? when? 2
¿cuánto/a? how much 2; **¿cuántos/as?** how many 2; **¿Cuánto cuesta(n) . . . ?** How much does it (do they) cost?
cuarto (m) 4; room 1
cuarto/a fourth
cubano/a Cuban
cubismo (m) cubism
cuchara (f) spoon 9

cuchillo (m) knife 9
cuello (m) neck 10
cuenta (f) account, bill 11; check 9; cuenta bancaria (f) bank account; cuenta corriente / de ahorros (f) checking / savings account 11
cuento (m) story, tale 8
cuerpo (m) body 10
cuestión (f) question
cuestionario (m) questionnaire
cuidado (m) care; cuidado de niños (m) childcare; cuidado prenatal (m) prenatal care 10; tener cuidado be careful 10
cuidar(se) take care of (oneself) 10
culinario/a culinary
cultivable arable
cultivar cultivate
cultivo (m) crop
cultura (f) culture
cultural cultural 4
cumpleaños (m) birthday 2
cumplido (m) compliment
cumplir turn (an age), carry out 8
curación (f) healing
curativo/a curative
curiosidad (f) curiosity 12; tener curiosidad be curious
currículum vitae (m) curriculum vitae, résumé 11
cursivo/a cursive
curso (m) course; curso universitario (m) university course
cursor (m) cursor 6

D

dama (f) lady
danza (f) dance
dar give 9; dar ánimo a alguien cheer someone up 10; dar asco be revolting, be unable to stand 9; dar hambre make hungry 9; dar la bienvenida welcome; dar miedo scare; dar sed make thirsty 9
datar de date from
datos (mpl) data; datos personales (mpl) personal data 11
de of, from 1; de . . . a . . . from . . . to . . . 2; de carácter personality-wise 3; de compras shopping 5; ¿De dónde eres? Where are you from? (fam.) 1; ¿De dónde es usted? Where are you from? (form.) 1; de habla inglesa English-speaking; de la mañana in the morning 2; de la noche in the evening / night 2; de la tarde in the afternoon 2; de mediana edad

middle-aged 3; de niño/a as a child 8; de (no) fumadores (non-)smoking 7; de seguridad security 7; de tu madre / padre your mother's / father's side 3; de última moda latest fashion; de vacaciones on vacation 7; ¿De veras? Really? 11; de vez en cuando once in a while
de compras: ir de compras go shopping 2
debajo de below, under 2
debatir debate
deber must / should 3
debido a due to
débil weak
debilitar debilitate
débito (m) debit
década (f) decade
decidir decide 7
décimo/a tenth
decir (i) say, tell 4; ¿Cómo se dice . . . en inglés? How do you say . . . in English? 1
decisión (f) decision
declarar declare
dedicación (f) dedication
dedicar dedicate; dedicarse a do (for a living), devote oneself to 8
dedos (mpl) fingers 10
deducir deduce
defender defend
déficit (m) deficit
definar define
definición (f) definition
definido/a defined
deforestación (f) deforestation 12
dejar leave (something somewhere) 4; dejar de (+ infinitive) stop . . . -ing 10
delante de ahead of, in front of 2
delantero/a front
delegación (f) delegation
delgado/a thin 3
delicioso/a delicious
demanda (f) demand
demás (mpl) the rest
demasiado too, too much 2, 5
demócrata (m/f) Democrat
democratización (f) democratization
demonstrativo/a demonstrative
dentista (m/f) dentist 10
dentro de within
denunciar denounce
departamento (m) department 11
depender (de) depend
dependiente / dependienta salesclerk 5
deportes (mpl) sports 2
deportista athletic, fond of sports 8
deportista (m/f) athlete 8
depositar deposit 11

depósito (directo) (m) (direct) deposit 11
depresión (f) depression 10
deprimido/a depressed
derecha (f) right; a la derecha de to the right of 2
derecho (m) right
derivado (m) derivative
desafortunadamente unfortunately 4
desaparición (f) disappearance
desarrollar develop 10
desarrollo (m) development 11
desastre (m) disaster
desastroso/a disastrous
desayunar eat / have breakfast 4
desayuno (m) breakfast 4, 7
descafeinado/a decaffeinated
descansar rest 2
descarga (f) data transfer 6
descargar download 6
descender descend
descifrable decipherable
desconectado/a disconnected
desconectar disconnect
desconocer not to know
desconocido/a unknown 2
desconocido/a (m/f) stranger
describir describe
descripción (f) description
desde . . . hasta (starting) from . . . until
desear want; wish, desire 2
desempleado/a unemployed
desempleo (m) unemployment
desequilibrio (m) imbalance
desesperanza (f) despair 10
desfile (m) parade
deshonesto/a dishonest
desnutrición (f) malnutrition
desordenado/a disordered; messy 4
desorganizado/a disorganized
despacio slow, slowly
despedida (f) farewell
despedir (i, i) fire 11; despedirse (i) say goodbye
despegar take off 7
despejado/a clear 5
despejar clear 5
despertarse (ie) wake up 5
después (de) after 2
destacar highlight
destino (m) destination
destruir destroy
desventaja (f) disadvantage
detalle (m) detail
detener detain
deteriorarse deteriorate
determinante determining
detrás de behind 2
devastación (f) devastation
devolver (ue) return to 11

día (*m*) day 2; **Buenos días.** Good morning. 1; **días laborales** work days; **hoy día** nowadays; **mediodía** noon 2; **todo el día** all day; **todos los días** every day 2

diabetes (*f*) diabetes 10

diablo (*m*) devil

diagnosticar diagnose

diálogo (*m*) dialogue

diario/a daily 2

dibujar draw 11

dibujo (*m*) picture

dibujos animados (*mpl*) cartoon

diccionario (*m*) dictionary 1

diciembre December 5

diente (*m*) tooth

dieta (*f*) diet 9

diferencia (*f*) difference

diferente different

difícil difficult 1

dificultad (*f*) difficulty 10

digestión (*f*) digestion

dígito (*m*) digit

dimensión (*f*) dimension

dinámica (*f*) dynamic

dinero (*m*) money 4; **dinero en efectivo** (*m*) cash 11

dirección (*f*) address 4

directo/a direct

director/a (*m/f*) director 11

dirigir direct

disciplina (*f*) discipline

discoteca (*f*) discotheque

discretamente discreetly

discreto/a discreet

discriminatorio/a discriminatory

¡Disculpe! Excuse me! Pardon me! 7

discurso (*m*) speech

discusión (*f*) discussion

discutir discuss

diseñador/a (*m/f*) designer; **diseñador/a de software** (*m/f*) software designer 8; **diseñador/a gráfico/a** (*m/f*) graphic artist 11

diseñar design 11

diseño (*m*) design 6; **diseño de páginas web** (*m*) web page design 11; **diseño gráfico** (*m*) graphic design

disfrutar enjoy

disgustado/a disgusted 6

disidente (*m/f*) dissident

disminuir diminish

disparidad (*f*) disparity

disponibilidad (*f*) availability 7

disponible available 7, 11

distancia (*f*) distance

distinguido/a distinguished

distinto/a different, distinct

distribución (*f*) distribution

distribuir distribute 11

distrito (*m*) district

diversidad (*f*) diversity

diversión (*f*) diversion

divertido/a fun 1

divertir(se) (ie, i) amuse, entertain; *refl* have fun, amuse oneself 5

divisa (*f*) currency

divorciado/a divorced 3, 4

divorciarse (de) divorce, get divorced (from) 5

divorcio (*m*) divorce

doble double

doctorado (*m*) doctoral degree

documento (*m*) document 11

dólar (*m*) dollar 11

doler (ue) hurt, ache 9

dolor (*m*) pain, ache 10

dolorido/a sore 10

doméstico/a domestic

domingo Sunday 2

dominicano/a Dominican

dominio (*m*) domain

dónde where? 2

dormir (ue) sleep 4; **dormir (ue) una siesta** take a nap 4

dormitorio (*m*) bedroom 4

dosis (*f*) dose

droga (*f*) drug

ducha (*f*) shower 7

ducharse shower, take a shower 5

dudar doubt 10

dueño/a (*m/f*) owner

dulces (*mpl*) sweets 9

duración (*f*) length

durante during 3

durar last 7

E

ecológico/a ecological

economía (*f*) economy 12

económico/a economic

economista (*m/f*) economist

ecoturismo (*m*) ecotourism 7

edad (*f*) age 8

edificio (*m*) building 1

editar edit

educación (*f*) education

educado/a polite

educador/a (*m/f*) educator

educar educate

educativo/a educative

efectivo (*m*) cash 11

efectivo/a effective

efecto (*m*) effect

eficacia (*f*) efficacy

egoísta selfish 3

ejemplo (*m*) example

ejercicio (*m*) exercise 1; **cuaderno de ejercicios** (*m*) workbook 1

ejotes (*mpl*) green beans 9

él he

elección (*f*) election 12

electricidad (*f*) electricity

electrónico/a electronic

elegante elegant

elemento (*m*) element

elevador (*m*) elevator

eliminar eliminate

ella she

ellos/as they

elocuente eloquent

elote (*m*) corn

elusivo/a elusive

embarazada pregnant; **estar embarazada** be pregnant 10

embarazo (*m*) pregnancy 10

embarque (*m*) boarding

emergencia (*f*) emergency

emisión (*f*) emission

emoción (*f*) emotion 11

emocionado/a excited 8

emocional emotional

emocionante moving, exciting, thrilling

emoticono (*m*) emoticon 6

emperador (*f*) emperor

empezar (ie) start, begin 4

empleado/a (*m/f*) employee 11

empleador/a (*m/f*) employer

empleo (*m*) employment, job 10; **empleo a tiempo completo / parcial** (*m*) full-time / part-time job 11

empresa (*f*) company, enterprise, business 11

empresario/a (*m/f*) businessman/woman

en at, in, on 1; **en casa** at home 4; **en cuanto a** as for 9; **en efectivo** in cash; **en el trabajo** at work 2; **en ese caso** in that case 7; **en forma** in shape 10; **en general** in general; **en la calle . . .** on . . . Street 2; **en la oficina** at the office 2; **en línea** online; **¿En qué puedo servirle?** How may I help you? 5; **en seguida** right away; **en vez de** instead of 9; **en vías de desarrollo** developing; **en vivo** live

enamorado/a in love, enamored 6

enamorarse (de) fall in love (with) 5

encabezado heading, headline

encantador/a enchanting

encantar love 9

encargado/a (*m/f*) person in charge, employer 7

encender (ie) turn on 11

enchiladas (*fpl*) enchiladas 9

encierro (*m*) running of the bulls

encima de on top of 2
encontrar(se) (ue) find 4; *refl* get together, meet up 5
encuesta *(f)* survey
encuestador/a *(m/f)* surveyor
endorfina *(f)* endorphin
energía *(f)* energy 9
enero January 5
enfermarse become ill; get sick 10
enfermedad *(f)* illness 10
enfermero/a *(m/f)* nurse 8
enfermo/a sick, ill 1, 4
enfrentar face; **enfrentarse (con)** confront
enfrente de across from, facing 2
enlace *(m)* link
enojado/a angry 2
enojarse get angry 5
ensalada *(f)* salad 9
ensayo *(m)* essay, paper 3
enseguida right away
enseñar teach
entender (ie) understand 4
entero/a entire, whole 9
entonces so, then, next 2
entrada *(f)* entrance 7; entry
entre among, between
entrenar train 11
entretenemiento *(m)* entertainment 12
entrevista *(f)* interview 11
entrevistado/a *(m/f)* interviewee
entrevistador/a *(m/f)* interviewer
entrevistar interview
envejecimiento *(m)* aging
enviar send 6, 7
enzima *(f)* enzyme
epidemia *(f)* epidemic
episodio *(m)* episode
época *(f)* epoch
equilibrado/a balanced 9
equipado/a equipped
equipaje *(m)* luggage
equipar equip
equipo *(m)* equipment; team 8
equitativo/a equitable
equivalente equivalent
equivaler amount to, be equivalent to
equivocado/a wrong, mistaken 11
erradicación *(f)* eradication
escala *(f)* scale; stopover; **hacer escala** make a stopover 7
escalera *(f)* stairs, staircase 7
escalfado/a poached
escandalizar scandalize
escándolo *(m)* scandal
escandaloso/a scandalous
escanear scan 11
escáner *(m)* scanner 11
escena *(f)* scene
esclavo/a *(m/f)* slave

escribir write 3; **¿Cómo se escribe?** How is that written? 1
escritor/a *(m/f)* writer
escritorio *(m)* desk 1
escrupulosamente scrupulously
escuchar listen (to) 2
escuela *(f)* school 4; **escuela normal** *(f)* elementary school 11; **escuela primaria** *(f)* elementary school 8, 11; **escuela secundaria** *(f)* secondary school 8
ese / esa (esos / esas) that (those) 3, 5
esencial essential
eslogan *(m)* slogan
espacio *(m)* space 4
espaguetis *(mpl)* spaghetti
espalda *(f)* back 10
España Spain
español *(m)* Spanish 1
español/a Spanish
español/a *(m/f)* Spaniard
espárragos *(mpl)* asparagus 9
especial special
especialista *(m/f)* specialist 10
especializar specialize
especialmente especially
específico/a specific
espejo *(m)* mirror 4
esperar hope 10; wait (for) 7
espinacas *(fpl)* spinach 9
espíritu *(m)* spirit
espiritual spiritual
esposo/a *(m/f)* spouse
esquiar ski 2
esquina *(f)* corner 7
esta noche tonight
esta semana this week 2
estabilidad *(f)* stability
estabilizar stabilize
establecer establish
establecimiento *(m)* establishment
estación *(f)* season 5; station; **estación de servicio** *(f)* service station, gas station 7
estacionamiento *(m)* parking lot 4
estacionar park 4
estadio *(m)* stadium
estado *(m)* state
estados físicos *(mpl)* physical states 10
Estados Unidos *(mpl)* United States
estadounidense American
estampilla *(f)* stamp
estante *(m)* shelf 1, 4
estar be 1; **estar a disposición** be available; **estar contento/a de que** be happy that 11; **estar de acuerdo** agree; **estar de buen / mal humor** be in a good / bad mood 11; **estar de moda** be in fashion 5; **estar embarazada** be pregnant 10; **estar en ayunas** fast; **estar**

encargado/a de be in charge of 11; **estar seguro/a** be sure 10; **estar triste de que** be sad that 11
estatua *(f)* statue
estatura mediana medium height 3
este / esta (estos / estas) this 2; this (these) 5
este *(m)* east 2; **al este de** east of 2
estéreo *(m)* stereo 1
estereotipo *(m)* stereotype
esteroides *(mpl)* steroids
estilo *(m)* style
estimación *(f)* estimation
estimado/a esteemed
estimar estimate
estimulante stimulating
estimular stimulate
estímulo *(m)* stimulus
estómago *(m)* stomach 10
estornudar sneeze 10
estrategia *(f)* strategy
estrella *(f)* star
estrés *(m)* stress 10
estresante stressful
estricto/a strict 3
estructura *(f)* structure
estudiante *(m/f)* student 1
estudiar study 2
estudiar en el extranjero study abroad
estudio *(m)* study
estudios *(mpl)* studies
estufa *(f)* stove 4
estupendo/a stupendous
eterno/a eternal
ética *(f)* ethics
etiqueta *(f)* etiquette
étnico/a ethnic
europeo/a European
evaluación *(f)* evaluation
evaluar evaluate 11
evento *(m)* event 3; **evento deportivo** sports event 3
evidente evident
evitar avoid 9
exagerado/a exaggerate
examen *(m)* exam; **examen parcial** *(m)* mid-term exam
examinar examine 10
excelente excellent
excepcionalmente exceptionally
excesivamente excessively
excesivo/a excessive
exceso *(m)* excess
excursión *(f)* excursion; **ir de excursión** go on an outing, go on a hike 7
excusa *(f)* excuse
exhalar exhale
exhausto/a exhausted
existir exist

éxito (m) success; **tener éxito** be successful
exótico/a exotic
expansión (f) expansion
expedición (f) expedition
experiencia (f) experience; **experiencia profesional** (f) professional experience 11
experto/a (m/f) expert
explicación (f) explanation
explicar explain 9
explotación (f) exploitation
exposición exhibition
expresar express
expresión (f) expression
exquisito/a exquisite
extender extend
extendido/a extensive
extensión (f) extension 6
extracto (m) extract
extranjero/a foreign
extraño/a strange
extraordinario/a extraordinary
extrovertido/a outgoing, extroverted 1
exuberante exuberant

F

fábrica (f) factory
fabricar make, manufacture
fácil easy 1
facilidad (f) facility
facilitar facilitate
fácilmente easily
factura (f) bill
facturar el equipaje check one's luggage 7
facultad (de medicina) (f) school (of medicine)
falda (f) skirt 5
fallar fail, be down 11
falsamente falsely
falso/a false
falta (f) lack; **falta de concentración / de interés** (f) lack of concentration / of interest 10
faltar (a) be absent, be missing, be needed 8
fama (f) fame
familia (f) family
familiar family member, relative 3; pertaining to family
famoso/a famous 8
fanático/a fanatic
farmacia (f) pharmacy 7
fascinante fascinating
fastidiar bother, annoy
fatiga (f) fatigue
favorecer favor

favorito/a favorite
febrero February 5
fecha (f) date 5; **fecha de nacimiento** (f) birthday
feliz happy
feminino/a feminine
fenómeno (m) phenomenon
feo/a ugly 1
feria (f) festival
ferrocarril (m) railway
fervor (m) fervor
festivo/a festive
fibra (f) fiber 9; **fibra óptica** (f) fiber optic
ficticio/a fictitious
fiebre (f) fever 10
fiesta (f) party 3; **fiesta de cumpleaños** (f) birthday party 8; **hacer una fiesta** have a party 3
filosofía (f) philosophy
fin de semana (m) weekend 2
final (m) end
finalmente finally
financiación (f) financing
financiar finance
financiero/a financial
firma (f) signature, firm, company
firmante (m/f) signer
firmar sign 11
física (f) physics
físicamente physically 3
físico/a physical
flan (m) flan 9
flexible flexible 3
flor (f) flower 4
floreciente flourishing
fluido/a fluid
flúor (m) fluoride
folleto (m) brochure
fondo (m) end, back; **al fondo de**
forma (f) forma; **en forma** in shape 10
formación académica (f) education 11
formar form
formato (m) format
formulario (m) form
foro (m) forum
fortuna (f) fortune
fosfato (m) phosphate
foto (f) photograph; **sacar una foto** take a picture 5
fotocopiadora (f) photocopier 11
fotografía (f) photography
fracción (f) fraction
francés (m) French
franco/a frank
frase (f) phrase
frecuencia (f) frequency
frecuente frequent
frenético/a frenetic
fresas (fpl) strawberries 9

fresco/a cool; fresh; **Hace fresco.** It's cool. 5
frigorífico (m) refrigerator
frijoles (mpl) beans 9
frío (m) cold; **Hace (mucho) frío.** It's (very) cold; 5 **tener frío** be cold 3
frío/a cold 3
frito/a fried
frívolo/a frivolous
frontera (f) border
frustración (f) frustration
fruta (f) fruit 9
frutillas (fpl) strawberries
fuente (f) font; source
fuera outside
fuerte strong 8
fuerza (f) force 12; strength 10
fumador/a (m/f) smoker
fumar smoke 4
funcionamiento (m) functioning
funcionar function; work (for machines, plans, or systems) 4
fundar found
furioso/a furious
fútbol soccer (football) 2; **fútbol americano** football 2
futbolista (m/f) soccer player 8
futuro (m) future

G

gafas (fpl) glasses 3; **gafas de sol** (fpl) sunglasses
galería (f) gallery
galleta (f) cookie 9
galón (m) gallon
ganar earn; win 8
ganas (fpl): **tener ganas de** feel like
garaje (m) garage 4
garantía (f) guarantee
garantizar guarantee
garganta (f) throat 10
gas (m) gas 4; **gasolina** (f) gasoline 7
gasolinera (f) service station, gas station 7
gastar spend (money) 5
gasto (m) expense
gástrico/a gastric
gastronomía (f) gastronomy
gato/a (m/f) cat
generación (f) generation
generalmente generally 2
generar generate
género (m) genre
generoso/a generous 3
genético/a genetic
genio/a (m/f) genius
gente (f) people 2

geografía (f) geography

gerente de fábrica (m/f) factory manager 8

gesto (m) gesture 8

gimnasio (m) gym(nasium) 1

globalización (f) globalization

globalizar globalize

gobernabilidad (f) governability

gobernador/a (m/f) governor

gobierno (m) government

gol (m) goal 8

golpear hit, strike 8

gordo/a fat 3

gorra (f) cap 5

gozar enjoy

grabación recording

grabar record

gracias thank you 1; **gracias a** thanks to

grado (m) degree; grade 8

graduación (f) graduation 8

graduarse graduate 8

gráfico (m) figure; **diseñador/a gráfico/a** (m/f) graphic artist 11; **diseño gráfico** (m) graphic design; graphic design program 11

grafiti (m) graffiti

gramática (f) grammar; grammatic

gramatical grammatical

gramo (m) gram

gran / grande big 1; large

grano (m) grain 9

grasa (f) fat 9

gratis free

gratuito/a free

grave serious, grave 10

gripe (f) flu

gris gray 3, 4

gritar yell

grupo (m) group

guapo/a good-looking, handsome 3

guardar keep; **guardar cama** stay in bed 10

guardia (m/f) guard

gubernamental governmental

guerillero/a (m/f) guerrilla 12

guerra (f) war

guía (f) guide; **guía (turística)** (f) (tourist) guidebook 7; **guía (turístico/a)** (m/f) (tourist) guide 7

guiar guide, drive

guineo (m) banana

guisantes (mpl) peas

guitarra (f) guitar 2

gustar be pleasing to, please 2; **Me gusta(n) . . .** I like; **Me gustaría(n)** I would like . . . 4; **(No) me gusta** (+ singular noun) I (don't) like . . . 1; **¿Te gusta** (+ singular noun)? Do you like . . . ? 1; **¿Te gustan** (+ plural noun)? Do you like . . . ? 1

gusto (m) taste

H

habichuelas (mpl) beans

habilidad (f) ability

habitación (f) room 7; bedroom; **habitación sencilla/doble** (f) single / double room 7

habitante (m/f) inhabitant

hábito (m) habit; **hábitos alimenticios** (mpl) eating habits

hablador/a talkative, chatty 4

hablar speak, talk 2

hace . . . . . . ago 7

hacer do, make 2; **Hace buen / mal tiempo.** The weather's good / bad. 5; **Hace fresco.** It's cool. 5; **Hace (mucho) calor.** It's (very) hot. 5; **Hace (mucho) frío.** It's (very) cold. 5; **Hace sol.** It's sunny. 5; **Hace viento.** It's windy. 5; **hacer clic** click; **hacer ejercicio** exercise 2; **hacer escala** make a stopover 7; **hacer esquí acuático** waterski 2; **hacer la carrera de . . .** get a degree in . . . 8; **hacer la maleta** pack one's suitcase 7; **hacer sol** be sunny; **hacer una fiesta** have a party 3; **hacer una pregunta** ask a question 3; **hacer un viaje** take a trip 3

Haití (f) Haiti

hambre (f) hunger; **dar hambre** make hungry 9; **tener hambre** be hungry 3

hamburguesa (f) hamburger 9

harina (f) flour 9

hasta until 2; **desde . . . hasta** (starting) from . . . until; **Hasta luego.** See you later. 1; **Hasta mañana.** See you tomorrow. 1; **Hasta pronto.** See you soon.; **hasta que** until 11

hay there is, there are / is there, are there 1

hecho (m) fact

helado (de vainilla) (m) (vanilla) ice cream 9

hemisferio (m) hemisphere

herencia (f) heritage

hermana (f) sister 3

hermanastro/a (m/f) stepbrother/sister

hermano (m) brother 3

hermanos (mpl) siblings 3

herramienta (f) tool

híbrido/a hybrid

hidratación (f) hydration

hidrógeno (m) hydrogen

hierba (f) herb

hija (f) daughter 3

hijo (m) son 3

hijos (mpl) children 3

hinchado/a swollen 10

hispano/a (m/f) Hispanic

historia (f) history; story

histórico/a historical

hogar (m) household

hoja de cálculo (f) spreadsheet 11

Hola. Hi. 1

hombre (m) man; **hombre de negocios** (m) businessman/woman 8

homeopatía (f) homeopathy

homogeneización (f) homogenization

honesto/a honest

hora (f) hour, time; 2; **¿A qué hora?** At what time? 2; **horas de oficina** office hours

horario (m) schedule 2

hormona (f) hormone

horóscopo (m) horoscope

hospedar lodge

hospicio (m) hospice

hospitalidad (f) hospitality

hostal (m) hostel

hotel (m) hotel 7

hoy today 1, 2

hoy día nowadays

hueso (m) bone 10

huésped (m/f) guest 7

huevo (m) egg 9

humanidades (fpl) humanities

humanitario/a humanitarian

humano (m) human being

humor (m) mood; **estar de buen / mal humor** be in a good / bad mood 11

humorístico/a humorous

huracán (m) hurricane

I

icono (m) icon 6

ida (f) outward flight 7

idea (f) idea 2, 8

idéntico/a identical

identidad (f) identity

identificable identifiable

identificación (f) identification 7

identificar identify

idioma (m) language 11

idiomático/a idiomatic

iglesia (f) church 2

igual equal

igualdad (f) equality

Igualmente. Likewise. 1

ilegal illegal

ilógico/a illogical

ilustración (f) illustration 4

imagen (f) image
imaginar imagine
imaginario/a imaginary
imbécil (m/f) idiot
(im)paciente (im)patient 1
impacto (m) impact
impecable impeccable
imperfecto (m) imperfect tense
impermeable (m) raincoat 5
implicar imply
imponer impose
importancia (f) importance
importante important
importar be important, matter 9
imposible impossible 10
impresión (f) impression
impresionante impressive
impresora (f) printer 4, 11
imprimir print 11
impuestos (mpl) taxes 11
impulsar drive, propel
impulso (m) impulse
incendio (m) fire
incidente (m) incident
incluido/a included 7
incluir include
incluso even; including
incorporar incorporate
incorrecto/a incorrect
increíble incredible
incrementar increase
indefenso/a defenseless
independencia (f) independence
independiente independent
independizarse become independent
indicación (f) indication
indicador (m) indicator
indicar indicate
indicativo/a indicative
índice (m) index
indiferente indifferent
indígeno/a indigenous
indignación (f) indignation 12
individuo (m) individual
indocumentado/a undocumented
industria (f) industry
industrializar industrialize
infancia (f) childhood
infantil children's
infectado/a infected 10
infectar infect
infidelidad (f) infidelity
infiel (m/f) unfaithful person, infidel
infinitivo (m) infinitive
inflación (f) inflation
influencia (f) influence
influir (en) influence 10

información (f) information 11
informar(se) report, inform; refl inform
  oneself
informática (f) computer science;
  computing 11; information
  technology 6
informativo/a informative
informe (m) report
ingeniería (f) engineering
ingeniero/a (m/f) engineer 8
inglés (m) English
ingrediente (m) ingredient
inhalación (f) inhalation
inhumano/a inhumane
inicial initial
iniciar initiate; start
iniciativa (f) initiative
inicio (m) start
injusticia (f) injustice
inmediatamente immediately
inmersión (f) immersion
inmigración (f) immigration 12
inmigrante (m/f) immigrant 8
inmigrar immigrate
inmunológico/a immunological
innecesario/a unnecessary
inocente innocent
inquieto/a worried
insertar insert 6
insignificante insignificant
insistir (en) insist (on) 10
insomnio (m) insomnia 10
inspirar inspire
instalar install
instantáneamente instantaneously
instantáneo/a instantaneous
institución (f) institution
instituto (m) high school
instrucción (f) instruction
instrumento (m) instrument
insuficiente insufficient
insultar insult
integral whole-grain 9
intelectual (m) intellectual 1
inteligente intelligent 1
intención (f) intention
intenso/a intense
interacción (f) interaction
interactivo/a interactive
interactuar interact
intercambiar exchange
interés (m) interest
interesado/a interested (in)
interesante interesting 1
interesar interest 9
internacional international
interrogativo/a interrogative

interrogatorio (m) interrogation
interrupción (f) interruption
intervalo (m) interval
íntimo/a intimate
intriga (f) intrigue
introducir introduce
introducir datos input data 11
inundación (f) flood 12
inusual unusual
invasión (f) invasion 12
investigación (f) investigation, research
investigar investigate
invierno (m) winter 5
invitado/a (m/f) guest 5
invitar invite 8
inyección (f) injection 10; shot
ir go 2; **ir a** + infinitive be going to + verb
  2; **ir de compras** go shopping 2; **ir de
  excursión** go on an outing, go on a
  hike 7; **ir de vacaciones** go on
  vacation 7
irresponsable irresponsible 1
irritabilidad (f) irritability 10
irritar irritate
irse leave, go away 5
isla (f) island
italiano/a Italian
itinerante traveling
itinerario (m) itinerary 7
izquierda (f) left; **a la izquierda de** to the
  left of 2

J

jamón (m) ham 9
japonés (m) Japanese
jaqueca (f) migraine
jardín (m) garden, yard 4
jeans (mpl) jeans 5
jefe/a (m/f) boss 11
joven young 3
joven (m/f) youth
jubilación (f) retirement 8; **pensión de
  jubilación** (f) retirement pension 11
jubilarse retire 8
judías verdes (fpl) green beans
jueves Thursday 2
juez (m/f) justice, judge
jugar (ue) play 4
jugo (m) juice; **jugo de naranja** (m)
  orange juice 9
julio July 5
junio June 5
junto a next to 7
juntos/as together 2
justicia (f) justice 12
justo/a right, correct

K

kilo *(m)* kilogram 9

L

la the, it
laboral pertaining to work
laboratorio *(m)* laboratory; **laboratorio de biología** *(m)* biology laboratory; **laboratorio de lenguas** *(m)* language laboratory 1
lado *(m)* side; **al lado de** next to 2; **por todos lados** everywhere 4
lago *(m)* lake 2
lamentar lament
lámpara *(f)* lamp 4
lápiz *(m)* pencil 1
largo/a long 3
lasaña *(f)* lasagna
lastimar(se) hurt (oneself) 10
lateralmente sideways
latino/a *(m/f)* Latino
Latinoamérica Latin America
lavabo washbasin
lavadero laundry room
lavadora washing machine
lavandería *(f)* laundry, laundromat 4
lavaplatos dishwasher
lavar wash 4; **lavarse el pelo / la cara** wash one's hair / one's face 5; **lavarse los dientes** brush one's teeth 5
le (to, for) you *(sing. / form.)*, him, her 6; **Le gusta(n) . . .** You like . . . ; He / She likes . . . 1; **Le gustaría . . .** He / She / You would like . . .
lección *(f)* lesson
leche *(f)* milk 9
lechuga *(f)* lettuce 9
lector/a *(m/f)* reader
lectura *(f)* reading
leer read 3
legislación *(f)* legislation
legumbres *(fpl)* legumes 9
lejos (de) far (from) 2
lengua *(f)* language
lenguaje *(m)* language
lentamente slowly
letra *(f)* letter
levantar lift, raise; **levantar pesas** lift weights 2; **levantarle el ánimo** lift someone's spirits 10; **levantarse** get up 5
ley *(f)* law 12
leyenda *(f)* legend
liberal liberal 3

liberar free
libertad *(f)* liberty, freedom
libre free
librería *(f)* bookstore 2
libro *(m)* book 1; **libro de texto** *(m)* textbook 3
licencia *(f)* license
licenciatura *(m)* degree
liceo *(m)* high school
líder *(m/f)* leader 6
liga *(f)* league
ligero/a light 9
limitar limit
limón *(m)* lemon 9
limonada *(f)* lemonade 9
limpiar clean 2
limpio/a clean 4
línea *(f)* line 11; **en línea** online
líquido *(m)* liquid
lista *(f)* list
listo/a ready 4
literatura *(f)* literature
litro *(m)* liter
llamada *(f)* call 7
llamado/a so-called
llamar(se) call; *refl* be named, called 3; **¿Cómo se llama usted?** What is your name? *(form.)* 1; **¿Cómo te llamas?** What is your name? *(fam.)* 1; **Me llamo . . .** My name is . . . 1
llave *(f)* key 7
llegada *(f)* arrival 7
llegar arrive 2
lleno/a full 4
llevar(se) take, carry, wear 5; *refl* take away 5; **llevarse bien (con)** get along well (with) 5
llorar cry 8
llover rain 5; **Llueve.** It rains. It's raining. 5
lluvia *(f)* rain
lo it; **lo antes posible** as soon as possible 11; **lo que** what, that which 8; **Lo siento.** I'm sorry. 4
localizar locate
loco/a crazy
lógica *(f)* logic
lógico/a logical
lograr achieve
los the 1; you, them; **los (lunes . . .)** on (Mondays) 1
luchar fight
luego next, then, later; **Hasta luego.** See you later. 1
lugar *(m)* place 4, 7
lunes Monday 2
luz *(f)* electricity, light 4

M

madrastra *(f)* stepmother
madre *(f)* mother 3
maestría *(f)* master's degree
maestro/a *(m/f)* teacher 8
magnífico/a magnificent
maíz *(m)* corn 9
mal bad(ly) 1
maleta *(f)* suitcase 7; **hacer la maleta** pack one's suitcase 7
malo/a bad 1
mamá *(f)* mama
mandato *(m)* command
mandón / mandona bossy 3
manejar drive 10; handle, manage
manera *(f)* way, manner
manga *(f)* sleeve
mango *(m)* mango 9
manicura *(f)* manicure
mano *(f)* hand 10
mantenimiento *(m)* maintenance
mantener(se) maintain 11; *refl* keep (oneself) 10
mantequilla *(f)* butter 9
manzana *(f)* apple 9
mañana *(f)* morning 2; tomorrow; **de la mañana** in the morning 2; **Hasta mañana.** See you tomorrow. 1; **por la mañana** in the morning 2
mapa *(m)* map
maquillarse put on make-up 5
mar *(m)* sea 7
maravilloso/a marvelous
marca *(f)* brand
marcar un gol score a goal 8
mareado/a dizzy, queasy 10
margen *(m)* margin
mariscos *(mpl)* seafood; shellfish 9
marrón (color café) brown 3
martes Tuesday 2
marxista Marxist
marzo March 5
más more, plus 1; **más . . . que** more . . . than 4; **más de + ** *number* more than + *number* 7; **más tarde** later; **más vale que . . .** one had better . . . 10
masa *(f)* mass
masaje *(m)* massage
mascota *(f)* pet 3
masivo/a massive
masticar chew
matemática *(f)* mathematics
materia *(f)* material
material de oficina *(m)* office supplies 11
materialista materialistic
materno/a maternal

matrimonio (*m*) matrimony, marriage
máximo/a maximum
mayo May 5
mayor older, oldest 3
mayoría (*f*) majority
mayormente mostly
me me, myself; (to, for) me 6; **Me gusta(n)** . . . I like; **Me gustaría(n)** . . . I would like . . . 4; **No me gusta(n)** . . . I don't like . . . 1
media hermana (*f*) half sister
medianoche (*f*) midnight 2
mediante by means of
medicamiento (*m*) medicine, medication 7, 10
medicina (*f*) medicine; **medicina preventiva** (*f*) preventive medicine 10
médico/a medical
médico/a (*m/f*) doctor, physician 8, 10
medida (*f*) measure
medio/a half
medio ambiente (*m*) environment 12
medio hermano (*m*) half brother
medio oeste (*m*) the midwest
mediodía noon 2
medios de comunicación (*mpl*) means of communication 3
mediterráneo/a Mediterranean
medusa (*f*) jellyfish
megáfono (*m*) megaphone
mejor better, best 3; **mejor amigo/a** (*m/f*) best friend 1
melodramático/a melodramatic
melón (*m*) melon 9
memoria (*f*) memory
memorizar memorize
mencionar mention
menor younger, youngest 3
menor (*m/f*) minor
menos minus, less, except 1; till 2; **menos . . . que** less . . . than 4
mensaje (*m*) message 7
mensajería instantánea (*f*) instant messaging
mensual monthly
mentalidad (*f*) mentality
mente (*f*) mind
menú (*m*) daily specials; menu
mercado (*m*) market; **mercado de trabajo** (*m*) job market
mes (*m*) month 2; **al mes** per month 2
mesa (*f*) table 1
mesero/a (*m/f*) server 9
meticuloso/a meticulous
metódico/a methodical
método (*m*) method
métrico/a metric
metropolitano/a metropolitan

mexicano/a Mexican 2
México Mexico
mezquita (*f*) mosque 2
mí me 2
micrófono (*m*) microphone
microondas (*m*) microwave oven 4
miedo (*m*) fear; **dar miedo** scare, frighten; **tener miedo (de)** be afraid of, fear 3; **tener miedo de que** be afraid that 11
miel (*f*) honey
miembro (*m*) member
mientras as 8; while, as long as 8, 11; **mientras tanto** meanwhile
miércoles Wednesday 2
migraña (*f*) migraine
migratorio/a migratory
mil (*m*) thousand
militar (*m/f*) soldier
millonario/a (*m/f*) millionaire
millón (*m*) million
mínimo/a minimum 11
ministerio (*m*) ministry
minoría (*f*) minority
minuto (*m*) minute
mío/a mine 9
mirar look at, watch 2
mi(s) my 1, 3
misión (*f*) mission
mismo/a same 1
mitad (*f*) half
mixto/a mixed
mochila (*f*) bookbag, backpack 1
moda (*f*) fashion; **estar de moda** be in fashion 5
modalidad (*f*) modality
modelo (*m*) model
moderar moderate
modernidad (*f*) modernity
moderno/a modern 1
modificación (*f*) modification
molestar bother 9, 11
molestia (*f*) discomfort
molesto/a upset, bothered 2, 4
momentáneo/a momentary
momento (*m*) moment
moneda (*f*) coin, money 11
monitor (*m*) monitor 11
monolingüe monolingual
montaña (*f*) mountain 2
montar mount
monumento (*m*) monument
morado/a purple 4
moreno/a dark-complexioned 3
morir (ue, u) die 8
mortalidad (*f*) mortality
motivación (*f*) motivation
motivo (*m*) reason 11
moto (*f*) motorcycle 8
motociclista (*m/f*) biker 8

motor de búsqueda (*m*) search engine
mover mover
móvil mobile
movimiento (*m*) movement
muchacha (*f*) girl 2
muchacho (*m*) boy, guy 2
mucho/a/os/as much, many, a lot of 1; **Mucho gusto.** Pleased to meet you. 1
mudarse move (residence), relocate 8
muebles (*mpl*) furniture 4
muerte (*f*) death 8
muerto/a dead 4
mujer (*f*) woman; **mujer de negocios** (*f*) businesswoman; **mujer policía** (*m/f*) policewoman 8
muletas (*fpl*) crutches 10
multiplicar multiply
multitarea (*f*) multitasking
mundial worldwide 6
mundo (*m*) world
músculo (*m*) muscle
musculoso/a muscular
museo (*m*) museum 2
música (*f*) music 2
músico (*m/f*) musician 8
musulmán Muslim
mutarse mutate
muy very; **muy bien** very well 1

N

nacer be born 8
naciente nascent, new
nacimiento (*m*) birth, Nativity scene 8; **fecha de nacimiento** birthday
nación (*f*) nation
nacional national
nacionalidad (*f*) nationality
Naciones Unidas United Nations 12
nada nothing, (not) anything 3, 4; **nada en especial** nothing in particular, nothing special 3
nadar swim 2
nadie no one; nobody, (not) anyone 4
naranja (*f*) orange 9
narcotraficante (*m/f*) drug trafficker
narcotráfico (*m*) drug trafficking
nariz (*f*) nose 10
narración (*f*) narration 8
natal native
nativo/a native
naturaleza (*f*) nature 7
navegar navigate
Navidad (*f*) Christmas
necesario/a necessary
necesidad (*f*) necessity 7
necesitar need 2, 10
negativo/a negative

negligencia (f) negligence
negociación (f) negotiation
negocio (m) business
negro/a black 3, 4
nervioso/a nervous 2, 4
nevar snow 5; **Nieva.** It snows. It's snowing. 5
nevera (f) refrigerator 4
ni nor 2; **ni . . . ni . . .** neither . . . nor 4; **ni un/a solo/a** not a single 8
nicaragüense Nicaraguan
nicotina (f) nicotine
nieta (f) granddaughter 3
nieto (m) grandson 3
nietos (mpl) grandchildren 3
ninguno / ninguna (ningún) no, none, not any 4
niñez (f) childhood 8
niño/a (m/f) boy / girl; child
nivel (m) level
no fumador/a (m/f) non-smoker
noche (f) evening, night 2; **de la noche** in the evening / night 2; **por la noche** in the evening / night 2
nocturno/a nocturnal
no-hispano/a non-Hispanic
nombrar name
nombre (m) name 11
normal normal 3
normalmente normally
noroeste (m) northeast
norte (m) north; **al norte de** north of 2
norteamericano/a (m/f) (North) American
nos us; (to, for) us; ourselves, each other, one another 6
nosotros/as we
nota (f) note
notablemente notably
notar note
noticias (fpl) news
noticiero (m) news provider 12
novato/a (m/f) beginner
novela (f) novel
noveno/a ninth
noviembre November 5
novio/a (m/f) boyfriend / girlfriend; fiancé(e) 1
nublado/a cloudy 5
nuestro/a(s) our 3; ours 9
Nueva Jersey New Jersey
Nueva York New York
nuevo/a new 1
Nuevo México New Mexico
número (m) number; **número de seguridad social** (m) social security number; **número de teléfono** (m) telephone number
numeroso/a numerous

nunca never 2
nutrición (f) nutrition
nutricional nutritional

O

o or 4
obesidad (f) obesity
objetivo (m) objective
objetivo/a objective
objeto (m) object
obligación (f) obligation
obligar obligate
obligatorio/a obligatory
obra (f) work
obrero/a (m/f) worker; **obrero/a de fábrica** (m/f), factory worker 8; **obrero/a de la construcción** (m/f), construction worker 8
observar observe
obstáculo (m) obstacle
obstetra (m/f) obstetrician 10
obtener obtain 11
ocasión (f) occasion
ocio (m) leisure
octavo/a eighth
octubre October 5
ocupado/a busy 1
ocurrir occur
oeste (m) west; **al oeste de** west of 2
ofensivo/a offensive
oferta (f) offer; **oferta de empleo** (f) job offer 11
oficina (f) office 2, 11; **en la oficina** at the office 2; **horas de oficina** office hours; **material de oficina** (m) office supplies 11; **oficina de correos** (f) post office 7
ofrecer offer 9
oído (m) inner ear 10
oír hear 3
Ojalá que . . . Let's hope that . . . 10
ojo watch out
ojo (m) eye 3
oliva (f) olive
onza (f) ounce
opción (f) option
operación (f) operation 10
opinar think, have an opinion
opinión (f) opinion
oportunidad (f) opportunity 11
oposición (f) opposition
optimista optimistic 1
oración (f) sentence 1
orden (m) order
ordenado/a neat, straightened up 4
ordenador (m) computer
ordenar order
ordinario/a ordinary

orégano (m) oregano
oreja (f) ear 10
organismo (m) body
organización (f) organization
organizar organize 11
orgullo (m) pride
orgulloso/a proud 8
orientación orientation
oriente (m) orient
origen (m) origin
originalmente originally
orquesta (f) orchestra; **orquesta sinfónica** (f) symphonic orchestra
ortografía (f) spelling
oscuro/a dark
ósmosis (m) osmosis
otoño (m) autumn, fall 5
otro/a other, another 1
oxígeno (m) oxygen
ozono (m) ozone

P

paciencia (f) patience
paciente patient 1
paciente (m/f) patient 10
padrastro (m) stepfather
padre (m) father 3
padres (mpl) parents 3
pagar pay 4
página (f) page; **página web** (f) web page
pago (m) pay 11
país (m) country
país extranjero (m) foreign country 7
palabra (f) word 1
palacio (m) palace
pan (m) bread 9
pandilla (f) gang
pánico (m) panic
pantalla (f) screen 11
pantalones (mpl) pants 5; **pantalones cortos** (mpl) shorts 5
papa (f) potato; **papa al horno / frita** (f) baked / fried potato 9; **papas fritas** (fpl) French fries
papel (m) (piece of) paper 1; role
papelera (f) waste basket
papitas (fpl) potato chips 9
paquete (m) package 7; packet
para for 1; by, in order to, to; in order to (+ infinitive) 8
parada de autobús (f) bus stop 4
paralización (f) paralysis
paramédico/a (m/f) paramedic 8
parcial partial 11
parecido/a similar
pared (f) wall 4
pareja (f) couple; pair

paréntesis (*m*) parenthesis(es)
parque (*m*) park
párquing parking
párrafo (*m*) paragraph
parrilla (*f*) grill; **a la parrilla** grilled
parte (*m*) part
participación (*f*) participation
participante (*m/f*) participant
participar participate 6
participio (*m*) participle
partido (*m*) game 2
partisano/a partisan 12
pasado/a past 7
pasaje (*m*) plane ticket 7
pasajero/a (*m/f*) passenger 7
pasaporte (*m*) passport 7
pasar happen 8; pass, spend (time) 2
pasatiempo (*m*) pastime 2
pasear walk, stroll
pasillo (*m*) aisle, hall 7
pasión (*f*) passion
paso (*m*) step
pastel (de chocolate) (*m*) (chocolate) cake 9
pastilla (*f*) tablet, pill 10
patata (*f*) potato
paterno/a paternal
pausa (*f*) pause
peatonal pedestrian
pecho (*m*) chest 10
pedir (i, i) ask for, order 4; order; request 10
pelea (*f*) fight
pelearse fight 5
película (*f*) film, movie 2
peligroso/a dangerous
pelirrojo/a red-haired 3
pelo (*m*) hair 3
peluquería (*f*) barber shop, hair salon 7
penicilina (*f*) penicillin
pensamiento thought
pensar (ie) think, intend 4; **pensar (en)** think (about) 4
pensativo/a pensive 6
pensión de jubilación (*f*) retirement pension 11
peor worse 4
pequeño/a little, small 1
percepción (*f*) perception
perder (ie) lose, miss 4
pérdida (*f*) loss
perdido/a lost
perezoso/a lazy 1
perfeccionar perfect
perfeccionista perfectionist
perfecto/a perfect 2
perfil (*m*) profile
periódico (*m*) newspaper 3; **periódico internacional** (*m*) international

newspaper 7; **quiosco de periódicos** (*m*) newsstand 7
periodista (*m/f*) journalist 12
permanecer remain
permanente permanent
permisivo/a permissive
permiso (*m*) permission 8
permitir permit, allow 7; **¿Me permite . . . ?** May I see . . . ? 7
pero but 1
perro/a (*m/f*) dog 3
persecución (*f*) persecution
persona (*f*) person 4
personaje (*m*) character
personalidad (*f*) personality
perspectiva (*f*) perspective
pertenecer belong; pertain
Perú Peru
pescado (*m*) fish 9
pescar fish 7
pesimista pessimistic 1
peso (*m*) peso 9
petróleo (*m*) petroleum
pie (*m*) foot 10; **pie de página** (*m*) footer
piel (*f*) skin 10
pierna (*f*) leg 10
pijama (*m*) pajamas 5
pimienta (*f*) pepper 9
pimiento verde (*m*) green pepper 9
pintar paint 11
pintor/a (*m/f*) painter 8
pintoresco/a picturesque
pintura (*f*) painting 4
piña (*f*) pineapple 9
pirámide (*f*) pyramid
piratería (*f*) piracy 6
piscina (*f*) pool; swimming pool 2
piso (*m*) floor
pizarra (*f*) blackboard 1; chalkboard
placa madre (*f*) motherboard 6
planear plan
planeta (*f*) planet
planificar plan
plano (*m*) map 7
planta (*f*) plant 1
planta baja (*f*) ground floor 7
plástico/a plastic
plátano (*m*) banana 9
plato (*m*) plate, dish 9; **plato hondo** (*m*) soup dish 9; **plato (llano)** (*m*) plate 9; **plato principal** (*m*) main dish, entrée 9; **plato regional** (*m*) regional dish 7
playa (*f*) beach 2
población (*f*) population
pobreza (*f*) poverty
poco (*m*) little, bit
poco/a/os/as little, few 1; **un poco cansado/a** a little tired 1
poder (*m*) power

poder (ue) be able to, can 4
poderoso/a powerful
poema (*m*) poem
policía / mujer policía (*m/f*) police officer 8
política (*f*) politics
político/a political
político/a (*m/f*) politician
pollo (asado) (*m*) (roasted) chicken 9
poner put, place, set 3; **poner la radio** turn on the radio 3; **ponerle una inyección a alguien** give someone a shot 10; **ponerse (la ropa)** put on (clothing)
popular popular 7
por for, on account of, because of, by, by way of, via, during; **por acá** over / through here 5; **por ciento** percent; **por ejemplo** for example; **por encima** above; **por eso** so, that's why, therefore, for that reason 8; **por favor** please 1; **por la mañana** in the morning 2; **por la noche** in the evening / night 2; **por la tarde** in the afternoon 2; **por parte de mi madre (padre)** on my mother's (father's) side 3; **por separado** separately; **por teléfono** on the telephone 11; **por todos lados** everywhere 4
¿por qué? why 2
porcentaje (*m*) percentage
porque because 2, 8
portarse behave 8
poseer possess
posesión (*f*) possession
posesivo/a possessive
posibilidad (*f*) possibility
posible possible 10
posición (*f*) position
positivo/a positive
posponer postpone
postal (*f*) postcard
postre (*m*) dessert 9
potencial potential
potenciar make possible
práctica (*f*) practice
prácticamente practically
practicar practice
práctico/a practical 4, 11
precaución (*f*) precaution
precio (*m*) price 5
precioso/a precious; lovely, beautiful
predador (*m*) predator
predeterminado/a predetermined
predicción (*f*) prediction
predominar predominate
preferencia (*f*) preference
preferible preferable 10
preferido/a favorite 9; preferred
preferir (ie, i) prefer 2, 4, 10

pregunta (*f*) question 3; **hacer una pregunta** ask a question 3
preguntar ask 9
prematuramente prematurely
prematuro/a premature
premio (*m*) prize
prender turn on
prensa (*f*) press
preocupado/a worried 8
preocupar(se) preoccupy; *refl* worry 10
prepa (*f*) high school
preparación (*f*) preparation
preparar prepare 2
preparativo (*m*) preparation
preparatoria (*f*) high school 11
presencia (*f*) presence
presentación (*f*) introduction; presentation
presentador/a (*m/f*) news anchor 12; presenter 12
presentar introduce; present; **presentarse** show up; be present; introduce oneself 5
presente indicativo (*m*) present indicative
presente progresivo (*m*) present progressive
preservación (*f*) preservation
presidente/a (*m/f*) president 12
presión (*f*) pressure; **presión arterial** (*f*) blood pressure 10
préstamo (*m*) loan 11
prestar lend 9
prestigio (*m*) prestige
presumido/a stuck-up 3
presupuestario/a estimated
pretendiente (*m/f*) suitor
pretérito (*m*) preterit tense
prevenir prevent
previamente previously
previo/a previous
primario/a primary
primavera (*f*) spring 5
primer(o)/a first; **Es (el) primero de . . .** It's the first of . . . 5
primo/a (*m/f*) cousin 3
principio (*m*) beginning; **al principio** at the beginning 8
prioridad (*f*) priority
prisa (*f*) hurry; **tener prisa** be in a hurry 3
privacidad (*f*) privacy 4
privado/a private
probabilidad (*f*) probability
probadores (*mpl*) fitting rooms 5
probar(se) (ue) try 7; *refl* try on 5
problema (*m*) problem
procesador de texto (*m*) word processor 6, 11
proceso (*m*) process
producción (*f*) production

producir produce
productividad (*f*) productivity
producto (*m*) product
productor/a (*m/f*) producer
profesión (*f*) profession
profesional professional 8
profesional (*m/f*) professional
profesor/a (*m/f*) professor
profundo/a deep 10; profound
programa (*m*) program; **programa de diseño gráfico** (*m*) graphic design program 11; **programa informática** (*f*) software 6
programación (*f*) programming
programador/a (*m/f*) programmer 8, 11
programar program 11
progreso (*m*) progress
prohibir forbid 10; prohibit
promedio (*m*) average
promedio/a average
prometador/a promising
prometer promise
prominente prominent
promoción (*f*) promotion
promocionar promote
promover promote
pronombre (*m*) pronoun 12
pronóstico del tiempo (*m*) weather forecast 12
pronto soon
pronunciar pronounce
propiedad (*f*) property
propio/a own 4
propósito (*m*) goal; resolution
propuesta (*f*) proposal 12
protección (*f*) protection
proteger protect
proteína (*f*) protein 9
protesta (*f*) protest
protocolo (*m*) protocol
proverbio (*m*) proverb
provocar provoke, cause
próximo/a next 1
proyecto (*m*) project
(p)sicología (*f*) psychology
psiquiatra (*m/f*) psychiatrist 10
psiquiatría (*f*) psychiatry
publicación publication
publicado/a published 11
públicamente publicly
publicar publish
publicidad (*f*) advertisement 11; advertising 11; publicity
publicitar publicize
público (*m*) public
público/a public; **concientización pública** (*f*) public awareness
pueblo (*m*) people
puerta (*f*) door 1; gate 7

puertorriqueño/a Puerto Rican
pues so 1; well
puesto (*m*) position 11
pulmones (*mpl*) lungs 10
pulmonía (*f*) pneumonia
punto (*m*) point
pupitre (*m*) student desk 1
puré purée(d), mashed
purificación (*f*) purification

Q

¿qué? what 2; **¿Qué clases tienes?** What classes do you have? 1; **¿Qué estudias?** What are you studying? 1; **¿Qué fecha es?** What is the date? 5; **¿Qué significa . . . en inglés?** What does . . . mean in English? 1; **¿Qué tal . . . ?** How is / are / was / were . . . ? 7; **¿Qué te pasa?** What's wrong with you? 10; **¿Qué tiempo hace?** What's the weather like? 5
que than; that 1
quedarse stay 5
quehacer (*m*) task; **quehacer doméstico** (*m*) chore 4
quemar(se) burn (oneself) 10
querer(se) (ie) love, want 2, 4, 10; *refl* love (each other) 5
Querido/a . . . Dear . . .
queso (*m*) cheese 9
quién(es) who, whom 2
química (*f*) chemistry
químico/a chemical
quinceañera (*f*) fifteenth birthday celebration
quinto/a fifth
quiosco de periódicos (*m*) newsstand 7
quizás perhaps, maybe 10

R

rábano (*m*) radish 9
radio (*f*) radio 3
radiografía (*f*) X-ray 10
raíz (*f*) root
ranchero/a (*m/f*) rancher
rápidamente rapidly
rapidez (*f*) rapidity
rápido/a rapid
raro/a weird 3
rato (*m*) while
ratón (*m*) mouse 11
ratos libres free time
razón (*f*) reason 3; **tener razón** be right 3
razonable reasonable 5
reacción (*f*) reaction 11
reaccionar react; reaction

realidad (f) reality
realista down-to-earth 3; realistic
realizarse come true; realize oneself
realmente really
recado (m) message 11
recámara (f) bedroom
recepción (f) front desk 7
recepcionista (m/f) receptionist 7
recesión (f) recession
receta (f) prescription 10
recetar prescribe 10
recibir receive 3
recibo de la luz (m) light bill 4
recién casados (mpl) newlyweds
reciente recent
recipiente (m/f) recipient
recíproco/a reciprocal
recoger pick up, gather 7
recomendación (f) recommendation
recomendar (ie) recommend 7, 10
recompensa (f) compensation
reconocer recognize
reconversión (f) reconversion
recordable memorable
recordar (ue) remember 4
recreo (m) recess 8; recreation
recuerdo (m) memory 8; souvenir 7
recurso (m) resource; **recursos humanos** (mpl) human resources 11
red (f) network; web 6
redacción (f) writing, composition
redactar write
reducción (f) reduction
reducir reduce
referencia (f) reference 11
referir refer
reflejar reflect
reflexión (f) reflection
reflexivo/a reflexive
reforma (f) reform
refresco (m) soft drink 9
refrigerador (m) refrigerator
refugio (m) refuge
regalar give as a gift 9
regalo (m) gift, present 2
reggaetón (m) reggae
régimen (m) regime
región (f) region
registrar register
regla (f) rule
regresar return 2
regulación (f) regulation
regular as usual 1
regularidad (f) regularity
regularmente regularly
relación (f) relationship
relacionar relate
relajado/a easy-going 3
relajarse relax 5

relativamente relatively
relatividad (f) relativity
relevante relevant
religioso/a religious
relleno/a stuffed
reloj (m) clock, watch 1
remedio (m) remedy
remedio casero (m) home remedy
rendir yield, give
renovable renewable
renovar renovate
renta (f) rent
rentar rent
reparación (f) repair
reparar repair
repasar review
repetir (i) repeat 4
repetitivamente repetitively
repetitivo/a repetitive
reportaje (m) report
reportero/a (m/f) reporter 12
represalia (f) reprisal
representante (m/f) representative
representar represent
reproducción (f) reproduction
reproductor de DVD (m) DVD player 4
República Dominicana (f) Dominican Republic
republicano/a (m/f) Republican
reputación (f) reputation
requerir (ie) require
reseña (f) review
reserva (f) reservation
reservado/a reserved 3; shy
reservar reserve 7
resfriado/a chilled, with a cold 10
resfriarse catch a cold 10
residencia (f) dormitory 1; residence hall 1
residente (m/f) resident
resistencia (f) resistance
resolución (f) resolution
resolver (ue) resolve 11
respaldo (m) back
respecto a with respect to
respetar respect
respeto (m) respect
respetuoso/a respectful
respirar breathe 10
respiratorio/a respiratory
responder respond
responsabilidad (f) responsibility 4
responsable responsible 1
responsable (m/f) person in charge 11
respuesta (f) answer, response 1
restaurante (m) restaurant 2, 9
resto (m) remainder, rest
restricción (f) restriction
resultado (m) result
resultar result

resumen (m) summary
retener retain
retirar remove; retire 11; withdraw 11
retiro (m) withdrawal 11
retraso (m) delay
retrato (m) portrait
reunir meet
revisar review
revisión dental (f) dental check-up 10
revista (f) magazine 3
revolución (f) revolution
revolucionario/a (m/f) revolutionary
rey (m) king
rezar pray 2
rico/a rich 6
ritmo (m) rhythm
robo (m) robbery
rodilla (f) knee 10
rojo/a red 3
rol (m) role
romántico/a romantic
romper(se) (el brazo) break (one's arm) 10
ropa (f) clothes 2, 5; **ponerse (la ropa)** put on (clothing)
rosa pink
rosado/a (rosa) pink 4
rubio/a blond 3
rueda (f) wheel
ruido (m) noise 4
ruidoso/a noisy 4
ruina (f) ruin
ruinas (fpl) ruins 7
rutina (f) routine; **rutina diaria** (f) daily routine 5

S

sábado Saturday 2
saber know, find out 7; **No sé.** I don't know. 1;
sacar take, take (out), get 7; **sacar una copia** make a copy 11; **sacar una foto** take a picture 5
sal (f) salt 9
sala (f) living room 4; room; **sala de chat** (f) chat room; **sala de espera** (f) waiting room; **sala de urgencia** (f) emergency room 10
salario (m) salary 11
salida (f) departure 7; outing
salir go out 2; leave 3; **salir en velero** go sailing 7
salmón (m) salmon
salón (m) hall, room; **salón de clase** (m) classroom 1
salsa (f) sauce
salteado/a sautéed
salud (f) health 9, 10

saludable healthy
saludar greet 8
saludo (*m*) greeting
salutación (*f*) salutation
salvadoreño/a Salvadoran
salvar save
salvo/a safe
sandalias (*f*) sandals 5
sangre (*f*) blood 10
sanidad (*f*) sanity
sano/a healthy 9
santo/a saintly 6
santo/a (*m/f*) saint
satisfacción (*f*) satisfaction
satisfacer satisfy
sazón (*m*) seasoning
se himself, herself, yourself, yourselves, themselves, each other, one another 5; to you, to him, to her, to you, to them 8; **¿Cómo se dice . . . en inglés?** How do you say . . . in English? 1; **¿Cómo se escribe?** How is that written? 1; **¿Cómo se llama usted?** What is your name? (*form.*) 1; **Se escribe . . .** It's written . . . 1; **Se llama(n) . . .** His / Her name is . . . (Their names are . . .); **se parece a . . .** He / She looks like . . . 3; **se puede** one can . . . 6
sección (*f*) section
secretario/a (*m/f*) secretary 8
secreto (*m*) secret
secuencia (*f*) sequence
sed (*f*) thirst; **dar sed** make thirsty 9; **tener sed** be thirsty 3
seducir seduce
segmento (*m*) segment
seguir (i, i) follow, continue 9
según according to
segundo/a second
seguridad (*f*) security 7; **número de seguridad social** (*m*) social security number
seguro/a safe 4; secure; **estar seguro/a** be sure 10
seguro médico (*m*) medical insurance 11
seleccionar select
sello (*m*) stamp 7
semana (*f*) week 2; **fin de semana** (*m*) weekend 2; **la semana pasada** (*f*) last week 7; **la semana que viene** (*f*) the coming week 2
semanal weekly
semestre (*m*) semester
Senado (*m*) Senate
senador/a (*m/f*) senator
sencillo/a single
sensación (*f*) sensation
sensacional sensational
sentarse (ie) sit down 5

sentimiento (*m*) feeling; sentiment
sentir (ie, i) feel 5; **Lo siento.** I'm sorry. 4; **sentir que** be sorry that 11
señalar signal
señor Mr., sir 1
señora (Sra.) Mrs., Mme. 1
señorita (Srta.) Miss 1
separado/a separate; **por separado** separately
septiembre September 5
séptimo/a seventh
ser be 1; **¡Así es!** that's right 9 **¿Cómo es . . . ?** How is . . . ?, What's . . . like? 1; **¿Cuántos son en . . . ?** How many are there in . . . ?; **¿De dónde eres?** Where are you from? (*fam.*) 2; **¿De dónde es?** Where are you from? (*form.*) 2; **ser operado/a** be operated on, have an operation 10; **son** equals; **Son las dos (tres).** It's one (two) o'clock. 2; **Soy . . .** I am, I'm . . . 1; **Soy de . . .** I'm from . . . 1
serenidad (*f*) serenity
serie policíaca (*f*) police series
serio/a serious 1, 3
servicio (*m*) service
servicio técnico (*m*) technical service 11
servilleta (*f*) napkin 9
servir (i, i) help 5; serve 4; **¿En qué puedo servirle?** How may I help you? 5
sesión session
sesionar meet, be in session
seudónimo (*m*) pseudonym
severo/a severe
sexismo (*m*) sexism
sexto/a sixth
sicología (*f*) psychology
siempre always 2, 4
siesta (*f*) nap
significado (*m*) significance
significar mean; **¿Qué significa . . . en inglés?** What does . . . mean in English? 1
siguiente following 1
silla (*f*) chair 1, 4
símbolo (*m*) symbol
similitud (*f*) similarity
simpático/a nice 1; pleasant
simulación (*f*) simulation
simultáneamente simultaneously
sin without 2; **sin embargo** nevertheless; **sin hogar** homeless 12
sinagoga (*f*) synagogue 2
síndrome (*m*) syndrome
sinónimo (*m*) synonym
sinónimo/a synonymous
síntoma (*m*) symptom 10
sistema (*m*) system 11

sistemáticamente systematically
sitio (*m*) site; **sitio histórico / turístico** (*m*) historic / tourist site 7; **sitio web** (*m*) web site
situación (*f*) situation
situar situate, locate
sobre over, about, on 9; **sobre todo** above all 8
sobrevivir survive
sobrina (*f*) niece 3
sobrino (*f*) nephew 3
socializar socializar
socialmente socially
sociedad (*f*) society
sociología (*f*) sociology
sofá (*m*) sofa 4
sofisticado/a sophisticated
sol (*m*) sun; **gafas de sol** (*fpl*) sunglasses; **Hace sol.** It's sunny. 5
soleado/a sunny
solicitar request
solicitud de empleo (*f*) job application 11
solidaridad (*f*) solidarity 12
sólo only 1
solo/a alone 2, 4
solsticio (*m*) solstice
soltero/a single 3
solución (*f*) solution
sombrero (*m*) hat 5
sonrisa (*f*) smile 8
soñar (ue) con dream of / about 8
sopa (*f*) soup 9
sorprender surprise 11
sorprendido/a surprised 2, 4, 6
sorpresa (*f*) surprise
sospechoso/a (*m/f*) suspect
subir a get on / in, go up 7
su(s) your (*sing. / form.*), your (*pl.*), his, her, its, their 3
súbito/a sudden
subjuntivo (*m*) subjunctive
subrayar underline
suburbano/a suburban
sucesivamente succesively
sucio/a dirty 4
sucursal (*f*) branch office 11
sudadera (*f*) sweatshirt 5
Sudamérica South America
sueldo (*m*) wage, salary 11
suelo (*m*) ground, floor 4
sueño (*m*) dream 8; sleep; **tener sueño** be sleepy
suerte (*f*) luck; **tener suerte** be lucky 3
suéter (*m*) sweater 5
suficiente sufficient
sufrir suffer
sugerencia (*f*) suggestion
sugerir (ie, i) suggest 10
superar overtake

superior higher
supermercado (*m*) supermarket
supersticioso/a superstitious
supervisor/a (*m/f*) supervisor 11
suplemento (*m*) supplement
sur (*m*) south; **al sur de** south of 2; south
suspenso (*m*) suspense
sustancia (*f*) substance
sustantivo (*m*) noun 4
sustituir substitute
suyo/a his, hers, yours (*pl.*), yours (*form. / sing.*) theirs 9

T

tabaco (*m*) tabacco
tabaquismo (*m*) smoking
tabla (*f*) table (graphic)
tal such; **¿Qué tal . . . ?** How is / are / was / were . . . ? 7; **tal vez** maybe, perhaps 10
talento (*m*) talent
talla (*f*) size 5
también also, too 1
tampoco neither 4
tan so; **tan . . . como** as . . . as 4; **tan pronto como** as soon as 11
tanto so much 10
tanto/a/os/as . . . como as much . . . as, as many . . . as 4
tarde late 2; **más tarde** later
tarde (*f*) afternoon 2; **de la tarde** in the afternoon 2; **por la tarde** in the afternoon 2
tarea (*f*) homework 1
tarifa (*f*) tariff
tarjeta (*f*) card; **tarjeta de débito** (*f*) debit card; **tarjeta de embarque** (*f*) boarding pass 7; **tarjeta telefónica** (*f*) phone card 7
tasa (*f*) rate; **tasa de interés** (*f*) interest rate 11
tatuaje (*m*) tatoo
taxi (*m*) taxi 7
taxista (*m/f*) taxi driver
taza (*f*) cup 9
te you, yourself (*fam.*) 1; **¿Te gusta** (+ *singular noun*)? Do you like . . . ? 1; **¿Te gustan** (+ *plural noun*)? Do you like . . . ? 1; **¿Te parece bien?** Does that seem okay to you? 2; **Te veo. . . .** You look . . . to me. 10
té tea; **té helado / caliente** (*m*) iced / hot tea 9
teatro (*m*) theater 2
teclado (*m*) keyboard 11
técnica (*f*) technique
técnico/a technical

tecnología (*f*) technology
telefonía telephony
telefónico/a telephonic
teléfono (*m*) telephone 2; **número de teléfono** (*m*) telephone number; **por teléfono** on the telephone 11; **teléfono público** (*m*) public telephone 7
telenovela (*f*) soap opera
teletrabajar telecommute
teletrabajo (*m*) telecommuting
televidente (*m/f*) television viewer
televisión (*f*) television
televisión (tele) (*f*) television (TV) 2
televisor (*m*) television; television set 1, 4
tema (*m*) theme
temático/a thematic
temer (que) fear (that) 11
temperamental moody 3
temperatura (*f*) temperature 10
temporal temporary
temprano early 2
tendencia (*f*) tendency
tenedor (*m*) fork 9
tener have 3; **(No) tengo . . .** I (don't) have . . . 1; **tener . . . años** be . . . years old 3; **tener calor** be hot 3; **tener cuidado** be careful 10; **tener curiosidad** be curious; **tener éxito** be successful; **tener frío** be cold 3; **tener ganas de** feel like; **tener hambre** be hungry 3; **tener miedo (de)** be afraid of, fear 3; **tener miedo de que** be afraid that 11; **tener prisa** be in a hurry 3; **tener que** have to, must; **tener razón** be right 3; **tener sed** be thirsty 3; **tener sueño** be sleepy; **tener suerte** be lucky 3; **Tengo . . .** I have . . . 1
tenis (*m*) tennis
tenis (*mpl*) sneakers 5; tennis shoes
tenista (*m/f*) tennis player
teoría (*f*) theory
terapeuta (*m/f*) therapist 10
terapia (*f*) therapy 10; **terapia de grupo** (*f*) group therapy 10
tercero/a third
terco/a stubborn 3
terminación (*f*) ending
terminar finish
término (*m*) term
terraza (*f*) terrace
terreno (*m*) land, terrain
territorio (*m*) territory
terrorismo (*m*) terrorism
terrorista (*m/f*) terrorist 12
testigo/a (*m/f*) witness
testimonio (*m*) testimony
texto (*m*) text
ti you 2
tía (*f*) aunt 3

tiempo (*m*) time; weather 5; **Hace buen / mal tiempo.** The weather's good / bad. 5; **pronóstico del tiempo** (*m*) weather forecast; **tiempo completo** (*m*) full-time 11; **tiempo libre** (*m*) free time 2; **tiempo parcial** (*m*) part-time 11; **tiempo verbal** (*m*) verb tense
tienda (*f*) store 2
tierra (*f*) land
timbre postal (*m*) stamp
tímido/a shy, timid 1
tío (*m*) uncle 3
típico/a typical
tipo (*m*) type
titular (*m*) headline
título (*m*) title
tocar play (music, musical instruments) 2
todavía still
todavía no not yet 11
todo/a/os/as all, every 1; **por todos lados** everywhere 4; **todo el día** all day 2; **todos** everyone 4; **todos los días** every day 2
Tokio Tokyo
tolerancia (*f*) tolerance
tomar drink, take 2; **tomar asiento** take a seat; **tomar el sol** sunbathe 2; **tomar una decisión** make a decision 10
tomate (*m*) tomato 9
tono (*m*) tone, beep 11
tonto/a foolish; stupid, silly 1
tortilla (de maíz / de harina) (*f*) corn / flour tortilla 9
tos (*f*) cough 10
toser cough 10
totalitario/a totalitarian
totalmente totally
trabajador/a hardworking 1
trabajador/a social (*m/f*) social worker 8
trabajar work 2
trabajo (*m*) job, work 2; **en el trabajo** at work 2
tradición (*f*) tradition
tradicional traditional
tradicionalismo (*m*) traditionalism
traducción (*f*) translation
traducir translate
traer bring 3
tráfico (*m*) traffic 4
tragedia (*f*) tragedy
traje (*m*) suit 5; **traje de baño** (*m*) swimsuit 5
trámite (*m*) transaction 11
tranquilidad (*f*) tranquility
tranquilo/a calm 3
transformación (*f*) transformation
transformar transform
transición (*f*) transition
transmisión (*f*) transmission

transmitir transmit
transparente transparent
transporte *(m)* transportation
transporte público *(m)* public transportation 4
tratamiento *(m)* treatment 10
tratar (de) treat, try (to) 8
trato *(m)* dealings
travieso/a mischievous 8
tren *(m)* train
triángulo *(m)* triangle
tribunal *(m)* jury
trigo *(m)* wheat
trimestre *(m)* trimester
triste sad 2, 4, 10; **estar triste de que** be sad that 11
tristeza *(f)* sadness 10
trompeta *(f)* trumpet
tú you *(sing. / fam.)*
tu(s) your *(sing. / fam.)* 1, 3
tuna university band
tuno university band member
turbulencia *(f)* turbulence
turismo *(m)* tourism
turista *(m/f)* tourist
tuyo/a yours *(sing. / fam.)* 9

U

u or (before words beginning with o)
ubicación *(f)* location 11
último/a last, latest 7
un/a a, an 1
una vez once 2
unido/a united
uniforme *(m)* uniform
unión *(f)* union
universidad *(f)* university 1
universitario/a university 8
unos/as some 1
urbano/a urban
urgente urgent 10
usar use 2
usario/a *(m/f)* user
usted you *(sing. / form.)*
ustedes you *(pl.)*
útil useful 1
utilidad *(f)* utility
utilización *(f)* use, utilization
utilizar use
uvas *(fpl)* grapes 9

V

vacaciones *(fpl)* vacation, holiday; **ir de vacaciones** go on vacation 7
valor *(m)* value
valoración *(f)* valuation
valorar value
vapor *(m)*: **al vapor** steamed
variado/a varied
variedad *(f)* variety
varios/as several 1
varón male
vaso *(m)* glass 9
vecindario *(m)* neighborhood 7
vecino/a *(m/f)* neighbor 4
vegetariano/a vegetarian
vehículo *(m)* vehicle
velero *(m)* sailboat 7
velocidad *(f)* velocity
vendedor/a *(m/f)* seller
vender sell 3
venir come 3
venta *(f)* sale
ventaja *(f)* advantage
ventana *(f)* window 1, 4
ventanilla *(f)* counter window 11; window (of a vehicle or box office) 7
ver see 2
verano *(m)* summer 5
verbo *(m)* verb
verdad true
verdadero/a true
verde green 3, 4
verduras *(fpl)* vegetables 9
verificar verify
versátil versatile
versión *(f)* version
vestido *(m)* dress 5
vestigio *(m)* vestige
vestirse (i, i) get dressed 5
vez *(f)*: **en vez de** instead of 9
vía via
viajar travel 7
viaje *(m)* trip 3; **hacer un viaje** take a trip 3
viajero/a *(m/f)* traveler
viceversa vice versa
víctima *(f)* victim
victoria *(f)* victory
vida *(f)* life 8; **vida nocturna** *(f)* night life
videojuego *(m)* videogame

viejo/a old 1, 4
viento *(m)* wind; **Hace viento.** It's windy. 5
viernes Friday 2
vigilar watch, be vigilant
vinagre *(m)* vinegar
vino *(m)* wine; **vino tinto / blanco** *(m)* red / white wine 9
viñeta *(f)* comic strip
violencia *(f)* violence
virtuoso/a *(m/f)* virtuouso
visita *(f)* visit
visitante *(m/f)* visitor
visitar visit 7
vista *(f)* view
vitalidad *(f)* vitality
vitaminas *(fpl)* vitamins 9
vivienda *(f)* housing, dwelling
vivir live 3
vivo live; **en vivo** live
vocabulario *(m)* vocabulary
vocal *(f)* vowel
voluntariamente voluntarily
voluntario/a voluntary
voluntario/a *(m/f)* volunteer
volver (ue) (a) return, . . . again 4
vomitar vomit, throw up 10
vosotros/as you *(pl. / fam.)*
votante *(m/f)* voter
votar vote
voz *(f)* voice
vuelo *(m)* flight 7
vuelta *(f)* returning flight 7
vuestro/a(s) your *(pl./ fam.)* 3

Y

y and 4
ya already 7
ya no no longer, not any more 10
yo I
yogur *(m)* yogurt

Z

zanahoria *(f)* carrot 9
zapatillas de tenis *(mpl)* tennis shoes
zapatos *(mpl)* shoes 5
zona *(f)* zone

English-Spanish Glossary

The **English-Spanish Glossary** includes all active vocabulary presented in *Hoy día,* as well as other high frequency words. Numbers following entries indicate the chapter where words are introduced. All translations separated by commas before a number are considered active in that chapter. Gender of nouns in Spanish is indicated by *(m)* for masculine and *(f)* for feminine. Nouns referring to people that have both masculine and feminine forms are indicated by *(m/f)*, and those that are generally used in the plural are followed by *(pl).*

A

a un/a 1
a lot of mucho/a/os/as 1
abandon abandonar
ability habilidad *(f)*
able: be able to poder (ue) 4, 7
about acerca de 8; sobre 9
above por encima
above all sobre todo 8
absent ausente; **be absent** faltar (a) 8
absolutely absolutamente
absurd absurdo/a 10
abuse abuso *(m)*
accede acceder
accelerate acelerar
accent acento 3; **with an accent** con acento 1; **without an accent** sin acento 1
accept aceptar
access acceso *(m)* 11
accessory accesorio *(m)* 4
accident accidente *(m)* 10
accompany acompañar
accomplice cómplice *(m/f)*
according to según
account cuenta *(f)* 11
accountant contador/a *(m/f)* 8, 11
accounting contabilidad *(f)*
accusation acusación *(f)*
accustom acostumbrar
accustomed acostumbrado/a
ache doler (ue) 9; dolor *(m)* 10
achieve lograr
across a través de; **across from** enfrente de 2
act actuar
action acción *(f)*
active activo/a
activist activista *(m/f)*
activity actividad *(f)* 2
actor actor *(m)* 8
actress actriz *(f)* 8
ad: classified ad anuncio clasificado *(m)*
adapt adaptar
adaptation adaptación *(f)*
addict adicto/a *(m/f)*

addiction adicción *(f)*
additional adicional
address dirección *(f)* 4
adjective adjetivo *(m)*
adjust to ajustarse a
administration administración *(f)*
administrator administrador/a *(m/f)*
admire admirar
admirer admirador/a *(m/f)*
admit admitir
adolescence adolescencia *(f)*
adopt adoptar
adult adulto/a *(m/f)*
advance avance *(m)*
advantage ventaja *(f)*
adventurous aventurero/a
adverb adverbio *(m)*
advertise anunciar
advertisement anuncio *(m)*; publicidad *(f)* 11
advertiser anunciante *(m/f)*
advertising publicidad *(f)* 11
advice consejo *(m)*
advise aconsejar 10
affect afectar
affectionate cariñoso/a 3
affirmation afirmación *(f)*
afraid: be afraid (of) tener miedo (de) 3; **be afraid that** tener miedo de que 11
African africano/a
after después 2; después (de) que 11
afternoon tarde *(f)* 2
afterwards después
again otra vez
against contra
age edad *(f)* 8
agency agencia *(f)*
agent agente *(m/f)*
aggressive agresivo/a
aging envejecimiento *(m)*
agitation agitación *(f)* 12
ago hace . . . 7
agree estar de acuerdo
agreeable agradable
agricultural agrícolo/a
agriculture agricultura *(f)*

ahead of delante de 2
air conditioning aire acondicionado *(m)*
airline aerolínea *(f)* 7
airplane avión *(m)* 7
airport aeropuerto *(m)* 7
aisle pasillo *(m)* 7
alarm alarma *(f)*
alarmed alarmado/a
alcoholic alcohólico/a
alcoholic drink bebida alcohólica *(f)* 9
alert alertar
algebra álgebra *(f)*
align alinear
all todo/a/os/as 1; **all day** todo el día 2
allergy alergia *(f)* 10
alleviate aliviar
allow permitir 10
almost casi 2
alone solo/a 2, 4
already ya 7
also también 1
alternative alternativo/a
although aunque
always siempre 2, 4
American estadounidense; (norte)americano/a *(m/f)*
among entre
amount to equivaler
amuse divertir
amuse yourself divertirse (ie, i) 5
an un/a
analgesic analgésico *(m)*
and y 4
angel ángel *(m)*
angry enojado/a 2
angry: get angry enojarse 5
animal animal *(m)*
animal feeder comedero *(m)*
animation animación *(f)*
announce anunciar
annoy fastidiar
annual anual
anonymity anonimato *(m)*
anonymous anónimo/a
another otro/a 1
answer contestar 2

answer respuesta (f) 1

antibiotics antibióticos 10

anticipate anticipar

antidepressant antidepresivo (m)

anti-inflammatory antiinflamatorio (m)

antonym antónimo (m)

anxiety ansiedad (f)

any alguno/a(s) 4; cualquier

apartment apartamento (m)

appear aparecer

apple manzana (f) 9

application aplicación (f) 6; **job application** solicitud de empleo (f) 11

apply aplicar

appointment cita (f) 10

appreciate apreciar

appropriate apropiado/a

approximate aproximar

April abril 5

arable cultivable

archeological arqueológico/a

architecture arquitectura (f)

archive archivo (m) 6

Are there . . . ? ¿Hay . . . ? 1

area área (f)

Argentine argentino/a (m/f)

arm brazo (m) 10

arms (military) armas (fpl)

around aldredor de

arrest arrestar

arrival llegada (f) 7

arrive llegar 2

art arte (m)

arthritis artritis (f) 10

article artículo (m)

artist artista (m/f)

as como 1; mientras 8; **as . . . as** tan . . . como 4; **as for** en cuanto a 9; **as long as** mientras 11; **as many . . . as** tanto/a/os/as . . . como 4; **as much . . . as** tanto/a . . . como 4; **as soon as** tan pronto como 11; **as soon as possible** lo antes posible 11; **as usual** regular 1

ask pedir (i, i) 10; preguntar 9; **ask a question** hacer una pregunta 3; **ask for** pedir (i, i) 4

asparagus espárragos 9

aspect aspecto (m) 11

aspirin aspirina (f) 10

assault asalto (m)

assign asignar

assistance asistencia (f); ayuda; **food assistance** ayuda alimentaria (f)

associate asociar

assure asegurar

asthma asma (f)

at en, a 1; **at the back of** al fondo de 7; **at the beginning** al principio 8; **at the end of** al fondo de 7; **at times** a veces 2; **At what time?** ¿A qué hora? 2; **at work** en el trabajo 2

athlete atleta (m/f); deportista (m/f) 8

athletic deportista (adj.) 8

Atlantic atlántico/a

ATM cajero automático (m) 11

atmosphere ambiente (m); atmósfera (f)

attack ataque (m)

attend asistir (a) 3; **attend to** atender (ie) 11

attention atención (f)

attitude actitud (f)

attract atraer

attraction atracción (f)

attractive atractivo/a

audience audiencia (f)

August agosto 5

aunt tía (f) 3

authentic auténtico/a

authenticity autenticidad (f)

author autor/a (m/f)

authority autoridad (f)

autobiographical autobiográfico/a

automatic automático/a

automobile auto (m); automóvil (m); carro (m); coche (m)

autumn otoño (m) 5

availability disponibilidad (f) 7

available disponible 7, 11; **be available** estar a disposición

average promedio (m); promedio/a

avoid evitar 9

away: take away llevarse 5

B

baby bebé (m)

back espalda (f) 10; respaldo (m)

backpack mochila (f) 1

bad malo/a 1

bad(ly) mal 1

baked / fried potato al horno 9

balanced equilibrado/a 9

balcony balcón (m) 7

banana banana (f); banano (m); guineo (m); plátano (m) 9

bank banco (m) 7

bank account cuenta bancaria (f)

banking banca (f) 11

banquet banquete (m)

bar bar (m) 3

barber shop peluquería (f) 7

base basar

baseball béisbol (m) 8

baseball player beisbolista (m/f) 8

basic básico/a

basketball básquetbol (m)

bath: take a bath bañarse 5

bathe bañarse 5

bathroom baño (m) 4

be estar; ser 1; **be able to** poder (ue) 4, 7; **be absent** faltar (a) 8; **be acquainted with** conocer 7; **be afraid of** tener miedo (de) 3; **be afraid that** tener miedo de que 11; **be available** estar a disposición; **be born** nacer 8; **be called** llamarse 3; **be careful** tener cuidado 10; **be cold** tener frío 3; **be curious** tener curiosidad; **be down** fallar 11; **be equivalent** equivaler; **be familiar with** conocer 7; **be happy that** alegrarse de que 11; estar contento/a de que 11; **be hot** tener calor 3; **be hungry** tener hambre 3; **be important** importar 9; **be in a good / bad mood** estar de buen / mal humor 11; **be in a hurry** tener prisa 3; **be in charge of** estar encargado/a de 11; **be in fashion** estar de moda 5; **be in session** sesionar; **be lucky** tener suerte 3; **be missing** faltar 9; faltar (a); **be named** llamarse 3; **be needed** faltar 9; **be operated on** ser operado/a 10; **be pleasing to** gustar 2; **be pregnant** estar embarazada 10; **be revolting** dar asco 9; **be right** tener razón 3; **be sad (that)** estar triste de (que) 11; **be sleepy** tener sueño; **be sorry that** sentir (ie, i) que 11; **be successful** tener éxito; **be sunny** hacer sol; **be sure** estar seguro/a 10; **be thirsty** tener sed 3; **be unable to stand** dar asco 9; **be vigilant** vigilar; **be . . . years old** tener . . . años 3; **How is . . . ?** ¿Cómo es . . . ? 1

beach playa (f) 2

beans frijoles (mpl) 9; habichuelas (mpl)

beard barba (f) 3

beautiful bello/a; precioso/a

beauty belleza (f)

because porque 2, 8; **because of** a causa de, por

bed cama (f) 1

bedroom alcoba (f); dormitorio (m) 4; habitación (f); recámara (f)

beep tono (m) 11

beer cerveza (f) 9

before antes (de)

begin comenzar (ie) 10; empezar (ie) 4

beginner novato/a (m/f)

beginning comienzo (m)

behave portarse 8

behind detrás de 2

believe (in / that) creer (en / que) 3, 10

bellboy botones (m)

belong pertencer

below debajo de 2
belt cinturón (m) 5
beneficial beneficioso/a
benefit beneficiar
benefit beneficio (m) 11
besides además 11
best mejor 3; **best friend** mejor amigo/a (m/f) 1
better mejor 3
between entre 1, 2
bicycle bicicleta (f) 4; **ride a bicycle** andar en bicicleta 4
big grande 1
biker motociclista (m/f) 8
bilingual bilingüe
bill billete (m) 11; cuenta (f) 9, 11; factura (f)
biology biología (f)
biology laboratory laboratorio de biología (m)
bird feeder comedero (m)
birth nacimiento (m) 8
birthday cumpleaños (m); fecha de nacimiento (f) 2; **birthday party** fiesta de cumpleaños (f) 8
bit poco (m)
black negro/a 3, 4
blackboard pizarra (f) 1
block (in a city) cuadra (f) 7
blond rubio/a 3
blood sangre (f) 10
blood pressure presión arterial (f) 10
blouse blusa (f) 5
blue azul 3, 4
board abordar 7
boarding embarque (m)
boarding pass tarjeta de embarque (f) 7
bodily corporal
body cuerpo (m) 10; organismo (m)
bone hueso (m) 10
book libro (m) 1
bookbag mochila (f) 1
bookstore librería (f) 2
boots botas (fpl) 5
border frontera (f)
bored aburrido/a 2, 4; **get bored** aburrirse 5
boring aburrido/a 1
boss jefe/a (m/f) 11
bossy mandón / mandona 3
bother fastidiar; molestar 9, 11
bothered molesto/a 2, 4
bottle botella (f) 9
boy chico (m); muchacho (m) 2; niño (m)
boyfriend novio/a (m/f) 1
brain cerebro (m) 10
branch office sucursal (f) 11
brand marca (f)
Brazil Brasil

bread pan (m) 9
break (one's arm) romper(se) (el brazo) 10
breakfast desayuno (m) 4
breathe respirar 10
brief breve
brilliant brillante
bring traer 3
broccoli brócoli (m) 9
brochure folleto (m)
bronchitis bronquitis (f)
brother (m) hermano (m) 3
brown café 3; castaño 3; marrón 3, 4
brush one's teeth lavarse los dientes 5
brusque brusco/a
buckle one's seatbelt abrocharse el cinturón 7
building edificio (m) 1
burn (oneself) quemar(se) 10
bus autobús (m) 4
bus stop parada de autobús (f) 4
business empresa (f); negocio (m)
business administration administración de empresas (f)
businessman/woman empresario/a (m/f); hombre / mujer de negocios (m) 8
busy ocupado/a 1
but pero 1
butter mantequilla (f) 9
button botón 6
buy comprar 2
by para; por; **by means of** mediante; **by way of** por
Bye. Chau.; Ádios. 5

C

café café (m) 2
cafeteria cafetería (f) 1
caffeine cafeína (f) 9
cake pastel (m) 9
calculate calcular 11
calculator calculadora (f) 1
calendar calendario (m)
call llamada (f) 7
call llamar
calm calmado/a; tranquilo/a 3
calories calorías 9
camel camello (m)
camp acampar 7
campaign campaña (f)
campus campus (m)
can poder (ue) 4, 7
Canada Canadá
cancel cancelar
candidate candidato/a (m/f)
cap gorra (f) 5
capacity capacidad (f)
capture captar

car auto (m); automóvil (m); carro (m) 4; coche (m) 3, 4
carbohydrates carbohidratos 9
care cuidado (m); **take care of (oneself)** cuidar(se) 10
career carrera (f)
careful: be careful tener cuidado 10
Caribbean caribeño/a
carpenter carpintero/a (m/f)
carpentry carpintería (f)
carpet alfombra (f)
carrot zanahoria (f) 9
carry llevar 5
carry out cumplir 8
cartoon dibujos animados (mpl)
case caso (m)
cash: in cash en efectivo 5
cash (a check) cobrar 11
cashier cajero/a (m/f) 11
cat gato/a (m/f)
cataract catarata (f)
category categoría (f)
cathedral catedral (f)
Catholic católico/a
cauliflower coliflor (m) 9
cause causar; provocar
celebrate celebrar
celebration celebración (f)
cell phone celular (m)
cello chelo (m)
censure censura (f)
census censo (m)
cent centavo (m) 9
center centro (m) 4
center centrar
centigrade centígrado (m)
central céntrico/a
Central America Centroamérica
Central American centroamericano/a (m/f)
centralized centralizado/a
cereal cereales 9
ceremony ceremonia (f)
certain cierto/a
chain cadena (f)
chair silla (f) 1, 4
chalkboard pizarra (f)
chamber of commerce cámara de comercio (f)
championship campeonato (m) 8
change cambio (m)
change cambiar
channel cadena (f); canal (m)
chapter capítulo (m)
character carácter (m) 3; personaje (m)
characteristic característica (f)
charge cargo (m) 11
charge (a fee) cobrar 11
chat chatear 6; **chat room** sala de chat (f)

chatty hablador/a 4
cheap barato/a 5
check cheque (m) 5; cuenta (f) 9
check one's luggage facturar el equipaje
checkbook chequera (f) 11
checking / savings account cuenta
    corriente / de ahorros (f) 11
checkup chequeo (m)
cheer someone up dar ánimo a alguien 10
cheese queso (m) 9
chemical químico/a
chemistry química (f)
chest pecho (m) 10
chest (of drawers) cómoda (f) 4
chew masticar
chicken pollo (m) 9
child niño/a (m/f); as a child de niño/a 8
childcare cuidado de niños (m)
childhood infancia (f); niñez (f) 8
children hijos (mpl) 3
children's infantil
chile pepper chile (m) 9
Chilean chileno/a
chilled resfriado/a 10
Chinese chino (m)
cholesterol colesterol (m) 10
chore quehacer doméstico (m) 4
Christmas Navidad (f)
church iglesia (f) 2
Ciao. Chau. 5
cigarette cigarrillo (m)
cinema cine (m) 2
circle círculo (m)
circuit circuito (m)
circulate circular
circulation circulación (f)
circumstance circunstancia (f)
city ciudad (f) 2
city map plano de la ciudad (m) 7
civilization civilización (f)
clarify aclarar
class clase (f) 1; classmate compañero/a
    de clase (m/f); classroom salón de
    clase (m) 1
classical clásico/a 2
classified ad anucio clasificado (m)
classify clasificar
clause claúsula (f)
clean limpio/a 4
clean limpiar
clear claro/a; despejado/a 5
clear despejar 5
click hacer clic
client cliente (m)
clientele clientela (f)
climate clima (m); climate change
    cambios climáticos (m)
climb ascender
clock reloj (m) 1

close cercana/o
close cerrar (ie) 4
closed cerrado/a 2
closet armario (m) 4; clóset (m)
clothing ropa (f) 2, 5
cloudy nublado/a 5
coast costa (f)
coat abrigo (m)
code código (m)
coffee café 3; black coffee café solo (m) 9
cognate cognado (m)
coherent coherente
coin moneda (f) 11
cold frío/a 3; frío (m); catarro (m) 10;
    be cold tener frío 3; catch a cold
    resfriarse 10; It's (very) cold. Hace
    (mucho) frío. 5
collapse colapsar
colleague colega (m/f) 11
college colegio (m)
colloquial coloquial
Colombian colombiano/a (m/f)
colonizer colonizador/a (m/f)
color color (m) 4; What color is it?
    ¿De qué color es?
column columna (f)
combat combatir
combination combinación (f)
combine combinar
come venir 3; come true realizarse
comedy comedia (f)
comfortable cómodo/a
comic cómico/a
comic strip viñeta (f)
command mandato (m)
commemorate conmemorar
comment comentar
commentary comentario (m) 6
commerce comercio (m); chamber of
    commerce cámara de comercio (f)
commercial comercial
commission comisión (f)
commit cometer; comprometer
committee comité (f)
common común 10
communicate (with each other)
    comunicar(se) 5
communication comunicación
community comunidad (f)
community (adj.) comunitario/a
community center centro comunitario (m)
companion compañero/a (m/f)
company compañía (f) 11; empresa (f) 11;
    firma (f)
compare comparar
comparison comparación (f)
compartment compartimento (m)
compatibility compatibilidad (f) 11
compatriot compatriota (m/f) 12

compensation recompensa (f)
compete competir
competition competición (f); concurso (m)
competitive competitivo/a
competitor concursante (m/f)
complement complementar
complete completo/a 11
complete completar
complex complejo (m)
complicated complicado/a
compliment cumplido (m)
composition redacción (f)
compression compresión (f) 6
computer computador (m);
    computadora (f) 1; ordenador (m)
computer science informática (f)
computing computación (f);
    informática (f) 11
concentrate concentrarse 10
concentrated concentrado/a
concentration concentración (f)
concept concepto (m)
concert concierto (m) 2
concise conciso/a
concrete concreto/a
condemn condenar
condiment condimento (m)
condition condición (f)
condition condicionar
conditional condicional
conference conferencia (f)
confess confesar
confidence confianza (f); have
    confidence in confiar
configure configurar
confirm confirmar
confirmation confirmación (f)
confront enfrentarse (con)
confused confundido/a 2
confusion confusión (f)
congested congestionado/a 10
congestion congestión (f) 10
Congress Congreso (m) 12
congressman/woman congresista (m/f)
conjunction conjunción (f)
connect conectar 8
connection conexión (f)
connectivity conectividad (f)
connotation connotación (f)
conquer conquistar
conquest conquista (f)
consequence consecuencia (f)
conservative conservador/a 3
conserve conservar
consist consistir
consonant consonante (f)
construction construcción (f) 8;
    construction worker obrero/a de la
    construcción (m/f) 8

consulate consulado (*m*)
consult consultar
consultation consulta (*f*)
consumer consumidor/a (*m/f*)
consumerism consumerismo (*m*)
consumption consumo (*m*)
contact contacto (*m*)
contact contactar
contain contener
container contenedor (*m*)
contaminate contaminar
contamination contaminación (*f*)
content contenido (*m*)
contestant concursante (*m/f*)
context contexto (*m*)
continue continuar; seguir (i, i)
contrary contrario (*m*)
contrast contraste (*m*)
contribute contribuir
contribution contribución (*f*)
control controlar 10
conversation conversación (*f*)
convert convertir
cook cocinar 2
cookie galleta (*f*) 9
cool fresco/a; **It's cool.** Hace fresco. 5
cooperation cooperación (*f*)
copy copiar; **make a copy** sacar una copia 11
cordially cordialmente
corn choclo (*m*); elote (*m*); maíz (*m*) 9
corn / flour tortilla tortilla (de maíz / de harina) (*f*) 9
corner esquina (*f*) 7
correct correcto/a; justo/a 7
correct corregir
correction corrección (*f*)
correspond corresponder
corresponding correspondiente
corruption corrupción (*f*)
cosmopolitan cosmopolito/a
cost costo (*m*); **cost of living** costo de vida (*m*)
cost costar (ue) 4
Costa Rican costarricense
costly costoso/a
cough tos (*f*) 10
cough toser 10
counsel consejo (*m*)
counselor consejero/a (*m/f*) 8
count contar (ue) 4
country campo (*m*) 4; país (*m*)
county condado (*m*)
couple pareja (*f*)
course curso (*m*)
court corte (*f*)
courtesy cortesía (*f*)
cousin primo/a (*m/f*) 3
crazy loco/a

cream crema (*f*) 9
create crear
creativity creatividad (*f*)
credit crédito (*m*)
credit card tarjeta de crédito (*f*)
crime crimen (*m*); criminalidad (*f*) (*in general*) 12
criteria criterios (*mpl*)
critic crítico/a (*m/f*)
criticize criticar
crop cultivo (*m*)
crutches muletas (*fpl*) 10
cry llorar 8
crystal cristal
Cuban cubano/a
cubism cubismo (*m*)
culinary culinario/a
cultivate cultivar
cultural cultural 4
culture cultura (*f*)
cup taza (*f*) 9
curative curativo/a
curiosity curiosidad (*f*) 12
curious: be curious tener curiosidad
currency divisa (*f*)
current event actualidad (*f*)
currently actualmente
curriculum vitae currículum vitae (*m*) 11
cursive cursivo/a
cursor cursor (*m*) 6
custom costumbre (*f*)
customer cliente / clienta (*m/f*) 5
cut cortar; **cut one's hair** cortarse el pelo 7; **cut the grass** cortar el césped 4; **cut (yourself)** cortar(se) 10
cybercafé cibercafé (*m*)
cybernetic cibernético/a

D

daily diario/a 2
daily routine rutina diaria (*f*) 5
daily specials menú (*m*)
dance baile (*m*); danza (*f*)
dance bailar 2
dangerous peligroso/a
dark oscuro/a
dark-complexioned moreno/a 3
data datos (*mpl*)
data transfer descarga (*f*) 6
database base de datos (*f*) 11
date cita (*f*); fecha (*f*) 5; **What is the date?** ¿Qué fecha es? 5
date from datar de
daughter hija (*f*) 3
day día (*m*) 2; **all day** todo el día 2; **every day** todos los días 2; **work days** días laborales

dead muerto/a 4
dealings trato (*m*)
Dear . . . Querido/a . . .
death muerte (*f*) 8
debate debatir
debilitate debilitar
debit débito (*m*)
debit card tarjeta de débito 5; tarjeta de débito (*f*)
decade década (*f*)
decaffeinated descafeinado/a
December diciembre 5
decide decidir 7
decipherable descifrable
decision decisión (*f*); **make a decision** tomar una decisión 10
declare declarar
dedicate dedicar
dedication dedicación (*f*)
deduce deducir
deep profundo/a 10
defend defender
defenseless indefenso/a
deficit déficit (*m*)
define definar
defined definido/a
definition definición (*f*)
deforestation deforestación (*f*) 12
degree grado (*m*); licenciatura (*m*); **get a degree in . . .** hacer la carrera de . . . 8
delay retraso (*m*) 7
delegation delegación (*f*)
delete button borrador (*m*)
delicious delicioso/a
demand demanda (*f*)
Democrat demócrata (*m/f*)
democratization democratización (*f*)
demonstrative demonstrativo/a
denounce denunciar
dental check-up revisión dental (*f*) 10
dentist dentista (*m/f*) 10
department departamento (*m*) 11
departure salida (*f*) 7
depend depender (de)
deposit depositar 11
deposit depósito (*m*) 11
depressed deprimido/a
depression depresión (*f*) 10
derivative derivado (*m*)
descend descender
describe describir
description descripción (*f*) 4
design diseño (*m*) 6; **graphic design** diseño gráfico (*m*); **graphic design program** programa de diseño gráfico (*m*) 11
design diseñar 11
designer diseñador/a (*m/f*)
desire desear 2

desk escritorio *(m)* 1; pupitre *(m)*
despair desesperanza *(f)* 10
despite a pesar de que
dessert postre *(m)* 9
destination destino *(m)*
destroy destruir
detail detalle *(m)*
detain detener
deteriorate deteriorarse
determining determinante
devastation devastación *(f)*
develop desarrollar 10
developing en vías de desarrollo
development desarrollo *(m)* 11
devil diablo *(m)*
devote oneself to dedicarse a 8
diabetes diabetes *(f)* 10
diagnose diagnosticar
dialogue diálogo *(m)*
dictionary diccionario *(m)* 1
die morir (ue, u) 8
diet dieta *(f)* 9
difference diferencia *(f)*
different diferente; distinto/a
difficult difícil 1
difficulty dificultad *(f)* 10
digestion digestión *(f)*
digit dígito *(m)*
dimension dimensión *(f)*
diminish disminuir
dining room comedor *(m)* 4
dinner cena *(f)* 2
direct directo/a
direct dirigir
direct deposit depósito directo *(m)* 11
direct / indirect object complemento
    directo / indirecto *(m)*
direction dirección *(f)*
director director/a *(m/f)* 11
dirty sucio/a 4
disadvantage desventaja *(f)*
disappearance desaparición *(f)*
disaster desastre *(m)*
disastrous desastroso/a
discipline disciplina *(f)*
discomfort molestia *(f)*
disconnect desconectar
discotheque discoteca *(f)*
discreet discreto/a
discreetly discretamente
discriminatory discriminatorio/a
discuss discutir
discussion discusión *(f)*
disgusted disgustado/a 6
dish plato *(m)*
dishonest deshonesto/a
dishwasher lavaplatos
disordered desordenado/a

disorganized desorganizado/a
disparity disparidad *(f)*
dissident disidente *(m/f)*
distance distancia *(f)*
distinct distinto/a
distinguished distinguido/a
distribute distribuir 11
distribution distribución *(f)*
district distrito *(m)*
diversion diversión *(f)*
diversity diversidad *(f)*
divorce divorcio *(m)*; **get divorced from**
    divorciarse (de) 5
divorced divorciado/a 3, 4
dizzy mareado/a 10
do hacer 2; **do (for a living)** dedicarse
    a 8
doctor médico/a *(m/f)* 8, 10
doctoral degree doctorado *(m)*
document documento *(m)* 11
dog perro/a *(m/f)* 3
dollar dólar *(m)*
domain dominio *(m)*
domestic doméstico/a
Dominican dominicano/a
Dominican Republic República
    Dominicana *(f)*
door puerta *(f)*
dormitory residencia *(f)* 1
dose dosis *(f)*
double doble; **double bed** cama doble *(f)*
    7; **double room** habitación doble *(f)* 7
doubt dudar 10
down abajo; **get down from** bajar de 7
download descargar 6
down-to-earth realista 3
downtown centro *(m)* 4
drag arrastrar
draw dibujar 11
drawer cajón *(m)* 11
dream sueño *(m)* 8; **dream of / about**
    soñar (ue) con 8
dress vestido *(m)* 5; **get dressed** vestirse
    (i, i) 5
drink bebida *(f)* 9
drink beber 3; tomar 2
drinkable bebible
drinking fountain bebedero *(m)*
drive circular; conducir; guiar; impulsar;
    manejar 10
drug droga *(f)*
drug trafficker narcotraficante *(m/f)*
drug trafficking narcotráfico *(m)*
due to debido a
during durante 3; por
DVD player reproductor de DVD *(m)* 4
dwelling vivienda *(f)*
dynamic dinámica *(f)*

E

each cada 1
ear oreja *(f)* 10
ear (inner) oído *(m)* 10
early temprano 2
earn ganar
easily fácilmente
east este; **east of** al este de 2
easy fácil 1
easy-going relajado/a 3
eat comer 2; **eat / have breakfast** desayu-
    nar 4; **eat / have dinner** cenar 4; **eat /**
    have lunch almorzar (ue) 4; **eat**
    heavily comer fuerte 9
eating habits hábitos alimenticios *(mpl)*
ecological ecológico/a
economic económico/a
economist economista *(m/f)*
economy economía *(f)* 12
ecotourism ecoturismo *(m)* 7
edible comestible
edit editar
educate educar
education educación *(f)*; formación
    académica *(f)* 11
educative educativo/a
educator educador/a *(m/f)*
effect efecto *(m)*
effective efectivo/a
efficacy eficacia *(f)*
egg huevo *(m)* 9
eighth octavo/a
election elección *(f)* 12
electricity electricidad *(f)*; luz *(f)* 4
electronic electrónico/a
elegant elegante
element elemento *(m)*
elementary school escuela primaria *(f)* 8
elevator ascensor *(m)* 7; elevador *(m)*
eliminate eliminar
eloquent elocuente
elusive elusivo/a
e-mail correo electrónico *(m)* 3
emergency emergencia *(f)*
emergency room sala de urgencia *(f)* 10
emission emisión *(f)*
emoticon emoticono *(m)* 6
emotion emoción *(f)* 11
emotional emocional
emperor emperador *(f)*
employee empleado/a *(m/f)*
employer empleador/a *(m/f)*; encar-
    gado/a *(m/f)* 7
employment empleo *(m)* 10
enamored enamorado/a 6
enchanting encantador/a
end final *(m)*

ending terminación (f)
endorphine endorfina (f)
energy energía (f) 9
engineer ingeniero/a (m/f) 8
engineering ingeniería (f)
English inglés (m); English-speaking
   de habla inglesa
enjoy disfrutar; gozar
enough bastante
enterprise empresa (f) 11
entertain divertir
entertainment entretenemiento (m) 12
entire entero/a 9
entrance entrada (f) 7
entrée plato principal (m) 9
entry entrada (f)
environment ambiente (m) 11; medio
   ambiente (m) 12
enzyme enzima (f)
epidemic epidemia (f)
episode episodio (m)
epoch época (f)
equal igual
equality igualdad (f)
equip equipar
equipment equipo (m)
equipped equipado/a
equitable equitativo/a
equivalent: be equivalent equivaler;
   equvalente
eradication erradicación (f)
eraser borrador
especially especialmente
essay ensayo (m) 3
essential esencial
establish establecer
establishment establicimiento (m)
esteemed estimado/a
estimate estimar
estimated presupuestario/a
estimation estimación (f)
eternal eterno/a
ethics ética (f)
ethnic étnico/a
etiquette etiqueta (f)
European europeo/a
evaluate evaluar 11
evaluation evaluación (f)
even aún; incluso
evening noche (f) 2
event acontecimiento (m) 8;
   evento (m) 3
every todo/a/os/as 1
every day todos los días 2
every time cada vez
everyone todos 4
everywhere por todos lados 4
evident evidente
exaggerate exagerado/a

exam examen (m); mid-term exam
   examen parcial (m)
examine examinar 10
example ejemplo (m)
excellent excelente
except menos 1, 2
exceptionally excepcionalmente
excess exceso (m)
excessive excesivo/a
excessively excesivamente
exchange cambiar 7; intercambiar
excited emocionado/a 8
exciting emocionante
excursion excursión (f)
excuse excusa (f)
Excuse me! ¡Disculpe! 7
exercise ejercicio (m); cuaderno de
   ejercicios workbook 1
exercise hacer ejercicio 2
exhale exhalar
exhausted exhausto/a
exhibition exposición
exist existir
exotic exótico/a
expansion expansión (f)
expedition expedición (f)
expense gasto (m)
expensive caro/a 4
experience experiencia (f)
expert experto/a (m/f)
explain explicar 9
explication explicación (f)
exploitation explotación (f)
express expresar
expression expresión (f)
exquisite exquisito/a
extend extender
extension extensión (f) 6
extensive extendido/a
extract extracto (m)
extraordinary extraordinario/a
extroverted extrovertido/a 1
exuberant exuberante
eye ojo (m) 3

F

face cara (f) 10
face enfrentarse (con) 7
facilitate facilitar
facility facilidad (f)
facing enfrente de 2
fact hecho (m)
factory fábrica (f)
factory manager gerente de fábrica (m/f) 8
factory worker obrero/a de fábrica (m/f) 8
fail fallar 11
fall otoño (m) 5

fall caer(se) 10; fall into caer a 8
fall in love (with) enamorarse (de) 5
false falso/a (m)
fame fama (f)
familiar: be familiar with conocer 7
family familia (f)
family member familiar 3
famous famoso/a 8
fanatic fanático/a
far (from) lejos (de) 2
farewell despedida (f)
farmer agricultor/a (m/f) 8
fascinating fascinante
fashion moda (f); latest fashion de
   última moda
fast estar en ayunas
fat gordo/a 3
fat grasa (f) 9
father padre (m) 3
fatigue fatiga (f)
favor favorecer
favorite favorito/a; preferido/a
fear temer 11; tener miedo (de) 3; fear
   that temer que 11
fear miedo (m)
February febrero 5
feel sentirse (ie, i) 5; feel like tener
   ganas de
feeling sentimiento (m)
feminine feminino/a
fertilizer abono (m)
fervor fervor (m)
festival feria (f)
festive festivo/a
fever fiebre (f) 10
few poco/a/os/as 1
fiancé(e) novio/a (m/f)
fiber fibra (f) 9; fiber optic fibra óptica
fictive ficticio/a
fifth quinto/a
fight pelea (f)
fight luchar; pelearse 5
figure cifra (f); gráfico (m)
file archivar 11
file (folder) carpeta (f) 11
filing cabinet archivador (m) 11;
   archivero (m)
film película (f)
finally finalmente
finance financiar
financial financiero/a
financing financiación (f)
find encontrar (ue) 4
find out saber 7
fine arts bellas artes (fpl)
fingers dedos 10
finish terminar
fire despedir (i, i) 11; incendio (m)
firefighter bombero/a (m/f) 8

firm firma *(f)*

first primer(o)/a; **It's the first of . . .** Es (el) primero de . . . 5

fish pescado *(m)* 9

fish pescar 7

fit en forma

fitting rooms probadores *(mpl)* 5

fix arreglar 4

flexible flexible 3

flight vuelo *(m)* 7

flight attendant asistente de vuelo *(m/f)* 7

flood inundación *(f)* 12

floor piso *(m)*; suelo *(m)* 4

flour harina *(f)*

flourishing floreciente

flower flor *(f)* 4

flu gripe *(f)*

fluid fluido/a

fluoride flúor *(m)*

follow seguir (yo sigo) 9

following siguiente 1

font fuente *(f)*

food alimento *(m)*; comida *(f)* 2, 9; **food assistance** ayuda alimentaria *(f)*

foolish tonto/a

foot pie *(m)* 10

football fútbol americano 2

footer pie de página *(m)*

for para 1; por; **for that reason** por eso

for example por ejemplo

for that reason por eso

forbid prohibir 10

force fuerza *(f)* 10, 12

forecast pronóstico *(m)*

foreign extranjero/a

foreign country país extranjero *(m)* 7

forest bosque *(m)* 7

fork tenedor *(m)* 9

form forma *(f)*; formulario *(m)*

form formar

format formato *(m)*

fortune fortuna *(f)*

forum foro *(m)*

found fundar

fourth cuarto/a

fraction fracción *(f)*

frank franco/a

free gratis; gratuito/a; libre

free liberar

free time ratos libres; tiempo libre *(m)* 2

freedom libertad *(f)*

French francés *(m)*

French fries papas fritas *(fpl)*

frenetic frenético/a

frequency frecuencia *(f)*

frequent frecuente

frequently con frecuencia 2

fresh fresco/a

Friday viernes 2

fried frito/a

friend amigo/a *(m/f)*

friendly amistoso/a 3

frightened asustado/a 8

frivolous frívolo/a

from de 1; **from . . . to** de . . . a . . . 2; **from . . . until** desde . . . hasta; **I'm from . . .** Soy de . . . 1

front delantero/a

front desk recepción *(f)* 7

fruit fruta *(f)* 9

frustration frustración *(f)*

full completo/a 11; lleno/a 4

full-time job empleo a tiempo completo *(m)* 11

fun divertido/a 1; **have fun** divertirse (ie, i) 5

function funcionar

functioning funcionamiento *(m)*

funny chistoso/a 3

furious furioso/a

furnished amueblado/a

furniture muebles *(mpl)* 4

future futuro *(m)*

G

gallery galería *(f)*

gallon galón *(m)*

game partido *(m)* 2

game show concurso *(m)*

gang pandilla *(f)*

garage garaje *(m)* 4

garden jardín *(m)* 4

gas station estación de servicio *(f)* 7; gasolinera *(f)* 7

gasoline gas *(m)* 4; gasolina *(f)* 7

gastric gástrico/a

gastronomy gastronomía *(f)*

gate puerta *(f)* 7

gather recoger 7

general: in general en general

generally generalmente 2

generate generar

generation generación *(f)*

generous generoso/a 3

genetic genético/a

genius genio/a *(m/f)*

genre género *(m)*

geography geografía *(f)*

German alemán *(m)*

gesture gesto *(m)* 8

get obtener, sacar 7; **get a degree in . . .** hacer la carrera de . . . 8; **get along well (with)** llevarse bien (con) 5; **get angry** enojarse 5; **get bored** aburrirse 5; **get divorced from** divorciarse (de) 5; **get down from** bajar de 7; **get**

dressed vestirse (i, i) 5; **get hot** calentarse (ie); **get married (to)** casarse (con) 5; **get off / out of** bajar de 7; **get on / in** subir a 7; **get sick** enfermarse 10; **get together** encontrarse (ue) 5; **get up** levantarse 5

gift regalo *(m)* 2

girl chica *(f)*; muchacha *(f)* 2; niña *(f)*

girlfriend novia *(m/f)* 1

give dar 9; rendir; **give as a gift** regalar 9; **give someone a shot** ponerle una inyección 10

glad contento/a 2

glass copa *(f)* 9; vaso *(m)* 9

glasses gafas *(fpl)* 3; **sunglasses** gafas de sol *(fpl)* 3

globalization globalización *(f)*

globalize globalizar

go ir 2; **go away** irse 5; **go on a hike** ir de excursión 7; **go on an outing** ir de excursión 7; **go on vacation** ir de vacaciones 7; **go out** salir; **go sailing** salir en velero 7; **go shopping** ir de compras 2; **go to bed** acostarse (ue) 5; **go up** ascender; subir a 7

goal gol *(m)* 8; propósito *(m)*

going to + *verb* ir a + *infinitive* 5; **It's going to rain / snow.** Va a llover / nevar. 5

good bueno/a

Good afternoon. Buenas tardes. 1

Good evening. Buenas noches. 1

Good morning. Buenos días. 1

Good night. Buenas noches. 1

Good-bye. Adiós. 1

good-looking guapo/a 3

gossip chisme *(m)*

gossipy chismoso/a 4

gourd calabaza *(f)*

governability gobernabilidad *(f)*

government gobierno *(m)*

governmental gubernamental

governor gobernador/a *(m/f)*

grade grado *(m)* 8

graduate graduarse 8

graduation graduación *(f)* 8

graffiti grafiti *(m)*

grain grano *(m)* 9

gram gramo *(m)*

grammar gramática *(f)*

grammatical gramatical

grandchildren nietos *(mpl)* 3

granddaughter nieta *(f)* 3

grandfather abuelo *(m)* 3

grandmother abuela *(f)* 3

grandparents abuelos *(mpl)* 3

grandson nieto *(m)* 3

grapes uvas 9

graphic artist diseñador/a gráfico/a *(m/f)* 11

graphic design diseño gráfico (m)

graphic design program programa de diseño gráfico (m) 11

grass césped (m) 4

grave grave 10

gray gris 3, 4

gray-haired canoso/a 3

green verde 3, 4

green beans ejotes (mpl); judías verdes (fpl)

greet saludar 8

greeting saludo (m)

grill parrilla (f); **grilled, on the grill** a la parrilla

ground suelo (m) 4

ground floor planta baja (f) 7

group grupo (m)

group therapy terapia de grupo (f) 10

grow crecer

growing creciente

guarantee garantía (f)

guarantee garantizar

guard guardia (m/f)

guerrilla guerillero/a (m/f) 12

guess adivinar

guest huésped (m/f) 7; invitado/a (m/f) 5

guide guía (f); guiar

guitar guitarra (f) 2

guy muchacho (m) 2

gym(nasium) gimnasio (m) 1

H

habit hábito (m)

hair pelo (m) 3

hair salon peluquería (f) 7

Haiti Haití (f)

half medio/a; mitad (f)

half brother medio hermano (m)

half sister media hermana (f)

hall pasillo (m) 7; salón (m)

ham jamón (m) 9

hamburger hamburguesa (f) 9

hand mano (f) 10

handle manejar

handsome bonito/a; guapo/a 3

happen pasar 8

happy contento/a 2; feliz; **be happy that** alegrarse de que 11; estar contento/a de que 11

hardware componentes físicos (m) 6

hard-working trabajador/a 1

harmoniously armoniosamente

hat sombrero (m) 5

have tener 3; **have a party** hacer una fiesta 3; **have an opinion** opinar; **have confidence in** confiar; **have fun** divertirse (ie, i) 5; **have just** acabar de; **have to** tener que ; **He has a mustache /**

beard. Tiene bigote / barba.; **He / She has glasses.** Tiene gafas. 3; **I have . . .** tengo . . . 1; **What classes do you have?** ¿Qué clases tienes? 1

he él

head cabeza (f) 10

heading encabezado (m)

headline encabezado (m); titular (m)

healing curación (f)

health salud (f) 9, 10

healthy saludable; sano/a 9

hear oír 3

heart corazón (m) 10

heat calentar (ie); calor (m)

height estatura 3; **medium height** estatura mediana 3

Hello. (on the telephone) Aló. 5

help ayuda (f)

help ayudar; servir (i) 5; **help (each other)** ayudar(se) 5; **How may I help you?** ¿En qué puedo servirle? 5

hemisphere hemisferio (m)

her ella 2; la; su(s) 1, 3; **(to, for) her** le, se

herb hierba (f)

herbalist botánco/a (m/f)

here acá; aquí 1; **over here** por acá

heritage herencia (f)

hers suyo/a 9

herself se 6

Hi. Hola. 1

high alto/a 3

high school colegio (m) 8; instituto (m); liceo (m); prepa (f); preparatoria (f) 11

higher superior

highlight destacar

highway carretera (f)

him él 1; lo; **(to, for) him** le, se

himself se 6

hire contratar 11

his su(s) 1; suyo/a 9

Hispanic hispano (m/f)

historic / tourist site sitio histórico / turístico (m) 7

historical histórico/a

history historia (f)

hit golpear 8

holiday vacaciones

home remedy remedio casero (m)

homeless sin hogar 12

homeopathy homeopatía (f)

hometown ciudad natal (f)

homework tarea (f) 1

homogenization homogeneización (f)

honest honesto/a

honey miel (f)

hope esperar 10

hormone hormona (f)

horoscope horóscopo (m)

hospice hospicio (m)

hospitality hospitalidad (f)

hostel hostal (m)

hot caliente; **be hot** tener calor 3; **get hot** calentarse (ie) **It's (very) hot.** Hace (mucho) calor. 5

hotel hotel (m) 7

hour hora (f) 2

house casa (f) 4

household hogar (m)

housemate compañero/a de casa (m/f)

housewife ama de casa (f) 8

housing vivienda (f)

How? ¿Cómo? 2; **How are you? (fam.)** ¿Cómo estás? 1; **How are you? (form.)** ¿Cómo está usted? 1; **How do you say . . . in English?** ¿Cómo se dice . . . en inglés? 1; **How is / are / was / were . . . ?** ¿Qué tal . . . ? 7; **How is . . . ?** ¿Cómo es . . . ? 1; **How is it going?** ¿Qué tal?; **How is that written?** ¿Cómo se escribe? 1; **How many?** ¿Cuántos/as? 2; **How may I help you?** ¿En qué puedo servirle? 5; **How much?** ¿Cuánto/a? 2; **How often?** ¿Con qué frecuencia? 2

hug abrazo (m)

hug (each other) abrazar (se) 5

human being humano (m)

human resources recursos humanos (mpl) 11

human rights derechos humanos (mpl)

humanitarian humanitario/a

humanitarian aid ayuda humanitaria (f) 12

humanities humanidades (fpl)

humorous humorístico/a

hundred cien(to)

hunger hambre (f)

hungry be hungry tener hambre 3; **make hungry** dar hambre 9

hurricane huracán (m)

hurry: be in a hurry tener prisa 3

hurt doler (ue) 9; **hurt (yourself)** lastimar(se) 10

hybrid híbrido/a

hydration hidratación (f)

hydrogen hidrógeno (m)

I

I yo; **I (don't) have . . .** (no) tengo . . . 1; **I don't know** No conozco a 4; **I don't know.** No sé. 1; **I (don't) like . . .** (No) me gusta / (+ singular noun) 1; (No) me gustan / (+ plural noun) 1; **I don't understand.** No comprendo. 1; **I have . . .** tengo . . . 1; **I like** Me gusta(n) **I need . . .** Necesito . . . 1;

I would like . . . Me gustaría(n) . . . 4;
I'm doing very well, thank you.
Estoy muy bien, gracias.; **I'm from . . .**
Soy de . . . 1; **I'm sorry.** Lo siento. 4;
I'm studying . . . Estudio . . . 1
ice cream helado (m) 9
icon icono (m) 6
idea idea (f) 2, 8
identical idéntico/a
identifiable identificable
identification identificación (f) 7
identify identificar
identity identidad (f)
idiomatic idiomático/a
idiot imbécil (m/f)
ill enfermo/a 1, 4; **become ill** enfermarse
illegal ilegal
illness enfermedad (f) 10
illogical ilógico/a
illustration ilustración (f) 4
image imagen (f)
imaginary imaginario/a
imagine imaginar
imbalance desequilibrio (m)
immediately inmediatamente
immersion inmersión (f)
immigrant inmigrante (m/f) 8
immigrate inmigrar
immigration inmigración (f) 12
immunological inmunológico/a
impact impacto (m)
impatient impaciente 1
impeccable impecable
imperfect tense imperfecto (m)
imply implicar
importance importancia (f)
important importante; **be important**
importar 9
impose imponer
impossible imposible 10
impression impresión (f)
impressive impresionante
impulse impulso (m)
in en 1, 2; **in advance** con antelación 7;
in cash en efectivo; **in front of**
delante de 2; **in general** en general;
in love enamorado/a 6; **in order to**
para + infinitive 8; **in spite of** a pesar
de que; **in that case** en ese caso 7
in order to para
in shape en forma 10
in that case en ese caso 7
incident incidente (m)
include incluir
included incluido/a 7
including incluso
incorporate incorporar
incorrect incorrecto/a
increase aumento (m)

increase aumentar; incrementar
incredible increíble
independence independencia (f)
independent independiente; **become**
independent independizarse
independently independientemente
index índice (m)
indicate indicar
indication indicación (f)
indicative indicativo/a
indicator indicador (m)
indifferent indiferente
indigenous indígeno/a
indignation indignación (f) 12
individual individuo (m)
industrialize industrializar
industry industria (f)
inexpensive barato/a
infect infectar
infected infectado/a 10
infidel infiel (m/f)
infidelity infidelidad (f)
infinitive infinitivo (m)
inflation inflación (f)
influence influencia (f)
influence influir (en) 10
inform informar; **inform oneself**
informarse
information información (f) 11
information technology informática (f) 6
informative informativo/a
ingredient ingrediente (m)
inhabitant habitante (m/f)
inhalation inhalación (f)
inhumane inhumano/a
initial inicial
initiate iniciar
initiative inciativa (f)
injection inyección (f) 10
injustice injusticia (f)
innocent inocente
input data introducir datos 11
insert insertar 6
inside adentro
insignificant insignificante
insist (on) insistir (en) 10
insomnia insomnio (m) 10
inspire inspirar
install instalar
instant messaging mensajería
instantánea (f)
instantaneous instantáneo/a
instead of en vez de 9
institution institución (f)
instruction instrucción (f)
instrument instrumento (m)
insufficient insuficiente
insult insultar
insurance seguro (m) 11

intellectual intelectual 1
intelligent inteligente 1
intend pensar (ie) 4
intense intenso/a
intention intención (f)
interact interactuar
interaction interacción (f)
interactive interactivo/a
interest interés (m)
interest interesar 9
interest rate tasa de interés (f) 11
interested (in) interesado/a
interesting interesante 1
international internacional
interrogation interrogatorio (m)
interrogative interrogativo/a
interruption interrupción (f)
intersection cruce (m)
interval intervalo (m)
interview entrevista (f) 11
interview entrevistar
interviewee entrevistado/a (m/f)
interviewer entrevistador/a (m/f)
intimate íntimo/a
intrigue intriga (f)
introduce introducir; presentar;
introduce oneself presentarse 5
introduction presentación (f)
invasion invasión (f) 12
investigate averiguar; investigar
investigation investigación (f)
invite invitar 8
irresponsible irresponsable 1
irritability irritabilidad (f) 10
irritate irritar
Is there . . . ? ¿Hay . . . ? 1
island isla (f)
it lo, la; **It rains. It's raining.** Llueve. 5; **It**
snows. It's snowing. Nieva. 5; **It's**
cool. Hace fresco. 5; **It's going to rain /**
to snow. Va a llover / nevar. 5; **It's**
sunny. Hace sol. 5; **It's the first of . . .**
Es (el) primero de . . . 5; **It's (very)**
cold. Hace (mucho) frío. 5; **It's (very)**
hot. Hace (mucho) calor. 5; **It's windy.**
Hace viento. 5
Italian italiano/a
itinerary itinerario (m) 7
its su(s) 3

J

jacket chaqueta (f) 5
January enero 5
Japanese japonés (m)
jeans jeans (mpl) 5
jellyfish medusa (f)
job empleo (m) 11; trabajo (m) 2; **full-**

time job empleo a tiempo completo (m) 11; **job application** solicitud de empleo (f) 11; **job market** mercado de trabajo (m); **job offer** oferta de empleo (f) 11; **part-time job** empleo a tiempo parcial (m) 11

joke chiste (m) 5
journalist periodista (m/f) 12
judge juez (m/f)
juice jugo (m)
July julio 5
June junio 5
junk food comida basura (f) 9
jury tribunal (m)
justice juez (m/f); justicia (f) 12

K

keep guardar; **keep (yourself)** mantenerse 10
key llave (f) 7
keyboard teclado (m) 11
kilogram kilo (m) 9
king rey (m)
kiss beso (m)
kiss (each other) besar (se) 5
kitchen cocina (f) 4
knee rodilla (f) 10
knife cuchillo (m) 9
know conocer 7; saber 7; **I don't know.** No conozco a 4; **I don't know.** No sé. 1
knowledge conocimiento (m)
known conocido/a

L

laboratory laboratorio (m); **biology laboratory** laboratorio de biología (m); **language laboratory** laboratorio de lenguas (m)
lack falta (f); **lack of concentration / of interest** falta de concentración / de interés (f) 10
lady dama (f)
lake lago (m) 2
lament lamentar
lamp lámpara (f) 4
land terreno (m); tierra (f)
land aterrizar 7
language idioma (m) 11; lengua (f); lenguaje (m)
large grande
lasagna lasaña (f)
last último/a 7
last durar 7
last name apellido (m) 11
last night anoche 7

last week semana pasada (f) 7
late con retraso 7; tarde 2
later luego; más tarde
latest último/a
Latin America Latinoamérica
Latino latino/a (m/f)
laundromat lavandería (f) 4
laundry lavandería (f)
laundry room lavadero
law ley (f) 12
lawn césped (m) 4
lawyer abogado/a (m/f) 8
lazy perezoso/a 1
leader líder (m/f) 6
league liga (f)
learn (to) aprender 3
learning aprendizaje (m)
leave dejar 4; irse 5; salir 3
left: to the left of a la izquierda de 2
leg pierna (f) 10
legend leyenda (f)
legislation legislación (f)
legumes legumbres (fpl) 9
leisure ocio (m)
lemon limón (m) 9
lemonade limonada (f) 9
lend prestar 9
length (time) duración (f)
less menos 1; **less ... than** menos ... que 4
lesson lección (f)
Let's hope that ... Ojalá que ... 10
letter carta (f); letra (f)
lettuce lechuga (f) 9
level nivel (m)
liberal liberal 3
liberty libertad (f)
library biblioteca (f) 1
license licencia (f)
lie down acostarse (ue) 5
life vida (f) 8
lift someone's spirits levantarle el ánimo 10
lift weights levantar pesas 2
light ligero/a 9
light luz (f)
like: I (don't) like ... (No) me gusta (+ singular noun) 1; (No) me gustan (+ plural noun) 1; **I would like ...** Me gustaría(n) ... 4
like como 1
likes to joke around chistoso/a 3
Likewise. Igualmente. 1
limit limitar
line línea (f) 11
link enlace (m)
liquid líquido (m)
list lista (f)
listen (to) escuchar 2
liter litro (m)

literature literatura (f)
little poco/a/os/as 1; **a little** poco (m)
little pequeño/a 1
live vivo; en vivo
live vivir 3
lively animado/a 4
living room sala (f) 4
loan préstamo (m) 11
locate localizar; situar
location ubicación (f) 11
lodge alojarse 7; hospedar
lodging alojamiento (m)
logic lógica (f)
logical lógico/a
logically lógicamente
long largo/a 3
look: look at mirar 2; **look for** buscar 5
lose perder (ie) 4
lose weight bajar de peso 9
loss pérdida (f)
lost perdido/a
love encantar 9; 11; **love (each other)** amor (m); querer (se) (ie) 5 querer (ie) 10; **in love** enamorado/a 6
lovable amable
lovely precioso/a
loving cariñoso/a 3
low bajo/a 3
luck: suerte (f)
lucky: be lucky tener suerte 3;
luggage equipaje (m)
lunch almuerzo (m) 9
lungs pulmones 10

M

magazine revista (f) 3
magnificent magnifico/a
mail correo
main dish plato principal (m) 9
maintain mantener 11
maintenance mantenimiento (m)
majority mayoría (f)
make fabricar; hacer 2; **make a copy** sacar una copia 11; **make a decision** tomar una decisión 10; **make a stopover** hacer escala 7; **make hungry** dar hambre 9; **make possible** potenciar; **make thirsty** dar sed 9
male varón
mall centro comercial (m) 2
malnutrition desnutrición (f)
mama mamá (f)
man hombre (m)
manage manejar
mango mango (m) 9
manicure manicura (f)
manner manera (f)

manufacture fabricar
many mucho/a/os/as 1
map mapa (m); plano (m)
March marzo 5
margin margen (m)
marinated adobado/a
market mercado (m) 9; **job market** mercado de trabajo (m)
marriage matrimonio (m)
married casado/a 3, 4
marry: get married (to) casarse (con) 5
marvelous maravilloso/a
Marxist marxista
mashed puré
mass masa (f)
massage masaje (m)
massive masivo/a
master's degree maestría (f)
material materia (f)
materialistic materialista
maternal materno/a
mathematics matemática (f)
matrimony matrimonio (m)
matter asunto (m)
matter importar 9
maximum máximo/a
May mayo 5
May I see . . . ? Me permite . . . ? 7
maybe quizás 10; tal vez 10
me me; mí 2
meal comida (f) 9
mean significar; **What does . . . mean in English?** ¿Qué significa . . . en inglés?
meanwhile mientras tanto
measure medida (f)
meat carne (f) 9
medical médico/a
medical insurance seguro médico (m) 11
medication medicamiento (m) 10
medicine medicamiento (m) 7; medicina (f)
medios de comunicación means of communication 3
Mediterranean mediterráneo/a
medium height estatura mediana 3
meet conocer 7; reunir; sesionar; **meet up** encontrarse (ue) 5
megaphone megáfono (m)
melodramatic melodramático/a
melon melón (m) 9
member miembro (m)
memorable recordable
memorize memorizar
memory memoria (f); recuerdo (m) 8
mental states estados mentales (m) 10
mentality mentalidad (f)
mention mencionar
menu carta (f) 9
message mensaje (m) 7; recado (m) 11
messy desordenado/a 4

method método (m)
methodical metódico/a
meticulous meticuloso/a
metric métrico/a
metropolitan metropolitano/a
Mexican mexicano/a 2
Mexico México
microphone micrófono (m)
microwave oven microondas (m) 4
middle-aged de mediana edad 3
midnight medianoche (f) 2
mid-term exam examen parcial (m)
midwest medio oeste (m)
migraine jaqueca (f); migraña (f)
migratory migratorio/a
milk leche (f) 9
million millón (m)
millionaire millonario/a (m/f)
mind mente (f)
mine mío/a 9
minimum mínimo/a 11
ministry ministerio (m)
minor menor (m/f)
minority minoría (f)
minus menos 1, 2
minute minuto (m)
mirror espejo (m) 4
mischievous travieso/a 8
miss perder (ie) 4
Miss señorita (Srta.) 1
missing: be missing faltar (a) 9
mission misión (f)
mistaken equivocado/a 11
mixed mixto/a
Mme. señora (Sra.) 1
mobile móvil
modality modalidad (f)
model modelo (m)
moderate moderar
modern moderno/a 1
modernity modernidad (f)
modification modificación (f)
moment momento (m)
momentary momentáneo/a
Monday lunes 2
money dinero (m) 4; moneda (f) 11; **(money in) cash** (dinero en) efectivo (m) 11
monitor monitor (m) 11
monolingual monolingüe
month mes 2; **per month** al mes 2
monthly mensual
monument monumento (m)
mood humor 11; **be in a good / bad mood** estar de buen / mal humor 11
moody temperamental 3
more más; **more . . . than** más . . . que 4; **more than** + *number* más de + *number* 7

morning mañana (f) 2; **in the morning** de / por la mañana 2
mortality mortalidad (f)
mosque mezquita (f) 2
mostly mayormente
mother madre (f) 3
motherboard placa madre (f) 6
motivation motivación (f)
motor motor (m)
motorcycle moto (f) 8
mount montar
mountain montaña (f) 2
mouse ratón (m) 11
mouth boca (f) 10
move mover
move (residence) mudarse 8
movement movimiento (m)
movie película (f) 2
moving emocionante
Mr. señor 1
Mrs. señora (Sra.) 1
much mucho/a/os/as 1; **as much . . . as** tanto/a/ . . . como 4
multiply multiplicar
multitasking multitarea (f)
murder asesinar
muscle músculo (m)
muscular musculoso/a
museum museo (m) 2
music música (f) 2
musician músico (m/f) 8
Muslim musulmán
must deber 3; tener que
mustache bigote (m) 3
mutate mutarse
my mi(s) 1, 3; **My name is . . .** Me llamo . . . 1
myself me 6

N

name nombre (m) 11
name nombrar; **What is your name?** (fam.) ¿Cómo te llamas? 1; **What is your name?** (form.) ¿Cómo se llama usted? 1
nap siesta (f); **take a nap** dormir (ue) una siesta 4
napkin servilleta (f) 9
narration narración (f) 8
nascent naciente
nation nación (f)
national nacional
nationality nacionalidad (f)
native natal; nativo/a
Nativity scene nacimiento (m)
nature naturaleza (f) 7
navigate navegar

near cerca; cerca de 2; cercana/o
neat ordenado/a 4
necessary necesario/a
necessity necesidad (f)
neck cuello (m) 10
necktie corbata (f) 5
need necesitar 2; **I need . . .** Necesito . . . 1
needed: be needed faltar 9
negative negativo/a
negligence negligencia (f)
negotiation negociación (f)
neighbor vecino/a (m/f) 4
neighborhood barrio (m) 4;
   vecindario (m) 7
neither tampoco 4; **neither . . . nor** ni . . .
   ni . . . 4
nephew sobrino (f) 3
nervous nervioso/a 2, 4
network red (f)
never nunca 2
nevertheless sin embargo
new naciente; nuevo/a 1
New Jersey Nueva Jersey
New Mexico Nuevo México
New York Nueva York
newlyweds recién casados
news noticias (fpl)
news anchor presentador/a (m/f) 12
news provider noticiero (m) 12
newspaper periódico (m) 3
newsstand quiosco de periódicos (m) 7
next a continuación; entonces; luego 8;
   próximo/a 1; **next to** al lado de 2;
   junto a 7
Nicaraguan nicaragüense
nice agradable 4; simpático/a 1
nicotine nicotina (f)
niece sobrina (f) 3
night noche (f); **last night** anoche 7
night club club nocturno (m) 2
night life vida nocturna (f)
ninth noveno/a
no no; ninguno / ninguna (ningún) 1
no longer ya no 10
no one nadie
nobody nadie 4
nocturnal nocturno/a
noise ruido (m) 4
noisy ruidoso/a 4
none ninguno / ninguna (ningún) 4
non-Hispanic no-hispano/a
non-smoker no fumador/a (m/f)
noon mediodía 2
nor ni 2
normal normal 3
normally normalmente
north norte; **north of** al norte de 2
(North) American
   norteamericano/a (m/f)

northeast noroeste (m)
nose nariz (f) 10
not no; **not a single** ni un/a solo/a 8; **not
  . . . any** ningún / ninguna 1, 4; **not any
  more** ya no 10; **not a single** ni un/a
  solo/a 8; **not yet** todavía no 11
not to know desconocer
notably notablemente
note anotar; notar
note nota (f)
notebook cuaderno (m) 1
nothing nada 3, 4; **nothing in particular**
  nada en especial 3; **nothing special**
  nada en especial 3
noun nombre (m) 4; sustantivo (m)
nourishing alimenticio/a
novel novela (f)
November noviembre 5
now ahora
nowadays hoy día
number cifra (f); número (m)
numerous numeroso/a
nurse enfermero/a (m/f) 8
nutrition nutrición (f)
nutritional nutricional

O

obesity obesidad (f)
object objeto (m)
objective objetivo (m)
objective objetivo/a
obligate obligar
obligation obligación (f)
obligatory obligatorio/a
observe observar
obstacle obstáculo (m)
obstetrician obstetra (m/f) 10
obtain obtener 11
occasion ocasión (f)
occur ocurrir
October octubre 5
of de 1
of course cómo no 5
offensive ofensivo/a
offer oferta (f); **job offer** oferta de
  empleo (f) 11
offer ofrecer 9
office oficina (f) 2, 11; **at the office** en la
  oficina 2; **office hours** horas de oficina;
  office supplies artículos de oficina
  (mpl) 11; material de oficina (m) 11
often: How often? ¿Con qué frecuencia? 2
old antiguo/a; viejo/a 1, 4
older mayor 3
oldest mayor 3
olive oliva (f)
on en 1, 2; sobre 9

on account of por
on top of encima de 2
once una vez 2
once in a while de vez en cuando
one had better . . . más vale que . . . 10
oneself se 6
onion cebolla (f) 9
online en línea
only solamente; sólo 1
open abierto/a 2, 4
open abrir 3
operation operación (f) 10
opinion: have an opinion opinar;
  opinión (f)
opportunity oportunidad (f) 11
opposition oposición (f)
optimistic optimista 1
option; opción (f)
or o 4; u
orange anaranjado/a 4; naranja (f) 9
orange juice jugo de naranja (m) 9
orchestra orquesta (f)
order comando (m) 6; orden (m);
  in order to para
order ordenar; pedir (i, i) 4
ordinary ordinario/a
oregano orégano (m)
organization organización (f)
organize organizar 11
orient oriente (m)
orientation orientación
origin origen (m)
originally originalmente
osmosis ósmosis (m)
other otro/a 1
ounce onza (f)
our nuestro/a(s) 3
ours nuestro/a(s) 9
ourselves nos 6
outdoors al aire libre 2
outgoing extrovertido/a 1
outing salida (f)
outside afuera 4; fuera
outskirts afueras (m/f) 4
outward flight ida (f) 7
over sobre 9
over here por acá 5
overcoat abrigo (m) 5
overlooking con vistas a . . . 7
overtake superar
own propio/a 4
owner dueño/a (m/f)
oxygen oxígeno (m)
ozone ozono (m)

P

pack one's suitcase hacer la maleta 7
package paquete (m) 7

packet paquete (m)
page página (f) 1
pain dolor (m) 10
paint pintar 11
painter pintor/a (m/f) 8
painting pintura (f) 4
pair pareja (f)
pajamas pijama (m) 5
palace palacio (m)
panic pánico (m)
pants pantalones (mpl) 5
paper ensayo (m) 3; (piece of)
    papel (m) 1
parade desfile (m)
paragraph párrafo (m)
paralysis paralización (f)
paramedic paramédico/a (m/f) 8
Pardon me! ¡Disculpe! 7
parenthesis(es) paréntesis (mpl)
parents padres (mpl) 3
park parque (m)
park estacionar 4
parking párquing
parking lot estacionamiento (m) 4
part parte (m)
partial parcial 11
participant participante (m/f)
participate participar 6
participation participación (f)
participle participio (m)
partisan partisano/a 12
part-time tiempo parcial (m) 11
part-time job empleo a tiempo
    parcial (m) 11
party fiesta (f) 3; birthday party fiesta
    de cumpleaños (f) 8; have a party
    hacer una fiesta 3
pass pasar 2
passenger pasajero/a (m/f) 7
passion pasión (f)
passionate apasionado/a
passport pasaporte (m) 7
password contraseña (f)
past pasado/a 7
pastime pasatiempo (m) 2
paternal paterno/a
patience paciencia (f)
patient paciente (m/f) 10
patient paciente
pause pausa (f)
pay pago (m) 11
pay pagar 4
peas arvejas (fpl); chícharos (mpl) 9;
    guisantes (mpl)
pedestrian peatonal
pen bolígrafo (m) 1
pencil lápiz (m) 1
penicillin penicilina (f)
pensive pensativo/a 6

people gente (f) 2; pueblo (m)
pepper pimienta (f) 9; pimiento (m) 9
per month / per year al mes / al año 2
percent por ciento
percentage porcentaje (m)
perception percepción (f)
perfect perfeccionar; perfecto/a 2
perfectionist perfeccionista
perfectly perfectamente
perhaps quizás 10; tal vez 10
permanent permanente
permission permiso (m) 8
permissive permisivo/a
permit permitir 7, 10
persecution persecución (f)
person persona (f) 4
person in charge encargado/a (m/f) 7;
    responsable (m/f) 11
personal data datos personales
    (mpl) 11
personality personalidad (f)
personality-wise de carácter 3
perspective perspectiva (f)
pertain pertenecer
Peru Perú
peso peso (m) 9
pessimistic pesimista 1
pet mascota (f) 3
petroleum petróleo (m)
pharmacy farmacia (f) 7
phenomenon fenómeno (m)
philosophy filosofía (f)
phone card tarjeta telefónica (f) 7
phosphate fosfato (m)
photocopier fotocopiadora (f) 11
photograph foto (f)
photographs; take photographs
    cargar fotos, sacar fotos
photography fotografía (f)
phrase frase (f)
physical físico/a
physical appearance aspecto físico 3
physical states estados físicos (mpl) 10
physically físicamente 3
physician médico/a (m/f) 8
physics física (f)
pick up recoger 7
picture dibujo (m); take a picture sacar
    una foto 5
picturesque pintoresco/a
pig cerdo/a (m/f)
pill pastilla (f) 10
pineapple piña (f) 9
pink rosa; rosado/a (rosa) 4
piracy piratería (f) 6
place colocar; lugar (m) 4, 7; poner 3
plan planear; planificar
plane ticket pasaje; boleto (m) 7
planet planeta (f)

plant planta (f) 1
plastic plástico/a
plate plato (m) 9
play jugar 4; (music) tocar
pleasant agradable 4; simpático/a
please por favor 1
please, be pleasing to gustar 2
Pleased to meet you. Mucho gusto. 1
plus más 1
pneumonia pulmonía (f)
poached escalfado/a
poem poema (m)
point punto (m)
police officer policía / mujer
    policía (m) 8
police series serie policíaca (f)
polite educado/a
political político/a
political science ciencias políticas (fpl)
politician político/a (m/f)
politics política (f)
pool piscina (f)
popular popular 7
population población (f)
pork carne de cerdo (m)
pork chop chuleta de cerdo (f) 9
portrait retrato (m)
position posición (f); puesto (m) 11
positive positivo/a
possess poseer
possession posesión (f)
possessive posesivo/a
possibility posibilidad (f)
possible posible 10; make possible
    potenciar
postcard postal (f)
post office oficina de correos (f) 7
postpone posponer
potato patata (f)
potato chips papitas (fpl) 9
potential potencial
poverty pobreza (f)
power poder (m)
powerful poderoso/a
practical práctico/a 4, 11
practice práctica (f)
practice practicar
pray rezar 2
precaution precaución (f)
precious precioso/a
predator predador (m)
predetermined predeterminado/a
prediction predicción (f)
predominate predominar
prefer preferir (ie, i) 2, 4, 10
preferable preferible 10
preference preferencia (f)
preferred preferido/a 9
pregnancy embarazo (m) 10

pregnant embarazada; **be pregnant** estar embarazada 10
premature prematuro/a
prenatal care cuidado prenatal (m) 10
preoccupy preocupar
preparation preparación (f)
prepare preparar 2
prescribe recetar 10
prescription receta (f) 10
presence presencia (f)
present presentar; regalo (m) 2
present indicative presente indicativo (m)
present progressive presente progresivo (m)
presentation presentación (f)
presenter presentador/a (m/f) 12
presently actualmente
preservation preservación (f)
president presidente/a (m/f) 12
press prensa (f)
pressure presión (f)
prestige prestigio (m)
preterit tense pretérito (m)
pretty bonito/a 1
prevent prevenir
preventive medicine medicina preventiva (f) 10
previous previo/a
price precio (m) 5
pride orgullo (m)
primary primario/a
primary school escuela normal (f) 11; escuela primaria (f) 11
print imprimir 11
printer impresora (f) 4, 11
priority prioridad (f)
prison cárcel (f)
privacy privacidad (f) 4
private privado/a
prize premio (m)
probability probabilidad (f)
problem problema (m)
process proceso (m)
produce producir
producer productor/a (m/f)
product producto (m)
production producción (f)
productivity productividad (f)
profession profesión (f)
professional profesional (m/f) 8
professional experience experiencia profesional (f) 11
professor profesor/a (m/f)
profile perfil (m)
profound profundo/a
profoundly profundamente
program programa (m); programar 11

programmer programador/a (m/f) 8, 11
programming programación (f)
progress progreso (m)
prohibit prohibir 10
project proyecto (m)
prominent prominente
promise prometer
promising prometedor/a
promote promocionar; promover
promotion promoción (f)
pronoun pronombre (m)
pronounce pronunciar
propel impulsar
property propiedad (f)
proposal propuesta (f) 12
protect proteger
protection protección (f)
protein proteína (f) 9
protest protesta (f)
protocol protocolo (m)
proud orgulloso/a 8
proverb proverbio (m)
provoke provocar
pseudonym seudónimo (m)
psychiatrist psiquiatra (m/f) 10
psychiatry psiquiatría (f)
psychology (p)sicología (f)
public público (m)
public público/a
public awareness concientización pública (f)
public transportation transporte público (m) 4
publication publicación
publicity publicidad (f)
publicize publicitar
publicly públicamente
publish publicar
published publicado/a 11
Puerto Rican puertorriqueño/a
pumpkin calabaza (f)
pupil alumno/a (m/f) 8
purchasing adquisitivo/a
purée(d) puré
purification purificación (f)
purple morado/a 4
purse bolsa (f) 5
put colocar; poner 3; **put on (clothing)** ponerse (la ropa); **put on make-up** maquillarse 5; **put on (one's clothes)** ponerse (la ropa) 5
pyramid pirámide (f)

qualified calificado/a
quality calidad (f); cualidad (f)
quantity cantidad (f)

queasy mareado/a 10
question cuestión (f); pregunta (f) 3
questionnaire cuestionario (m)
quiet callado/a 4

radish rábano (m) 9
railway ferrocarril (m)
rain lluvia (f)
rain llover 5; **It rains. It's raining.** Llueve. 5; **It's going to rain / snow.** Va a llover / nevar. 5
raincoat impermeable (m) 5
raise aumento (m) 11
rancher ranchero/a (m/f)
rapid rápido/a
rapidity rapidez (f)
rapidly rápidamente
rate tasa (f)
react reaccionar
reaction reacción (f) 11
read leer 3
reader lector/a (m/f)
reading lectura (f)
ready listo/a 4
real estate bienes raíces (mpl)
realistic realista
reality realidad (f)
realize oneself realizarse
Really? ¿De veras? 11
really realmente
reason motivo (m) 11
reasonable razonable 5
receipt recibo (m) 4
receive recibir 3
recent reciente
recently recientemente
receptionist recepcionista (m/f) 7
recess recreo (m) 8
recession recesión (f)
recipient recipiente (m/f)
reciprocal recíproco/a
recognize reconocer
recommend recomendar (ie) 7, 10
recommendation recomendación (f)
reconversion reconversión (f)
record grabar
recording grabación
recourse recurso (m)
recreation recreo (m)
recreation area área recreativa (f)
red rojo/a 3, 4
red-haired pelirrojo/a 3
reduce reducir
reduction reducción (f)
refer referir
reference referencia (f) 11

reflect reflejar
reflection reflexión (f)
reflexive reflexivo/a
reform reforma (f)
refrigerator frigorífico; nevera (f) 4;
  refrigerador (m)
refuge refugio (m)
reggae reggaetón (m)
regime régimen (m)
region región (f)
regional dish plato regional (m) 7
register facturar; registrar
regularity regularidad (f)
regularly con regularidad 10;
  regularmente
regulation regulación (f)
relate relacionar
relation relación
relationship relación (f)
relative familiar 3
relatively relativamente
relativity relatividad (f)
relax relajarse 5
relevant relevante
religious religioso/a
relocate mudarse
remain permanecer
remainder resto (m)
remedy remedio (m)
remember recordar (ue) 4
remove retirar
renewable renovable
renovate renovar
rent alquiler (m) 4; renta (f)
rent alquilar 4; rentar
repair reparación (f)
repair reparar
repeat repetir (i) 4
repetitive repetitivo/a
repetitively repetitivamente
report informe (m); reportaje (m)
report informar
reporter reportero/a (m/f) 12
represent representar
representative representante (m/f)
reprisal represalia (f)
reproduction reproducción (f)
Republican republicano/a (m/f)
repulse dar asco 9
reputation reputación (f)
request pedir (i, i) 10; solicitar
require requerir
research investigación (f)
reservation reserva (f)
reserve reservar 7
reserved reservado/a 3
residence hall residencia 1
resident residente (m/f)

resistance resistencia (f)
resolution propósito (m); resolución (f)
resolve resolver (ue) 11
respect respetar; respeto (m)
respectful respetuoso/a
respiratory respiratorio/a
respond responder
responsability responsabilidad (f)
response respuesta (f) 1
responsibility responsabilidad (f) 4
responsible responsable
rest (los) demás; resto (m)
rest descansar 2
restaurant restaurante (m) 2, 9
restriction restricción (f)
result resultado (m)
result resultar
résumé currículum vitae (m) 11
retain retener
retire jubilarse 8; retirar 11
retirement jubilación (f) 8
retirement pension pensión de
  jubilación (f) 11
return devolver (ue) 11; regresar 2;
  volver (ue) 4
returning flight vuelta (f) 7
review repasar; revisar
review reseña (f)
revolution revolución (f)
revolutionary revolucionario/a (m/f)
revulsion asco (m) 9
rhythm ritmo (m)
rice arroz (m) 9
rich rico/a 6
ride a bicycle andar en bicicleta 4
right correcto/a 7; justo/a; be right
  tener razón 3; to the right of a la
  derecha de 2
right away enseguida
right (legal) derecho (m)
roasted asado/a
robbery robo (m)
role papel (m); rol (m)
romantic romántico/a
room cuarto (m) 1, 4; sala (f); salón (m);
  double room habitación doble (f);
  single room habitación sencilla (f)
roommate compañero/a de cuarto (m/f)
root raíz (f)
rope ropa (f)
routine rutina (f)
rug alfombra (f) 4
ruin arruinar; ruina (f)
ruins ruinas 7
rule regla (f)
run correr 3
running corriente
running of the bulls encierro (m)

sad triste 2, 4, 10; be sad that estar triste
  de que 11
sadness tristeza (f) 10
safe salvo/a; seguro/a 4
sailboat velero (m) 7
saint santo/a (m/f)
saintly santo/a 6
salad ensalada (f) 9
salary salario (m) 11; sueldo (m) 11
sale venta (f)
salesclerk dependiente / dependienta 5
salmon salmón (m)
salt sal (f) 9
salutation salutación (f)
Salvadoran salvadoreño/a
same mismo/a 1
sandals sandalias (f) 5
sanity sanidad (f)
satisfaction satisfacción (f)
satisfy satisfacer
Saturday sábado 2
sauce salsa (f)
sautéed salteado/a
save ahorrar 11; salvar
say decir (i) 4; How do you say . . . in
  English? ¿Cómo se dice . . . en inglés? 1
saying goodbye despedidas
scale escala (f)
scan escanear 11
scandal escándolo (m)
scandalize escandalizar
scandalous escandaloso/a
scanner escáner (m) 11
scare dar miedo
scared asustado/a 8
scene escena (f)
schedule horario (m) 2
school colegio (m); escuela (f) 4
school of medicine facultad de
  medicina (f)
science ciencia (f)
scientist científico/a (m/f) 8
score a goal marcar un gol 8
screen pantalla (f) 11
scrupulously escrupulosamente
sea mar (m) 7
seafood mariscos (mpl)
search buscar; búsqueda (f)
search engine buscador (m); motor de
  búsqueda (m)
seasoning sazón (m)
seasons estaciones (fpl) 5
seat asiento (m) 7; take a seat tomar
  asiento
seat belt cinturón (m)
seaweed alga (f)

second segundo/a
secondary school escuela secundaria (f) 8
secret secreto (m)
secretary secretario/a (m/f) 8
section sección (f)
secure seguro/a
security seguridad (f) 7
security check control de seguridad (m) 7
seduce seducir
see ver 2
See you later. Chau.; Ádios.; Hasta luego. 1
See you soon. Hasta pronto.
See you tomorrow. Hasta mañana. 1
seem parecer 2
segment segmento (m)
select seleccionar
self-discipline autodisciplina (f)
selfish egoísta 3
self-medicate automedicarse
self-medication automedicación (f)
self-portrait autorretrato (m)
sell vender 3
seller vendedor/a (m/f)
semester semestre (m)
Senate Senado (m)
senator senador/a (m/f)
send enviar 6, 7
sensation sensación (f)
sensational sensacional
sentence oración (f) 1
sentiment sentimiento (m)
separate separado/a; separar
separately por separado
September septiembre 5
sequence secuencia (f)
serenity serenidad (f)
serious grave 10; serio/a 1, 3
serve servir (i, i) 4, 5
server mesero/a (m/f) 9
service servicio (m)
service station estación de servicio
    (f) 7; gasolinera (f) 7
session sesión
set poner 3
seventh séptimo/a
several varios/as 1
severe severo/a
sexism sexismo (m)
share compartir 3
shave afeitarse
she ella
shelf estante (m) 1, 4
shellfish mariscos 9
shirt camisa (f) 5
shoes zapatos (mpl) 5
shopping de compras 5
shopping center centro comercial (m) 2
short corto/a 3

short (in height), low bajo/a 3
shorts pantalones cortos (mpl) 5
shot inyección (f) 10
shower ducha (f) 7
shower ducharse 5; take a shower
    ducharse 5
shrimp camarones 9
shy reservado/a; tímido/a 1
siblings hermanos (mpl) 3
sick enfermo/a 1, 4; get sick
    enfermarse 10
side lado (m); on my mother's / father's
    side por parte de mi madre / padre 3
sideways lateralmente
sign firmar 11
signal señalar
signature firma (f)
signer firmante (m/f)
significance significado (m)
silent callado/a 6
silly tonto/a 1
similar parecido/a
similarity similitud (f)
simple sencillo/a
simulation simulación (f)
simultaneously simultáneamente
sincerely atentamente
sing cantar 2
singer cantante (m/f) 8
single sencillo/a; soltero/a 3
sir señor 1
sister hermana (f) 3
sit down sentarse (ie) 5
site sitio (m)
situate situar
situation situación (f)
sixth sexto/a
size talla (f) 5
ski esquiar 2
skin piel (f) 10
skirt falda (f) 5
slave esclavo/a (m/f)
sleep sueño (m)
sleep dormir (ue) 4
sleepy: be sleepy tener sueño
sleeve manga (f)
slogan eslogan (m)
slow despacio
slowly lentamente, despacio
sluggishly perezosamente
small pequeño/a 1
smile sonrisa (f) 8
smoke fumar 4
smoked ahumado/a
smoker fumador/a (m/f)
smoking tabaquismo (m)
sneakers tenis (mpl) 5
sneeze estornudar 10

snow nevar 5; It snows. It's snowing.
    Nieva. 5; It's going to snow. Va a
    nevar. 5
so pues 1; entonces 2; por eso 8; tan
so much tanto 10
soap opera telenovela (f)
so-called llamado/a
soccer (football) fútbol 2
soccer player futbolista (m/f) 8
sociable sociable 3
social sciences ciencias sociales (fpl)
social security number número de
    seguridad social (m)
social worker trabajador/a social (m/f) 8
socialize socializar
socially socialmente
society sociedad (f)
sociology sociología (f)
socks calcetines (mpl) 5
sofa sofá (m) 4
soft drink refresco (m) 9
software aplicación informática (f) 6;
    programa informática (f) 6
software designer diseñador/a de
    software (m/f) 8
soldier militar (m/f)
solidarity solidaridad (f) 12
solstice solsticio (m)
solution solución (f)
some alguno/a(s) 4; unos/as 1
someone alguien 4
something algo 2, 4
sometimes a veces 2, 4
son hijo (m) 3
song canción (f)
soon pronto
sophisticated sofisticado/a
sore dolorido/a 10
sorry: be sorry that sentir (ie, i) que 11;
    I'm sorry. Lo siento. 4
soup sopa (f) 9
soup dish plato hondo (m) 9
source fuente (f)
south sur (m); south of al sur de 2
South America Sudamérica
souvenir recuerdo (m) 7
space blanco (m); espacio (m) 4
spaghetti espaguetis (mpl)
Spain España
spam correo no deseado (m) 6
Spaniard español/a (m/f)
Spanish español (m) 1
Spanish español/a
Spanish class clase de español (f) 1
speak hablar 2
special especial
specialist especialista (m/f) 10
specialize especializar

specific específico/a
speech discurso *(m)*
speed up acelerar
spelling ortografía *(f)*
spend (money) gastar 5
spend (time) pasar 2
spinach espinacas *(f)* 9
spirit espíritu *(m)*
spiritual espiritual
spoon cuchara *(f)* 9
sports deportes *(mpl)* 2; **fond of sports** deportista (adj.) 8; **sports event** evento deportivo 3
spouse esposo/a *(m/f)*
spreadsheet hoja de cálculo *(f)* 11
spring primavera *(f)* 5
squash calabacín *(m)* 9
stability estabilidad *(f)*
stabilize estabilizar
stadium estadio *(m)*
staircase escalera *(f)* 7
stairs escalera *(f)* 7
stamp estampilla *(f)*; sello *(m)* 7; timbre postal *(m)*
star estrella *(f)*
start comenzar (ie) 10; empezar (ie); iniciar
start inicio *(m)*
state estado *(m)*
station estación *(f)*
statue estatua *(f)*
stay quedarse 5; **stay at (on a trip)** alojarse en 7; **stay in bed** guardar cama 10
steak bistec *(m)* 9
steamed al vapor
stemmed glass copa *(f)* 9
step paso *(m)*
stepbrother hermanastro *(m)*
stepfather padrastro *(m)*
stepmother madrastra *(f)*
stepsister hermanastra *(f)*
stereo estéreo *(m)* 1
stereotype estereotipo *(m)*
steroids esteroides *(mpl)*
still todavía
stimulate estimular; estímulo *(m)*
stimulating estimulante
stomach estómago *(m)* 10
stop . . . -ing dejar de + *infinitive* 10
stopover escala *(f)*; **make a stopover** hacer escala 7
store tienda *(f)* 2
story cuento *(m)* 8; historia *(f)*
stove estufa *(f)* 4
straighten out / up arreglar 4
straightened up ordenado/a 4
strange extraño/a
stranger desconocido/a *(m/f)*
strategy estrategia *(f)*
strawberries fresas 9; frutillas *(fpl)*

street calle *(f)* 4
street map plano de la ciudad *(m)* 7
strength fuerza *(f)* 10
stress estrés *(m)* 10
stressful estresante
strict estricto/a 3
strike golpear 8
stroke (swimming) brazada *(f)*
stroll pasear
strong fuerte 8
structure estructura *(f)*
stubborn terco/a 3
stuck-up presumido/a 3
student alumno/a *(m/f)* 8; estudiante *(m/f)*
student desk pupitre *(m)* 1
studies estudios *(mpl)*
study estudiar 2; **I'm studying . . .** Estudio . . . 1; **study abroad** estudiar en el extranjero; **What are you studying?** ¿Qué estudias? 1
study estudio *(m)*
stuffed relleno/a
stuffed pepper chile relleno *(m)* 9
stupendous estupendo/a
stupid tonto/a 1
style estilo *(m)*
subject asunto *(m)*
subjunctive subjuntivo *(m)*
substance sustancia *(f)*
substitute sustituir
suburban suburbano/a
succesively sucesivamente
success éxito *(m)*
successful: be successful tener éxito
sudden súbito/a
suffer sufrir
sufficient suficiente
sugar azúcar *(m)* 9
suggest sugerir (ie, i) 10
suggestion sugerencia *(f)*
suit traje *(m)* 5
suitcase maleta *(f)* 7
suitor pretendiente *(m/f)*
summary resumen *(m)*
summer verano *(m)* 5
sun sol *(m)*
sunbathe tomar el sol 2
sunblock bloqueador solar *(m)*
Sunday domingo 2
sunglasses gafas de sol *(fpl)*
sunny soleado/a; **be sunny** hacer sol; **It's sunny.** Hace sol. 5
supermarket supermercado *(m)*
superstitious supersticioso/a
supervisor supervisor/a *(m/f)* 11
supplement suplemento *(m)*
support apoyo *(m)*
Supreme Court Corte Suprema *(f)*
sure seguro/a; **be sure** estar seguro/a 10

surgeon cirujano/a *(m/f)* 10
surgery cirugía *(f)* 10
surprise sorpresa *(f)*
surprise sorprender 11
surprised sorprendido/a 2, 4, 6
survey encuesta *(f)*
surveyor encuestador/a *(m/f)*
survive sobrevivir
suspect sospechoso/a *(m/f)*
suspense suspenso *(m)*
suyo/a their
sweater suéter *(m)* 5
sweatshirt sudadera *(f)* 5
sweets dulces 9
swim nadar 2
swimming pool piscina *(f)* 2
swimsuit traje de baño *(m)* 5
swollen hinchado/a 10
symbol símbolo *(m)*
symphonic orchestra orquesta sinfónica *(f)*
symptom síntoma *(m)* 10
synagogue sinagoga *(f)* 2
syndrome síndrome *(m)*
synonym sinónimo *(m)*
synonymous sinónimo/a
system sistema *(m)* 11
systematically sistemáticamente

T

tabacco tabaco *(m)*
table mesa *(f)* 1
table (graphic) tabla *(f)*
tablet pastilla *(f)* 10
take llevar 5; sacar; tomar 2; **take a bath** bañarse 5; **take a nap** dormir (ue) una siesta 4; **take a picture** sacar una foto 5; **take a seat** tomar asiento; **take a shower** ducharse 5; **take a trip** hacer viaje 3; **take away** llevarse 5; **take care of (yourself)** cuidar(se) 10; **take off** despegar 7; **take photographs** cargar fotos, sacar fotos
tale cuento *(m)* 8
talent talento *(m)*
talk hablar 2
talkative hablador/a 4
tall alto/a 3
tariff tarifa *(f)*
task quehacer *(m)*
taste gusto *(m)*
tattoo tatuaje *(m)*
taxes impuestos *(mpl)* 11
taxi taxi *(m)* 7
taxi driver taxista *(m/f)*
tea té 9; **hot tea** té caliente *(m)* 9; **iced tea** té helado *(m)*
teach enseñar

teacher maestro/a (*m/f*) 8
team equipo (*m*) 8
technical técnico/a
technical service servicio técnico (*m*) 11
technique técnica (*f*)
technology tecnología (*f*)
telecommute teletrabajar
telecommuting teletrabajo (*m*)
telephone teléfono (*m*) 2; **on the telephone**
　por teléfono 11; **public telephone**
　teléfono público (*m*) 7; **telephone**
　number número de teléfono (*m*)
telephonic telefónico/a
telephony telefonía
television (TV) televisión (tele) (*f*);
　televisor (*m*)
television set televisor (*m*) 1, 4
television viewer televidente (*m/f*)
tell contar (ue) 4; decir (i) 4
teller cajero/a (*m/f*) 11
temperature temperatura (*f*) 10
temporary temporal
tendency tendencia (*f*)
tennis tenis (*m*)
tennis court cancha de tenis (*f*)
tennis player tenista (*m/f*)
tennis shoes tenis (*mpl*); zapatillas de
　tenis (*mpl*)
tenth décimo/a
term término (*m*)
terrace terraza (*f*)
terrain terreno
territory territorio (*m*)
terrorism terrorismo (*m*)
terrorist terrorista (*m/f*) 12
testimony testimonio (*m*)
text texto (*m*)
textbook libro de texto (*m*) 3
than que
thank you gracias 1
thanks to gracias a
that que 1; **that (those)** ese / esa (esos /
　esas) 3; **that (those) (over there)**
　aquel / aquella (aquellos / as) 5; **that**
　which lo que 8; **that's right** así es 9;
　that's why por eso 8
the el, la, los, las
theater teatro (*m*) 2
their su(s) 3
theirs suyo/a 9
them ellos / ellas 2; les, se; los, las 6
thematic temático/a
theme tema (*f*); tema (*m*)
themselves se 6
then entonces 2; luego 8
theory teoría (*f*)
therapist terapeuta (*m/f*) 10
therapy terapia (*f*) 10
there allí, allá

there is, there are hay 1
therefore por eso 8
they ellos/as 1
thin delgado/a 3
thing cosa (*f*) 1
think opinar; **think (about)** pensar (ie)
　(en) 4
third tercero/a
thirsty: be thirsty tener sed 3; **make**
　thirsty dar sed 9
this (these) este / esta (estos / as) 5
thought pensamiento
thousand mil (*m*)
thrilling emocionante
throat garganta (*f*) 10
through here por acá
throw up vomitar 10
Thursday jueves 2
thus así
ticket billete (*m*) 7; boleto (*m*) 7;
　pasaje (*m*) 7
till menos; hasta 2
time hora (*f*) 2; tiempo (*m*)
times: at times a veces
timid tímido/a 1
tired cansado/a 1, 4
title título (*m*)
to para
to where adónde
today hoy 1, 2
together juntos/as 2; **get together**
　encontrarse (ue) 5
Tokyo Tokio
tolerance tolerancia (*f*)
tomato tomate (*m*) 9
tomorrow mañana
tone tono (*m*) 11
tonight esta noche
too demasiado 2, 5; también 1
too much demasiado 2, 5
tool herramienta (*f*)
tool bar barra de herramientas (*f*)
tooth diente (*m*)
totalitarian totalitario/a
totally totalmente
tourism turismo (*m*)
tourist turista (*m/f*)
tourist guide guía (turístico/a) (*m/f*) 7
tourist guidebook guía (turística) (*f*) 7
tradition tradición (*f*)
traditional tradicional
traditionalism tradicionalismo (*m*)
traffic tráfico (*m*) 4
tragedy tragedia (*f*)
train tren (*m*)
train entrenar 11
tranquility tranquilidad (*f*)
transaction trámite (*m*) 11
transform transformar

transformation transformación (*f*)
transition transición (*f*)
translate traducir
translation traducción (*f*)
transmission transmisión (*f*)
transmit transmitir
transparent transparente
transportation transporte (*m*)
trash basura (*f*) 4
travel viajar 7
travel agency agencia de viajes (*f*) 7
traveler viajero/a (*m/f*)
traveler's check cheque de viaje (*m*)
traveling itinerante
treat tratar (de) 8
treatment tratamiento (*m*) 10
tree árbol (*m*) 4
triangle triángulo (*m*)
trimester trimestre (*m*)
trip viaje (*m*) 3; **take a trip** hacer viaje 3
true cierto/a; verdad; verdadero/a
trumpet trompeta (*f*)
trust confiar
try probar (ue) 7; tratar (de) 8; **try on**
　probarse (ue) 5
T-shirt camiseta (*f*) 5
Tuesday martes 2
tuna atún (*m*)
turbulence turbulencia (*f*)
turn (an age) cumplir 8
turn off apagar 11
turn on encender (ie) 11; poner 3; prender
type tipo (*m*)
typical típico/a
typically típicamente

U

ugly feo/a 1
ultimately últimamente
uncle tío (*m*) 3
under debajo de 2
underline subrayer
understand comprender 3; entender (ie) 4;
　I don't understand. No comprendo. 1
understanding comprensivo/a 3
undocumented indocumentado/a
unemployed desempleado/a
unemployment desempleo (*m*)
unfaithful person infiel (*m/f*)
unfortunately desafortunadamente 4
uniform uniforme (*m*)
union unión (*f*)
united unido/a
United Nations Naciones Unidas (*mpl*) 12
United States Estados Unidos (*mpl*)
university universidad (*f*)
university (adj.) universitario/a

university band tuna
university band member tuno
university course curso universitario (m)
unknown desconocido/a 2
unnecessary innecesario/a
unpleasant antipático/a 1
until hasta 2; hasta que 11
unusual inusual
up arriba
upon: a; **upon . . . ing** al + *infinitive* 7; **upon request** a petición 11
upset molesto/a 2, 4
urban urbano/a
urgent urgente 10
us nos 6; nosostros/as 2
use usar 2; utilizar
use utilización (f)
useful útil 1
user usario/a (m/f)
utility utilidad (f)
utilization utilización (f)

V

vacation: on vacation de vacaciones 7
valuation valoración (f)
value valor (m); valorar
varied variado/a
variety variedad (f)
vegetables verduras (fpl) 9
vegetarian vegetariano/a
vehicle vehículo (m)
velocity velocidad (f)
verb verbo (m)
verb tense tiempo verbal (m)
verify verificar
versatile versátil
version versión (f)
very muy; **very well** muy bien 1
vestige vestigio (m)
via por; vía
vice versa viceversa
victim víctima (f)
victory victoria (f)
videogame videojuego (m)
view vista (f)
view of . . . vistas a . . . 7
vigilant: be vigilant vigilar
vinegar vinagre (m)
violence violencia (f)
virtuouso virtuoso/a (m/f)
visit visita (f); visitar 7
visitor visitante (m/f)
vitality vitalidad (f)
vitamins vitaminas 9
vocabulary vocabulario (m)
voice voz (f)
voice mailbox buzón de voz (m) 11

voluntarily voluntariamente
voluntary voluntario/a
volunteer voluntario/a (m/f)
vomit vomitar 10
vote votar
voter votante (m/f)
vowel vocal (f)

W

wage sueldo (m) 11
wait esperar 7; **wait on** atender (ie) 11
waiter camarero/a (m/f); mesero/a (m/f)
waiting room sala de espera (f)
wake up despertarse (ie) 5
walk caminar 10; pasear
wall pared (f) 4
want desear; querer 2; querer (ie) 4, 10
war guerra (f)
wardrobe armario (m) 4
warm cálido/a; caluroso/a
warm up calentar; calentarse (ie)
warn advertir
warning advertencia (f)
wash lavar 4; **wash one's hair / one's face** lavarse el pelo / la cara 5
washbasin lavabo
washing machine lavadora
waste basket papelera (f)
watch reloj (m) 1
watch mirar, ver 2; vigilar
watch out ojo
water agua (f, el) 4
waterfall catarata (f)
waterski hacer esquí acuático 2
way manera (f)
we nosotros/as
weak débil
wear llevar 5
weather tiempo (m) 5; **The weather's good / bad.** Hace buen / mal tiempo. 5; **What's the weather like?** ¿Qué tiempo hace? 5
weather report pronóstico del tiempo (m) 12
web red (f) 6
web page página web (f)
web page design diseño de páginas web (m) 11
web site sitio web (m)
wedding boda (f) 8
Wednesday miércoles 2
week semana (f) 2; **last week** semana pasada (f) 7
weekend fin de semana (m) 2
weekly semanal
weird raro/a 3
welcome bienvenido/a 7

welcome dar la bienvenida
well bien 1, 4; pues; **I'm doing very well, thank you.** Estoy muy bien, gracias.
well-being bienestar (m)
west oeste (m); **west of** al oeste de 2
What? ¿Cuál(es)? 2; ¿Qué? 2; **What are you studying?** ¿Qué estudias? 1; **What classes do you have?** ¿Qué clases tienes? 1; **What color is it?** ¿De qué color es?; **What does . . . mean in English?** ¿Qué significa . . . en inglés?; **What is the date?** ¿Qué fecha es? 5; **What is your name?** (fam.) ¿Cómo te llamas? 1; **What is your name?** (form.); ¿Cómo se llama usted? 1; **What's . . . like?** ¿Cómo es . . . ? 1; **What's the weather like?** ¿Qué tiempo hace? 5; **What's wrong with you?** ¿Qué te pasa? 10
wheat trigo (m)
wheel rueda (f)
When? ¿Cuándo? 2
Where? ¿Dónde? 2; **Where are you from?** (fam.) ¿De dónde eres? 1; **Where are you from?** (form.) ¿De dónde es usted? 1
Which? ¿Cuál(es)? 2
while mientras 8, 11
while rato (m)
white blanco/a 4
white-haired canoso/a 3
Who? ¿Quién(es)? 2
whole entero/a 9
whole-grain integral 9
Whom? ¿Quién(es)? 2
Why? ¿Por qué?
win ganar 8; **win the heart of** enamorar
wind viento (m)
window ventana (f) 1, 4; **counter window** ventanilla (f) 11; **window (of a vehicle or box office)** ventanilla (f) 7
windy: It's windy. Hace viento. 5
wine vino (m) 3; **red / white wine** vino tinto / blanco (m) 9
wine glass copa (f) 9
wine shop bodega (f)
winter invierno (m) 5
wish desear 2, 10
with con 1, 2; **with an accent** con acento 1; **with attention** con atención 8; **with me** conmigo 2; **with respect to** respecto a; **with you** contigo 3
withdraw retirar 11
withdrawal retiro (m) 11
within dentro de
without sin; **without an accent** sin acento 1
witness testigo/a (m/f)

woman mujer *(f)*; **businesswoman** mujer de negocios *(m)* 8; **policewoman** mujer policía *(m)* 8

woods bosque *(m)* 7

word palabra *(f)* 1

word processor procesador de texto *(m)* 6, 11

work obra *(f)*; trabajo *(m)* 2

work funcionar 4; trabajar

work days días laborales

workbook cuaderno de ejercicios *(m)* 1

worker: construction worker obrero/a de la construcción *(m/f)* 8; **factory worker** obrero/a de fábrica *(m/f)* 8; **social worker** trabajador/a social *(m/f)* 8

world mundo *(m)*

worldwide mundial 6

worried inquieto/a; preocupado/a 8

worry preocupar(se) 10

worse peor 4

write anotar; escribir 3; redactar; **How is that written?** ¿Cómo se escribe? 1

writer escritor/a *(m/f)*

writing redacción *(f)*

wrong equivocado/a 11

X-ray radiografía *(f)* 10

yard jardín *(m)* 4

year año *(m)*; **be . . . years old** tener . . . años 3; **per year** al año 2

yell gritar

yellow amarillo/a 4

yesterday ayer 7

yield rendir

yogurt yogur *(m)*

you *(pl.)* ustedes

you *(pl. / fam.)* vosotros/as

you *(sing. / fam.)* (to/for) **you** ti 2

you *(sing. / fam.)* tú; **How are you?** *(fam.)* ¿Cómo estás? 1; **You like . . .** Te gusta(n) . . . 2; **You look . . . to me.** Te veo . . . 10

you *(sing. / form.)* usted; **How are you?** *(form.)* ¿Cómo está usted? 1

young joven 3

younger menor 3

youngest menor 3

your *(pl. / fam.)* vuestro/a(s) 3

your *(sing. / fam.)* tu(s) 1, 3

your *(sing. / form.; pl.)* su(s) 3

yours *(pl.)*, **yours** *(sing. / form.)* suyo/a 9

yours *(pl./fam.)* vuestro/a 9

yours *(sing./fam.)* tuyo/a 9

youth joven *(m/f)*

zone zona *(f)*

Credits

© Emiliano Rodriguez / Shutterstock; **(bottom right, bottom)** © Radovan / Shutterstock; **p. 216 (top)** © GoldPitt LLC; **(middle)** GoldPitt LLC; **(bottom)** © GoldPitt LLC; **p. 220** © Todd Warnock / Jupiter Images Royalty Free; **p. 222 (top left)** © Andresr / Shutterstock; **(top right)** © Felix Mizioznikov / Shutterstock; **(bottom left)** © Lee Morris / Shutterstock; **(bottom right)** © Monkey Business Images / Shutterstock; **p. 227** © iStockphoto; **p. 228 (top left)** © CC Studio / Science Photo Library / Photo Researchers, Inc.; **(top right)** © Tony Freeman / PhotoEdit Inc.; **(bottom left)** © Tony Freeman / PhotoEdit Inc.; **(bottom right, top)** © Spencer Grant / PhotoEdit Inc.; **(bottom right, bottom)** © Brand X Pictures / Fotosearch.com, LLC / Royalty Free; **p. 240 (top left)** © A. Ramey / PhotoEdit Inc.; **(top middle)** © Michael Newman / PhotoEdit Inc.; **(top right)** © David Young-Wolff / PhotoEdit ; **(middle left)** © Bob Daemmrich / The Image Works; **(middle middle)** Lynton Gardiner © Dorling Kindersley; **(middle right)** © Juan Carlos Ulate / REUTERS / Archive Photos; **(bottom left)** © Ljupco Smokovski / Shutterstock; **(bottom right)** © Walter Hodges / Getty Images Inc. / Stone Allstock; **p. 244** © Photos.com; **p. 247** © Jack Hollingsworth / Corbis / Royalty Free; **p. 248 (top)** © GoldPitt LLC; **(middle)** © GoldPitt LLC; **(bottom)** © GoldPitt LLC; p. 252 © John Neubauer / PhotoEdit Inc.; **p. 259** © Jupiter Unlimited; **p. 263** © Photos.com; **p. 266 (top left)** © Jupiter Unlimited; **(top right)** © Dave King / Dorling Kindersley Media Library; **(middle left)** © Sian Irvine / Dorling Kindersley Media Library; **(middle middle)** © Dave Rudkin / Dorling Kindersley Media Library; **(middle right)** © Tim Ridley / Dorling Kindersley Media Library; **(bottom left)** © Tim Ridley / Dorling Kindersley Media Library; **(bottom right)** © Roger Phillips / Dorling Kindersley Media Library; **p. 276** © Jupiter Unlimited; **p. 278** © Jenny Mills / Photolibrary. com; **p. 280 (top)** © GoldPitt LLC; **(middle)** © GoldPitt LLC; **(bottom)** © GoldPitt LLC; **p. 284** © Photos.com; **p. 286 (top left)** © Jupiter Images Royalty Free; **(top right)** © Dorling Kindersley; **(bottom)** © Andy Crawford and Steve Gorton / Dorling Kindersley Media Library; **p. 287** © Jupiter Unlimited; **p. 292 (top left)** © Andy Crawford / Dorling Kindersley Media Library; **(top middle)** ©

Jupiter Unlimited; (top right) © Jupiter Unlimited; **(middle left)** © Jupiter Images Royalty Free; **(middle middle)** © Jupiter Images Royalty Free; **(middle right)** Jupiter Images Royalty Free; **(bottom left)** © Dorling Kindersley / Dorling Kindersley Media Library; **(bottom right)** © Dorling Kindersley / Dorling Kindersley Media Library; **p. 293** © Jupiter Unlimited; **p. 297** © Alexander Raths / Shutterstock; **p. 298** © Yuri Arcurs / Shutterstock; **p. 299** © Jupiter Unlimited; **p. 301** © Andy Crawford / Dorling Kindersley Media Library; **p. 303** © Jupiter Unlimited; **p. 304 (top left)** © Dorling Kindersley / Dorling Kindersley Media Library; **(top right)** © Steve Gorton / Dorling Kindersley Media Library; **(bottom left)** © Jupiter Images Royalty Free; **(bottom right)** © Andy Crawford / Dorling Kindersley Media Library; **p. 305** © Jupiter Images Royalty Free; **p. 309** © Rob Marmion / Shutterstock; **p. 310** © Will & Deni McIntyre / Getty Images Inc.-Stone Allstock; **p. 311** © Imcsike / Shutterstock; **p. 312 (top)** © GoldPitt LLC; **(middle)** © GoldPitt LLC; **(bottom)** © GoldPitt LLC; **p. 316** © Shutterstock; **p. 318** © Jupiter Unlimited; **p. 321** © Jupiter Unlimited; **p. 323 (left)** © Steve Gorton / Dorling Kindersley Media Library; **(right)** © Dorling Kindersley /Dorling Kindersley Media Library; **p. 324 (top left)** © Sarah Ashun / Dorling Kindersley Media Library; **(top right)** © Dorling Kindersley / Dorling Kindersley Media Library; **(bottom left)** © jamalludin / Shutterstock; **(bottom right)** © Steve Gorton / Dorling Kindersley Media Library; **p. 327** © Jupiter Unlimited; **p. 330 (top left)** © PBJ Pictures / Getty Images, Inc.-Stone Allstock; (top middle) © AVAVA / Shutterstock; (top right) © vgstudio / Shutterstock; (bottom left) © Elena Rooraid / PhotoEdit Inc.; (bottom middle) © Edw / Shutterstock; (bottom right) © Michael Newman / PhotoEdit Inc.; **p. 331** © Andresr / Shutterstock; **p. 335** © Mike Cohen / Shutterstock; **p. 336 (left)** © Jupiter Images Royalty Free; **(right)** © Jupiter Images; **p. 337 (top)** © Jeff Banke / Shutterstock; **(bottom)** © Jupiter Unlimited; **p. 340** © Jupiter Unlimited; **p. 342 (left)** © iofoto / Shutterstock; **(right)** © Gautier Willaume / Shutterstock; **p. 344 (top)** © GoldPitt LLC; **(middle)** © GoldPitt LLC; **(bottom)** © GoldPitt LLC; **p. 348** © Mikhail Zahranichny / Shutterstock; **p. 350 (top left)** ©

Index

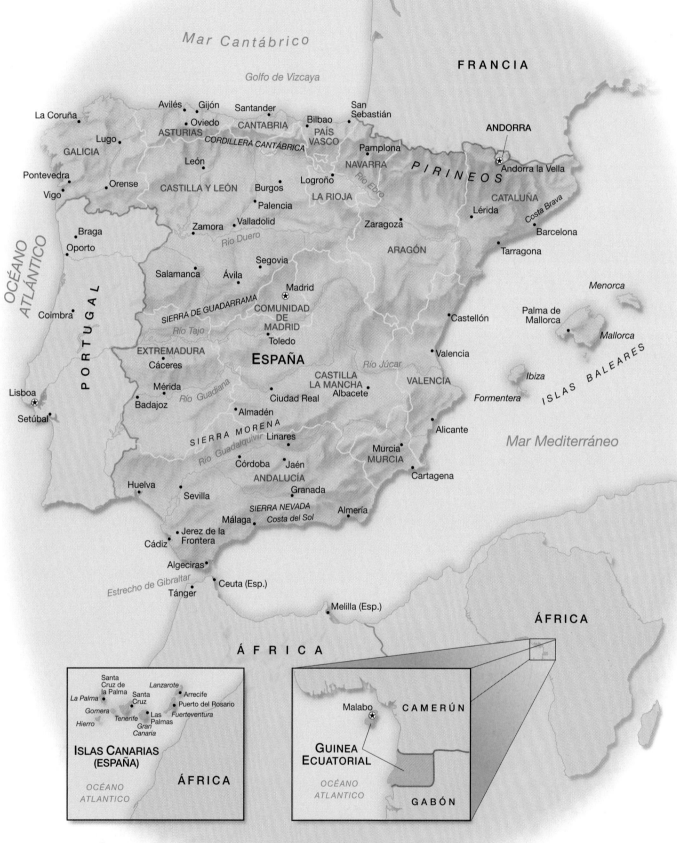

España y África

Mar Caribe

OCÉANO ATLÁNTICO

Barranquilla
Cartagena
Maracaibo
Caracas
Barquisimeto
Medellín
VENEZUELA
Río Orinoco
Georgetown
Paramaribo
Cayenne
GUYANA
SURINAM
GUAYANA FRANCESA (Francia)
Manizales
Salto Ángel
Cali
Bogotá
COLOMBIA
CORDILLERA DE LOS ANDES
Quito
ECUADOR
Ecuador
Guayaquil
Cuenca
Iquitos
Río Amazonas
Manaus
Belém
Fortaleza
Islas Galápagos (Ec.)
Cajamarca
Río Madeira
Trujillo
Río Branco
BRASIL
PERÚ
Recife
Lima
Machu Picchu
Ayacucho
Cuzco
Salvador
Arequipa
BOLIVIA
Lago Titicaca
La Paz
Brasília
Cochabamba
Santa Cruz

OCÉANO PACÍFICO
I. Pinta
I. Fernandina
I. Marchena
I. San Salvador
Santa Cruz
I. Santa Cruz
I. Isabela
Puerto Ayora
I. San Cristóbal
Puerto Villamil
Puerto Baquerizo Moreno
ISLAS GALÁPAGOS (ECUADOR)

Arica
Sucre
Potosí
Belo Horizonte
Iquique
PARAGUAY
São Paulo
Río de Janeiro
Antofagasta
Salta
Asunción
Santos
Trópico de Capricornio
Salto Iguazú
CHILE
San Miguel de Tucumán
Pôrto Alegre

OCÉANO PACÍFICO
Cabo Norte
Volcán Katiki
Hanga Roa
Cabo Cumming
Mataveri
ISLA DE PASCUA (CHILE)

Coquimbo
ARGENTINA
Río Paraná
Rivera
Córdoba
Río Uruguay
Valparaíso
Rosario
URUGUAY
Santiago
Mendoza
Buenos Aires
Montevideo
Concepción
La Plata
Río de la Plata
OCÉANO ATLÁNTICO
Bahía Blanca
CORDILLERA DE LOS ANDES
Desierto de Atacama

OCÉANO PACÍFICO

Puerto Montt

Estrecho de Magallanes
Islas Malvinas (Br.)
Punta Arenas
TIERRA DEL FUEGO
Cabo de Hornos

América del Sur

ESTADOS
UNIDOS

Mexicali
Tijuana
Nogales
Ciudad
Juárez
Río Bravo del Norte
Río Grande
Nuevo Laredo
SIERRA MADRE OCCIDENTAL
Baja California
Golfo de California
SIERRA MADRE ORIENTAL
Monterrey
MÉXICO
Golfo de
México
Guadalajara
Comala
México, D.F.
Veracruz
Mérida
Península
de
Yucatán
Taxco
Palenque
Be
Acapulco
Oaxaca
Tikal
Belm
BEL
GUATEMALA
Cop
Quetzaltenango
Volcán Izalco
Guatemala
San
Salvad
EL
SALVADOR

OCÉANO

PACÍFICO

Islas
Galápagos
(Ec.)

México, América Central y el Caribe